Negotiating Belongings

Dear C[illegible]opher,

Enjoy the journey.

Mel

STUDIES IN INCLUSIVE EDUCATION
Volume 30

Scope

This series addresses the many different forms of exclusion that occur in schooling across a range of international contexts and considers strategies for increasing the inclusion and success of all students. In many school jurisdictions the most reliable predictors of educational failure include poverty, Aboriginality and disability. Traditionally schools have not been pressed to deal with exclusion and failure. Failing students were blamed for their lack of attainment and were either placed in segregated educational settings or encouraged to leave and enter the unskilled labour market. The crisis in the labor market and the call by parents for the inclusion of their children in their neighborhood school has made visible the failure of schools to include all children.

Drawing from a range of researchers and educators from around the world, Studies in Inclusive Education will demonstrate the ways in which schools contribute to the failure of different student identities on the basis of gender, race, language, sexuality, disability, socio-economic status and geographic isolation. This series differs from existing work in inclusive education by expanding the focus from a narrow consideration of what has been traditionally referred to as special educational needs to understand school failure and exclusion in all its forms. Moreover, the series will consider exclusion and inclusion across all sectors of education: early years, elementary and secondary schooling, and higher education.

Negotiating Belongings

Stories of Forced Migration of Dinka Women from South Sudan

Melanie Baak
University of South Australia, Australia

SENSE PUBLISHERS
ROTTERDAM/BOSTON/TAIPEI

A C.I.P. record for this book is available from the Library of Congress.

ISBN: 978-94-6300-586-9 (paperback)
ISBN: 978-94-6300-587-6 (hardback)
ISBN: 978-94-6300-588-3 (e-book)

Published by: Sense Publishers,
P.O. Box 21858,
3001 AW Rotterdam,
The Netherlands
https://www.sensepublishers.com/

All chapters in this book have undergone peer review.

Printed on acid-free paper

For the women, Kuol and all those who have experienced displacement from their homes.

And to my parents, Henry and Lynda. Thank you for instilling in me a love of learning.

TABLE OF CONTENTS

PREFACE

I met William Kuol Baak on the first day that I went to see the first family from Sudan that I ever met.[1] It was 2004. I had volunteered to support a family during their process of re-settlement in Australia, a duty that William had been undertaking until that time as one of the few members of the Mading Aweil[2] community in South Australia who could read, write and speak English. I took over supporting this family from the man who introduced himself to me as William. Subsequently I bumped into William occasionally when I took the family that I was assisting to visit other families, and we would greet each other cordially. I met many *Jëëng*[3] families during the period that I was volunteering, and I was always received very warmly, and given tea, food and much hospitality. The women, men and children with whom I chatted would tell me stories of their lives, and I felt that we were engaged in intimate exchanges, friendships and knowledge sharing.

At the end of 2004 I spent four months in Nairobi. While staying with a Sudanese family who were living there as refugees, I met a man who was picking up the flight tickets for his family who had been accepted to come to Australia under Australia's resettlement program.[4] He said that a man called Kuol Baak in Adelaide had sponsored his family to go to Australia. At the time I had no idea who he was talking about. The man in Nairobi asked for my phone number and said that when he got to Australia he would call me. I thought nothing more of it.

Several months later I had settled back into my university studies and was in the process of moving out of home. I distinctly remember standing in the trailer outside my parent's house as my mum came running out with the phone saying 'I think it's someone from Africa'. I answered the phone, and it turned out it was the man I had met in Nairobi. He had arrived in Adelaide with his family and wanted me to come and meet them. I went to visit the family with a car full of second-hand sheets, blankets, clothes and anything else my mum thought would be useful for a newly arrived family. When I arrived, I found William playing with six children in the front yard. It was then that I discovered William was in fact Kuol Baak.

I started visiting the family frequently, three or more times a week. William, who from then on became known as Kuol, practically lived there as his house was just around the corner. He would help the children with their homework and the parents with reading and filling in forms as well as just providing them with general emotional support during the sometimes challenging experience of resettlement in Australia. On my visits I would help the children with homework, take them shopping, eat with them, watch TV with them, chat, play and laugh. It was during these frequent visits that my relationship with Kuol developed. One thing lead to another, and Kuol and I ended up living together, and in the *Jëëng* sense this meant we were husband and wife.

This was the beginning of a difficult period in both Kuol's and my lives; we went from being central to this family's life, and the *Jëëng* community (in Kuol's case), to being outsiders and ostracised by the community. Before Kuol and I started living together, Kuol would receive at least ten phone calls a day from people in the *Jëëng* community in Australia wanting assistance or just wanting to chat, invitations to community gatherings and functions, and calls from *Jëëng* in Africa most commonly requesting financial support. As soon as we started living together Kuol's phone stopped ringing. I recall even checking on several occasions to make sure it was still working. We had both crossed the perceived 'boundary' that lay between 'us' and 'them'. Kuol, by living with, and therefore in the eyes of the *Jëëng* marrying, a *khawaja*, a 'white'[5] person, was considered lost to the 'other'. And I suddenly went from being a nice 'white' volunteer who supported the Sudanese community but was still sufficiently distant so as not to pose a threat, to a 'white prostitute' who had stolen one of their good men.

When we attended community gatherings I would be shunned, and people whom I had previously drunk tea and laughed with would not even talk to me. More than anything I wanted our relationship to be recognised as a legitimate relationship between a man and a woman regardless of our skin colour and backgrounds. I wanted to be recognised as a *Tiengjäng*, a Dinka wife, to feel some sense of belonging within the *Jëëng* community, but it seemed that the harder I tried to belong, the more I was rejected.

We were excluded through the ways that the community treated Kuol, including comments such as 'the *khawaja* have stolen you', said not only to reflect the belief that as a 'white' woman I controlled Kuol, but also the perception that he was lost from his own people and his own culture. We were excluded through the ways the community treated me. I was no longer invited to gatherings which I had previously been invited to as a volunteer, and when I visited families whom I had previously supported, they were noticeably uneasy in my presence. While, at first appearances, Kuol and I had apparently lessened the divide between 'black' and 'white', 'Australian' and 'Sudanese', my personal everyday lived experiences told me that never before had the divide been so great. While Kuol and I had created our own little union, we ultimately felt excluded from the very communities of which we desired to be a part.

Kuol continued to tell me 'Just wait, as time passes things will get better'. As time passed, our relationship with the community slowly started to heal. It was different, but some trust and understanding began to creep back in. My efforts to learn *Thuongjäng* and behave in a manner deemed appropriate for a 'good' *Tiengjäng* were recognised. Eleven years later, we have had to work hard to earn back the respect of the community members that we took for granted prior to our marriage. We have made four trips to Africa together including three to Sudan, we have three children with whom we have made a concerted effort to teach *Thuongjäng* and to socialise with the *Jëëng* community, but we are still both constantly negotiating our belonging, whether in Sudan, in other countries in Africa or in Australia. Things have certainly changed since that fateful day in 2005 and while on one day I can think 'Yes, I am *Tiengjäng*, I belong', the very next day I can feel as much an outsider as ever.

Within the *Jëëng* community in Australia, Kuol is still sometimes thrown the taunt that he has become a *khawaja*, as a criticism of some of his actions and ways of thinking which people perceive have changed because he married a 'white' woman, but his phone is back to ringing many times a day. My position in the community has clearly shifted from being the nice, friendly, helpful, 'white', volunteer girl, to being a member of the *Jëëng* community, a *Tiengjäng* who can be loved, criticised, backstabbed and adored just like any other member of the community.

Regardless of our frequent visits to Sudan and our financial support of Kuol's family, Kuol is still considered 'lost' to his family and community in Sudan, and I will always be *nyan khawaja*—'the white girl'. And yet every time we return to Sudan we return to our family, our friends and our community—a community of which I have become a part through my marriage and through my ongoing interactions with the people and the place. It seems that, regardless of birthright, marriage, kinship, community or any other factor, belonging remains an emotionally charged, contested desire and the question remains—is it ever really possible to belong?

NOTES

1 Since the mid 1990s, 27,679 people who identify their birth place as Sudan have migrated to Australia (Department of Immigration and Citizenship, 2011a), with a majority having been resettled under Australia's Humanitarian Entrant Program. The peak years of resettlement of Sudanese-born migrants was in the period from 2003 to 2006. These figures do not include the large numbers of children born to those of Sudanese origin while living in countries of exile such as Kenya, Ethiopia, Egypt and Uganda. Department of Immigration and Citizenship (2011b) statistics suggest that since 1991, 12,279 people who resettled in Australia were of Dinka (*Jëëng*) ethnicity, with the main concentrations being born in Sudan (10,137), Kenya (1,141), Egypt (709), Uganda (149) and Ethiopia (123). It is therefore difficult to put an exact figure on the number of people currently living in Australia who identify as being of 'Sudanese' or 'Dinka' background. Of the 27,679 Sudanese-born people, 2,341 (Department of Immigration and Citizenship, 2011c) initially settled in South Australia. However this figure does not account for internal migrations across state borders subsequent to the initial settlement nor for those who were born of Sudanese parents in other African countries (Baak, 2011c).

2 A regionally based sub-community of southern Sudan.

3 *Jëëng* are a group of people originating from South Sudan who share a common language and culture with some territorial variations. Jëëng are referred to outside of Sudan as 'Dinka' but, as with many groups of people, they have come to be known in the West by a name with which they did not recognise themselves (Southall, 1976). There are an estimated 2.5–3 million *Jëëng* predominantly living in South Sudan but also dispersed globally particularly in the United States, Canada, the UK and Australia (Gurtong, 2011).

4 Under the Australian Department of Immigration and Citizenship Offshore Special Humanitarian Program, a sponsor who is a permanent resident or citizen in Australia may propose an applicant who is living outside their home country, and is subject to discrimination in their home country, for consideration to be accepted to Australia as a Special Humanitarian Entrant (Department of Immigration and Citizenship, 2009).

5 I use inverted commas around words such as 'white', 'black' and 'race' to acknowledge both the contested nature of these terms and their status as social constructs (Maylor, 2009, Peach, 2000).

ACKNOWLEDGMENTS

The journey through writing this book and conducting the research has been exhilarating, devastating, joyous, heart breaking and life changing, among a myriad of other emotions. But the journey would not have been possible without the support of the host of people with whom I have felt some degree of belonging over the course of the project.

First and foremost, to the women, thank you for joining me on my journey and sharing your journeys with me. Your guidance, friendship, teaching, understanding and honesty have taught me more than you can imagine. I hope that when your children read your stories they better understand your journeys.

Associate Professor Robert Hattam and Dr Vicki Crowley, thank you both for guiding me through the journey. You showed me the routes, signposts and markers to follow, and let me get lost when I needed to, but you were always there to redirect me and remind me that somewhere, sometime, at least for the sake of the research, the journey had to end.

The journey through the research was shaped through crossing paths with many academics who may not necessarily be aware of how significantly they contributed to my thinking. I am grateful for the opportunity to present seminars at both the Refugee Law Project (Makerere University, Uganda) and the Forced Migration Studies Programme (University of the Witwatersrand, South Africa) during a University of South Australia–funded trip to Africa. The academics and participants present at those seminars challenged me to look at my research through a broader lens. Special thanks to Veerle Dieltiens, Lorena Nunez Carrasco and Lyandro Komakech for your conversations and hospitality. Thank you also to those academics and people both closer to home and abroad who have offered (unknowingly or knowingly) their advice and time: Professor Vron Ware, Professor Marie Brennan, Dr Kim Huýnh, Associate Professor Susanne Schech, Dr Sophia Rainbird, Stephanie Riak Akuei, Dr Jenny Barnett, Dr Pius Ojara, Sarah Rose, Peter Cassidy and Dr Alison Edwards.

Pan da, my home of birth, Mum, Dad and Steph. You started me on the journey long before any of us knew where it would lead. Yet through all the twists and turns it has taken you have never left my side. *Dziękuję, спасибо*, thank you.

Last, but most certainly not least, to my husband Kuol and children Akon, Achol and Yuew. Words cannot express the gratitude I feel for everything you have shared with me over the journey through this research and book writing. *Wek aa ca leec* is the best I can do. From the endless journeys between Port Pirie and Adelaide where gauntlets were thrown down, battles were fought, and worlds were changed, to the journeys we took together to interstate conferences and learnings in Africa, and who could forget the late night translations. The journey would not have been possible without the innumerable ways in which you have stood by me, supported me and challenged me when I needed challenging. Kuol, your belief in me encouraged me to begin the journey. Your strength, patience and devotion saw it completed. I hope that this book is only the beginning of my journey to become a better *Tiengjäng*, and that in some small way it will help to improve our belongings as a transnational, 'mixed-race', 'cross-cultural' family.

EXPLANATION OF KEY DINKA WORDS

Ciɛɛŋ (written in anglicised form as cieng and pronounced chieng)—It is very difficult to formulate a concise definition of *cieng*, and this will be explored further in the body of the book. *Jëëng* anthropologist Francis Mading Deng (1984, 1998, 2007, 2009) provides a very broad definition. He suggests that, as a verb, *cieng* means 'to look after, to order, to rule, to inhabit, to treat [a person], and to relate to a person', and as a noun it means 'human relations, conduct, behaviour, habit, personality, custom, law, rule, way of life, culture, essence, and nature' (Deng, 1984, p. 185).

Dhëëŋ (written in anglicised form as dheeng and pronounced as written)—'a concept of normative and aesthetic dignity' encompassing 'individual and collective pride, honour and dignity' (Deng, 2009, p. 42).

Jääŋ (singular) *Jëëŋ* (plural) (*written in anglicised form as Jääng* (singular) *Jëëng* (plural) *and pronounced as written*)—a group of people originating from South Sudan who share a common language and culture with some territorial variations. *Jëëng/Jääng* is translated as meaning person or people. In everyday conversation, *Jëëng* people commonly refer to themselves as *Muonyjäng* (*Jääng* man). However in more recent years, particularly in academic and scholarly fields, the word *Jëëng* has been acknowledged as the gender-inclusive term. This term has not yet gained wide acceptance in everyday usage. *Jëëng* are referred to outside of Sudan as Dinka but, as with many groups of people, they have come to be known in the West by a name with which they did not recognise themselves (Southall, 1976). There is much debate over where the name Dinka originated from. Some have said that the English is a corrupted version of the Arabic name for the *Jëëng* which is *Dengka* or *Dengkawi* (Seligman & Seligman, 1932; Jackson, 1923). However, some groups of the 'Arab' north call the *Jëëng* by names stemming from *Jëëng*, such as the Baggara name *Jäängi* (Howell in Southall, 1976). *Jëëng* sources suggest that the name Dinka stemmed from the interaction between a *Jëëng* chief, Deng Kak, and British colonisers in the early 1900s. Deng Kak is said to have introduced himself to the British after which the British began referring to all *Jëëng* as Dinka (perhaps an anglicisation of Deng Kak).

Muonyjäŋ (singular) *Muonyjëëŋ* (plural) (*written in anglicised form as Muonyjäng* (singular) *Muonyjëëng* (plural) *and pronounced as written*)—the name that *Jëëng* (male and female) use to refer to themselves as a group of people in everyday conversation. Literally *Jääng* man/*Jëëng* men. *Jëëng* is the gender-inclusive term which has been adopted in more recent academic and scholarly fields but has not yet gained wide acceptance in everyday usage.

Khawaja—Arabic word adopted by *Jëëng* to refer to 'white' people.

Pan Muonyjäŋ (*written in anglicised form as Pan Muonyjäng and pronounced as written*)—literally means the home (*pan*) of the man (*muony*) of the people (*jäng*). Originally used to refer to any part or the whole of the territories inhabited by *Jëëng*. However usage since colonisation has changed so that *Pan Muonyjäng* now specifically refers to village (rural) areas of Dinka lands, and towns are referred to by their individual names.

Thuɔŋjäŋ (*written in anglicised form as Thuongjäng and pronounced as written*)—the *Jëëng* language (commonly referred to in English as Dinka). As with the words *Jääng* and *Muonyjäng*, the phrase *Thong Muonyjäng* is most commonly used in everyday usage. However, *Thuongjäng* has been recognised as the gender-inclusive term in recent scholarly fields.

Tik (singular—becomes *tieng* when combined with another word), *Diäär* (plural)—woman or wife. A female only becomes *tik* once she has had sexual intercourse for the first time, which is traditionally not meant to occur until she is married.

Tieŋjäŋ (singular) *Diäärjäŋ* (plural) (*written in anglicised form as Tiengjäng* (singular) *Diäärjäng* (plural) *and pronounced as written*)—literally the wife of the people. Means both *Jëëng* woman and *Jëëng* wife. *Jëëng* do not differentiate linguistically between a woman who is *Tiengjäng* by birth and a woman who is *Tiengjäng* by marriage.

MAPS

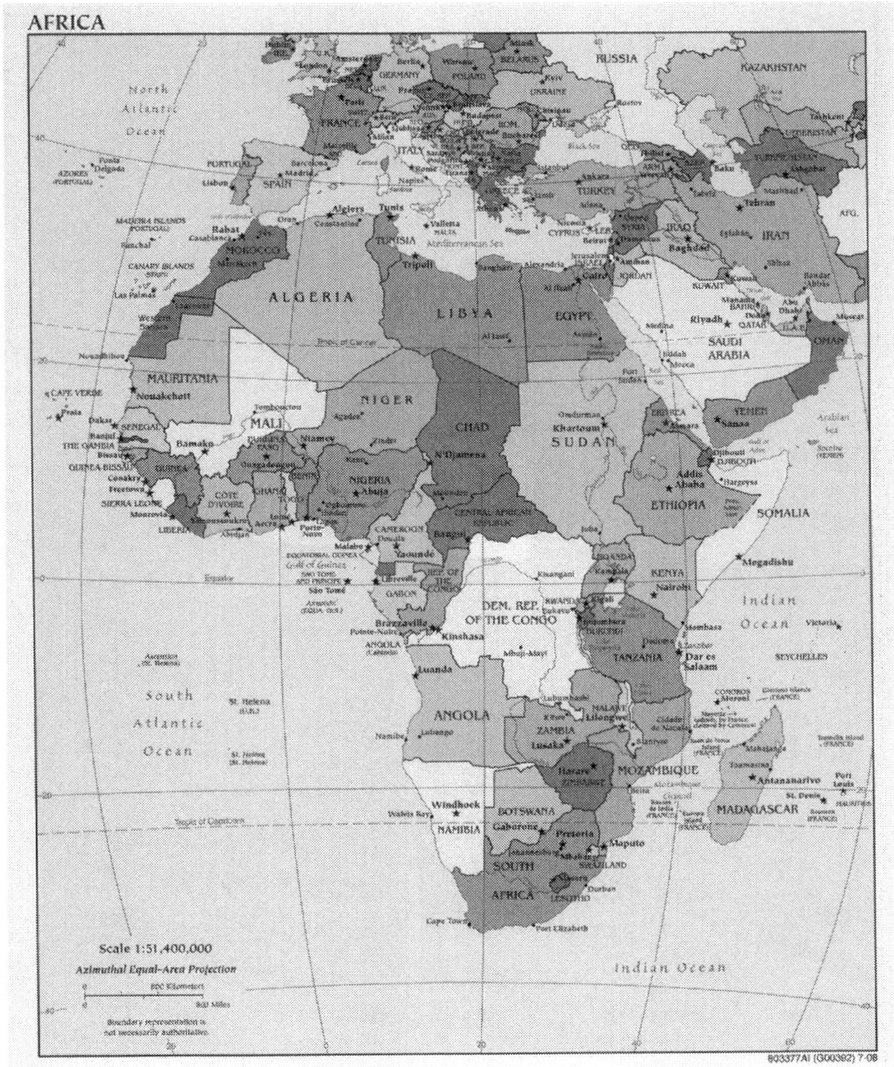

Figure 1. Map of Africa (U.S. Central Intelligence Agency, 2008)

The location of Sudan and the main countries of initial asylum of the women, Ethiopia, Egypt, Kenya and Uganda.[1]

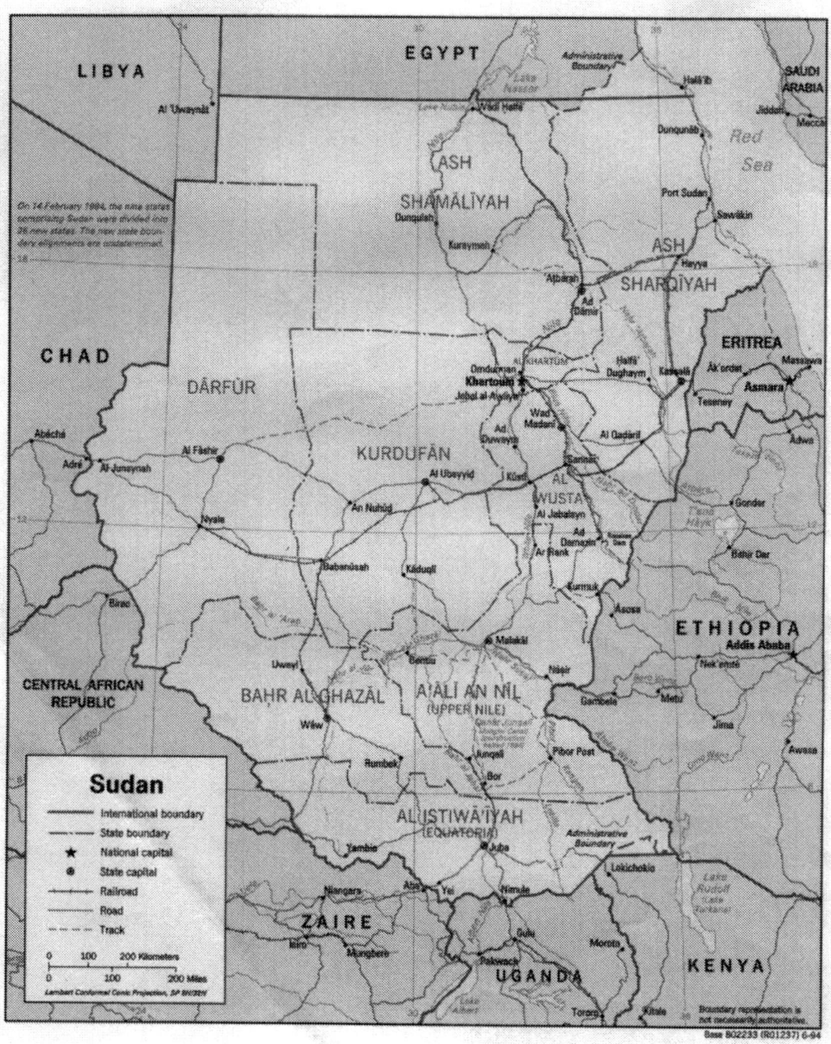

Figure 2. Colonial States of Sudan (U.S. Central Intelligence Agency, 1994)

The states of Sudan as defined by the British including Bahr el Ghazal (spelt Bahr al Ghazal on this map), the original state with which all of the women in this research had a connection.

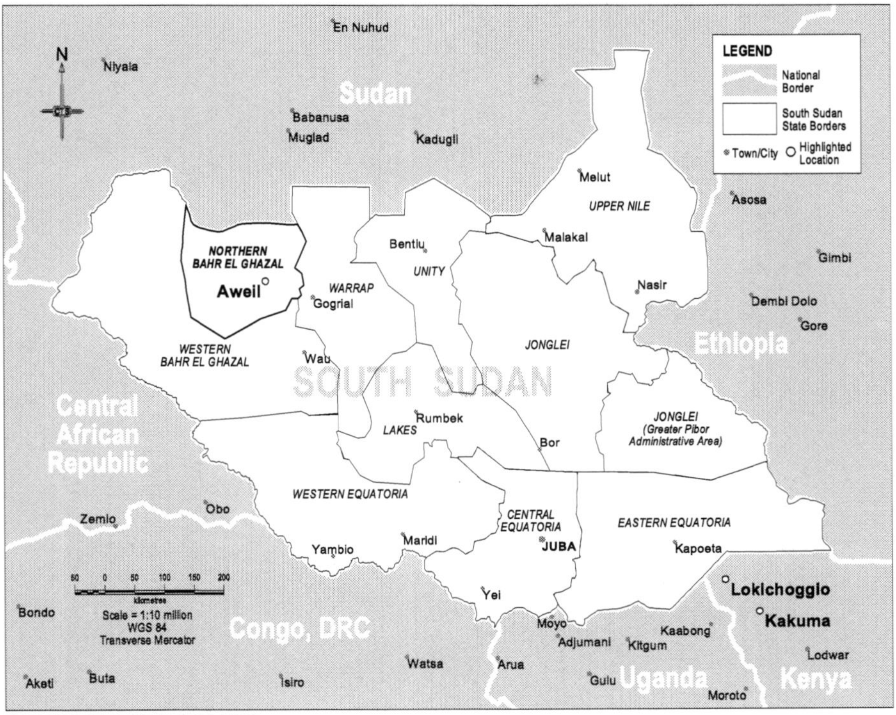

Map compiled by CartoTech Services Pty Ltd, Adelaide

Figure 3. States of South Sudan 1993–2015

This map shows Northern Bahr El Ghazal, the region with which all of the women identified (referred to as Mading Aweil by the women). Also on this map is Lokichoggio, the processing centre at which some of the women were registered as refugees before being transferred to Kakuma refugee camp.

NOTE

1 Sudan was divided into the new countries of Sudan and South Sudan on July 9th, 2011. However, for the substantive period of this research including the data collection period, as well as for most of the duration of the lives of the women involved in the project Sudan was one country. As such, the map illustrates the pre-2011 country of Sudan.

CHAPTER 1

HAUNTED JOURNEYS

Being, Becoming and Belonging

> All lands are haunted. Every place bears its ghosts. All flesh has a surface that is penetrated. All borders are real but provisional. We are all hybrid, on a journey somewhere. And all the nations of the world—all its races, religions, creeds—travel constantly in search of certainty. On that journey we set down anchor lines, roots, traces of neglect and hope. These journeys—call them songlines if you must—create a web that we get tangled in, connecting us, joining the reluctant masses, even as we claim separation, difference, distance. To acknowledge such connections, however, is not to spin a humanist tale. It isn't to make a claim for universals. Rather it is to acknowledge the palimpsest of journeys and the way they shape and texture interactions. (Turcotte, 2007, pp. 110–111)

INTRODUCTION

The concept of belonging has been frequently explored in recent years (see for example Anthias, 2015; hooks, 2009, Pries & Pauls, 2013; Yuval-Davis, 2006a; Probyn, 1996; Yuval-Davis, 2009, 2011), particularly with relation to migration. Belonging is an issue that affects us all, but for those who have been displaced, unsettled or made 'homeless' by the increased movements associated with the contemporary globalising era, 'the ideas and practices associated with belonging are under constant challenge' (Ilcan, 2002, p. 1). As Pollock (1994) has suggested, 'we all have "a dream of belonging", made acute not because of tourism but precisely because of the twentieth century's epidemic condition of migration, refugeeism, diaspora' (p. 84). Migration throws into question not only the belongings of those who physically migrate, but also, particularly in a postcolonial context, of the indigenous and the 'settlers' of destination countries, of subsequent generations born to migrants, and of those who are left behind in countries of origin.

If we all have a 'dream of belonging' (Pollock, 1994, p. 84), a thorough questioning of what this belonging entails for particular individuals is timely and necessary. Belonging has frequently been examined through isolated consideration of disparate categories such as citizenship, nationality, gender, ethnicity, community and family, but how do these multiple and sometimes conflicting belongings operate at one and the same time for people who have been displaced and unsettled by the current era of migration? This book considers this question by exploring the negotiations of belonging of six *Diäärjäng* (Dinka women/wives) across multiple categories, in multiple locations, through stories of whole lives. Five of these *Diäärjäng* were born in the Dinka lands of southern Sudan before subsequently migrating to Australia through a variety of pathways. The sixth is me, who as a 'white' Australian woman who married a Dinka man has, in the words of my mother-in-law, '*raan cë ye cök jɔt bë mɛt wun jëëŋ*' (started a journey to join/become a Dinka person).

This introduction begins with an overview of the development and conceptualisation of my research, before introducing the main theoretical tools and lenses that I utilise and explore throughout the book. The ideas that are outlined in this introduction continue to grow, shift, unfold and 'become' throughout the remainder of the book.

Initially this research grew from a desire to explore and present the stories I had heard from many *Diäärjäng* in the period since I commenced my involvement with the *Jëëng* community in 2004. The stories I had heard were full of difficulty, trauma, hardship, injustice, pain and exclusion, yet these stories also revealed resiliency, agency, love, luck, perseverance, determination, camaraderie and humanity. The stories that I wanted to tell were those that were largely absent from discourses of Sudanese migration to Australia, of refugee women and of African women. They were stories of *Diäärjäng* who continued to negotiate their everyday lives when the everyday seemed impossible. To explore these stories I considered the narrative stories of life[1] of five women (Nyanut, Abuk, Nyalong, Achol and Atong)[2] originally from southern Sudan. As I began to explore these narratives, two challenges became increasingly apparent.

First, the women's narratives clearly illustrate, as Gordon (2008) has articulated, that 'even those who live in the most dire circumstances possess a complex and oftentimes contradictory humanity and subjectivity that is never adequately glimpsed by viewing them as victims or, on the other hand, as superhuman agents' (p. 4). Gordon's further observes that '[i]t has always baffled me why those most interested in understanding and changing the barbaric domination that characterizes our modernity often—not always—withhold from the very people they are most concerned with the right to complex personhood' (p. 4). The challenge became how to understand and present the women's narratives in a way which acknowledged this right to complex personhood.

To acknowledge and articulate the complex personhoods of the women was a challenging task in the academic realm where, as Krog (2011) describes it, one becomes aware of 'how the quality of "on-the-ground experience"' is 'being crushed into a dispirited nothingness through weak English and the specific format of academic papers', how 'an important story' easily dies 'within the corset of an academic paper, how a crucial observation' is 'nothing without a theory, and how a valuable experience dissolved outside a discipline' (p. 383). Respecting the complex personhood of the women required a particular way of hearing, doing and writing the research which will be outlined in Chapter 2. It required a form of interdisciplinarity described by Barthes (cited in Clifford & Marcus, 1986):[3]

> Interdisciplinary work, so much discussed these days, is not about confronting already constituted disciplines (none of which, in fact, is willing to let itself go). To do something interdisciplinary it's not enough to choose a 'subject' (a theme) and gather around it two or three sciences. Interdisciplinarity consists in creating a new object that belongs to no one. (p. 1)

As Gordon (2008) argues, this type of interdisciplinarity is '[n]ot owned by anyone yet, this interdisciplinarity is in the public domain, which does not guarantee anything except that there is still some room to claim rather than discipline its meaning into existence' (p. 7). *Negotiating belongings* draws on fields as diverse as migration, ethnic, kinship, family, critical whiteness, African feminist, globalisation, cultural and gender studies, and on sociology, African philosophy and literature. All of these fields are overburdened with particular theories, particular ways of knowing and particular ways of doing, that obscure the complexities that are inherent in the everyday lived experiences of the women. So, while this book draws on all of these fields, it neither originates from nor sits comfortably within any of them. Rather *Negotiating belongings* grew from a desire to be able to understand and articulate adequately the complex personhoods of six women, the result of which has been 'a new object that belongs to no one' (Barthes, cited in Clifford & Marcus, 1986, p. 1). In addition to this interdisciplinarity, respecting the complex personhoods of the women has also required a particular constellation of theoretical tools which I will outline later in the introduction.

The second challenge that arose as the research proceeded was a recognition that I had another, perhaps initially unconscious, research interest. As I began to listen to the women's narratives, what struck me time and again were the portions of their stories which centred on desires and negotiations for belonging. On questioning what it was that drew me to these narratives of belonging I was forced to acknowledge that, as a woman who had 'started a journey to join/become a Dinka person', my desire to understand the women's lives went much deeper than simply wanting to tell their stories. Rather, I thought, or even hoped, that through listening to and better understanding the other women's stories I would learn something that would make my own journey as a becoming *Tiengjäng* (Dinka woman/wife) somewhat easier. In addition, I found that to understand the women's narratives of belonging adequately I also had to reflect on my own journey that had made my desire to belong so strong. On the whole, the experiences of 'white' women in 'mixed-race' relationships are hugely under-researched, leaving women such as myself to forge our own alliances and make our way through somewhat isolated struggles. While this book is not singularly or explicitly an exploration of the deeply troubling, vexed and compromised issue of my journey as a 'white' woman 'being/becoming other' through my 'mixed-race' marriage, it is haunted by my journey and experiences as a becoming *Tiengjäng.*

Negotiating belongings therefore became a dual exploration, as it became clear that I could not hear the narratives of the women outside of my own experiences, desires and negotiations for belonging. The book explores the narrative stories of lives of the five women alongside my own autoethnographic reflections. While my narrative autoethnography overlaps and intertwines with the women's narratives, it is important to note that I am not aiming for any sort of equivalence between mine and the women's stories. Rather I interweave my narrative with theirs as a means to understand my own relationship with the women and their narratives, as well as adding layers to the theoretical concepts which unfold throughout the book. Through the six narratives, the book examines various sites of belonging: from belonging within and among friends to belonging in nation-states and ethnic groups, from 'glocal' place-based belongings to belonging within and among family and kin. Exploring how the journeys towards desired belongings are haunted by various 'social' processes such as colonisation, power, 'race', class, gender and sexuality, I argue that human beings are constantly moving between being and becoming, a movement which is shaped not only by the self, but also by others.

There are three main arguments that are explored throughout *Negotiating belongings*. Each argument unfolds in a different way. The first and most salient argument that is made through a variety of different explorations is that belonging is not fixed, but is a continual negotiation and process of becoming. This argument builds on the work of Elspeth Probyn (1996) and Ann-Marie Fortier (2000), who consider belonging as an ongoing process negotiated through the combined processes of being and becoming. This book offers new ways of considering the intersections between being, becoming and belonging. Through examining belonging to different sites from friendship (Chapter 2), to the nation-state (Chapter 3), to gendered ethnicities (Chapter 4), to 'glocal' place-based communities (Chapter 5), to families and kin (Chapter 6), *Negotiating belongings* presents ways to rethink some of the taken-for-granted notions around belonging. By considering the experiences of belonging through the diverse and multiple in-depth narratives of migration of six *Diäärjäng*, the book provides increased depth and layers of understanding to what is a continually developing and increasingly important body of academic work in the fields of belonging and migration. Each woman's story of life told a different narrative of the complexities of being, becoming and desired belongings which shifted and changed throughout the journey through her life. The women described a shifting in importance of different modes of belonging depending on context, place and people, and the women's stories were never simply about feeling a sense of belonging and inclusion, but also very much about exclusion and not belonging.

Each of the women's narratives focused on journeys toward particular belongings which held the most significance for that woman, either through the difficulties and challenges it had given her in her life, or through the support and comfort that site of belonging provided her. Abuk's narrative centred around difficulties in negotiating a sense of belonging on a national level in Sudan, then in Egypt (the country in which she initially sought asylum), and finally in Australia. Nyalong's narrative focused on her challenges in negotiating belonging within the 'glocal' community of Mading Aweil in exile in Kenya following the death of her husband. Atong's narrative centred on place and regionally based belonging, as she married a man who was from a different region of Sudan than her family of birth. Achol's narrative centred on several sites of belonging including the challenges in being the granddaughter of an immigrant to the Dinka lands as well as how she negotiated her gender-based belonging as a Dinka woman who found it difficult to become pregnant. Nyanut's narrative centred on the importance of her immediate family (father, mother and siblings) in maintaining a sense of belonging, and how this had been challenged and impeded as a direct result of the civil war in Sudan, her experiences in exile and finally her resettlement in Australia. Finally, my own narrative centred around a perpetual search for belonging which led me on the journey to and through this research. Each chapter of the book explores one particular site to which the women described desiring and negotiating their belongings.

The second of my main arguments is a demand for 'new' ways of doing research that encompass 'new' and different ways of listening to and really hearing the narratives of the 'subaltern' (Spivak, 1988). This argument draws on the work of Antjie Krog (2008, 2011) and is most salient in Chapters 2 and 7. Throughout the book I use the term 'new' in inverted commas when referring to 'new' ways of doing, hearing and knowing in research. I use 'new' in acknowledgement that what I am calling for is not really new. For over thirty years, scholars (particularly postcolonial and feminist) such as Clifford and Marcus (1986), Denzin (1995) and Haraway (1991) have been calling for new and different ways of doing research that acknowledge the partiality and situatedness of knowledge, and the difficulties and challenges of really hearing research participants.[4] While the approach I am calling for is not really new, this research approach still remains to be taken up successfully and widely within the fields of research in which this research is situated. As such, I continue to refer to it as 'new'. For me, this 'new' way of doing research required that I engage a methodological process which included ethnography, autoethnography and listening to what I call the 'living oral (hi)stories of life' of the five women. These 'new' ways of 'doing' research allow and even require an intense challenge to many of the ways in which 'subaltern' groups are understood and 'known'. Hearing the stories of the women who participated in this research through these 'new' ways of listening challenges many of the ways in which these women are commonly understood whether as, among other things, women, refugees, Africans, 'black' or mothers. Hearing the narratives in this way returns to the women a respect for their complex personhoods. In addition, these 'new' ways of doing research involve a degree of reflexivity which recognises the inability of the researcher ever to write themselves out of their research. This book explores both the challenges and necessity of this reflexivity, as well as providing an example of one way to articulate this reflexivity. Hearing narratives in these 'new' ways also requires particular translations and interpretations that are often not possible through hearing these stories through Western epistemologies and Western lenses. Learning how to understand a narrative through an epistemology that is not embedded in Western ontology and philosophy is perhaps the most challenging aspect of these 'new' ways of hearing. However, to be able to do so ultimately leads to the third revelation of the book.

While the links between belonging and the negotiated journey of becoming receive most attention throughout the body of the book, the third main argument was initially 'hidden' by the limitations of my own Western epistemologies. As the research evolved, and I gave precedence to the importance of 'new' ways of listening, a particular aspect emerged as the most important in understanding not only the women's negotiations for belonging, but the very ways in which they 'are' in the world. Understanding the ways in which Nyanut, Abuk, Achol, Atong and Nyalong negotiated their belongings was not possible without an understanding of the *Jëëng* ontology that governed their ways of being in the world. As such, this book is also an exploration of *cieng*, a key concept of relationality for *Jëëng* that emphasises a relational ontology underpinned by a relational ethical responsibility which underscores the way in which *Jëëng* exist in the world. The salience of this ontology became clear towards the conclusion of the research process and writing of the book. As such, the concept unfolds throughout the book with a detailed exploration in Chapter 7. The women's narratives and my own experiences within the *Jëëng* community provided particular ways to interrogate the intersections of being and becoming on the haunted journey to belonging, and the relational ontology of *cieng* provided an added layer to the understanding that was developed.

The following sections introduce the three main theoretical tools and lenses that are utilised and explored throughout the book. The first concept which is outlined is belonging and its intersections with being and becoming. Second, the phrase 'haunted journeys', which includes the theoretical ideas of both haunting and journeying, is introduced. Finally, the *Jëëng* concept of *cieng* is explored. All of these sections serve only as introductions to these concepts, and all are further built upon throughout the book.

DESIRING BELONGING AND ITS POLITICS

> [I]n common usages, the term belonging moves from 'being the property of someone, something' to the sense of 'fitting in socially', 'being a member', and that 'belongings' designates 'possessions' and 'baggage'. Belonging for me conjures a deep insecurity about the possibility of really belonging, truly fitting in. But then, the term 'belongings' also forefronts the ways in which these yearnings to fit in will always be diverse: at times joyous, at times painful, at times destined to fail. Perhaps more immediately, belonging brings forth images of leaving, carting one's possessions and baggage from place to place. Thus, while belonging may make one think of arriving, it also always carries the scent of departure—it marks the interstices of being and going. (Probyn, 1996, p. 2)

While experiences of belonging have been extensively examined in recent years,[5] the meaning of the concept itself is often implicitly assumed and is certainly not uniform. My conceptual understanding of belonging resonates with the above quotation from Probyn.[6] Probyn emphasises the diversity of the term belonging, but also signifies most of the key dimensions. First, she uses the word 'belongings' to illustrate the multiplicity of belonging. Secondly, she refers to the relationality of belonging through connections to people, places and objects. Thirdly, she alludes to both the affective dimensions of belonging and the politics of belonging by emphasising the insecurities and instabilities of belonging. Finally, she observes that belonging is linked with the movement of leaving and arriving. This emphasises the processual nature of belonging, its ongoing development and negotiation through movement. I draw on these points to elaborate my understanding of belonging below.

First, belongings are multiple. 'People can "belong" in many different ways and to many different objects of attachments' (Yuval-Davis, 2006a, p. 199). This multiplicity of belongings was evident in the narratives of all the women, who described negotiating belongings on many different levels—from the nation-state, to the ethnic group, to the family. However, it is also through this multiplicity that belonging is frequently conflated with identity, and it is important here to clarify and differentiate between the two briefly. While identity is undeniably linked to the question of belonging (Mason, 2007, p. 274), belonging 'cannot be reduced to identities and identifications' (Kannabiran, Vieten, & Yuval-Davis, 2006, p. 189). As Anthias (2006) has argued, it is possible to identify and not feel that one belongs or, alternatively, to feel like one belongs but not identify with a particular group. Additionally, Probyn (1996) has argued that the idea of identity describes 'categories of belonging' (pp. 152–153) and therefore does not engage with the singular specificity in which individuals and groups live out their belongings. Fortier's (2000) description is particularly useful in clarifying the intersections between belonging and identity. She asserts that '[i]ncluded in the formation of belonging, then, is identity as a momentary positionality which is always already becoming' (p. 2). The idea of identity as a 'momentary positionality' in the ongoing negotiation/formation of belonging is therefore central to understanding the connections between being, becoming and belonging.

Secondly, belonging is a process which is always located in place (hooks, 2009). Reflecting on her first experiences of a geographical shift from her home in Kentucky to university in California, hooks (2009) recalls 'I felt for the first time the way in which geographical origins could separate citizens of the same nation. I did not feel a sense of belonging at Stanford University, I constantly felt like an unwanted outsider' (p. 12). Probyn (2005) uses the phrase 'being out-of-place' to describe this process of '[w]hen you feel like a fish out of water', a process 'the body registers in social and cultural contexts when it doesn't belong' (p. xvi). For the women involved in my research, belongings were always negotiated in places and place always underscored the recollections in which belongings were recalled.

From their descriptions of exclusion from national belonging in Sudan, based in part on geographical location as southern Sudanese in a nation dominated politically and economically by northern Sudanese (Chapter 3) to their 'glocal' belongings in Australia which were shaped by allegiances to small, local regions and villages of birth in Sudan (Chapter 5), place-based belongings permeated their stories.

Thirdly, belonging occurs not only in place, but also among people (Nsamenang, 2008; hooks, 2009; Rose, 2000; Probyn, 1996; Garbutt, 2009). hooks (2009) also alludes to these relational experiences of belonging. She recalls her efforts to build a sense of belonging with a 'white' male student from a Mormon background at Stanford, a young man who was also 'more often than not alone and isolated' (p. 14). This negotiation for belonging was based on a shared religious upbringing in which she suggests:

> We talked to one another and endeavoured to make each other feel less like strangers in a strange land. We talked scripture. But talking scripture was not powerful enough to erase the barriers created by racism that had taught us to fear and beware difference. (p. 14)

This begs the question, then, when are the similarities between the self and the other enough to override the differences so that a sense of belonging can be felt? Are the differences between people from different 'race', class and gender backgrounds, for example, so great that there can never be any sense of belonging across these divides? The women's narratives posed more questions than answers in relation to belonging within and among groups of people. From belonging among the *Jëëng* community in Australia (Chapter 4) to belonging among kin and family (Chapter 6), reflections on belonging with relation to 'others' all signified that 'belonging cannot be an isolated and individual affair' (Probyn, 1996, p. 13).

This relational nature of belonging means that belonging can never be stable. It is 'tenacious and fragile' (Probyn, 1996, p. 8) and performed in the knowledge that one can be excluded from belonging just as quickly as one is included. In this way, negotiating belongings is always processual. One's belonging is never fixed. This vulnerability and instability of belonging also results in the strong affective connections and connotations that belonging holds (Kannabiran, Vieten, & Yuval-Davis, 2006; Anthias, 2006; Ilcan, 2002). As Probyn (1996) has acknowledged, belonging 'designates a profoundly affective manner of being, always performed with the experience of being within and in-between sets of social relations' (p. 13). This book considers how these affective dimensions of belonging underscore the desires of the women to belong and ultimately unsettles the very possibility of 'ever really and truly belonging' (Probyn, 1996, p. 8).

The instability of belonging also results in what has frequently been termed the 'politics of belonging' (Alinia, 2004; Castles & Davidson, 2000; Crowley, 1998; Geschiere & Nyamnjoh, 1998; Yuval-Davis, 2006a). Several authors have argued that it is important to differentiate between belonging and the politics of belonging (Crowley, 1998; Castles & Davidson, 2000; Yuval-Davis, 2006a, 2009, 2011).[7] As

Yuval-Davis (2006a) has argued, '[b]elonging tends to be naturalized and becomes articulated and politicized only when it is threatened in some way' (p. 197; see also Yuval-Davis, Kannabiran, & Vieten, 2006). The women in this research described various ways in which they felt excluded from belonging across all levels, from the nation-state to the family, and through this exclusion their belongings were threatened and became politicised.

Crowley (1998) has described the politics of belonging as 'the dirty work of boundary maintenance' (p. 30). Yuval-Davis (2006a) has elaborated on this by explaining that '[t]he boundaries that the politics of belonging is concerned with are the boundaries of the political community of belonging, the boundaries that separate the world population into "us" and "them"'(p. 204). The borders and boundaries that mark and maintain the difference between 'us' and 'them', who does or does not belong to a particular group, are fraught with complexity. To begin with, the types of borders are limitless. There are 'geographical borders, cultural borders, national borders, linguistic borders, generic borders, specular borders, and disciplinary borders' (Henderson, 1995b, p. 2), borders as metaphors 'for psychological, sexual, spiritual, cultural, class and racialised boundaries' (Brah, 1996, p. 198), and borders 'between outside and inside, self and other, public and private, subject and object' (Henderson, 1995b, p. 2). Borders are

> arbitrary dividing lines that are simultaneously social, cultural and psychic; territories to be patrolled against those whom they construct as outsiders, aliens, the Others; forms of demarcation where the very act of prohibition inscribes transgression; zones where fear of the Other is the fear of the self; places where claims to ownership—claims to 'mine', 'yours' and 'theirs'—are staked out, contested, defended, and fought over. (Brah, 1996, p. 198)

These borders and boundaries are not fixed, which is in part what makes belonging so malleable. The very nature of their social construction and maintenance determines that there is a continual 'staking out' and contestation of their location—not only by those located inside the borders, but also by those who are outside.

Brah (1996) has emphasised, however, that the critical questions lie in interrogating 'when and where these borders are imagined and instituted, or how they may shift, change, weaken or dissolve' (p. 175). Interrogating these questions provides insight into how the politics of belonging operates. This is central to my argument. This research explores the lives of six women as they move, shift and are shifted across borders and boundaries (both physical and metaphorical), negotiate and desire various belongings and blur the boundaries between being and becoming. The book provides a means for rethinking and adding depth to some of the ideas around belonging which are currently taken for granted, primarily the notion of belonging as a process of becoming (Fortier, 2000; Probyn, 1996), as well as the multiplicity of beings, becomings and belongings.

INTERLUDE I: ON DESIRING BELONGING[8]

As I have been considering the belongings of the other women I am haunted by my own experiences of belonging and not belonging. I am repeatedly drawn back to an issue that I have tried to ignore. I am not quite sure how or even if I should examine it in light of the women's stories. The women's words of suffering and hunger throughout the war and their years in exile are always heard by me as something that was done to them; something outside of their control. I can see the larger picture of what led to their suffering and periods of hunger. On the other hand, because I lived my own experience of suffering and hunger and because of the stereotypical connotations that go along with these, I feel almost self-indulgent considering it in light of what I have heard of the women's experiences. However, finally something forced me to.

It was a day I'd spent studying like any other, mostly contemplating *Jëëng* identity, examining some early writings of British colonisers about *Jëëng* women. I went to pick up my daughter Akon from childcare and thought I'd grab a copy of *Adelaide's Child*, a magazine for parents about all things child related. I scanned the articles on the first page and found one about recovering from anorexia nervosa. I flicked through the magazine until I came to the article; a sketch of a skeletal young woman sitting at the bottom of a well greeted me. I started reading. One paragraph, I stopped, turned away. Started reading again, the bottom dropped out of my stomach. I turned away again. I made it through one more paragraph before tears came into my eyes. I walked away. I could not keep reading. I sat with the article open on the table next to me but struggled to keep reading. This is what has shaped a part of my life, my own search for a sense of belonging, and as much as I think I've recovered, reading the article written by another anorexia survivor brings back memories I'd rather forget. I thank Rachael Hyde (2009) for putting into words what I can still so painfully and vividly remember. Her words ring true to my experience down to every last word. 'I had lost my health, my hair, my self-esteem, my energy, my height, my ambition, my friends, my ability to think, to reason, my trust in myself, others' trust in me, my pride—in short, my identity' (p. 14). This sentence made me realise that if I am to consider my own negotiations for belonging, emphasised by my identities at given points, I must consider what first alerted me to the intense desire I have to belong.

I had to examine all of my previous experiences of belonging and not belonging before I could understand my journey of becoming a *Tiengjäng*. I do not see myself still as having an 'anorexic' identity, and I also do not feel as if I have a sense of belonging with survivors of anorexia. Perhaps because anorexia is such a competitive, distortive and selfish illness, it is impossible to see yourself as having connections and a shared identity with any other sufferers. Plus, to me, anorexia is a negative, self-destructive identity, one that I no longer wish to have any sense of belonging with. I do not want to go to great lengths to examine my experience with anorexia, but I do want to acknowledge my own personal battle to, as Hyde (2008) puts it, 'regain an identity for yourself' (p. 14).

BEING AND BECOMING: THE CHANGING SAME

> The changing same seizes the ways in which the tension between having been, being, and becoming is continually negotiated, conjugated and resolved. (Fortier, 2000, p. 49)

In the current era of increased global movement there is a growing trend towards understanding identities and belongings as mobile and not fixed; as processes of becoming (see for example Malkki, 1995a; Hall, 1996; Sarup, 1994; Kannabiran, Vieten, & Yuval-Davis, 2006). We are all engaged in journeys through life that in various ways define, shift and change who we are, who we want to be and how we are seen by the world. However, this understanding of identities (and belongings) as transient processes of becoming obscures that fact that, right here and now, we are only ever being.[9] There are some things that we just are, that we cannot change (as much as we may like). For example, I am 'white', and the five other women are 'black'.[10] However, what this 'whiteness' or 'blackness' means shifts and changes depending on locational politics which vary over time and space. At other times, we may become something that we have never previously been, for example by marrying Kuol I began my journey to becoming a *Tiengjäng*. At certain points in time, in certain places, we are who we are, but these beings continue to be haunted, negotiated processes of becoming.

Arguably, being and becoming operate hand in hand. At certain points in time we must simply be, whether or not we are content with what this being means. On this theme Paul Gilroy (2000) uses the idea of 'the changing same' (p. 129).[11] To me this phrase emphasises both being, as the sameness we have once been or continue to be, and becoming, as the changing movement and shift towards becoming something else.

> The changing same is not some invariant essence that gets enclosed subsequently in a shape-shifting exterior with which it is casually associated. It is not the sign of an unbroken, integral inside protected by a camouflaged husk … The same is present, but how can we imagine it as something other than an essence generating the merely accidental? Iteration is the key to this process. The same is retained without needing to be reified. It is ceaselessly reprocessed. It is maintained and modified in what becomes a determinedly nontraditional tradition, for this is not tradition as closed or simple repetition. (Gilroy, 2000, p. 129)

Through the idea of the 'changing same', where neither being nor becoming can exist without the other, it becomes clearer, for example, how the always already there 'blackness' or 'whiteness' has changed in relation to how it is understood or shapes the lives of the women depending on location and other circumstances surrounding their positionality at any given moment (Wright, 2004). Exploring the various sites in which the women have negotiated and desired their belongings illustrates this quivery nature of being and becoming, and illustrates that belonging is an ongoing negotiation which is always produced 'through the combined processes of being and becoming' (Fortier, 2000, p. 2).

HAUNTED JOURNEYS

The women told their recollections of being, becoming and belonging in times and places that were at times far from where these experiences originated. Therefore I needed a conceptual framework that would help understand the nature of these retrograde reflections and how they shaped the present. Utilising theories of journeying (hooks, 2009; Clifford, 1997, 1989) and haunting (Gordon, 2008) I consider the undeniably haunted belongings of myself and the five other women—belongings which not only journey across spatial and temporal transitions but belongings that are haunted by many of the larger 'social' phenomena that have shaped the era of modernity: colonisation, 'race', power, gender and class.

Journeying

> [R]econstructing an archaeology of memory makes return possible, the journey to a place we can never call home even as we reinhabit it to make sense of present locations. Such journeying cannot be fully encompassed by conventional notions of travel. (hooks, 2009, p. 99)

Travel theories have proliferated in recent years[12] and these diverse observations on travel reflect the unsettled nature of an era '[w]hen the "Third World" is no longer maintained at a distance "out there" but begins to appear "in here"' (Chambers, 1994b, p. 2). This is an era in which the world has experienced significant global restructuring, resulting in many new kinds of movement (Hart, 2005). From the way that theories travel (Said, 1983), to the way that ethnographic research is affected by movements of people (Clifford, 1989, 1997), to travel as a way of understanding 'race' (hooks, 2009), travel theories have permeated the social sciences. As Knapp (2005) suggests, theories of travel have become their 'own exemplary case of a fast moving idea' (p. 250).

Following hooks (2009), I utilise the term journey in preference to travel. hooks (2009) suggests that forms of travel undertaken by people which encompass the terrors of experiences such as 'rites of passage, immigration, enforced migration, relocation, enslavement, and homelessness' (p. 100) cannot be easily evoked under the word travel with its leisurely connotations. The journeying of the women—enforced flight from devastation, destruction and danger, as well as my own journeying—at times physical, at other times metaphorical but always confrontational, is best understood through the idea of journeying which recuperates travel theory from the 'conventional notions of travel' (p. 99), providing a more inclusive concept for understanding the complex journeys of the women.[13]

Travel, journeying and movement also allow for an undoing of the notion that belonging is always rooted in place. As Clifford (1997) has observed, there has long been an assumption in the social sciences that 'social existence is, or should be, centered in circumscribed places … Dwelling was understood to be the local ground of collective life, travel a supplement; roots always precede routes' (p. 3). However, recent efforts in travel theory have worked to unsettle this notion, with more and more theorists recognising that, as Chambers (1994b) has described,

> [o]ur sense of being, of identity and language, is experienced and extrapolated from movement: the 'I' does not pre-exist this movement and then go out into the world, the 'I' is constantly being formed and reformed in such movement in the world … In this movement our sense of identity can never be resolved. I might self-consciously try to halt the journey and seek shelter in the comforting categories of being … But the movement in which we all are caught, the languages and histories into which we are thrown, and in which we appear, lies beyond such individual volition. (pp. 24–25)

For the women in this research, it was precisely the displacement from roots and the thrust into routes that catapulted them into their ongoing search for belonging. They are constantly renegotiating the 'I' in the movements which they undertake; from home to exile to diaspora, the 'I' is constantly reconstructed to 'make sense of the present location' (hooks, 2009, p. 99). This is not only an experience common to the five women originally from Sudan who were forcibly displaced from the place of their roots, but also for me as the grandchild of immigrants to Australia, living in a colonial nation to which I, as a 'white' immigrant Australian, can claim no roots. In fact in the current era rootlessness seems to affect virtually everyone to some extent: 'Virtually everywhere one looks, the processes of human movement and encounter are long-established and complex' (Clifford, 1997, p. 3).

Haunting

While journeying provides a framework for considering the movement of people, material objects and concrete ideas across places and time, the concept of haunting allows for a consideration of what Gordon (2008) has referred to as the 'ghostly matters' that haunt. She describes haunting as a 'way in which abusive systems of power make themselves known and their impacts felt in everyday life' (p. xvi). In the foreword to Gordon's book, Radway (2008) suggests that Gordon is calling for a new sociology that acknowledges that individual 'subjectivity is always and inevitably haunted by the social and most especially by those repressions, disappearances, absences, and losses enforced by the conditions of modern life' (pp. x–xi).[14] By observing and listening to the 'echoes and murmurs of that which has been lost but which is still present among us in the form of intimations, hints, suggestions, and portents' (p. x), haunting provides a way to 'reveal and to learn from subjugated knowledge' (Gordon, 2008, p. xvii), the knowledge that is always already present, but repressed, disqualified or marginalised.

'[T]o be haunted', argues Turcotte (2007), 'is to be visited by ghosts' (p. 111). He continues, suggesting that:

> Ghosts, one would have to say, are as present today as they've always been. They stand as an intangible fact, a luminal presence between the here and now, the now and then … They reassure us only of the insubstantiality of borders, the lie of geography, the myth of purity, the fragility of place. And in a contemporary time framed by the certainties of poststructuralist uncertainties, they are the only universal force—signatures that write across languages, races, bloodlines and maps. The ghost is a tattoo that lives on, within, and beyond the skin. It marks, it covers over; it transforms through its inscription. And yet it is profoundly and at once a part of and alien to—the self and the not self; the other and the same. (p. 109)

These 'ghostly matters', the ghosts and spectres of the past, are 'everywhere but the ground' (Michaels, 1996, p. 8). They are 'in our dreams, our language, our ideas, our habits and rituals, our books and paintings' (Ruitenberg, 2009, p. 297); they are in our stories, our memories, they are everywhere—if we only learn to observe them and to listen to what they are telling us. The question then becomes, how 'do we work productively with the spirits that course through our veins: that infect us, reflect us, threaten and reassure?' (Turcotte, 2007, p. 111).

In order to work productively with these spirits and ghosts, I have endeavoured to adopt and adapt Gordon's new sociology—her 'ghostly matters'—as a

> method of knowledge production and a way of writing that could represent the damage and the haunting of the historical alternatives and thus richly conjure, describe, narrate, and explain the liens, the costs, the forfeits, and the losses of modern systems of abusive power in their immediacy and worldly significance. (2008, p. xvii)

By considering the hauntings of modern systems of abusive power including colonialism, racism, capitalism and patriarchy I have drafted a meditation that acknowledges, understands, represents and narrates the ghosts that haunt the always-present past of six women's lives. These 'ghostly matters' are present in the times, events and places that led to the initial displacement of the women from their homes, they are present in their reflections on exile in their countries of initial asylum and they continue to permeate their experiences in Australia. Following, acknowledging and writing about these ghosts has, for me, been a profound experience which has significantly shifted my ways of thinking and understanding of both my own and the women's narratives. Considering these hauntings has located 'a profound and durable practice of thinking and being and acting toward eliminating the conditions that produce the nastiness in the first place' (Gordon, 2008, p. xvii).

Turcotte's (2007) observation that these ghostly matters 'infect us, reflect us, threaten and reassure' (p. 111) encapsulates the multiple affective dimensions of haunting and ghosts. My understanding and use of these terms does not include just the negative connotation that is frequently associated with Western ghosts. Haunting and ghostly matters are not purely negative, but involve side by side, contradictory affect; both affections and fear, reassurance and loss. Haunting and ghostly matters should not be read and understood as having a singular meaning.

At times, both the women's journeys and my own took us to locations and through experiences which forced us to change the places and groups with which we desired belonging. For example, my relationship with Kuol resulted in me desiring belonging within the *Jëëng* community, while the women's migration to Australia resulted in them desiring belonging as Australians. Our journeys towards these desired belongings were haunted, and these hauntings made belonging to particular groups exceptionally complex. Appiah (2005) argues that there are

> constraints on how we may live that derive from our historical circumstances and our physical and mental endowments: I was born into the wrong family to be a Yoruba chief and with the wrong body for motherhood; I am too short to be a successful professional basketball player, insufficiently dexterous to be a concert pianist. But even when we have taken these things into account, we know that each human life starts out with many possibilities … And for a person of a liberal disposition these choices belong, in the end, to the person whose life it is. (p. xii)

Appiah, however, does not appear to take into consideration the full extent to which historical circumstances and physical and mental endowments limit the ability for some people to make choices about what sort of life they want to live and to which groups they wish to belong. While every person endeavours to 'make' their lives (Appiah, 2005, p. 15), some lives are haunted to such an extent that there are severe limits to just how they 'make' their lives.

The stories of the women in my research illustrate that certain lives are haunted in a way that ultimately limits how they can 'make' their lives. While they continue to negotiate and resist many of the ghosts that haunt them, the ghosts are always already there. To be born with 'black' skin or 'white' skin, for example, can haunt individuals in particular ways—these ghosts took centuries to come into being and will take centuries of resistance to cease to exist.

INTERLUDE II: ON HAUNTED JOURNEYS

The particular moment detailed below forced me to consider the prevalence of 'ghostly matters' in my own everyday life.[15] It also made me think beyond the scope of my haunted belonging in relation not only to *Jëëng*, but to the readings of our bodies in haunted spaces. In this moment I was forced to realise the haunted nature of the space in which I live. Australia is haunted by the ghosts of a colonial past. To acknowledge the space in which I am writing, researching and living means also to acknowledge the haunted nature of the space in which we exist. This was a haunted journey in which I became profoundly aware of the nature of what I was researching.

> I was catching the bus from Port Pirie to Adelaide[16] for an Australian Critical Race and Whiteness Studies Association Symposium (ironic considering what follows). The bus had driven through from Ceduna, some 550 kilometres from Port Pirie, and was already mostly full. Kuol carried Akon, our one-year-old daughter, onto the bus as he usually does while I loaded the bags. He went to our allocated seats of 5C and 5D, but found that they were already occupied by some blankets and bags on the floor in front of the seats. He asked what I wanted to do. I said 'I guess we'll move them' because there were no people around who took ownership of them and no other spare seats. A young guy said he was sitting in a seat he was not meant to be in, but that was not the seat we were allocated. I put my luggage in the overhead rack and started putting the other blankets and things up there as well. Kuol put Akon into the seat. Then an Aboriginal woman who had been out for a smoke got back onto the bus and started talking to another Aboriginal woman who was sitting in the seat in front of us holding a baby. They were speaking in a combination of an Aboriginal language spliced with English, so I could not understand what they were saying, but it was the kind of talking where you begin to think you've done something wrong without necessarily understanding what it is. Perhaps it was in the body language, the facial expressions or the tone. I got that feeling you get when you're trying to do the right thing, aware, perhaps too aware, of the racial nature of what is unfolding. A 'white' woman, a 'black' man—foreigners, invaders—two 'black' women—natives, the invaded—and two babies—could they have been neutral? Then the bus started to move and Kuol was still on board so he quickly left and I sat down. The lady in front of me was still talking to the other lady, who had since sat opposite in the seat that had been occupied by the young man. It turned out that the blanket and bags belonged to the woman who had been out for a smoke, but during their long drive from Ceduna, the passengers had all spread out and occupied other seats, and that lady had occupied the seat allocated to me.
>
> The women kept talking to each other, and although I could not understand everything, I could understand enough English words in their conversation to know that they were still talking about me and the seat. Feeling uncomfortable

and guilty, as if I needed to justify my actions, I said 'I'm sorry I did not realise this was anybody's seat. There were no other seats that did not have people sitting in them, so I took the only seat I found, and the one that was allocated to me'. The response caught me off guard, especially given my relation to Kuol and Akon. One of the women said 'That's the difference between black women and white women'. I responded saying 'It didn't have anything to do with race or skin colour, I simply sat in the only seat I could find'. She said 'Black women would sit in any seat they found'. I decided not to respond to this simply saying 'I think we'll leave it there'.

As a person who has spent so much of their life trying perhaps to deceive myself that there is no difference between 'black' women and 'white' women, I was taken aback. I spent the rest of the trip in silence, contemplating the incident and the exchange of words and thinking what a terrible 'white' woman I must be. I wondered if the exchange would have been different if Kuol was 'white', I wondered what I could have said or done differently, but most of all I wondered if there really was a difference between 'black' women and 'white' women. I sat for the three-hour journey deep in thought, but also listening to the ongoing conversation of the two women, wondering if they would say something that revealed to me why 'black' and 'white' women were different.

They were sitting in front of me and talking at a level that could be heard by most people surrounding them. They arrived at a point in their conversation that struck me, as not only had they shaken me with their off-hand remarks about 'blackness' and 'whiteness', which most likely they have not thought about since, but they then began talking about ghosts. Granted, the ghosts they were talking about were slightly different to the sociological nature of the ghosts that I had been considering, but they were ghosts that were present in the everyday lives of these women nonetheless. One spoke of going in to her baby at night and finding him tucked into bed but knowing that neither her nor her partner had tucked him in. They spoke of feeling the presence of people who have died, sometimes protective, other times violent. One of them asked the other if she had ever asked one of the ghosts what they wanted, because maybe there was something they needed.[17]

That was when I realised that we all have ghosts; ghosts of different sorts, ghosts that show themselves in different ways, we all have different ways of acknowledging and dealing with our ghosts. But just as much as those two women had acknowledged their ghosts, even if they did not know why they were haunting them, I too have my ghosts. My ghosts haunt me in a way that I had never previously been aware of, but now that I was aware I found them everywhere. Gordon (2008) has argued that '[f]ollowing the ghosts is about making a contact that changes you and refashions the social relations in which you are located' (p. 22). Once I had begun 'following the ghosts' I was struck by their presence in conversations, in altercations, in movies, in books, in everyday exchanges; they were always already there. Perhaps I had previously been aware of them, but by acknowledging them as ghosts I was finally able to appreciate that these were the links between institution and individual, social structure and subject, and history and biography that constitute the haunted nature of my life (Gordon, 2008). Examining some of my past was critical to understanding the haunted process of my becoming a *Tiengjäng*.

◈

CIENG: A *JËËNG* ONTOLOGY AND EPISTEMOLOGY

As argued above, belonging is a relational concept. As such, it became clear towards the end of the research process that it is impossible to consider the negotiated belongings of a group of six *Diäärjäng* without considering a key concept of relationality for *Jëëng*. This is expressed in the *Thuongjäng* word *cieng* which emphasises relational ethical responsibility. For *Jëëng* this encompasses a particular way of being in the world. It is difficult to formulate a concise definition of *cieng*. *Jëëng* anthropologist Francis Mading Deng (1984, 1998, 2007, 2009) provides a very broad definition. He suggests that, as a verb, *cieng* means 'to look after, to order, to rule, to inhabit, to treat [a person], and to relate to a person', and as a noun it means 'human relations, conduct, behaviour, habit, personality, custom, law, rule, way of life, culture, essence, and nature' (Deng, 1984, p. 185). He further argues that *cieng* underscores all human relationships for *Jëëng* and, in essence, is the 'concept of ideal human relations' (Deng, 1984, p. 185, 2009, p. 42). 'At the core of *cieng*', Deng (2007) states, 'are the ideals of human relations, family and community, dignity and integrity, honor and respect, loyalty and piety and the power of the word' (p. 100). For the women in this research *cieng* remained a very important element underscoring how they negotiated their belongings through the ways in which they existed in relation with others.

Cieng, argues Deng (2009), exists alongside another term *dhëëng*,[18] which he interprets as being 'a concept of normative and aesthetic dignity' encompassing 'individual and collective pride, honour and dignity' (p. 42). He suggests that

> *cieng* provided standards for evaluating conduct, while *dheeng* classified people according to that conduct; *cieng* requires that one should behave in a certain way. While *dheeng* labels one virtuous for behaving in that way; *cieng* is a normative concept, a means; while *dheeng* is a concept of status, an end. (p. 42)

To understand *cieng* and how and why it operates, it is important then to understand it in the context of *dhëëng*. For *Jëëng* '[r]espect for human dignity', or *dhëëng*, 'is an integral part of the principles of conduct that guide and regulate human relationships and constitutes the sum total of the moral code and the social order' (p. 45). To be recognised as *adheng* (a person living with *dhëëng*), a desirable status, one must practise and live in *cieng path* (good *cieng*) but, as Deng (2007) has argued, *cieng* 'is largely an aspiration that is only partially adhered to and, indeed, is often negated' (p. 100). So not every person practises *cieng path* at every moment in time. It is a desired way of living that is not always adhered to in its fullest. The presence of *cieng* as a *Jëëng* way of life certainly does not mean that all *Jëëng* live in ways or practise acts that are commensurate with the ideals of *cieng* at all times. When people do not practise or live in the ideal ways of *cieng* it is referred to as *cieng rac* (bad *cieng*).

Unfortunately, aside from Deng's definitions, there is a scarcity of research on the concept of *cieng*, and what does currently exist is problematic and far from extensive. With the exception of Biong Deng (2010),[19] who briefly describes *cieng* both as the 'traditional Dinka way of life' (p. 233) and 'social relations' (p. 234), all of the current writing on *cieng* draws on the original definition from Deng (1984).[20] With such a broad definition, it is easy to see how the term could be misappropriated and misunderstood. For example, Swedish health researchers Jeppsson and Hjern (2005) utilised the concept of *cieng* to try to 'contrast the Western medical model of traumatic stress with the particular political and cultural context of the Dinkas of southern Sudan' (p. 67). They formulated their understanding of *cieng* based on the work of Deng, and arrived at the following definition:

> The Dinkas have a way of describing the balance between the aggressive and the compassionate, the egoistic and the social—in other words, the world in harmony. When things are in balance the world is in accordance with *cieng*. The accompanying feeling is *adheeng*. *Cieng* literally means home, a place and a situation where things are well-known, in unity and harmony, as opposed to places and situations where things are not so. It is a concept of ideal human relations. It starts in the relations and good manners in the family but acquires, in the context of the wider society, the meaning of law. As circles widen it becomes blurred, aggressiveness being acceptable against peoples that are foreign to the Dinka. (pp. 69–70)

Jeppsson and Hjern then surveyed 147 Dinka children aged between 10 and 18 years who were living in Kakuma Refugee Camp in Kenya to try to understand how these children made sense of traumatic events that had occurred in their lives and how they sought comfort and support in the refugee camp. In their findings, they stated that, for *Jëëng*, a definition of mental health should be 'based on whether life was in accordance with *cieng* and *adheng*' (2005, p. 77). Finding that 90 per cent of their cohort stated 'that their current lifestyle was in accordance with the traditional concepts of *cieng* and *adheng*' (p. 74), they argued that this, in part, described the remarkable resilience to adversity and trauma that many of the children seemed to have. This understanding of *cieng* as a mental health concept is very limiting and certainly does not encapsulate how I have come to understand *cieng* through my involvement with the *Jëëng* community. While living in *cieng* may be one aspect which contributes to *Jëëng* perceptions of well-being, this is by no means the only way of understanding *cieng*, nor is *cieng* the only marker of mental health for *Jëëng*. In addition, arguably it would be very difficult to find a *Jëëng* who said that they did not live in accordance with the concepts of *cieng* and *dhëëng*, as these in fact underscore what it means to be *Jëëng* in relation to others.

Drawing directly from this article is Pickard's (2006) PhD thesis entitled *Southern Sudanese concepts of cieng/ciang in America: The transcultural experience of well-being and adaptive functioning.*[21] Pickard uses the concept of *cieng* to explore the mental well-being of Dinka and Nuer[22] resettled in the US. He examines *cieng* from a psychological standpoint and argues that *cieng* represents a 'set of values or ideals existing at one end of a continuum of well-being' (p. 2). He suggests that when a 'southern Sudanese' is what he refers to as 'in *cieng*' they will be in 'a state of well-being' (p. 56) and when they are 'out of *cieng*' they will be in a 'state of distress' (p. 58). Pickard's thesis is problematic on more levels than there is scope to detail here. However, I do wish to address two major problems that I fear may hinder further developments in the understanding of the concept of *cieng*. First is the conflation of two uses of the word *cieng* into a 'southern Sudanese concept'. Throughout the thesis Pickard utilises the Nuer and Dinka concepts of *cieng* as synonymous. This is not the case. As Deal (2010) has argued, '[c]ieng, as I found expressed and defined among the Dinka Agaar, is distinct from the identical word used by the nearby Nuer' (p. 571). For the Nuer, *cieng* signifies differing descriptions of physical places of 'home' encompassing 'homestead, hamlet, village, and tribal sections of various dimensions' (Evans-Pritchard, 2010, p. 81). While it appeared from his literature review that Pickard was utilising the *Jëëng* concept of *cieng*, his conflation of the *Jëëng* and Nuer terms with these differing meanings was highly problematic and meant that it was hardly surprising that Pickard's participants had obvious difficulty in enunciating a description of *cieng*. Secondly, by drawing on Jeppsson and Hjern's (2005) research on *cieng* which defined *cieng* as predominantly a mental health–related concept, Pickard's thesis once again presents a narrow understanding of *cieng* which focuses on just one possible outcome of living in *cieng*, which is positive mental health and well-being.

Three additional articles have provided particular case studies of the enactment of *cieng* in various locations. The first is Deal's (2010) captivating article 'Torture by *cieng*: Ethical theory meets social practice among the Dinka Agaar of South Sudan', which captures the notion of *cieng* well, but unfortunately due to the particular case study presents the negative outcomes of *cieng* in an extreme situation. The other two are articles I have recently published (Baak, 2011c, 2011b) which reflect on the experiences of the *Jëëng* community in Australia following the murder of a young *Jäăng* man in 2009. Like Deal's article, my articles also reflect on community responses in a negative and extreme situation. In these articles I argue that *cieng* encompasses a relational ethical responsibility that underscored how the community mourned the death of this young man. In his article Deal reflects on a series of experiences he had during a period he spent living and working in the Dinka lands of South Sudan from 2003 to 2008. Early in his paper, Deal details 'A lesson in *cieng*' in which he was summoned by the local community elders of a Dinka village in which he had recently opened a medical clinic. The elders requested that he account for why he had opened the clinic without liaising with the community leaders. Deal articulates that '[t]hey [the community leaders] observed that we were acting independently, rather than as members of the community, and it made them uncomfortable' (2010, p. 565). He further reflects that he

> had been called before the community's leaders not because of the product of our decisions but because of the process we used to reach them. In my mind, our decisions had resulted in the correct actions and were therefore proper. In the minds of the elders, however, the process that brought us to act as we did was devoid of *cieng* and therefore improper—regardless of the rightness of the eventual decision. (p. 565)

This reflects the communal mentality inherent in *cieng*, in which decisions that impact on particular individuals or communities should not be made in isolation without consulting with and involving members of that community within the decision-making process.

Following the detailing of this experience, Deal continues in his article to explain his observations of the tensions and violence that occurred between two sections of the Agaar Dinka. This violence resulted in the deaths of over fifty people from the two communities (including a chief) in a series of retributional attacks. Subsequently a number of people who had not been directly involved in the violence were imprisoned and flogged by the army that was responsible for governing the region at that time. These people included the mother and other relations of the man who was accused of killing the chief. These people were imprisoned 'because of their clan affiliations with the murderers, rather than any individual infraction' (p. 568). Deal was surprised and confronted by the imprisonment and beating of people 'without a trial or any reasonable idea that they had committed a crime' (p. 568). In the months following the violence and imprisonment Deal interviewed in excess of 112 people and found that

> the sociocentric ideas, positively expressed as *cieng*, accounted for coalitional guilt not in the need for the accused murderer to turn himself in but, rather, in the widespread justification by both victims and perpetrators of violence of the punishment of the entire clan. Within this framework of reason, no innocent person was being punished: there was a guilty family being punished using the body of an individual mother as the receptacle of wrath. (p. 568)

This is an extreme example of the communalism that *cieng* defines. In order for the communities to live together, those who are related to the individual who has committed the crime can be held accountable, as these relations mean that there is a sense of coalitional guilt and responsibility. From his experience, Deal surmises that 'the concept of *cieng* may be best understood here to mean that the good of the group supersedes the needs or even safety of the individual. *Cieng* puts material values and individual welfare subordinate to social human values and community interests' (p. 571). From this conclusion, it starts to become clearer that *cieng* represents a form of communal ontology which challenges the Western focus on individualism (Swanson, 2009; Keevy, 2008; Krog, 2004; Kamwangamalu, 1999).

This description draws much closer to the way that I have come to understand *cieng* as a way of life which is relational to others. However, it is not only a way of life; it is a way of being, a way of thinking and a way of looking at and understanding the world. It is a component of a philosophy, an ontology, an epistemology, which requires a particular relational ethic and governs how *Jëëng* exist in the world. As such it very closely (if not precisely) equates with other similar African notions[23] such as *ubuntu* in the Nguni languages (Caracciolo, 2009; Gade, 2010; Swanson, 2007; Tutu, 1999), *uMunthu* in Chichewa (Sharra, 2009), *hunhu* in Shona (Taringa, 2007), *botho* in Sotho (Metz & Gaie, 2010) and the many other indigenous African terms that represent this way of being that, it has been argued, exists in most regions of sub-Saharan Africa (Metz & Gaie, 2010; Taringa, 2007). Much has been written on all of these terms and I will briefly explore just some of the increasing body of literature on these terms, most specifically how they relate to *cieng* and to belonging. All of these terms signify a particular relational ontology, and this relational ontology has much to contribute to the ways in which belonging is understood and negotiated.

Ubuntu has undergone the most thorough analysis of any of the linguistic terms that identify this epistemology and ontology, perhaps as a result of its use as a founding aspect of the South African Truth and Reconciliation Commission (TRC). One of the most frequently cited definitions of *ubuntu* is Archbishop Desmond Tutu's (1999) description in his reflection on the TRC process:

> *Ubuntu* is very difficult to render into a Western language. It speaks of the very essence of being human. When we want to give high praise to someone we say, '*Yu, u nobumtu*'; 'Hey, he or she has *ubuntu.*' This means they are generous, hospitable, friendly, caring and compassionate. They share what they have. It also means my humanity is caught up, is inextricably bound up, in theirs. We belong in a bundle of life. We say, 'a person is a person through other people'. It is not 'I think therefore I am'. It says rather: 'I am human because I belong.' I participate, I share. A person with *ubuntu* is open and available to others, affirming of others, does not feel threatened that others are able and good; for he or she has a proper self-assurance that comes from knowing that he or she belongs in a greater whole and is diminished when others are humiliated or diminished, when others are tortured or oppressed, or treated as if they were less than who they are. (pp. 34–35)

This description is by no means exhaustive, but does encompass many of the main aspects of *ubuntu* and other related discourses. First, it encompasses the humanity or humanism underscored by these terms (Swanson, 2007, 2009; Gade, 2010; Ramose, 2001; Kamwangamalu, 1999). Secondly, it illustrates that there can be varying degrees to which someone can practise or 'have' *ubuntu*, and that practising *ubuntu* results in people being recognised in particular positive ways including being generous and hospitable (this reflects the practice of *cieng* and resulting *dhëëng* outlined by Deng which are detailed above). Thirdly it illustrates the relational, interdependent, communal nature of these concepts through the phrase 'a person is a person through other people' (Swanson, 2007, 2009; Nussbaum, 2003; Kochalumchuvattil, 2010; Gade, 2010; Metz & Gaie, 2010; Kamwangamalu, 1999). This phrase is captured in the *Thuongjäng* saying '*Raan ee ya raan ë raan dä*' (literally a person is a person in reliance on another person). Fourth, it alludes to the ways in which *ubuntu* provides a possible site of belonging (Taringa, 2007; Segrest, 2002). Finally, it elucidates some of the diminishing outcomes of not practising *ubuntu* including torture and oppression (Ramose, 2001).

My understanding and use of *cieng* (and related concepts) will be developed further throughout this book. I argue that *cieng* offers a different way both to conduct research as well as to co-exist ethically in the world. *Cieng* offers a 'new'[24] way not only to understand relational ethics but also to formulate an understanding of how we can all belong in the world as human beings. This way of living together offers a way of being and belonging that would enable Others to simply become others, co-existing unhampered by the confines of citizenship, nationality, 'race', gender, class, sexuality or the many other ghosts which haunt modes and ways of belonging.

OUTLINE OF THE BOOK

The introduction has set out the main theoretical and conceptual ideas that underscore the book. The remainder of the book explores different sites and ways in which the women negotiated their belongings.

Chapter 2 considers how friendship, as one articulation of *cieng*, formed a key component of both my research methodology and method and became the grounds for what Gandhi (2006) has referred to as 'the co-belonging of nonidentical singularities' (p. 26). The chapter begins to engage with some of the questions of belonging that unravel over the following chapters through considering how I was positioned as an inside-out/outside-in researcher and how this reflected my ongoing negotiations for belonging as a *Tiengjäng*. It also considers how the research was conducted in an 'ethic of friendship' (Tillmann-Healy, 2003). This chapter forms the basis of the argument for 'new' ways of hearing narratives, conducting research and learning about and understanding Others.

The terms citizenship, nationality and ethnicity are frequently conflated or subsumed under other concepts. Many of the current writers on concepts of belonging in relation to migration do not clearly differentiate between the uses of these three concepts (see, for example, Fortier, 2000; Salih, 2003; Yuval-Davis, 2006a, 2009). While, arguably, there is overlap in how these various categories operate to control and determine belongings, both Oommen (1997) and Castles and Davidson (2000) suggest that careful differentiation between these particular categories is needed. The women's stories further signified the importance of differentiating between citizenship, nationality and ethnicity, illustrating how each operated in particular ways to shape their journeys and negotiations for belonging. Chapters 3 and 4 emphasise the distinctions between nationality, citizenship and ethnicity and they are explored further in the two chapters.

Chapter 3 considers belonging to the nation-state through lenses of citizenship and nationality. Chapter 3 was shaped most significantly by Abuk's narrative of desiring belonging through the rights and responsibilities most commonly associated with citizenship, while she also recognised the impossibilities and challenges of obtaining these in Sudan, Egypt and Australia. In addition, this chapter came about through an intense consideration of what it was that made it so difficult for the women to feel a sense of belonging to the larger unit of the nation-state in all of the locations in which they had lived. Through the women's narratives, it became clear that nationality and citizenship operated in different ways to control these belongings.

Chapter 4 was predominantly drawn from one word which haunted not only the women's stories, but also my own experiences: *Diäärjäng*. *Diäärjäng* (or its singular form *Tiengjäng*) is a compound word which draws together *Diäär* (women/wives) and *Jääng* (Dinka person)—in this way making a consideration of ethnicity outside of gender virtually impossible. While gender operated in every realm of the women's lives to shape how their belongings were negotiated, the women's stories illustrated that it was particularly salient in how they negotiated their belongings as *Jëëng*. Therefore Chapter 4 considers how they negotiated belonging through both gender and ethnicity. By considering the women's reflections on what it has meant to be female in the *Jääng* context across the spatial and temporal transitions they have made during their lives, this chapter questions whether there is any one way of being *Diäärjäng*, and therefore whether there is really any way to categorise who exactly belongs as *Diäärjäng*.

There is a general assumption in much of this literature that more 'global' sites of belonging in transnational migration override the more 'local' sites of belonging (Robertson, 1995). Chapters 5 and 6 consider some of these more 'local' sites of belonging. These are the levels in which everyday interactions frequently take place, and in which communities are constituted less through the 'imagined' (Anderson, 1991) and more through the physicality and intimacy of knowing, face-to-face, others who negotiate their belongings in these sites.

Chapter 5 considers how 'local' regionally based communities in South Sudan continue to haunt the women's lives on a global scale. It considers how these 'glocal' sites become increasingly significant as a result of migration and then explores the politics and contestations of belonging within that site across a range of locations. Chapter 5 explores how the 'local' region of Mading Aweil continues to haunt the women's belongings through their global migrations. The chapter centres around the narratives of three of the women which describe not only how these glocal communities were produced through 'global' migrations but also how belongings within these communities are politicised through the hauntings of family histories, fear and jealousy. Ultimately the chapter illustrates how the politics of belonging results in an impermanency and complexity even within this 'local' site belonging.

Chapter 6 considers the women's negotiations for belonging within and among their families and kin of birth. It begins by arguing for a broader conception of kin and family and then examines how the women negotiated their belongings within this site in spite of the global dispersion of their family and kin. Chapter 6 explores the most intimate of the sites in which the women negotiated their belongings, the family. It focuses particularly on negotiating belongings within and among *kooc pan da* (the family and kin of birth), first suggesting that even who is considered kin and family is never permanent and then arguing that migration further complicates belongings within and among family and kin.

Finally, Chapter 7 draws together the various themes which permeate the book, arguing for the need for 'new' ways of 'hearing' in order to hear narratives within the embeddedness within particular ontologies and epistemologies. Through this, I argue for the importance of indigenous epistemologies, such as *cieng*, to understanding the haunted journeys through being, becoming and belonging.

NOTES

1. I utilised this methodology which I have described in long form as 'living oral (hi)stories of life', abbreviated to stories of life, which draws on the narrative methodologies of life history, living stories and oral history.
2. Pseudonyms have been used for the names of the women and for some place names that could identify the women. Although some of the women were happy to be identified, others were not, so I made the decision to make all of the women as anonymous as possible as I thought that this was ethically in the best interests of each woman, her family and myself in the small and often politically turbulent *Jëëng* community in Australia.
3. This quotation is drawn from an article originally published in French (Barthes, 1972) and appears to have first been translated into English by Clifford and Marcus (1986).
4. See also, for example, Abu-Lughod (1993), Behar (1996), Collins (1990), Couldry (2009) and Lammers (2005).
5. For some key examples see Anthias (2006, 2009a, 2009b), Bailey (2012), Castles and Davidson (2000), Fortier (1999, 2000, 2006), Geschiere (2009), hooks (2009), Probyn (1995, 1996) and Yuval-Davis (2006a, 2009, 2011).
6. This description is also similar to that of a number of other authors including Yuval-Davis, Kannabiran and Vieten (2006). They describe belonging as referring to 'patterns of trust and confidence' relating to community and society. Within this, they suggest 'we have to think about the shifting meaning of identity, family, the influence of spatial (migration) and existential (material) displacement and, further, the actually confused (and diffused) longing for stable emotional attachments as they are articulated in national, ethnic, cultural and religious affiliations' (p. 4).
7. See also Alinia (2004), Berg (2010), Geschiere and Nyamnjoh (1998), Nyamnjoh and Rowlands (1998), and Yuval-Davis et al. (2005, 2006).
8. Throughout the book I draw on a literary technique of Markus Zusak (2005) in his incredible hauntology *The book thief.* In this text, Zusak splices the main text with interjections from the narrator, who identifies himself as Death. Zusak uses indented passages, highlighted by the use of bold and italic script, to interpose particular information into the story. These are used to signify narrative shifts or as an aside from Death. The first interjection, for example is:

   *** *HERE IS A SMALL FACT* ***
   You are going to die. (p. 1)

The final note from Death is

I am haunted by humans. (p. 584)

I use this technique to splice the main body of the book with autoethnographic vignettes (labelled as interludes) which illustrate my personal experience of the pertinent themes being discussed. In this introductory chapter, there are two interludes which illustrate my connection with two of the key themes. Chapters 3 to 7 each begin with an interlude which illustrates my own experience of negotiating belonging in relation to the site of belonging discussed subsequently in the chapter.

9 Much philosophical work has been done on 'being' (for example Heidegger, 1962; Lévinas, 1991; Warburton, 2001; Overgaard, 2004; Sartre, 2005; Lovejoy, 2009; Merleau-Ponty, 2002). While I acknowledge that my work draws on the contributions of these authors, I do not attempt to attend to the debate on 'being'.

10 For an interesting further exploration of this concept see Krog's (2009) *Begging to be black.*

11 Gilroy draws this term from the work of LeRoi Jones (1967) who traces the continuities in forms of 'black' music. McDowell (1995) also uses this term to explore 'black' women's fiction from the nineteenth century to the present.

12 See, for example, Chambers (1994a), Clifford (1989, 1997), Dube (1999), hooks (2009), Howe (2003), Kaplan (1996), Mouffe (1994), Pollock (1994), Said (1983, 2000), Sarup (1994), and Trinh (1994).

13 The physical journeys of migration made by the individual women as well as the root causes of their displacement are explored in Appendix A.

14 The notions of haunting, ghosts and spectres have been used by many different writers in a variety of fields. These range from Derrida's (1994) argument for a hauntology through which ghosts and spectres are considered to transcend time in his consideration of the spectres of Marx in philosophy, to Morrision's (2006) use of ghosts in her American literary classic *Beloved*, from Ronnell's (1993) examination of the hauntings of Goethe in the writings of Freud and Eckermann, to O'Riely's (2007) consideration of the use of haunting in postcolonial theory. Much other work has also been done on the concepts of haunting, spectres and ghosts (see, for example, Davis, 2005; Etking, 2009; Hart, 2006; Hofmeyr, 2007; Holland, 2001; Kenway et al., 2006; Lai, 2011; Mansfield, 2008; Munos, 2011; Bell, 1997; Labanyi, 2001; Matsuoka & Sorenson, 2001; Taiwo, 1998). While I have considered all of these texts, I draw most strongly on the work of Gordon (2008), whose feminist analysis of 'ghostly matters' most robustly resounds with the lives and stories of the women in this research.

15 This particular moment, as with most of the autoethnographic reflections detailed in the interludes in the book, provided moments that Barthes (1981) might describe as 'punctum' (p. 27). This multilayered encounter provided a moment in which identity, 'race', ghosts, journeys and belonging collided in one punctumous moment.

16 For a majority of the research period I lived in Port Pirie, a regional town of South Australia approximately 240 kilometres north of South Australia's capital city of Adelaide.

17 Ghosts play an important role in Indigenous Australian cosmology and dreaming. While these do not parallel Western ghosts or haunting, it is nonetheless salient given the ways in which my journey was haunted by this ghostly occurrence. Clarke (2007) reports:

> Contemporary Aboriginal people ... inform me that they believe ghosts are the spiritual remains of people who were once alive. In the case of southern Aboriginal people, they have told me that during the period immediately after death, the person's spirit is torn between the desire to stay with loved ones still alive and the imperative to return to the Spirit World where it merges with the Ancestors ... The spirits of the dead are still said to be able to have an impact upon human lives. (p. 148)

He further suggests that '[n]ot all contemporary ghost sightings in southern Australia are necessarily seen as negative. Aboriginal people consider that the dead often appear to close family members and friends to console them' (p. 153).

[18] I write this term as *dhëëng* (the commonly accepted current *Thuongjäng* nomenclature). Deng (1984, 1998, 2007, 2009) writes it as *dheeng* so I leave direct quotations from Deng in this format. Jeppsson and Hjern (2005) term it *adheng*, which again I leave in direct quotations.

[19] Luka Biong Deng is also a *Jääng* and is not related to Francis Mading Deng.

[20] While not referenced, it would appear that Deng's definition draws, in part, on the work of Godfrey Lienhardt (2004), who writes that the Dinka 'have a word, *cieng* or *cieng baai*, which used as a verb has the sense of "to look after" or "to order", and in its noun form means "the custom" or "the rule"' (p. 106).

[21] Pickard (2006) states that, to his knowledge, the concept of *cieng* has been examined only once in the literature, citing Jeppsson and Hjern (2005).

[22] Nuer are an 'ethnic' group of South Sudan whose home regions neighbour *Jëëng* lands. *Jëëng* and Nuer (Nath in the Nuer language) are both Nilotic groups who have lived in neighbouring regions for many centuries. As such they share some linguistic and cultural characteristics (Evans-Pritchard, 1940, 2010). Kelly (1985) suggests that '[t]he Nuer and Dinka speak genetically related Western Nioltic languages that are derived from a common proto-language' (p. 10). However, he further argues that 'Nuer and Dinka would have ceased to be mutually intelligible dialects of the same language' between approximately 'A.D. 700 and 1300' (p. 11).

[23] Two other writers (Asante, 2011; de Ngor, 2006) have very briefly alluded to the similarities between *cieng* and *ubuntu*.

[24] Again, I use the word 'new' in inverted commas, this time because it is not 'new' for everyone. Relational epistemologies and ontologies are at the forefront of many indigenous ways of knowing and being. However, they offer 'new' ways for those of us situated within Western epistemologies and ontologies to understand relationality.

CHAPTER 2

FRIENDSHIP AND NEGOTIATING BELONGINGS THROUGH RESEARCH

> 'Friendship,' I suggest, is one name for the co-belonging of nonidentical singularities. (Gandhi, 2006, p. 26)

INTRODUCTION

Research is a dirty word for many of those who have been affected by colonialism and its legacies. Linda Tuhiwai Smith (2003) suggests that 'the term "research" is inextricably linked to European imperialism and colonialism' (p. 1). In many ways qualitative research methods of participant observation, interviewing and ethnography historically served as the 'scientific' basis for objectifying 'natives' and justifying colonisation and are therefore implicated in the project of racism (Denzin & Lincoln, 2008). How then, was I going to conduct 'research' with a group of women who have suffered the consequences of colonialism from a postcolonial standpoint if research was a dirty word?

Swanson (2007) argues that in order to disrupt and decolonise the dominant meanings and 'deficit discourse' (Bernstein, 2003a, 2003b) inherent in much research which produces meanings from particular privileged perspectives it is essential to find 'less objectifying ways of being in research' (p. 62). She further acknowledges that in her South African–based research:

> Ubuntu provided a vision and framework for me for respectful engagement in research of this nature; one that permitted reflexivity, reciprocity, community connectedness, and cross-cultural understanding, through a sense of 'humble togetherness'. (p. 62)

This research was underscored by friendship. I had been a friend or acquaintance of all five women before commencing the research relationships and, over the course of the research, these friendships became ways through which the women and I negotiated our belongings. Derrida (1988), however, suggests that friendship is always an aspiration; it is desired but never fully achieved. It 'is never a given in the present; it belongs to the experience of waiting, of promise, or of commitment' (p. 636). It is negotiated, evolving and a process of becoming. The research was a process through which the women and I negotiated these belongings. Through these friendship negotiations, the women and I built deeper knowledges of each other through sharing stories and experiences, listening, crying, and showing sympathy, compassion and a multitude of other emotions. While the women and I negotiated our belongings through friendship during the research, the research process was also underscored by this friendship. Through the practices of aspiring to and negotiating friendships with the five women, the research methodologies and methods evolved, and friendship thereby came to underscore the very ethic and method of the research. As *ubuntu* (and *cieng*) emphasise a sense of 'togetherness in forms of friendship and hospitality' (Fox, 2011, p. 82; see also Sackey, 2012), friendship provided a way of conducting the research in a 'humble togetherness' (Swanson, 2007, p. 62) which kept the relational ethic, epistemology and ontology of *cieng* at the forefront of the research process and research relationships.

For me, research conducted in an ethic of friendship which grew from an ethic and epistemology grounded in *cieng* provided one aspect of the framework to 'decolonize the research act' (Caracciolo, 2009, p. xiii). As Swanson (2007) has further argued:

> Ubuntu contributes to disrupting and decolonizing hegemonic meanings, and provides an opportunity for renewal and transformation in our desire for egalitarianism and human dignity. It affords a way of knowing that helps us learn to become human. (p. 65)

Making the relationships and friendships that I shared with the women central to the methodology kept the women's humanity central to the research. It provided a way of knowing, learning about and hearing the narratives of the women that emphasised human dignity.

This chapter explores how friendship as both ethic and method informed the research methodology and method. The chapter illustrates how friendship, over the course of the research, was an ongoing negotiation, a process of becoming, which ultimately underscored the 'co-belonging of nonidentical singularities' (Gandhi, 2006, p. 26) between the women and myself.

When I began this research project, I set out to examine the lives and identities of 'other' *Jëëng* women. When I began to examine why it was that I wanted to consider 'other' *Jëëng* women's lives, I realised that, in part, it was to try to gain a better understanding of my own experiences of becoming a *Tiengjäng*. I discovered that I could not examine the life of the other without examining the life of the self. As Portelli (1991) suggests, '[t]he recognition of the other, which is the foundation of anthropology, is at best limited unless it implies also a questioning and redefinition of the anthropologist's (or historian's) own identity' (p. 43). As such, this project brought together three methodologies: stories of life and ethnography to examine the lives of the 'other' women, and autoethnography, to analyse the experiences and interpretations of the 'self'. These methodologies were underset by what I labelled an ethic of friendship, and it was through this ethic of friendship that the women and I negotiated our belongings during the research.

The research draws on the approaches of narrative researchers (Bruner, 1986; Clandinin, 2007; Clandinin & Connelly, 2000).[1] Clandinin and Murphy (2009) suggest that this approach begins 'with an ontology of experience' (p. 599). Clandinin and Rosiek (2007), drawing on the work of Dewey (1981), further suggest that:

> The narrative inquirer takes the sphere of immediate human experiences as the first and most fundamental reality we have ... and focuses on the way the relational, temporal, and continuous features of a pragmatic ontology of experience can manifest in narrative form, not just in retrospective representations of human experience but also in the lived immediacy of that experience ... Following from this ontology, the narrative inquirer arrives at a conception of knowledge ... of human experience that remains within the stream of human lives. (p. 44)

In addition, Clandinin and Murphy (2009) argue that '[n]arrative research is relational research ... Ontological commitment to the relational locates ethical relationships at the heart of narrative inquiry. The ethical stance of narrative inquirers is best characterized by a relational ethics' (pp. 599–600). As such, this approach was particularly appropriate for research with friends that aimed to explore relational concepts such as belonging and *cieng*.

This chapter begins by exploring my negotiations as what I call an 'inside-out/outside-in' researcher. These negotiations shaped the research process, my research relationships and my continual negotiation of becoming a *Tiengjäng*. The second section considers what using an ethic of friendship entailed and how this underscored the entire research methodology. This section also considers how various power differentials between myself and the women were negotiated through an ethic of friendship. I then consider how I selected the five women before turning to explore how I conducted the research with friendship as method (Tillmann-Healy, 2003).

LIVING ON THE EDGE: THE INSIDE-OUT/OUTSIDE-IN RESEARCHER

> living as we did—on the edge—we developed a particular way of seeing reality. We looked both from the outside in and from the inside out. (hooks, 1984, p. vii)

Griffith (1998) suggests that 'different knowledges are imbedded in both the researcher's biography and the social relations of power and privilege in which the researcher is located' (p. 363). This haunted nature of knowledge, person, place and relations sees the researcher continuously moving backward and forward, negotiating and renegotiating their position on the insider–outsider spectrum, emphasising and de-emphasising certain identities and positionalities at different times and in different places. This section examines the position of researcher as insider and outsider, living on the edge (hooks, 1984), and how I was positioned and positioned myself as an 'inside-out/outside-in' researcher (Smith, 2003, p. 5). However my positioning as an 'inside-out/outside-in' researcher over the course of this research was never removed from my journey to become a *Tiengjäng* and my search for belonging.

Much has been written on the researcher as insider or outsider in the community being researched.[2] Insider-outsiderism was first proposed by Merton (1972) as a dichotomous means of understanding the issue of access to the community in which research takes place. It was suggested that insiders have exclusive knowledge and privileged access to the community due to a previous association with that community (Labaree, 2002; Zavella, 1993). Outsiders, on the other hand, are more detached from the group under study and could hence more readily acquire objectivity (Labaree, 2002; Collins, 1986). This dichotomous division has been revised in more recent years, with Deutsch (1981), for instance, suggesting that researchers can be multiple insiders and outsiders, and Surra and Ridley (1991) suggesting that being an insider or an outsider rests on various points along a continuum.

The physical and social commonalities that are shared with participants (i.e. 'race', class, gender, age, etc.) are not enough to make a researcher an insider. As Riessman (1987), Beoku-Betts (1994), Styles (1979), and Zavella (1993) all found, it was not enough simply to share gender, skin colour, sexuality or ethnicity with their participants to be considered insiders. While I shared the position of being a woman and aspiring *Tiengjäng* with my participants, I was still constantly negotiating my position on the spectrum of insiderness and outsiderness.

Not only is the researcher involved in a continual negotiation of their own position as an insider or outsider, research participants and community members also position the researcher in certain ways. Humphrey (2007) wrote of her experiences 'sliding along' and being 'shunted along' the insider–outsider continuum. This encapsulates the idea that it is not only the researcher who determines their own placement on the continuum by 'sliding' but research participants and others position us along the continuum by 'shunting' us into places that we may or may not be comfortable with. I experienced this 'shifting' and 'shunting' many times during my research by both positioning and being positioned as insider and outsider.

However, there are four people without whom it would have been much more difficult for me to negotiate any degree of insider status. The first is my husband Kuol, without whom I would not be *Tiengjäng*, and the others are my children, Akon, Achol and Yuew, without whom I would not be the mother of *Mïthjäng* (*Jëëng* children). While the period of time that I have known the *Jëëng* community in Australia granted me some degree of inside knowledge, I have witnessed the changes in how I am treated by the community both when I became Kuol's wife and when I became Akon, Achol and Yuew's mother and my subsequent shift along the insider continuum. Aside from this, as I wrote in the Preface, I will always be considered as *nyan khawaja*—'the white girl', and being a 'white' girl has its legacies. hooks (2009) has proposed that, while 'black people' have never

> gathered as anthropologists and/or ethnographers to study whiteness, black folks have, from slavery on, shared in conversations with one another 'special' knowledge of whiteness gleaned from close scrutiny of white people. Deemed special because it was not a way of knowing that has been recorded fully in

> written material, its purpose was to help black folks cope and survive … black people … have maintained steadfast and ongoing curiosity about the 'ghosts,' 'the barbarians,' these strange apparitions. (pp. 89–90)[3]

Against this backdrop of 'special' knowledge of whiteness that *Jëëng* share, I try to negotiate my 'shifting' and 'shunting' along the insider–outsider spectrum, and ultimately I negotiate my belonging as a *Tiengjäng*.

The researcher brings multiple identities to the research and can only be in a position of insiderness with relation to particular lives and events (Beoku-Betts, 1994). While I have shared many experiences with the women, from pounding grain in Sudan to the deaths of members of our community in Australia, there are also many experiences that I have been unable to share with them. At times, the closest I could come to sharing their experiences was to relate them to something I had seen in a movie. As a result of this, different moments in the research saw me positioning myself and being positioned in different places along the insider–outsider continuum. Even within a single interview, I shifted between being an insider and an outsider. For example, if a participant was talking about the duties and expectations of a new wife in *Pan Muonyjäng*, an experience she knew she shared with me and I knew I shared with her, I was an insider. On the other hand, if a participant was talking about her experiences running from attacks by soldiers and fearing for her life, she spoke to me as someone who knew nothing of the experience she was speaking of and I heard her story only as a spectator. These were experiences I was clearly outside of.

Likewise, during my participant observation, I was constantly renegotiating my position between insider and outsider. While sitting, drinking tea and chatting with the women and their families in their homes where I have visited them many times, I felt relaxed and comfortable. These were the moments that I felt like an insider, like I belonged. On the other hand, sometimes when I attended larger community events, such as memorial gatherings, where there were people whom I did not know, I would feel awkward and uncomfortable, as if I was engaged in a performance to negotiate and prove myself in the community. It was at these times that I felt like an outsider, like I did not belong.

Many researchers have argued for the importance of being an insider, at least to some degree (see Trinh, 1990; Haniff, 1985; Herod, 1999; Labaree, 2002; Zavella, 1993). It is often perceived that the insider's view 'bears within itself a seal of approval' (Trinh, 1990, p. 373). Being an insider, however, brings with it a number of ethical and methodological dilemmas.

While Labaree (2002) suggested that being an insider allows the researcher to discover a deeper understanding and greater clarity on what is being studied, at times it can also cloud the researcher's view (Collins, 1986). There were moments during the research where I had to step back to try to consider the data from an outsider perspective in an effort to clarify ideas that were blurred by my insiderness. I had to learn actively to question familiarities.

My sometimes insider status with the community, particularly by marriage, also meant that, at times, what was going on in my personal life was reflected in my research, from the ways and moods in which I collected data, to my analysis and ultimate development of key themes and my writing. There was never any clear distinction between the subjective and the objective in my research, and the permanently blurred boundaries between my insider and outsider status only served to confirm this (Ifekwunigwe, 1999).

POWER AND AN ETHIC OF FRIENDSHIP

> Within this context of entangled power relations, research ethics that are deployed in collaborative methodologies need to be relational and contextual, a product of reciprocity between researchers and researched, negotiated in practice. (Routledge, 2004, p. 86)

The salience of ethics in research is underscored by the identification of power imbalances that exist between the researcher and participants. As Faubion (2001) has identified, '[t]here is no thinking of ethics without thinking of power, or rather of powers' (p. 97). Power negotiations within the researcher–participant relationship have been written about extensively (Ali, 2006; Gupta & Ferguson, 1997).[4] A number of postmodern (Foucault, 1982, 1991), feminist (Stacey, 1988; Alcoff, 1991) and postcolonial (Spivak, 1988) writers have suggested that researchers have an ethical obligation to acknowledge the hierarchical and power-laden relations of research. Acknowledging and attempting to counter the power imbalances between myself and the women was central to this study of the belongings of a diverse group of women. To do so, I adopted what Tillmann-Healy (2003) refers to as an 'ethic of friendship'. An 'ethic of friendship' forced me to consider the potential colonising effects of power differentials in the research relationships. By attempting to acknowledge and account for these power differentials I struggled to 'decolonise' the methodology I utilised—an act which Caracciolo (2009) argues 'strives for Ubuntu's open spirit of respect and the honouring of all members of the human community as part of the research act' (p. xiii).

While I went to great lengths to ensure that my research complied with the requirements of the university ethics committee,[5] Portelli (1997) has suggested that 'ethical and legal guidelines only make sense if they are the outward manifestation of a broader and deeper sense of personal and political commitment to honesty and to truth' (p. 55). An ethic of friendship allowed me to focus on both the power imbalances and the broader personal and political commitments with which I am concerned.

As in any type of research, there was a power imbalance between myself and the women who participated in this project. While many researchers attribute a majority of the power in a research relationship to the researcher, Limerick et al. (1996) believe that such dichotomous understandings of power relations do not capture the total dynamics of the research relationship. In my experience the power dynamics between researcher and participants continued to shift and change throughout the duration of the research project. These shifts and changes in the power dynamics were felt across two significant and distinct locations during the research process. The first was in the 'field' as a researcher conducting interviews and participant observations. The second was through the actual research process of how I conceived of, theorised and wrote the research.

In the 'field', my position as not only a researcher but also a friend and young *Tiengjäng* complicated the power dynamics between the women and me. As a 'white', educated, middle-class woman who has lived most of her life in Australia, where the five women have migrated, I had what Spivak (1990) refers to as privilege. These privileges saw the women requesting assistance from me for things ranging from driving lessons to air-conditioner installation, filling in forms to career advice, but most importantly they impacted on the way that I asked questions of the women and on the questions that I asked, as well as how I heard their answers. My privilege also influenced my everyday interactions with *Jëëng*, and the way *Jëëng* perceived my privilege influenced how they interacted with me. By observing how these privileges have helped and hindered me, as well as how they have consolidated or mitigated the power differentials that exist between myself and the women, I have embarked on the project which Spivak (1990) terms 'un-learning our privilege as our loss' (p. 9).

A further ethical issue was the vulnerability of the women who participated in the research. As members of a marginalised community in Australia, and given the often traumatic nature of some of their past experiences, the women were vulnerable participants. They made themselves even more vulnerable by opening up to me and telling me about their lives. My response to this was to be as open as possible to the women, sharing my experiences with them, and becoming what Behar (1996) has termed a 'vulnerable observer'. By doing this I tried to find 'that place of shared vulnerability' in which 'there is the possibility for recognition, respect, and mutual partnership' (hooks, 2009, p. 87) necessary to begin to understand the complexities of the negotiations for belonging which have taken place in all of our lives. We built and developed friendships through this shared vulnerability in which we also formed a sense of belonging (Gandhi, 2006).

These friendships, however, did also bring with them additional ethical concerns. All five participants were women with whom I had friendships that predated the research and continued after the research was completed. Ellis (2007) suggests that this can be a difficult ethical quandary to acknowledge and deal with, as many of the ethical guidelines for research are developed for research with 'strangers with who we have no prior relationships and plan no future interaction' (p. 3). To try to counter this dilemma and the issues with power in the research relationships, I adopted an ethic of friendship. This ethic seeks to undermine the potential for colonisation and exploitation in research with power imbalances (Tillmann-Healy, 2003).

Tillmann-Healy (2003) argues that to conduct research with an ethic of friendship the researcher must adopt 'a stance of hope, caring, justice, even love … a level of investment in participants' lives that puts fieldwork relationships on par with the project' (p. 735). Through an ethic of friendship I tried to acknowledge my personal 'stakes and investments' in the research relationships, the 'frustrations, anxieties, and disappointments' (Luttrell, 2000, p. 515) that occurred in the relationships, and my process of trying to understand the difference between self and other (Portelli, 1991). An ethic of friendship meant that I attempted to treat my participants 'with respect, honor their stories, and try to use their stories for humane and just purposes' (Tillmann-Healy, 2003, p. 745).

My status as an 'inside-out' researcher meant that the power imbalances in the research were more complex than simply considering my power as a 'white' Anglo researcher with 'vulnerable' participants. There was also an ethical need to ensure that I accounted for cultural protocols, values and behaviours as a part of my methodology (Smith, 2003). Accounting for these cultural protocols meant, for example, behaving in a way that acknowledged my junior position in relation to the women with respect to age, length of marriage and number of children. As a result of this I had a cultural obligation while at the women's houses and community events to do things such as washing the dishes, cooking the food, making the tea and taking care of children. These are some of the reasons why it was never possible simply to go to a woman's house, do an interview and leave. I had ethical and cultural obligations that required me to undertake other duties as a younger *Tiengjäng* in the homes of my elders. Additionally, as a result of this aged-based hierarchy, this group of women would not traditionally share all of their personal and intimate experiences with me. This was highlighted in an informal conversation with one of the women immediately after requesting her participation in the research. She told me that usually she would not talk to me about all of her life experiences as she is older than me, but for the purposes of the research and because she thought the research was important she would be as truthful, open and honest with me as possible.

In addition to this age-based power hierarchy, the women also have a degree of power due to their insider status within the *Jëëng* community. Although the women's negotiations for belonging in the community are also complex and shifting by virtue of their place of birth and kinship ties, their insiderness within the *Jëëng* community is unquestionably more comprehensive than mine. Where it is based on birthright, it is incommensurable with mine, yet it is not without moments of sharedness. As relative insiders, the women were able to facilitate both my inclusion and, at times, my exclusion from community events, politics and discussions. The women had the power to change my status along the insider–outsider spectrum in response not only to their individual perceptions of me, but also in relation to internal hierarchies and micro-politics within the community (Limerick, Burgess-Limerick, & Grace, 1996). These self–other and interpersonal and community power negotiations existed not only in my role as researcher, but also in my day-to-day life as a *Tiengjäng*.

An additional way in which power necessitated that I conducted the research with an ethic of friendship was in the ways in which I conceived of, theorised and wrote about the research. First, while the oral stories and lived experiences belonged to the participants who were able to choose which information to disclose and which to withhold, ultimately it was me, as the researcher, who wrote the stories and this book. Many researchers have reported that it is ultimately the researcher who conceives of, initiates, writes, analyses, publishes and benefits professionally from the publication of the research (Ellis, 2007; Bateson, 1989).[6] As the researcher, my power in the research relationship was present from my choice of participants, to the ways that I conducted interviews, to the selection of which parts of their stories to include and how I wrote about them.

As a researcher, another ethical issue that I encountered was the struggle to ensure the anonymity of the participants. While some of the women were happy to be identified, others were adamant that no-one should know who they were. I made the decision to make all of the women as anonymous as possible, even those who were happy to be identified, as I thought that this was ethically in the best interests of each woman, her family and me in the small and often politically turbulent *Jëëng* diaspora. Given the very individual nature of their lived experiences and subsequent narratives, and the small *Jëëng* community in South Australia, this was difficult. The use of pseudonyms and changing place names in many instances did not ensure anonymity. I therefore used a form of analysis which may detract from the overall coherence of individual life stories, but ensures, as much as possible, anonymity of the women as well as a greater capacity for theory building.

Combining the women's stories with theory also brought its own set of ethical challenges. Duneier and Back (2006) suggest that part of their

> criticism of ethnography as a frame theory for doing theory for theory's sake is not simply that the people in the studies can't recognize themselves in the work but they don't even have any sense of how they mattered. I mean how did it matter, why did it matter that this ethnographer spent all this time with me? So he could enter into a dialogue with a theory that is utterly trivial, even by academic standards? What is the ethics of that? (p. 564)

I have tried to be cognisant of the fact that the root of this book stems from the stories of six women. My hope is that it remains clear that these stories came from these women and were part of their everyday lived experiences and that they are not lost in the muddy mess of theory (Gamson, 1998) with which they are in dialogue.

Finally, as a member of the *Jëëng* community, friend to the five women who were my participants, and researcher, I often had conflicting responsibilities on how and what to report of the data (Haniff, 1985; Portelli, 1997; Zavella, 1993). Ultimately, at times of conflict, using an ethic of friendship, I chose my responsibilities to the women and the community over those I had as a researcher. This meant sometimes making decisions not to use stories that I had written or recorded. While these stories may have provided the reader with a more in-depth understanding, I decided that using those stories would cause too much harm to the women involved, or myself as a member of the community, to justify their inclusion in this book (Zavella, 1993; Tillmann-Healy, 2003).

CHAPTER 2

ABUK, ACHOL, ATONG, NYALONG AND NYANUT: THE WOMEN

Bateson (1989) suggests that the women who collaborate with us on our research projects are, in fact, our 'truest colleagues' (p. 101) and this is why words such as 'interviewees', 'subjects' and 'informants' often feel so wrong. The five women who worked with me on this project started out as my friends, acquaintances or distantly related relatives. As already noted, over the course of the project, the women became my teachers, confidants, colleagues, students, helpers, allies and so much more. Given the nature of my pre-existing relationships with the women and the even deeper relationships that developed over the duration of the research project, I have found it difficult to refer to the women as participants, interviewees or any of the other commonly used social science terms for research participants. While Bateson (1989) uses the term collaborators to refer to the women involved in her research, I struggle with the use of this term given the nature of the fact that ultimately I am the one who initiated the research process, and has done the writing of the stories and book. While the women have collaborated with me in the recording and telling of their stories of life, I must take ownership of how I have ultimately presented the stories on paper. Instead of naming the women as participants or interviewees, I have commonly called them 'the women' or by their individual pseudonyms: Abuk, Achol, Atong, Nyalong and Nyanut.

Initially, my selection criteria was to include six *Jëëng* women who had been living in South Australia for between three and seven years and who had experienced a variety of migration pathways, including through refugee camps or cities in Kenya, Egypt and northern Sudan. The women were to be selected from a group of women that I had known and formed relationships with since 2004. The need to talk with women who had taken a variety of migration pathways was summed up by Achol, in an interview, who commented that:

> You like every woman here coming from Ethiopia, you talking from her. Other woman coming from Khartoum, talking with her. This one, other woman coming from Khartoum will give you other something. Different story, similar from this one. You collect them.[7]

Talking with women from a variety of migration pathways provided me with a 'different story', an 'other something' that would give me a more rounded idea of how *Jëëng* women's experiences of belonging have been shaped, transformed and experienced through a variety of experiences of migration.

When I first began trying to identify participants, I thought that of all the *Jëëng* women I had formed relationships with since 2004 it would be easy to identify six to invite to participate. What I discovered as I began my identification process was just how complicated my relationships with the women and the *Jëëng* community were. My selection process was haunted by my pre-existing relationships and my history with the community. When I began approaching the women to request participation, I found that I could easily select the first five women and quickly requested and obtained consent from them, but despite a number of preliminarily visits to other women, I was not able to find a suitable sixth participant. Each of the five women that I recruited suggested other women whom I could approach to talk to, but for a variety of reasons I found that I was not comfortable in inviting participation of any of these women. These reasons need to be addressed here, as they illustrate the complexity of my negotiations for belonging within the *Jëëng* community as well as the significance of my relationships with the five women who were selected.

First, I address why the first five women were so easy to approach. One of the reasons for my intimate relationship with these five women was their links to the Mading Aweil region and community (see Figure 3). I am married to a man from Mading Aweil. Four of the women are daughters of Mading Aweil and married to Mading Aweil men, and the fifth is a daughter of Wau (a region neighbouring Mading Aweil) and married to a Mading Aweil man. This regional link, a link to place, is important in the development and maintenance of relationships, as I discuss in more detail in Chapter 5. To consider subsequent reasons, I will briefly consider my relationship with each individual woman.

The first woman that I approached, Nyanut, I came to know soon after her arrival in Adelaide with her family in 2005. For six months after they arrived I visited them frequently. During this six-month period, my relationship with Kuol also developed and in July 2005, when Kuol and I started living together, our friendship with the family went through a difficult period. As they (and the community) began to come to terms with the relationship between Kuol and me, the friendship began to re-kindle. By 2008 Nyanut would talk to me about almost anything and was one of my most ardent teachers on becoming a *Tiengjäng*. When Akon was born, she was the first *Jëëng* to come to visit us and was waiting on our doorstep with her family when we brought Akon home from hospital. There were periods during the research where I had to make very clear decisions about what Nyanut had talked to me about as a friend and what she had talked to me about as a researcher.

The second woman that I approached, Achol, I had known since 2005, when I brought some photos of one of her relatives back from Africa with me and dropped them at her house. She was one of the few women who, during the early days of mine and Kuol's relationship, still maintained our friendship. I recall one evening, at the end of a community party in late 2005 I was the last young woman left cleaning up the hall after everyone else had gone. We were giving Achol a lift home, so she was waiting for us. She commented to Kuol that 'Mel is really a good girl, she works very hard. She's better than most of our Dinka girls.' This meant a lot to me at that particular point in time when I was being ostracised by most of the rest of the community who were struggling to come to terms with my relationship with Kuol, and I was struggling with my commitment to becoming a *Tiengjäng*.

The third woman that I approached, Nyalong, I had known since 2005 but my friendship with her deepened in 2006 when she asked me to assist her with one of the women's community group projects. I have learnt much about the politics of the *Jëëng* community from Nyalong, sharing the headaches of trying to run a community group with *Jëëng*.

The fourth woman that I approached, Atong, I have known since 2005. I can still recall one of my early conversations with her, when I had just returned from Kenya. We were discussing the difficulties for her raising her children in Australia without her husband. Our friendship has always been very open and I have always felt that she has treated me as a younger sister. She too is a relative outsider to the Mading Aweil community, as a daughter of the Wau region who is married to a Mading Aweil man, and I think this has helped deepen our friendship through the commonality of being relative outsiders but insiders by marriage.

The final woman that I invited to participate, Abuk, I came to know most recently. I met Abuk for the first time in late 2006 at a community meeting. At the time of our wedding in 2007, Kuol did not know her as she had recently moved to Adelaide from interstate, so we did not send her an invitation. Despite this, and the fact that there was much community gossip going on about the wedding, she came to the wedding and the reception and patiently waited at the gate with her son for spare seats of those who did not show up. Among everything that went on during our wedding day, I can clearly remember her excitement at the marriage and meeting my family, most particularly my paternal grandmother who was wheelchair bound. Since the wedding we have visited her infrequently as she lives some distance from us, but whenever we see her she is always very happy to see us. One of the barriers to my friendship with Abuk is language. She is slightly older than the other participants and has struggled to learn English. She talks to me in *Thuongjäng*, which I can understand, but my spoken *Thuongjäng* is limited so it is difficult to hold an in-depth conversation with her.[8]

Finally, there were two women I visited on precursor visits to consider inviting their participation, and many other women who were suggested as potential participants, but whom I did not feel comfortable approaching. Again, the reason for my caution and inability to identify a sixth participant was summed up in an interview:

> Achol: Other woman go to, it's look for a good woman. Other woman, not good. You talking with you, maybe you talking other something.
>
> Melanie: Some funny stories. Yes, I tried to be careful. Someone that I know and I know that they can tell me the good story, not some other story.

I was sure that my friendship with these five women was strong and enduring enough that they would not be 'talking other something'. They would not tell me stories that they thought I wanted to hear. The risk with some of the other potential participants with whom my friendship was either not as deep, or complicated by community politics, was that they would tell me what they thought I wanted to hear. This was experienced in one of the interviews with Nyalong, where two other women were present and engaged in the conversation. Some aspects of the discussion became a reiteration of cultural stereotypes of what the women believed a 'white' woman would want to hear about *Jëëng* women's experiences. Guerin and Guerin (2007) suggest that this is common when participants perceive the researcher as being in a position of power. They frequently experienced the standard answers given by members of refugee communities where the interviewee is trying to please the researcher by providing what they think the researcher 'wants' to hear (Guerin & Guerin, 2007; Guerin et al., 2003).

Tillmann-Healy (2003) suggests that '[i]n friends, we seek trust, honesty, respect, commitment, safety, support, generosity, loyalty, mutuality, constancy, understanding, and acceptance' (p. 731), and through the existence of these traits in relationships formed with these five women over an extended period I felt comfortable embarking on the project of our lives. I was certain that I had strong enough relationships with the five women that I had selected to ensure that they would be truthful with me and we would be able to work together in an honest, collaborative venture. I was sure that the mutual respect we shared would enable us to work on a project that would be as open, truthful and sensitive as I foresaw the project being.

FRIENDSHIP AS METHOD

> Moving toward friendship as method may be as simple as turning off the tape recorder and cooking dinner with participants; investing more of ourselves in their emotional, relational, and political welfare; inviting respondents further into our lives than we ever dared before; hanging around longer; writing texts that are as enlightening and useful to our research, local, and global communities as to our academic careers; and/or approaching participants as we would potential or actual friends: with a desire for mutual respect, understanding, examination, and growth. (Tillmann-Healy, 2003, p. 746)

Having identified the importance of friendship in my research ethic and participant selection, I now consider how friendship as method informed the way that I carried out the research project. Friendship as method is a term which was coined by Lisa Tillmann-Healy (2001) in her book *Between gay and straight: Understanding friendship across sexual orientation.* She suggests:

> Calling for inquiry that is open, multivoiced, and emotionally rich, friendship as method involves the practices, the pace, the contexts, and the ethics of friendship. Researching with the practices of friendship means that although we employ traditional forms of data gathering (e.g., participant observation, systematic note taking, and informal and formal interviewing), our primary procedures are those we use to build and sustain friendship: conversation, everyday involvement, compassion, giving, and vulnerability. (2003, p. 734)

While Tillmann-Healy (2003, p. 735) suggests that one of the limits to friendship as method is the time it takes to build the friendships, for me the friendships were already built before commencing the research. Friendship as method for me then meant sustaining the friendships that I already had with the women, but also deepening them through spending hours engaged in in-depth conversation learning about each other's lives, hopes, dreams and tragedies, through sharing cups of tea, meals, laughter, tears, joys and traumas, and through a reciprocal relationship of shared learning and knowledge construction, underscored by the interdependence and relational ethic of *cieng*. Through using friendship as method, 'the lines between researcher and researched blur, permitting each to explore the complex humanity of both self and other' (p. 733), enabling us to strengthen and deepen our friendships through a better understanding of each other.

Interviews and visits were always more than simply interviews and participant observation. For example, during a visit to Abuk, for which she had specially prepared a time-consuming traditional dish of *kisira* (flat pancake-like bread) and *kadang riing* (meat stew), I washed the dishes, including all of her family's dishes of that day, which any *Tiengjäng* who is related to her would be expected to do. She replied with '*Shurkuran ting wämääth*' (Thank you the wife of my brother). This expectation and obligation were underscored by *cieng* through which, as a young wife, I had certain relational responsibilities. The friendships and relationships I shared and continued to develop with the women required knowing, learning and responding to the particular way of being through *cieng*, and the cultural expectations of me as a *Tiengjäng*. If I had visited Abuk as the wife of her brother, recorded her story, eaten her food and left without performing the duties required of me as *ting wämääth*, I would have damaged the relationship, the friendship and the future research relationship.

Another important component of friendship as method is that 'a project's issues emerge organically, in the ebb and flow of everyday life' (Tillmann-Healy, 2003, p. 735). When I began this project, I initially intended it to be an investigation of the educational experiences of Sudanese women. However, through conversations with the women in the Sudanese community in the early months of the project, I learnt that education for the women was not necessarily one of the most pressing issues for them in their lives. Through using a methodology of stories of life coupled with ethnographic approaches and friendship as method, the key issues began to emerge through our ongoing conversations and everyday interactions. One of the challenges to this, however, was that the issues never stopped emerging and changing, so at a certain point I drew the line at any new and emerging issues and focused instead on the issues that had emerged up to that point.

Not only did my friendships and relationships with the individual women deepen throughout the research, but my relationships with their families and with the wider community deepened as I developed a better understanding of them, and them of me. These are relationships which will continue to grow, develop and change for many years to come.

HEARING THROUGH 'NEW' WAYS OF LISTENING

> We have to find ways in which the marginalized can enter our discourses in their own genres and their own terms so that we can learn to hear them. They have a universal right to *impart information and ideas through any media regardless of frontiers*, and we have a duty to listen and understand them through engaging new acts of becoming. (Krog, 2011, p. 384 [original emphasis])

The five 'other' women who participated in this research are members of the large group of people whom Spivak (1988) has referred to as the 'subaltern'. These are the peoples at the margins 'of the circuit marked out by this epistemic violence' of colonialism. They are the 'men and women among the illiterate peasantry, the tribals, the lowest strata of the urban subproletariat … the oppressed' (p. 25). She goes on to suggest that these are the peoples who 'cannot speak'. They are disadvantaged and muted by their gender, 'race', ethnicity, location, sexuality, education, class and many other factors. Krog (2011), however, suggests that it is not that the 'subaltern cannot speak' but rather that they cannot be heard by the privileged. She argues, as quoted above, that for the marginalised and the subaltern to 'speak', the privileged must be prepared to listen and hear.

As a privileged 'white' Australian woman my challenge, my duty, and my ethical responsibility as a fledgling/becoming *Tiengjäng* and friend of the women that I engaged in the research, was to find a way through which what this particular group of 'subaltern' women had to say could enter the privileged discourses of the Western academy. I had to ensure that not only could they speak, but they could be heard. Central to this imperative of listening and really hearing 'is that all human beings have the capacity for voice, to give an account of their lives. This is an irreducible part of their human agency' (Couldry, 2009, p. 580). Really 'hearing' the women's stories was 'embodied in the process of mutually recognizing our claims on each other as reflexive human agents, each with an account to give, an account of our lives that needs to be registered and heard' (p. 580).

This required particular research methodologies, and the research had to be conducted in a way that was cognisant of the women's 'own genres'. The traditional genre through which *Jëëng*, including the women in this research, impart information is through conversations and storytelling. Therefore 'living oral (hi)stories of life' were a critical way of 'hearing'. However, engaging only with this methodology would not have allowed me to understand the indigenous epistemology of *cieng* that governed the ways in which the narratives were told and therefore how they needed to be understood and interpreted. I had to find other tools that allowed me to understand and 'translate' their narratives from the indigenous epistemology in which they were told (Krog, 2008). To do this I used a combination of ethnography and autoethnography. Through reflecting on my own experiences as a becoming

Tiengjäng I engaged in what Krog (2011) refers to as 'new acts of becoming'. Recognising how my continual negotiation as an inside-out/outside-in researcher, constantly shifting and being shifted along the spectrum of insiderness, was reflected also in my negotiations for belonging within the community of *Jëëng* with whom I resided and researched.

Acting as a 'methodological bricoleur' (Denzin & Lincoln, 2008, p. 5), I wove together the methodologies of stories of life, ethnography and autoethnography. I adopted, adapted, discarded and amended components of each methodology to endeavour to account for some of the limits to each of the individual methodologies, while also providing a depth to the data that would not have been possible through using each methodology independently. None of the methodologies operated outside the other. Visiting a woman to conduct an interview for her 'living oral (hi)story of life' was never done outside of reflecting on my own position in the interview, as an inside-out/outside-in researcher, and as someone who was also negotiating a journey to belong. In addition, my everyday life and interactions with my husband, his family and the extended 'Sudanese' community became sites in which I viewed and remembered both my own journey towards belonging as well as those of others. Through combining these three methodologies, the research process became not just an analysis of the other women's lives and stories, but a journey through our variously shared desires for belonging.

In addition, grounding these methodological approaches in an ethic of friendship allowed me to conduct the research in a 'humble togetherness' (Swanson, 2007, p. 56), rooted in an ethic and epistemology of *cieng*. In listening to and really 'hearing' the women's stories and reflecting on my experiences as a becoming *Tiengjäng* and friend and kin to many people in the global *Jëëng* community, and through hearing and experiencing these stories through the epistemology of *cieng* in which they were told, I recognised that these were not simply narratives of trauma, disempowerment and victimisation, an understanding which is inherent in many analyses of both subaltern women as well as forced migrants, but they were stories of agency, subjectivity, individuality, resiliency, resentment, fear, hate, love, passion, vulnerability, strength, courage, challenge and humanity. My approach enabled a way of hearing the women's narratives that emphasised the complexities in their lives and the ways in which they negotiated their belongings. Recognising this complexity is an essential step in acknowledging the humanity of research participants, particularly the 'subaltern' (Halpern & Weinstein, 2004).

As researcher, friend, family and simply fellow human being I had an ethical responsibility to hear the voices of those least often heard, to recognise the complexities of the stories they tell and the lives they live, and through this to 'realize that there are no Others, only others, finding their way through their ordinary everyday lives' (Wise, 2008, p. 154).

CONCLUSION: BUILDING BELONGING AND FRIENDSHIP THROUGH RESEARCH

> There is no belonging or friendly community that is *present*, and first present *to itself, in act*, without election and without selection. (Derrida, 1988, p. 21)

Throughout the research process, my friendship with the women took precedence and, as Routledge (2004) has argued, such a relational ethic

> requires that we are sensitive to the contingency of things, and that our responsibility to others and to difference is connected to the responsibility to act … Such a responsibility, within the context of political struggle, implies that researchers take sides, albeit in a critical way. (p. 86)

Understanding these relational ethics, such as friendship through *cieng*, is one of the aims of the research, and as such it was pertinent to keep it at the forefront of how the research was conducted.

However, as Derrida (1988) has observed, friendship cannot be present without the active selection of those with whom friendship is desired and the election by both parties to participate in the friendship. As such, through my selection of a particular group of five women with whom I built stronger friendships over the course of the research, the research, as well as my negotiations for belonging within the *Jëëng* community, was haunted by this selection. By including these five women, I actively chose to exclude other women. While I negotiated closer friendships with these five women, I did so to the detriment of building friendships with other women within the wider *Jëëng* community. In this act using friendship as a method became politicised as it involved including some women and excluding others. This reflected the broader ways through which friendship became a site in which belonging was negotiated.

Throughout the research process, my selection of these particular women, their election to participate in the research project, and my election to enact particular research methods became ways not only to carry out research, but also methods through which we negotiated belongings. By enacting these selection and election processes of building friendships and belonging, I ensured not only that the data was more rigorous, but most importantly that the sense of belonging that I had established with the women throughout the research process did not end when the research ended. By the time of completion of the writing of this book, approximately eight years after the first of my ‘precursor visits’, my friendships with all five of the women were stronger and closer than they were before the research began. The journeys which we have been on together have meant that, while undeniably the friendships remain evolving processes in which we continue to negotiate our co-belongings through becoming, ultimately we have shared an experience which has strengthened the foundations on which friendship and belonging are built.

NOTES

1 See also Berger (2001), Beverley (2008), Chase (2008), Franzosi (1998), Gedalof (2009) and Shacklock and Thorp (2005).

2 See, for example, Collins (1986), De Andrade (2000), Deutsch (1981), Griffith (1998), Haniff (1985), Herod (1999), Humphrey (2007), Labaree (2002), Merton (1972), Naples (1997), Nyaba (2000), Schipper (1999), Smyth (2005), Trinh (1990) and Zavella (1993).

3 As an example, in Chinua Achebe's (2010) critically acclaimed novel *No longer at ease*, there is a passage in which he writes of marriages between black men and white women. When the character Obi returns to his village in Nigeria after four years studying in England, the elder males in his village gather to celebrate his return. During this gathering the following conversation takes place:

> Matthew Ogbonna, who had been a carpenter in Onitsha and was consequently a man of the world, said they should all thank God that Obi had not brought home a white wife.
> 'White wife?' asked one of the men. To him it was rather far-fetched.
> 'Yes. I have seen it with my two eyes,' said Matthew.
> 'Yes,' said Obi. 'Many black men who go to the white man's country marry their women.'
> 'You hear?' asked Matthew. 'I tell you I have seen it with my own two eyes in Onitsha. The woman even had two children. But what happened in the end? She left those children and went back to her country. That is why I say a black man who marries a white woman wastes his time. Her stay with him is like the stay of the moon in the sky. When the time comes she will go.'
> 'Very true,' said another man who had also travelled. 'It is not her going away that matters. It is her turning the man's face away from his kinsmen while she stays'. (p. 193)

4 See also, Grossberg (1996), Hand (2007), Limerick, Burgess-Limerick and Grace (1996), Porter (2007) and Soderqvist (1991).

5 For example Kuol translated the Information Sheet and Consent Form into *Thuongjäng* despite the fact that none of the women could read or write Thuongjäng.

6 See also, Alcoff (1991), Chow (1998, 1993), Schipper (1999) and Tierney (1999).

7 There are a number of different forms in which the women's narratives are presented in the book. Where the narratives were originally spoken in *Thuongjäng* and then translated, this has been noted. Narrative excerpts which were spoken in English are presented verbatim, or near verbatim, which in some instances may be difficult for the reader to understand. Where I have deemed necessary I have included my interpretation in square brackets following the woman's words.

8 The language issues related to the research are discussed in more in Appendix B, which considers issues of translation and interpretation in the research.

CHAPTER 3

BECOMING NATIONALS, BEING AND BECOMING CITIZENS

Searching for Belonging in the Nation-State[1]

And even if there comes a peace between us and the Arabs we won't be happy. Only someone who has no relative that has been killed could be happy. Anyone whose relatives have been killed will never be happy. I am certain there is no Dinka who doesn't have a relative that *Maram*[2] has killed … Even Egypt is not a good place because when you just walk on the way, the Egyptians pick up stones and stone you. They stone you with stones, while you are walking in the road. And they can also abuse you verbally. Someone can just slap you while you are walking on the street … Now that we are here in Australia we like to participate in the Australian way of life, like we can vote if people are having elections, and if there are things like foreign relations and representing Australia internationally we can do that, and if there is war we can go there and defend Australia. And if you are not a citizen, how can you participate? Because nobody knows you as part of the society. Only the immigration people know you because when you came through they know your form.[3] But we've been here for years and we are not refugees anymore. Now I've been here for about five years and I'm not a citizen, I'm still a refugee. I'm still a refugee, how can I vote? (Abuk, Kuol translated)

INTERLUDE III: AM I UN-AUSTRALIAN?

Australia Day. Our first one in regional 'country' Australia. Our first one as a family. We put on our best clothes and head down to the beach where the Port Pirie Australia Day celebrations take place. I get there and I'm instantly embarrassed. Shorts, t-shirts, thongs and bathers are the order of the day. My knee-length, autumn-coloured, favourite 'nice' skirt blows up in the wind. If it was not so hot, onlookers would have seen me blush. Kuol, Akon and I look lost. We feel lost. Everyone else is chatting, laughing, having fun, but we have no-one to laugh with. What is one meant to do on Australia Day when you do not look or feel Australian? We move off the path, under the shade of a tree and gather our thoughts. Everyone else has picnic rugs, picnic chairs, shorts,

> t-shirts and bathers. I go home, collect our picnic rug, put on my shorts and t-shirt and go back.
>
> I find Kuol and Akon under the same tree as I left them, standing alone, trying to look like they're enjoying themselves. We go and lay our rug under another tree and friends find us—another 'refugee' and his un-Australian feeling wife and son. We laugh, we have fun, and our children play oblivious to the meaning of the day, a celebration of the day the British colonised Australia. The day Australia first became a nation of homeless. We are joined by another couple and their baby. They look Australian, they sound Australian, but do they feel Australian? They look as lost as we feel, so maybe not. Maybe it's not that we're not Australian enough; maybe we're not Piriean enough? Maybe this is not just Australia Day, but Pirie Day as well, a celebration of what it means to be Piriean. Paddling rafts on the beach, watermelon eating competitions, a minute's silence for an esteemed local Piriean who had passed away. Pirie, Australia, what's the difference anyway?
>
> The event winds down at about 11 am, so we go our separate ways. Kuol calls his cousins to invite them over. I thought I'd said to invite them for dinner as I'd only got the roast out of the freezer in the morning and it takes time to defrost. He invites them for lunch. The relevant chaos ensues. He tells me I do not like *Jëëng*, I tell him he's not part of my family. Is it at these moments that we speak the truth, what we really believe, or do we say what we know will hurt the most?
>
> They come for lunch. I cook a *Jëëng* dish and feel even less Australian and even less *Jëëng*.

In many ways, I initially thought that my sense of belonging to the nation would be the least complicated. I was born in Australia, I look and speak like a mainstream 'Aussie', but does this automatically give me a sense of belonging in Australia? In my experience, no. I am the grandchild of migrants to Australia; my maternal grandparents were from England, and my paternal grandparents were from Poland and the Ukraine/Russia. My identity grew from so many disparate places and groups that I could not just identify with one.

Jackson (1995) writes of his experience of home:

> I had an ambivalent relationship with my homeland. You feel estranged from your European roots yet cannot identify wholeheartedly with the indigenous culture of the land. You live betwixt and between, uneasy about your origins, unsure of where you stand, in two minds about your identity and allegiance. (p. 4)

This uneasiness about my origins has shaped my own sense of belonging in Australia. I guess it's hard to feel like you belong to someone else's stolen country. My belonging in Australia is haunted by Australia's colonial past, a past that I am not sure of my affiliations to. As a 'white' person in Australia today, I acknowledge that I am positioned in a certain way that is shaped by history, culture and power. By virtue of my place of birth and my skin colour, I am a 'white' Australian. This brings with it many privileges that must be acknowledged. Growing up 'white' in Australia meant that I immediately had access to forms of capital not available to other members of the Australian society. But as the grandchild of four immigrants to Australia, I have never been convinced of my direct implications in the colonial project (I am still working this out as I write).

If my relationship with homeland as a direct reading of land is ambivalent, I begin to wonder where I do feel at home. Do I have a relationship with any sort of home to which I do not feel ambivalent? Where do I feel a sense of belonging? As a citizen of Australia and part of the 'white'-Anglo hegemonic norm, my belonging to the nation-state in Australia seems unquestionable. My personal experience tells me otherwise. My own confusion over belonging to the nation-state seems to be prevalent globally, particularly in the current era. As bell hooks (2009) has observed

> Again and again as I travel around I am stunned by how many citizens in our nation feel lost, feel bereft of a sense of direction, feel as though they cannot see where our journeys lead, that they cannot know where they are going. (p. 1)

While the reasons for my ambivalent sense of belonging to the nation-state of Australia are different to those of the women (hence the reason I explore them separately to the women's stories), the stories together, no doubt, illustrate the vulnerability of belonging in the nation-state.

INTRODUCTION

When I began this research, I had little idea of where it would lead. I was led primarily by the women's stories. Arriving home after having completed my first interview with Abuk, I felt a little deflated, as if everything she spoke of was superficial and anecdotal and was not a reflection on her personal life story. It was not until I began to analyse the transcripts in more detail that I realised that perhaps the main reason for this feeling of distance between the story Abuk told, in comparison to the intimacy I felt when listening to the stories of the other women, was the level on which she was seeking a sense of belonging. Abuk's narrative focused almost entirely on the yearning to belong through the nation-state. Abuk's story illustrated not only the lived ambivalence, longing and desire for belonging to the nation-state in multiple locations, but also how her belongings were controlled, determined and made unstable by various powers outside her control.

The notion of the nation-state has been contested in recent times, with many authors discussing both the apparent threat of globalisation to the nation-state (Mann, 1997; Castles & Davidson, 2000), and how the state responds to these threats through forms of nationalism (Babacan, 2010; Breuilly, 1993; Wimmer & Glick Schiller, 2002). As a result of the complexities and contestations over what the nation-state is (Davidson, 1992; Davidson & Munslow, 2004; Mann, 1997), how it operates (Keely, 1996; Rotberg, 2002; Wimmer & Glick Schiller, 2002), and how belongings are negotiated in relation to it (Castles & Davidson, 2000, Butler & Spivak, 2007; Bauder, 2013), there has been a proliferation of research and academic writing on these topics. Partly because of the plethora of academic material on this topic, this chapter was one of the most difficult for me to write. However, one of the other difficulties I faced was that there was no singular description of how belonging is negotiated in relation to the nation-state that resounded with the women's descriptions of their experiences. As such, I drew together materials, ideas and tools from a vast array of fields, including cultural studies, sociology and philosophy, to attempt to understand the women's narratives.

Two texts, in particular, provided good starting points for my understanding, but both had their limits. Castles and Davidson's (2000) *Citizenship and migration: Globalization and the politics of belonging* is a seminal text in the field, and served as a useful tool to consider the ways in which belonging to the nation-state through citizenship has been transformed, questioned and reshaped in the current era of increased global mobility. However, through their main argument in the book that 'a theory of citizenship for a global society must be based on the separation between nation and state' and that '[c]itizenship should therefore not be connected to nationality' (p. 24) they do not provide a complete way of understanding the women's experiences which were shaped by both citizenship and nationality. Butler and Spivak's (2007) conversation in *Who sings the nation-state?* provided a crucial tool for considering the power of the state in controlling who can or cannot belong to the nation-state through both prescriptions of citizenship as well as formations of particular national identities. However, relating their deeply philosophical reasonings to the women's narratives of everyday lived experiences required assistance from a variety of academic intermediaries. As such, it may appear as if the theoretical underpinnings for this chapter come from a disparate selection, but this was what was required to understand the complex themes and arguments that came out of the women's narratives.

The multiplicity and complexity of how the women's belongings were negotiated and controlled in relation to the nation-state created more questions than answers. In Abuk's story I was not sure whether she yearned to belong as a Sudanese, or an Egyptian, or a Sudanese in Egypt, or an Australian, or a Sudanese-Australian. None of these labels seemed to really define the sense of belonging she was seeking. Was it citizenship that she desired, as she reflected in her narrative? Or was it a sense of belonging to a national identity? As McCrone and Kiely (2000) question, 'If someone asked what your nationality was, how would you answer? And your citizenship? Would you treat these questions as identical?' (p. 19). Arguably, nationality and citizenship are not synonymous,[4] and they have become even less so in the era of increased global movements of people across state borders (Tetreault & al-Mughni, 1995; Oommen, 1997). Brettell (2006) has claimed that, with the increasing number of people of various nationalities living as citizens within the borders of nation-states, there has been a decoupling between national identities and the rights and responsibilities of citizenship. She continues, suggesting that '[t]he conceptual distinction between citizenship and nationality represents this decoupling. It is clear that the differences between political belonging and cultural belonging are embedded in this contrast between citizen and national' (pp. 71–72). As will become clear throughout the remainder of this chapter, the women's stories illustrate that belonging on the basis of both nationality and citizenship is continually negotiated and that without both working conterminously a full sense of nation-state belonging cannot be achieved.[5]

While arguably there is significant overlap between how nationality and citizenship operated to determine the belongings of the women in relation to the nation-state, I have separated them into two distinct sections in the remainder of this chapter to highlight the slightly different ways in which they functioned. The first section, '"New Racisms" and Nationalism in Becoming Nationals', considers negotiating belongings to the nation-state through nationality. Through descriptions of how the women were constructed and targeted as cultural, ethnic and linguistic minorities in Sudan,[6] exile and Australia, in this section I argue that the women had never been able to belong through nationality in any country. While they had journeyed towards becoming nationals, ultimately the hauntings of 'race', ethnicity, culture and religion meant that it was virtually impossible for them to achieve national belonging (Butler & Spivak, 2007). The second section, 'Violence, Quasi-citizenship and "Feeling" in Being and Becoming Citizens', illustrates how, in Sudan, exile and Australia, the women's experiences of citizenship emphasised the processes of both being and becoming. While in some locations, either by birth rights or naturalisation, some of the women were able to be citizens in the official sense of the term, the hauntings of violence, state bureaucracy and barriers such as education meant that in every location they have been engaged in a continual process of becoming citizens.[7] The women continued to negotiate their belongings in relation to the nation-state across the transnational movements they made, which resulted in a complex web of being and becoming in relation to both nationality and citizenship.

'NEW RACISMS' AND NATIONALISM IN BECOMING NATIONALS

The ideal of the nation-state has always been based on the 'one state, one nation' principle (Bauman, 2001, p. 90). Ideally, within a nation-state there should be sufficient cultural homogeneity to enable a sense of a national identity or nationality (Castles & Davidson, 2000). However in most countries globally this has never been possible. Most nation-states, particularly those formed through colonisation, were cobbled together from diverse linguistic and cultural nations (Meredith, 2005;

Schnapper, 1999) under the legal and institutional authority of the state (Butler & Spivak, 2007). In the current era of intensified globalisation with increased numbers of people from diverse nations living within the borders of nation-states from which they did not necessarily originate, the 'one state, one nation' principle becomes even more problematic. When individuals living within nation-states do not necessarily identify with or conform with the hegemonic national identity of the 'one state, one nation' principle, the state works to bind 'in the name of the nation, conjuring a certain version of the nation forcibly, if not powerfully' (Butler & Spivak, 2007, p. 4). The state thereby attempts to produce a type of essentialised national identity to enable the continuity of the nation-state. It is this state operation, to try to produce the ideal of a national identity, that is referred to as nationalism (Breuilly, 1993; Hage, 2003).

Through nationalism many residents within nation-states find that their belongings to the nation-state are questioned. Castles and Davidson (2000) suggest:

> Most nation-states have had groups on their territory not considered capable of belonging and therefore either denied citizenship or alternatively forced to go through a process of cultural assimilation in order to belong. Moreover, even those with formal membership have often been denied some of the rights vital to citizenship, so they have not fully belonged. Discrimination based on class, gender, ethnicity, race, religion and other criteria has always meant that some people could not be full citizens. (p. vii)[8]

Exclusive forms of nationalism in many instances preclude minority groups and immigrants from gaining full belonging (Spinner, 1994). Nationalism becomes the political means through which the state 'imagines the community in a particular way (as national), asserts the primacy of this collective identity over others, and seeks political power in its name' (Spencer & Wollman, 2002, p. 2). The process of nationalism becomes a process through which those who do not 'fit inside the nation' (p. 2) are emphasised just as much as those who do.

The markers for inclusion or exclusion from national belonging are frequently based on 'race', ethnicity, culture and religion. The activation of these markers as categories of exclusion from nation-state belonging have been increasingly well examined in recent years (see for example Bauder, 2013; Gilroy, 1990, 1993, 2003; hooks, 1990, 2009; Pries, 2015; Pries & Pauls, 2013).[9] Wimmer and Glick Schiller (2002) suggest that 'it was a central part of the nation-state project to define all those populations not thought to represent the "national culture" as racially and culturally different, producing an alterity that contributed to efforts to build unity and identity' (p. 306). While 'race' as a biological construct has been disproven, rendering differentiations on the basis of 'race' more difficult, many have argued that there have been new forms of 'racism' in the form of 'culturalization of race' and 'ethnicization of race thinking' (Jackson, 2005, p. 393).[10] The dominant theme of these new forms of racism, or what Balibar (2007) terms 'neo-racism',

> is not biological heredity but the insurmountability of cultural differences, a racism which, at first sight, does not postulate the superiority of certain groups or peoples in relation to others but 'only' the harmfulness of abolishing frontiers, the incompatibility of life-styles and traditions. (p. 84)

These new forms of racism, Hall (1993) suggests, bring together and condense 'into a single discourse questions of race and ethnicity with questions of nation, national and cultural belonging: "Cultural belongingness" … has replaced genetic purity and functions as the coded language for race and colour' (p. 357). The women's narratives all highlighted how the state, as well as state enforcement bodies such as the police and local populations, activated these forms of neo-racisms.

The women described how neo-racism operated in various ways as a form of nationalism to exclude them from national belonging in all of the nation-states in which they had lived. Forms of nationalism which emphasised particular 'race', cultural, linguistic and religious identities as belonging inside the nation ultimately emphasised the women as outside this 'imagined' hegemonic identity. None of the women described feeling as if their way of being fitted with the national identity in any of the locations they had lived in. Although at times they endeavoured to shift their own identities to be more commensurate with the perceived national identity, invariably they never quite belonged. They were involved in continual negotiations to try to become.

Interestingly, while the women described never having felt as if they belonged to the Sudanese national identity while living in Sudan due to the persecution they faced from the northern-based government, they described at some points while living in exile and in Australia being both labelled with and, sometimes, feeling some identification with a 'Sudanese' national identity. Most commonly this 'Sudanese' identity was ascribed to the women by others in an attempt to categorise or label them. Infrequently, the women used being 'Sudanese' to try to imagine a united, diasporic identity; however this was usually as a direct reaction to the threat to their other identities, such as their identities as Australians. What remained clear was that becoming 'Sudanese' in exile and in Australia, as well as negotiating belonging in relation to the nation in all locations, entailed a continual becoming.

The following three subsections explore how national belongings were controlled and negotiated in relation to the nation-state through forms of 'new racism' and nationalism. The first subsection explores the women's experiences in Sudan, the second subsection considers the women's experiences in exile and the third subsection explores the women's experiences in Australia.

Not Being Sudanese in Sudan

The women told many stories of state-led violence that ultimately displaced them from their homes. However, it is the basis for this violence that illustrates how nationalism operated in Sudan. The women did not talk a lot about the reasons for the violence; rather it was left implicit and assumed in their stories. I can only guess that because the women all knew of my involvement and knowledge of Sudan, they assumed I knew the reasons for the war and fighting.

A diverse range of scholarly work has been carried out from a variety of perspectives examining the complexities of national identity in Sudan (see for example Jok, 2007; Hutchinson, 2001; Deng, 1995).[11] These books consider how 'race', religion, colonisation, migratory processes, power and many other factors have resulted in conflict over who 'belongs' in the nation of Sudan. It is very difficult to summarise the complexities of both the history of Sudan and the debates on national identity without oversimplifying and essentialising the basis for the differences on which hegemonic and minority identities are based. However, it is necessary, to some extent, for the purposes of this book. The majority of the population in the north of Sudan are Muslim and identify as 'Arab'. The majority of the population in the south of Sudan hold traditional or Christian beliefs and identify as 'African'. Since the departure of the British colonisers in 1950, state power has largely been held by northerners, and the state has been engaged in a process of attempting to 'dominate, Islamize, and Arabize the South' (Deng, 1995, p. 11). These attempts at assimilation and oppression have been met with great resistance in the South. The result has been what Deng (1995, p. 11) refers to as an 'internecine war of visions'[12] in which 'state-supported racialization of social relations has been a deadly project … and has prompted people to carry out terrible acts of violence, to deny services, and to determine a person's status in the nation' (Jok, 2007, p. 12).

The women's stories all highlighted the distinction between the 'Arabs'[13] and themselves. For example:

> Aluel: The *Muonyjäng* they can't live with the Arab, Arab they can't live with this *Muonyjäng*, kill them. That the problem.
>
> Melanie: So if you're friend to the Arab it's OK.
>
> Aluel: If you're like a Muslim one, you stay with Arab.
>
> Melanie: Yeah I wondered how some people could stay in Aweil town and most people had to go, but some people could stay.
>
> Nyalong: Yeah that is politics. You have to sell yourself to the Arab one.

While this conversation suggested religion (i.e. 'if you're like a Muslim one') as the basis for this differentiation, religion was not the only signifier of difference. According to Achol's description, the key signifiers of difference between the warring groups were territorial location (i.e. the south and the north).

> Achol: When I was in Sudan, I am Muslim.
>
> Melanie: OK.

> Achol: When I will run away. When I will born my son … when I will born my son, when I will pregnant in Kenya, when I will born my son in I am coming to Christian.
>
> Melanie: OK. When you were Muslim in Aweil, how was it? Like because some people were making fighting with the Arab, how was it for you in Aweil?
>
> Achol (Kuol translated): When people were fighting, it was not Christian and Muslim. It was in the end, it was one of the factors that people mentioned was the cause for fighting, but it was basically the south and the north, and the Muslims in the south were southerners, so many of them were fighting against the northerners. So I was part of southerners even though I was a Muslim. We are not Arabs. A lot of people in Aweil are Muslim.

Achol identified as a Muslim southerner, but was clear to identify that she was not an 'Arab'. For the women, while the basis of their differentiations between 'Arabs' and others might have been different, all the women largely based the differentiations on territorial divisions between north and south and supposed 'racial', cultural, linguistic and ethnic group markers that defined someone as either 'Arab' or 'African'.

What resounded in all of the women's stories was that as a southerner, unless they were willing to assimilate with the state-desired hegemonic identity as Muslim and 'Arab',[14] they did not belong in the nation-state of Sudan. The state made this clear through the use of violence which targeted those who could be identified as southerners through either their location in the south of Sudan, or by other cultural, linguistic and phenotypical markers. Abuk (Kuol translated), for example, recalled:

> Even in Khartoum, if you find an educated southerner in Khartoum, the intelligence just come and get him and kill him. A lot of people are lynched and nobody knows what killed them. You just find someone walking today and then you hear tomorrow so and so is dead and you don't even know where or how he died. A person from the intelligence can just come at night and find you inside the house and say 'come' and put you in the car. They put you in a black car. Then they just take you and kill you. That thing is in Khartoum until today as we speak, it is there. A lot of people are dying in Khartoum.

Nyanut used the terms 'the Arabs', '*Maram*' and '*Marahaleen*' interchangeably in describing how this state-led extreme nationalism ultimately forced her to flee Sudan.

> Nyanut (Kuol translated): Before I left *Pan Muonyjäng*, I was once chased by the Arab militia, called *Marahaleen*.
>
> Nyanut (speaks English): Do you know *Maram*?
>
> Melanie: Yeah, the *Maram*.

> Nyanut (speaks *Thuongjäng*—Kuol translated): *Maram* chased me. It was 4 o'clock pm. They found me pounding grains. When I was pounding grains, I heard the sound of the gun, I heard it 'coh' and I raised my ears and said what is that? I did not think it was a big thing, I thought it was just a small thing. Normal. Then I saw 2 horses coming, running and the person was on them, so I ran. And when I ran, I ran with another woman. When we ran, the *Marahaleen* shot someone next to me. I kept running. I ran. I ran and when I got to a mound which I could hide behind, I hid myself behind that mound, and then blood came out of my mouth from running. Another woman came with a water container and put some water in my ears. On that day, *Maram* killed a lot of people and retreated. Then I returned. I wouldn't have come here if I didn't survive that day.

***

> Nyanut (Kuol translated): When I saw that even if I stay in Sudan, and the Arabs keep coming every day like that, and we were keeping cows. The Arabs may kill us or kidnap us and take the cows. When I thought about that and my brother-in-law said that he was leaving and he offered to take us. He said to my sister 'If I leave your brother and your sister behind, they may be killed when we leave. Or some people will take advantage of them.' And because of that, we had to leave with my brother-in-law.

While facing this ongoing threat from the 'Arab' north, on whom the ideal of the 'Sudanese' identity was based, the women could feel no sense of belonging to the Sudanese nation. They were forced to flee the country of their birth as a result of persecution.

'Passing' and Becoming Sudanese in Exile

Having fled Sudan the women sought asylum in various African countries bordering Sudan. On reflecting on their time in exile, the women expressed a kind of desire not so much to belong as nationals within the nation in which they sought asylum, but to belong enough that they could 'pass'[15] as nationals and avoid being targeted by state forces, such as the police, for their difference.[16] In Atong's narrative, for example, she described how during her monthly bus trips between a regional Kenyan town, where she resided, and Kakuma Refugee Camp, which she made to collect her United Nations High Commissioner for Refugees (UNHCR) distributed rations, buses were frequently pulled over by Kenyan police and documentation would be requested from those who looked or sounded like foreigners:

> Atong: But Kenya, he have a lot of racie.[17] If can you caught the bus with another people, the police he can take the Sudanese outside. Then he leave

> the Kenyans inside. Then when you come outside, he need something, he say 'I need document'. If can you don't have any document like passport, the paperwork, they can say 'Bring the money'. It's very racie.
>
> Melanie: And how do they know that this one is Sudanese and this one is Kenyan?
>
> Atong: He knows. They know Sudanese. The colour, then if can you don't know Kiswahili. Last time I went I live in Eldoret, I know Kiswahili. Sometimes I pretend I'm a Pokot.[18] Pokot, if you can see Pokot, like Sudanese. If can you see the woman from Pokot, you say this one is Sudanese woman. It's black like us. It's look like Sudanese. If can you pretend like Pokot and you know Kiswahili, you don't tell, you can go.
>
> Melanie: Is that the first time in your life that you had someone treat you like a different person because your skin colour?
>
> Atong: Yep, it's the first time. In Kenya, it's the first time I know this one… some police is very racie.

Atong used her appearance and language skills to try to 'pass' as Pokot, a Kenyan ethnic group, albeit a minority group, in her country of asylum. At times this would work well enough for her to survive a bus trip without being targeted by state authorities; however, even this served to illustrate just how much she did not belong. At least for that moment she engaged in a performance[19] which saw her 'pass' as Kenyan. Atong described how the police recognised and targeted people as 'Sudanese' based on their 'colour'[20] and whether or not they could speak Kiswahili, the national language of Kenya.

For the women such as Atong, who had been systematically targeted by the state in Sudan as not being 'Sudanese', it was ironic that suddenly on entering another nation-state they became 'Sudanese' through how they were framed and recognised. Through this recognition as 'Sudanese', they once again became targets of the state as non-nationals in the nation-state in which they resided. To be clear, however, it must be acknowledged that, while Atong described being identified as 'Sudanese', she did not describe feeling a sense of belonging as 'Sudanese'. A distinction needs to be made between the women's processes of becoming 'Sudanese' through being labelled by another as 'Sudanese' and actually feeling a sense of belonging as 'Sudanese' themselves.

All of the women identified that skin colour and physical appearance were used to mark them as outside national belonging in countries of exile. For example, Nyalong commented of her experience in Ethiopia that, 'when I stayed in Ethiopia briefly in 1990, they did not ask for money but they would throw stones at us calling out "black person".' This was similar to the description Abuk gave of her experience in Egypt (quoted in the opening epigraph of the chapter) where she experienced having stones thrown at her and being verbally abused as she walked down the road.

Both Abuk and Nyalong described how they were identified on the basis of their appearance in countries of asylum as being outside the hegemonic norm.

Appearance and language clearly operated to identify the women as minorities who did not belong as nationals in their countries of exile. However, it was also apparent how, even from outside Sudan, the women were engaged in a continual process of becoming 'Sudanese'.

Sudanese in Australia and Sudanese Australians: The Quandary of 'Black' Australians

The backdrop against which the women negotiated their belongings in relation to the Australian nation is complex and has been extensively explored elsewhere (see, for example, Baak, 2011c; Hage, 2000, 2002, 2003, 2009).[21] This backdrop includes a colonial, migratory and 'race' history of which the women have become a part. Since colonisation, Australia has and continues to be a nation of settlers (Ahluwalia, 2001) and its national identity continues to be unsettled by the migration of those who do not conform to the hegemonic 'white' Anglo-Celtic norm. Historically, refugees that arrive in Australia have been socially constructed as different, deviant and a danger to 'the Australian nation and national identity' (McMaster, 2001, p. 34).

As the first ever large intake of migrants or refugees from Africa to Australia, those from 'Sudanese' backgrounds rapidly became a visibly different minority group in the predominantly 'white' Australia. The Australian national identity was, until relatively recently, considered exclusively of 'white'-Anglo heritage. Belonging to the Australian nation was, and continues to be, racialised (Mares, 2002; Moreton-Robinson, 2003). As Moreton-Robinson (2003) suggests, '[w]ho belongs, and the degree of that belonging, is inextricably tied to "white" possession. The right to be here and the sense of belonging it creates are reinforced institutionally and socially' (p. 37). For the women, being 'black' became a means through which they were regularly forced to question their belonging in Australia. Achol, for example, explained how in an incident at her daughter's school her 'blackness' as well as her background as a refugee were used as a means to question both her daughter's and her own status in Australia.

> Achol: But when I was moving here this house, I take children to Greenhills Primary School. Other girls to fighting with the Ayak in the school. Other woman coming, she tell me 'This one refugees, refugees …'
>
> Achol (speaks *Thuongjäng*—Kuol translated): 'This black refugee. How could she beat my child? So if you are angry about your child, let your child go and stay at home.' Then I was called to the meeting, there was a translator, and I had already been informed by Ayak that there was a woman who was angry with me in the school. Then the headmaster asked me through the interpreter, and I replied that 'If you people say you don't want my child in the school because she is a black refugee, then I will take her to another school.' The

headmaster pleaded with me and said let her finish this term, so she finished that term and then I took her to St John's. After my small son was 5 years old, I sent him to St John's as well.

Melanie: And she didn't have any problem in St John's?

Achol (speaks English): St John's, she don't have any problem, but the children not good. Children the same. Kids are the same. But St John's is good, children talking not tell this one the black people, teacher he tell me, this one I beat you now. St John's is OK.

Melanie: So the teachers are [pause]

Achol: strong teacher.

Melanie: Yeah it's hard for the children when the other children are not good.

Achol: Yeah it's Dau is small …

Achol (speaks *Thuongjäng*—Kuol translated): When Dau was in reception, kids used to tell him 'Don't come here, don't come here, don't join our group. Just stay away. You are black. Don't come to us.' When he was told that, he used to fight. Then the headmaster called me in and I asked Dau 'Why do you fight with kids?' Dau said 'I'm told not to join the group or come near people because I'm black.' Dau said 'I may be black, but I'm just like you. I was created by the same God that created you and I'm not anyone different.' So I told Dau not to fight and I told the headmaster that I talked to Dau about it, then the headmaster also talked to the kids and now everyone is friends with Dau and calls him 'Dau, Dau' [with Australian accent—laughs].

Melanie: That's better. Now once they know them. Maybe they feel scared when they don't know the children, it just seems like somebody different, but when they know it's just another person and like that, they should be good.

Achol (speaks *Thuongjäng*): Children are not good. Children are not good.

Melanie: Sometimes children are not nice.

Achol: Mm not nice. Other children is good, other children not nice. For other people is telling… [speaks *Thuongjäng*] 'How can this black refugee fight with my child?'

Achol's narrative provided side-by-side examples of both how her and her family have been Othered through categorisation as 'black refugees' but also how, in one particular situation, her son was able to overcome his Othering by emphasising that he was 'not anyone different'. As Achol's narrative above outlines, Othering took place not only on the basis of 'racial' differentiation but also through categorisation of the women and their children as 'refugees'. This categorisation as 'refugees' took place as a result of public access to particular images and representations of 'refugees' primarily in the media. As bell hooks (2009) has noted, '[n]owadays, mass media is the location where most folks gather information about the "other," that is folks who are different from themselves' (p. 57). Photojournalism, film, the media and the state have all shaped the positioning of 'refugees' in particular ways (Rajaram, 2002). Some argue that these discourses have seen refugees positioned as 'universal victims' (Rajaram, 2002; Malkki, 1995b, 1996) and 'objects of humanitarian intervention' (Limbu, 2009, p. 268), while others suggest that refugees are 'undesirable elements disruptive to the national order of things' (Limbu, 2009, p. 268) who are recognised through 'racializing schemes that serve to blacken and stigmatize' (Ong, 2003, p. 13). Regardless of the frame of recognition, being categorised as a 'refugee' served to position Achol and her daughter outside of national belonging as Australians. However, while Achol began this particular story by emphasising a negative experience which significantly destabilised her family's belonging in Australia, she concluded with her son's story which emphasised how it is possible to shift towards more ethical relational ways of being together through understanding.

In Australia, as with many other Western nations, conceptions of national identity, and the identities of minority groups, are not only formed and enforced by the state, but also by the media. The explanation of the media as a source describing, positioning and framing[22] 'Sudanese' in Australia is evident in the following conversation with Nyalong. This conversation took place shortly after the murder of a young man, Alex Ngong Akol,[23] who was originally from Sudan, by a group of Australian youths.[24]

> Nyalong: You know, somewhere, everywhere is the same. Good people, bad people. Good people. Even like they said racist, I said even in Kenya, they just call 'refugees, go home'. In Ethiopia, the same. In Uganda, the same. So that is not even, they good in school, same thing. So, everywhere. But the bad one to kill someone is not good. Is not good. Because we run away from problems, we don't want any problems. We are not coming here to make a problem. We just running for safety, not to …
>
> Melanie: Yeah and for education.
>
> Nyalong: Yeah. So that is the problem for us. It's a new …
>
> Melanie: New problem.
>
> Nyalong: And it's getting worse.
>
> Melanie: I don't know why. I wonder why? Why is it now getting worse?
>
> Nyalong: Even me, I don't know, maybe it's in the news, you know. In the news when they say African or black or Sudanese like this. So people, someone they got it wrong, you know.

Nyalong speculates that it was the media's framing of people as 'African', 'black' or 'Sudanese' that resulted in them being targeted in certain ways. Nyalong's observations are well supported by research into the media reporting following the murders of four young men from Sudanese backgrounds during the period from 2007 to 2010.[25]

While discussion about people from Sudanese backgrounds has been present in media, academic and governmental discourses since the peak period of their arrival in Australia in the early 2000s, this discourse became more prevalent and negative following the murders of four young men from Sudanese backgrounds. Media, governmental and academic responses surrounding the murders categorised those from Sudanese backgrounds in Australia under the labels of 'Sudanese' or 'Sudanese refugees', suggesting that, as 'part of a homogenized moral collective, they share "race", educational deficits and pre-arrival deprivations in common' (Hanson-Easey & Augoustinos, 2010, p. 307). It is argued that these media reports suggest that those from Sudanese backgrounds perform 'frequent category-bound asocial and violent acts' (p. 307).[26] These essentialising claims, which positioned 'Sudanese' as a homogenous group based on shared culture and ethnicity, meant that all those who could be categorised as 'Sudanese', a categorisation which in everyday life and media discourse invariably took place on the basis of skin colour, were positioned through forms of new racism as 'other' to the 'white' Anglo-Celtic Australian norm. As with their countries of asylum, the women (and other people from Sudanese backgrounds) were once again identified by others as 'Sudanese'. Being 'Sudanese' was used as a mechanism to render them outside belonging to the Australian nation.

Following Ngong's murder, Nyalong was the first and only woman to mention the desire for a united 'Sudanese' identity in the diaspora. While complaining about micro-politics within the 'Sudanese' sub-communities following Ngong's death, Nyalong commented:

> He died here, so here all of us, even if you are north Sudan, we are all Sudanese, and he's a young man, you know, he's a young boy. So I don't want that your politics.

While Nyalong described a desire for a united 'Sudanese' community in Australia at this time, what was actually taking place in the community showed the opposite.[27] Perhaps the feeling Nyalong was relating was the response that Anthias (2006) has described:

> it is precisely when we feel destabilised, when we seek for answers to the quandaries of uncertainty, disconnection, alienation and invisibility that we become more obsessed with finding, even fixing, a social place that we feel at home in, or at least more at home with; where we seek for our imagined roots, for the secure haven of our group, our family, our nation writ large. (p. 21)

When completely destabilised from any sense of belonging to the Australian nation, Nyalong sought a sense of national belonging to her 'imagined roots' to the nation of Sudan, while still acknowledging the complexities of these in her comment 'even if you are north Sudan'.

For the women, national belonging in Australia seemed to be virtually impossible. By virtue of their 'black' skin and cultural and linguistic differences in a nation which may pride itself on being multicultural, but in reality is still hegemonically 'white' (Hage, 2000, 2003, 2009), the women's stories told of the everyday lived impossibilities of fully belonging as Australian nationals. While inadvertently they have become more 'Sudanese' through their framing by the Australian media, political and academic discourse, their belonging as 'Sudanese' remained problematic and incomplete.

The women's stories illustrate the ambivalence and ambiguity of their belonging to the nation-state through nationality. Nationality is, no doubt, a complex and contested category, which when based on the idea of a hegemonic national identity results in those from cultural, linguistic and visibly different minorities being, sometimes forcefully, left outside belonging. While the individuals who are rendered outside national belonging are continually engaged in a process of trying to become nationals, ultimately it seems that there is an impossibility, for the women involved in this research, of ever really fully belonging as nationals in the nation-state.

VIOLENCE, QUASI-CITIZENSHIP AND 'FEELING' IN BEING AND BECOMING CITIZENS

While the women's stories described never having conformed to hegemonic national identities, they did describe having been citizens at some points in some of the locations in which they had lived. However, as Castles and Davidson (2000) have suggested,

> there is no clear cut-off between the process of becoming a citizen and the condition of being a citizen. Nor is there an absolute distinction between being and not being a citizen … The construction of in-between categories, like denizens and margizens, is a reflection of the real ambiguity of citizenship status. (p. 103)

For the women, this meant that, while in some locations they were citizens, at least formally, through either birth or naturalisation, they were still all engaged in processes of becoming citizens. This becoming was haunted by state policies, actions and decisions. While 'the state is supposed to service the matrix for the obligations and prerogatives of citizenship' (Butler & Spivak, 2007, p. 3), it can also 'be precisely what expels and suspends modes of legal protection and obligation' (p. 5) thereby unbinding, releasing, expelling and banishing particular populations within the nation-state. It was this shift between the need for the state to bind the populations living within the territory of the nation-state, and unbind those who did not conform with hegemonic national identities, that ultimately resulted in the negotiations for the women between being and becoming citizens. This section explores how through state-based violence in Sudan, labelling as 'refugees' in countries of exile, and citizenship testing and the affect associated with citizenship in Australia, the women journeyed through being and becoming citizens.

As with many theorists on citizenship (see, for example, Batrouney & Goldlust, 2005; Boatcă & Roth, 2015; Castles & Davidson, 2000; Ceuppens & Geschiere, 2005; Geschiere, 2009; Steiner, 2009), the women had varying views of how citizenship should be understood. Abuk, quoted in the epigraph at the beginning of this chapter, for example, described desiring citizenship in Australia so that she could vote, represent Australia internationally, defend Australia during war and be recognised as a part of the society. This resounds with the definition of one of the most frequently cited theorists of citizenship, T. H. Marshall (1998, p. 94), who describes citizenship as entailing a sense of belonging through political, civil and social membership, as well as associated rights and responsibilities, within a particular community. While Marshall's theory has been criticised, particularly in its appropriateness to countries other than Britain, where it emerged from (Turner, 1992), it is nonetheless pertinent to have some sort of conceptualisation of citizenship for this section. While formal citizenship is commonly conferred by access to political and civil rights, social membership within the nation-state is much more difficult to achieve and is underset by nationalism as outlined above (Castles & Davidson, 2000). As Balibar (2001) has observed, 'the important question is permanent access to rather than simply entitlement to citizenship, and therefore humanity … It is an active and collective civil process, rather than a simple legal status' (p. 28; see also Hage, 2002; Ong, 2003). The women's stories identified the absence of full civil, political and social membership, and the associated rights and responsibilities necessary for full belonging as citizens across all the nation-states they had resided in. Ultimately, it was clear that becoming citizens for the women was an ongoing journey haunted by the power of the state.

Citizens by Birth, Non-Citizens by Violence

Much has been written on the role of citizenship in liberal, democratic nation-states (Spinner, 1994; Halfmann, 1998; Faist, 2000; Soysal, 2001; Hartnell, 2006). Considerably less has been written on citizenship in postcolonial nation-states, particularly those nation-states whose postcolonial existence has been marred by instability and contestation over national identity (for a notable example, see Hansen & Stepputat, 2005). During the period in which the women lived in Sudan, citizenship was defined by the Sudanese Nationality Act 1957. This Act stated that people could become Sudanese nationals[28] either through descent or naturalisation. All of the women were born in the nation-state of Sudan to fathers of Sudanese descent, which, according to this Act, qualified them as nationals and citizens of Sudan. Their lived experiences, however, illustrated that, while they had entitlement to citizenship, they did not have access to the accompanying rights and political, civic and social membership critical for full belonging as citizens. This section explores how state-supported violence against the women and other southerners, in the name of national identity, denied them access to full nation-state belonging through citizenship.

Butler (2007) suggests that when the state 'unbinds' certain populations within the territory of the nation-state, individuals 'are deposited in a dense situation of military power in which juridicial functions become the prerogative of the military' (p. 5). This 'particular formation of power and coercion ... is designed to produce and maintain the condition, the state, of the dispossessed' (p. 5). Abuk's narrative described how this military power operated in the name of the state not only to displace her from her home in the south of Sudan, but then to further dispossess her by continuing to kill 'her people'. Abuk was one of the estimated four million people who were internally displaced within Sudan as a result of the war. She moved to Khartoum, in the north, with her children after her husband, an SPLA [Sudan People's Liberation Army] soldier, was killed in fighting between the northern government army and the SPLA. Abuk recalled the ideological conflict between trying to live in Khartoum, the city of the 'Arab' northerner, while knowing that they were killing 'her people' in 'her home' in *Pan Muonyjäng*:

> Abuk (Kuol translated): The *Muonyjäng* that are staying in Khartoum are not happy. They are not happy because *Maram* goes to *Pan Muonyjäng* and kills people. And the people that *Maram* goes to kill in *Pan Muonyjäng* are our own people. When they go to the Dinka land to go and kill people they may go and kill your cousins or your brother who is still at home, or any of your relatives while you are displaced in Khartoum. That way you can't be happy. But you can just stay because if you are in Khartoum there is no way Arabs can single you out and kill you. But the ones still staying at home are killed. The public guard force, *Difashabi*, used to go with *Maram* and kill people. This *Difashabi*, they are trained in Khartoum and then they go to *Pan Muonyjäng*. The leader, the president of Sudan, instructs them from Khartoum to go to *Pan Muonyjäng* and kill people. *Difashabi* cannot be camouflaged as militia or tribal militia, they are a well-trained, armed army that the president is aware of. It is the *Difashabi* that kills us, it's the one that has finished our people. Our people who were left home, those are the ones they were targeting. And if you were in Khartoum and you want to go back to *Pan Muonyjäng*, they will meet you on the way and kill you and take whatever you got from Khartoum that you were taking home. Then you just die there. If you stay in Khartoum, no one can target and kill you, but if you want to go to *Pan Muonyjäng*, someone will target and kill you. Someone will kill you on the way. You can be killed and your children can be taken so that they can work for Arabs to look after their cows or work on their farm as slaves.

Through Abuk's story, as with the stories of the other women and most literature on postcolonial Sudan, it becomes obvious that, regardless of whether a southern Sudanese lived in *Pan Muonyjäng* in the south or Khartoum in the north (see another quotation from Abuk on page 53 in which she discusses the murder of educated southerners in Khartoum), they remained victims of state-sanctioned violence. This state-led violence against particular populations dispossessed southerners not only from their land and their homes, but also from the civil, social and political rights and membership that would signify their status as citizens in the nation-state of Sudan. As Yuval-Davis et al. (2006) have argued, '[v]iolence is central to projects of belonging' (p. 3). By utilising violence as a means to dispossess and displace southerners through the military operations of the state and its alliances, the people of *Pan Muonyjäng* were forced into statelessness through the destruction and removal of their livelihoods, violence, slavery and murder.

While all of the women's stories illustrated a general sense of feeling excluded from belonging in Sudan, the following comment from Nyanut enunciated how the state-based violence which undermined her rights to citizenship ultimately undid the possibility of her ever belonging in Sudan through citizenship:

> Nyanut: The *Maram* is very hard. When sometimes, you hiding in under *noon* [long grass], he bring the fire to put in the *noon*. Burn, he burn the grass. When you hiding in grass, he burn grass. Then he call 'Abuk, Achol [common *Jëëng* girls' names], I see you now. *Yïn ca tïng* [I can see you]. *Ɣɛn daai yïïn* [I see you].' Nothing. When he say he see you for real, but no. Nothing, he doesn't see you. When you coming to run, he shoot, shoot someone like that. *Maram* is very hard …
>
> Melanie: And they don't care if it's girls or women or men, they just kill anyone?
>
> Nyanut: Kill anyone. The baby, put in the *dong* [wooden mortar used to pound grains in] and then [demonstrates pounding]. Yes. In Sudan, the *Maram* do that a lot. Or put the someone in the *luak* [cattle byre], then burn the *luak*. Like that. It's very hard in Africa, *Maram* is do any a lot of things. Even now I don't like. I couldn't think to go back in Africa, no.
>
> Melanie: Never?
>
> Nyanut: Never.
>
> Melanie: You never want to go back?
>
> Nyanut: Because very scared. You think the place you go, your place, you think the people died there, here, here and here.

While this feeling was not common to the other women, some of whom had already made return trips to Sudan or were in the process of planning return trips, it demonstrated the ambivalent belonging felt by most of the women in relation to the nation-state of Sudan. Nyanut's belonging to Sudan seemed irreparably damaged by the hauntings of the atrocities she experienced and witnessed while living in Sudan. These atrocities were based on the state's belief, rooted in the legacy of colonial power imbalance, that the maintenance of an 'Arab' national identity in the nation-state of Sudan made southerners' lives disposable.

Quasi-Citizenship in Exile

When the women became stateless non-citizens in their country of birth, they were forced into exile[29] in neighbouring countries. When an exile first crosses the border from their home country to a country in which they seek refuge from any sort of real or perceived threat to their safety or security, they become an asylum seeker (US Committee for Refugees, 2001; McMaster, 2001; Australian Human Rights Commission, 2008). They seek asylum, but their status as official refugees is yet to be determined. Asylum seekers are neither citizens nor refugees and as such are positioned 'outside and between sovereign states' (Haddad, 2003, p. 8). They 'do not belong to a particular state and thus do not have the means of claiming the rights associated with membership of a political community' (Haddad, 2003, p. 8) nor do they conform with the 'quasi-citizenship' of being a refugee. As Corfield (2008) identifies, 'asylum seekers occupy a period of intense liminality' (p. 10), which, quoting Turner (1982), she suggests is a 'period and area of ambiguity, a sort of social limbo' (p. 10).

Abuk's story of the time she spent in exile in Egypt awaiting 'classification' as a refugee resonated with this concept of liminality. As soon as Abuk arrived in Egypt, she sought recognition as a refugee at the UNHCR office in Cairo. It took several years for her application to be processed during which time, as an asylum seeker, she was not protected by any authorities:

> Abuk (Kuol translated): Yes in Egypt if you stay until you get the UN card,[30] then they can respect, or they can be afraid of UN so they won't do anything to you. If someone does something to you on the street, you can call the police and show your card to the police. In that way, the police can catch that person and punish them, but if you don't have the card and someone beats you up and you call the police, the police will ask where the card is, and if you don't have the card, the police will put you in prison. But if you are carrying a UN card you will be safe. If someone hurts you and you have a card you can go to the UN and the police can come and get that person and punish them. If there is something bad that you don't like, you can always go to the UN and the UN can support you.
>
> Melanie: Is it difficult to get that card, the UN …?
>
> Abuk (Kuol translated): The UN works closely with the Egyptian security and for that reason you have higher protection if you have that card. If you don't have a UN card, no Egyptian would even care if you exist. You could just be killed on the street and no-one cares.

This radical liminality, the feeling that 'no Egyptian would even care if you exist', underscores the difficulty for asylum seekers in negotiating any sense of belonging in a nation-state in which one's very being seems to be of no importance.

The granting of refugee status to asylum seekers is determined by the government of the country in which asylum is sought (Jacobsen, 1996). Governments are guided by policies and recommendations set down by the UNHCR. These guiding principles stem from the 1951 UN Refugee Convention which defined a refugee as a person who,

> owing to a well-founded fear of being persecuted for reasons of race, religion, nationality, membership of a particular social group, or political opinion, is outside the country of his [sic] nationality, and is unable to or, owing to such fear, is unwilling to avail himself [sic] of the protection of that country. (United Nations High Commissioner for Refugees, 1996, p. 16)[31]

While Malkki (1995a) has argued in her seminal work on refugees in Tanzania that 'refugees are at once no longer classified and not yet classified' (p. 7), I argue that by nature of the above definition and the processes which asylum seekers must undergo to be identified as refugees, refugees are in fact classified.[32] In the current era of globalisation, wars on terror and perceived threats to national security, governments are particularly wary of those who reside within their borders who are not classified and documented, whether through citizenship or some other label (Haddad, 2003; Jacobsen, 1996; McMaster, 2001; Richmond, 2002; Castles & Davidson, 2000). Documenting refugees therefore becomes a process through which governments exert control over who can remain legally in a country of asylum and who must either return to their country of origin or remain illegally in the country of asylum. Haddad (2003) suggests, therefore, that the 'refugee regime can be seen as an attempt to make refugees into "quasi-citizens"' (p. 9). She goes on to argue further that categorisation of people as refugees

> is a corrective mechanism set up by states to prevent further disturbance of the internationally accepted model of belonging to a political community … Granting refugees a special status has the aim of overcoming the anomalous and threatening position of 'not belonging' that refugees pose. (Haddad, 2003, p. 9)

Some governments are more indiscriminate in their granting of refugee status to asylum seekers than others, and some governments take much longer to assess the refugee status of asylum seekers than others. Abuk explained that in Cairo the process of applying for and being granted refugee status took several years. For Nyanut, Atong and Achol the process of being determined refugees was faster and easier. Once they crossed the border from Sudan into Kenya they were directed to the UNHCR Lokichoggio Transit Centre, where they were documented, registered and received their UNHCR registration and ration cards and became 'refugees'. They were then dispatched in convoys of trucks 100 kilometres from the Sudan border to Kakuma Refugee Camp (see Figure 3).

Categorisation as a refugee gave the women a status as 'quasi-citizens'; they were entitled to some of the civic, political and social rights and memberships associated with citizenship. However, many of these rights were provided by the UNHCR. The UNHCR operated as a surrogate state which functioned within the nation-state in which the women were seeking asylum to ensure the women's status as quasi-citizens. Quasi-citizenship, therefore, did not provide the women with a means through which they could feel a sense of belonging within their nation-states of asylum. Quite the opposite: it provided a label through which they could be easily identified as not belonging, as 'different' to the majority population of the host country. As Victoria, a *Jëëng* refugee from Mading Aweil commented (cited in Salbi, 2006), '[b]eing a refugee is a terrible experience. People treat you like you are nothing, like you have no value in the world' (p. 170).

The women's status as refugees, with their accompanying UNHCR documentation, was meant to ensure their status as legitimate residents in their countries of asylum and offer some protection. However, this was not always the case. I heard on many occasions during my time in Kenya in 2005 that the police would ignore or even tear up the refugee documentation of Sudanese refugees. This is supported by a Human Rights Watch (2002) report that comments that, even once refugees in Kenya obtain documentation of their refugee status, these pieces of paper are often 'ignored and even destroyed by the Kenyan police' (p. 16). In addition to this, supporting the comments of Atong and Nyalong who suggested that the Kenyan police would request *kitu kidogo* (something small) as well as seeing their documentation, Human Rights Watch (2002) identified that '[a]lmost all refugees ... must pay bribes' (p. 16).

The women's stories illustrated that, in countries of exile, they were not able to access the full range of civic, political and social membership deemed necessary for full citizenship. As 'refugees' they were made quasi-citizens, becoming part citizens without fully belonging.

Becoming but not Feeling Like Citizens

> Becoming a citizen represents a commitment to Australia and its people. It gives a sense of belonging because you can fully participate in all aspects of Australian life. (Department of Immigration and Citizenship, 2006)

The women were all accepted for resettlement by the Australian government prior to their departure from Africa. They travelled with documents issued by the Australian government which granted them status as 'Special Humanitarian Entrants'. This meant that they arrived in Australia as permanent residents. Permanent residents are entitled to many of the rights involved in citizenship, such as access to welfare, employment and education. However, as Abuk's narrative in the opening epigraph suggests, they are not recognised as citizens. Permanent residency, like refugee status, operates as a form of quasi-citizenship through which people living within the nation-state of Australia can be categorised without fully belonging.

In order to qualify for formal citizenship status in Australia, the women had to meet residency requirements,[33] complete an application and, as of October 2007, sit a citizenship test.[34] Becoming citizens in Australia was, therefore, not a simple process for the women. As Abuk (Kuol translated) recounted:

> I have heard that if you want to become an Australian citizen you go and do a test on the computer, but we don't know anything about computers. Even when we were interviewed to come to Australia, you sign with your fingerprint and you don't know anything about computers. Most of the older women who have come here do not read or write and they even used to sign with a fingerprint. And even me, when I was accepted to come to Australia I signed with a fingerprint. And now, how come I have to do a citizenship test on the computer? I hate this way of testing, maybe it should be changed so that maybe you can just be asked with questions. And if you can say anything through interpreter you can say that. They can provide you with a translator and help you to say what you can say. Because now that we are here we are Australians.

Again, Abuk explained her desire to become an 'Australian', but emphasised that this was made very difficult through the government policy of citizenship testing. As she described, these tests were done on computers and demanded reasonable levels of literacy in order to complete the test.[35] This severely restricted the chances of women like Abuk, whose literacy levels were minimal, in gaining Australian citizenship.

At the time of the interviews conducted for this research, Atong, Achol and Nyalong held formal citizenship status in Australia while Nyanut and Abuk were struggling to obtain citizenship. When Atong, Achol and Nyalong were asked if having 'official' citizenship made them feel as if they were 'Australian', they all hesitated. While they held formal citizenship which entitled them to participate in the civic and political roles of a citizen, they lacked a sense of full social membership which resulted in them not fully 'feeling' Australian. Atong's response illustrated this feeling:

> Melanie: Are you an Australian citizen?
>
> Atong: (intonation unsure) Yep.
>
> Melanie: Do you feel like Australian person or not?
>
> Atong: (laughs) I feel sometimes I feel Australia citizen, sometimes I'm not feel because some Australian, if can you not working, you don't know the people. If can you get the job, you can know the people. Some people, if can

> you work, some people is not treat the people equal. It's not good. Now I think it's about the colour.

For Atong, simply being a citizen was not enough to ensure a sense of belonging. While Atong was an Australian citizen, she expressed that sometimes she did not feel like an Australian citizen because of how she was treated in the workplace. Atong suggested that in the workplace she was not treated equally with other employees, further suggesting that this occurred on the basis of her skin colour. This illustrated that, while being a 'formal' citizen, Atong continued to negotiate her full belonging as a citizen in trying to negotiate her access to full social membership in the workplace.

Citizenship in Australia was therefore underscored by negotiations between both being and becoming. Even being a citizen in Australia did not ensure a full sense of belonging through citizenship within the nation-state. Belonging through citizenship continued to be haunted by feelings of exclusion.

CONCLUSION: IS IT POSSIBLE TO BELONG TO THE NATION-STATE?

I have argued two main points in this chapter. First, for national minorities or those without birthright, belongings in relation to the nation-state are continually negotiated. They are negotiated through processes in which individuals are positioned and position themselves in particular ways in relation to both the nation—through nationality—and the state—through citizenship. Arguably, none of the women in this research had ever been able to belong to any nation-state as a national. As cultural and linguistic minorities in all of the locations in which they had resided, they had only been able to engage in processes of trying to *become* nationals through assimilation and integration. Their negotiations for belonging as nationals were haunted by nationalism and old and 'new racisms' which have worked to exclude them in all of the locations in which they lived. Their processes of negotiating their belongings through citizenship were haunted by the power of the state. While the women had been quasi-citizens and even citizens, at some points in the locations in which they had resided, this 'formal' tag of *being* citizens had not equated with being treated as citizens. This meant that, in spite of being 'formal' citizens, the women were continually negotiating their belongings and becomings as citizens to try to belong more fully through citizenship to the nation-state.

Secondly, while the women in this research were still engaged in continual processes to negotiate their way towards desired belongings to the nation-state, ultimately their stories illustrated that, through the models of nation-state belonging currently in operation, they will never be able to obtain full belonging within any nation-state. Like cultural and linguistic minorities in every current nation-state (as of the period of data collection) on earth, they will never be able to belong through nationality. And, even though potentially their belonging as citizens is attainable, without the social belonging that nationality entails, belonging to the nation and the state cannot be conterminous, and therefore the women will never belong to any (current) nation-state.

If there is an impossibility for any of the women in this research to belong to the nation-state within the current confines of the term, on what level do they then seek belonging? As Butler (2007) has questioned, 'are there modes of belonging that can be rigorously non-nationalist? I think it has to be the case, because the critique of nationalism is so profound ... What would non-nationalist modes of belonging be?' (pp. 49–50). While many current writers have moved towards ideals of transnational and cosmopolitan belongings,[36] these sorts of, sometimes overly idealistic, models do not resonate with the daily lived experiences of the women. As Gikandi (2010) has observed:

> The refugee is Other of the cosmopolitan; rootless by compulsion, this figure is forced to develop an alternative narrative of global cultural flows, functioning in a third zone between metropolis and ex-colony, producing and reproducing localities in the centres of metropolitan culture itself. Missing the very states they fled in the first place, refugees do not want to be cosmopolitan because they have no idiom for this experience; instead they set out to demarcate a zone of ethnicity and locality. Yet they are global because they cannot return to their old spaces of identity and must somehow learn to live outside both the nations that have rejected them and those that have adopted them. (p. 26)

The forced migratory experiences of those, such as the women, who have experienced rejection by both their nation-state of birth as well as the nation-states in which they seek asylum or are resettled necessitates a rethinking of notions of cosmopolitan belonging. Derrida (2001) has argued that there is a contradictory imperative in the notion of cosmopolitanism. This contradiction reveals why a cosmopolitan belonging is currently impossible for those who do not belong within any nation-state. On one side of this contradictory imperative Derrida argues that cosmopolitanism requires a universal 'ethic of hospitality' (p. 16), in which

> [h]ospitality is culture itself and not simply one ethic amongst others. Insofar as it has to do with the *ethos*, that is, the residence, one's home, the familiar place of dwelling, inasmuch as it is a manner of being there, the manner in which we relate to ourselves and to others, to others as our own or as foreigners. (pp. 16–17)

In contrast, however, Derrida argues that this 'unconditional Law of hospitality would be in danger of remaining a pious and irresponsible desire, without form and without potency, and of even being perverted at any moment' (pp. 22–23). In order to overcome the dangers of 'unconditional hospitality' then, 'hospitality, whether public or private, is dependent on and controlled by the law and the state police' as well as being 'dependent on treaties between states' (p. 22).

Derrida's 'ethic of hospitality' resounds with the notion of *cieng* in which hospitality is just one component of the relationality ethic that governs how human beings should co-exist. Ideally, such an ethic would provide a means through which both nations and individuals within a nation could relate to Others as others. However *cieng* is a human concept. It is an epistemology and ethic practised by humans in relation to other humans. While there have been efforts by the nation-state to adopt these practices (such as through *ubuntu* in the interim constitution, Truth and Reconciliation Commission and legal cases in South Africa: see Keevy, 2008[37]), there are limits to the ways in which the nation can adopt and enact a human concept. An unconditional practice of *cieng* would pose too many threats and dangers to the nation-state, just as unconditional hospitality does. An unconditional practice of *cieng* by the nation-state would mean an embracing of foreigners, aliens, non-nationals, non-citizens and Others as belonging, a practice which would go against the very foundations of current conceptions of nation-states.

The search for different ways of belonging in relation to the nation-state, particularly for national minorities, must continue and I envisage that these will have to encompass forms of transnational, diasporic, cosmopolitan or at least non-national belonging. However this research exists in the here-and-the-now of the everyday lived experiences of a group of women. These women recognised the current impossibility of their belongings at the level of the nation-state, which did not reduce their desire to belong at this level, but ultimately this impossibility forces the consideration of how belongings are negotiated at other levels to other groups.

NOTES

1 This chapter draws on ideas I have published in a journal article (Baak, 2011c) and presented in various forums and conferences (Baak, 2010, 2011a, 2011d, 2011e, 2011f).

2 The plural is '*Marahaleen*'. The *Marahaleen* were initially a group of Baggara (a nomadic ethnic group who live along the border region between the north and south of Sudan) who were trained and armed by the northern government to attack the *Jëëng* lands in the south. Through the duration of the war *Maram* came to represent any 'Arab' militia (Deng, 1995, p. 340).

3 Immigration application form.

4 There is no single, agreed-upon definition for either nationality or citizenship. As such, my use of these two terms in understanding belonging to the nation-state may be contrary to some other writers (for example McMaster, 2001). I have drawn on the stories of the women and argue that, in this instance, the women's stories describe a particular distinct operation of both citizenship and nationality in positioning them in relation to the nation-state. These understandings will further unfold through the dialogue that follows.

5 Many academics have written on how nationality and citizenship operate in relation to belonging and the nation-state, particularly in relation to migration (see, for example, Anthias, 2006; Babacan, 2010; Baumeister, 2003; Bond, 2006; Brettell, 2006; Butler & Spivak, 2007; Castles & Davidson, 2000; Ceuppens & Geschiere, 2005; Geschiere, 2009; Hage, 2002; Hartnell, 2006; Ifekwunigwe, 1999; O'Neill & Spybey, 2003; Pearson, 2005; Siu, 2005; Yuval-Davis, 2006a, 2009; Yuval-Davis, Anthias, & Kofman, 2005; Steiner, 2009). This chapter contributes to this body of work by looking at the reflective experiences of the five women involved in this research across a multitude of locations and stages in the migration process.

6 Sudan was divided into two nations on 9 July 2011 (Republic of South Sudan and Republic of the Sudan). The data collection for this research took place before this division and, as such, the women's belongings are considered in relation to the previously united Sudan, albeit at civil war.

7 All of the women, particularly in Australia, expressed a desire to obtain 'formal' citizenship status, but this chapter does not only explore the negotiations for 'formal' citizenship, as I further explain.

8 See also Spinner (1994) and Yuval-Davis (1997) who highlight the difficulties of people from various racial, cultural, ethnic and gender backgrounds in having full citizenship in the nation-state.

9 See also Anthias and Yuval-Davis (1992), Akyeampong (2006), Ang and Stratton (2001), Hall (1993), Hickman and Walter (1995), Ifekwunigwe (1999), Oommen (1997) and Wimmer and Glick Schiller (2002).

10 See also Anthias (1992), Balibar (2005, 2007), Giroux (1993, 2006), Hall (1993) and Modood (2005).

11 See also Ahmed and Rahman (1979), Bassil (2009), Biong Deng (2005), Breidlid (2005a, 2005b), C. Collins (1976), R. O. Collins (2007), Deng (1995), Garang (1992), Holt and Daly (1988), Hutchinson (2000, 2007), Johnson (2003), Jok (1999b), Madut-Arop (2006), Nyaba (2000), Ruay (1994), Scroggins (2004), Sharkey (2008), and Zuor and Chan (2006).

12 In Sudan this has resulted in civil wars between the north and the south from 1955 to 1972 and again from 1983 to 2005, and more recently in the Dafur region since 2003.

13 All of the women seemed indifferent about the distinctions between the categorisations of 'northerners', 'Arabs', and '*Maram*' (plural is '*Marahaleen*'). Abuk also referred to the '*Difashabi*' (National Guard) but identified that these were people who were specially trained in the north as a national army to come and fight in the south in whereas the *Marahaleen* were a militia from whom the northern government could attempt to claim no allegiance.

14 The state attempted to enforce Muslim Arabic identities through enforcing *shari'a* law, converting people to Islam and requiring the use of Arabic as the national language.

15 Ginsberg (1996) describes passing as 'about identities: their creation or imposition, their adoption or rejection, their accompanying rewards or penalties. Passing is also about the boundaries established between identity categories and about the individual and cultural anxieties induced by boundary crossing' (p. 2).

16 It seems to be assumed by both the women and by academics in this field that it is impossible for refugees to belong in countries of asylum by virtue of being 'refugees'. As such there is very little research on refugees negotiating belonging in relation to the nation in countries of asylum (see, for example, Landau, 2006; Landau & Freemantle, 2010; Landau & Jacobsen, 2004; Malkki, 1995a, 1997).

17 Atong used the term 'racie' as a single term which covered racism and racist.

18 Pokot are a Nilotic ethno-linguistic group of central-western Kenya (Finke, 2000–2003). Being a Nilotic group they share some aspects of physical appearance with the *Jëëng* who are also a Nilotic group.

19 Much work has been done on performativitiy in relation to identity (see, for example, Fortier, 1999; Harris & Nyuon, 2010), drawing on the seminal work of Judith Butler (1997). I will not engage with performativity in great detail.

20 *Jëëng* typically have darker skin than many of the local populations in Egypt, Ethiopia, Uganda and Kenya and they are often quite tall and thin which further marks their physical difference from the local populations in countries of exile.

21 See also Ahluwalia (2001), Babacan (2010), Castles (1992), Due (2008), Harris and Nyuon (2010), Matereke (2009), McMaster (2001), Moran (2002, 2005a, 2005b), Moreton-Robinson (2003), Phillips (2010) and Windle (2008).

22 The notion of framing has been used to explore how groups of people are understood and portrayed in popular culture, films and media (Trinh, 1992; Henderson, 1995a; Butler, 2010).

23 As with most of the Sudanese community in Australia, I knew Alex by his *Thuongjäng* name, Ngong, and this is how I will refer to him in the rest of the book.

24 For further discussion on this murder and the consequences for the Sudanese community in Australia see Baak (2010, 2011b, 2011c).

25 The first murder was that of Liep Gony in Melbourne, Victoria in 2007. The second was the 2008 murder of Daniel Thongjang Awak in Adelaide, South Australia. The third was the 2009 murder of Ngong Akol Akok, which is explored here. The fourth was the 2010 murder of Asama Manyang in Perth, Western Australia. The media responses to these murders have been explored in a number of

publications, for example, Baak (2010, 2011b, 2011c), Due (2008), Hanson-Easy and Augoustinos (2010), Marlowe (2009a, 2009b, 2010a, 2010b), Matereke (2009), Ndholovu (2009) and Westoby (2005, 2008).

26 See Baak (2010, 2011c) and Marlowe (2010a, 2010b) for further analysis of these descriptions. See Australian Associated Press (2008a, 2008b) and Lower and Akerman (2008) for examples of these descriptions in media sources.

27 For a further examination of this see Baak (2011b, 2011c).

28 Interestingly, this act equated citizenship with nationality. Whoever was a Sudanese by nationality was also deemed to be a citizen. Oommen (1997) argues that, while nationality is frequently invoked to refer to citizenship in state and UN documents, this conflation is problematic for many reasons.

29 There has long been categorical confusion between exiles, refugees, asylum seekers, migrants and the multitude of other names given to those who leave the borders of one 'home' and journey to another location (see for example Allender, 1998; Richmond, 2002; Australian Human Rights Commission, 2008). These categories depend on the situation under which a person leaves their 'home', the reasons they journey to the other location and the grounds on which they are accepted into that new location. While I have used the term exile as the most generic term to encompass all of the women's experiences of living outside of their 'home' country, their categorisation as refugees, asylum seekers and migrants becomes important in considering how the women negotiated their belongings in relation to the nation-state in these countries.

30 This is the registration card obtained from the UNHCR that identifies an asylum seeker as a refugee.

31 The initial definition was formulated in the UN Refugee Convention in 1951 and amended in a protocol in 1967 (United Nations High Commissioner for Refugees, 1996).

32 Zetter (2007) has referred to this as labelling.

33 In 2007 this was increased from two years to four years (Betts & Birrell, 2007).

34 The introduction and implementation of this test and its impacts on people from migrant and refugee backgrounds in obtaining citizenship have been well critiqued elsewhere (see, for example, Fozdar & Spittles, 2009; Haggis & Schech, 2010; Macintyre & Simpson, 2009; Betts & Birrell, 2007; Bennett & Tait, 2008).

35 Following an independent assessment of the 2007 citizenship testing amendments, the testing system was again amended in 2009 to make it easier for women such as Abuk to obtain citizenship. Subsequent to these changes (and after the completion of formal data collection for this research project) Abuk was able to gain formal citizenship in Australia.

36 See, for example, Derrida (2001), Gilroy (2005), Hall (2002), Ignatieff (1993), Salih (2001, 2003), and Wimmer and Glick Schiller (2002).

37 In South Africa, *ubuntu* has arguably been used as a nation-building concept rather than as an ethic which the nation-state practises (Blankenberg, 1999).

CHAPTER 4

BEING AND BECOMING *DIÄÄRJÄNG*

Melanie: Like when you were a child, what did people expect the woman to be like?

Nyalong: I think they just expect like, just to married and bring a cows. That is in mind that I think so. And have children. And you have your house. They just thought that one yeah. But I don't know.

Melanie: What about now, what do you think, what do people expect a good woman now, is it the same? …

Nyalong: I think it's a little bit the same. Like for me, I hope for my kids they will grow up and they will get their houses and they will live there. And the one I don't believe that now is like marriage like before. Because I don't know now, they will marry a white one or they will marry a black one or they will marry a different, because we don't know. But before in Sudan, you know that your daughter will marriage anyone there and she will bring you a lot of cow and what, but here now, no.

Aluel: We not thinking about marriage, we thinking about education. And see her chose, when you getting married, her choice. To bring the man from white, from whatever, the same to her. Because when we were still very young, what happened to us is not good. Because we are married still young. We don't know anything about the life. But now, we know about the life, we don't want the children to be married.

Nyalong: We wish them to have a good life.

Amath: We want to finish school. Finish school and then go to help them.

Aluel: When you at your mum's house it's a good life. When you coming to your husband, it's not good. Like me, I'm not happy. Because to my house I'm not happy. I don't want my children to be like me again. I want them to finish school, education, and still, you know anything about her life. And then it's getting married. When she chose the marriage, when you finish the school is go to work and whatever. But I don't want again to be like me.

Nyalong: I think so Mel, like when you go to Africa, you still young the first time. But we don't have that chance when we were young. They take young girl to go and see something, they just think young girl going are bad. But here now, like our girls they have more choices, they can finish school, they can go to Sudan, they can go to America, they can go to what. So that is to learn what is the life going on. And they will work. Like me now is my first time to come and do work here. So it's very hard.

INTERLUDE IV: BETWEEN BEING AND BECOMING A *TIENGJÄNG*

On Being

Mum dropped me at the Central Market to run in and get some almond croissants for Christmas morning. While I was there I decided I wanted to get some okra because we cannot get any in Port Pirie. I went to the Asian grocer where I usually get the okra and while I was selecting my four bags a *Jëëng* woman walked past. I did not recognise her except to recognise that she was *Jëëng*. She looked at me with some sort of recognition, but then kept walking into the shop to select what she wanted. I was waiting at the cashier, and the *Jëëng* lady came and stood behind me. She said a greeting in *Thuongjäng*, but I had my back to her and did not know she was there. My guess is she was not quite sure if it was me, so she said '*Ye ka da*?' [How are you?] and if I had not responded she would have left it at that. But I responded and we greeted each other. She got very excited laughed and said '*Yïn ee tiŋ Muɔnyjäng*' [You are *Tiengjäng*]. Then she went to pay for the thing she was buying and left before I got to talk to her. I finished my shopping and then rang Kuol, very excited because '*Ɣɛɛn ee tiŋ Muɔnyjäng*' [I am *Tiengjäng*].

... And Becoming

I returned to Atong's house, as we had arranged, to continue reading through her story. Her daughter answered the door and I went and sat in the sitting room. Her daughter said that Atong had gone to pick up her son from school and would be back soon. I sat waiting, chatting with the daughter. Atong came in with her friend, one of the other women who had left Wau with her in the early 1980s to join the SPLA. They sat down and started playing with the Foxtel remote. Each day they recorded *The young and the restless* and in the afternoon they watched it together. I sat there watching with them. I was fascinated by the apparent addiction they have to the show. I asked them what they like about it. They said it has a lot of history, 'life history'. Also their English teacher had told them to watch TV so that they could learn about Australia, Australian language and the Australian way of life. They are very careful to point out to me the Australian man in *The young and the restless*, but it was one of the most poorly performed Aussie accents I had ever heard in my life.

What fascinated me the most was Atong and her friend's constant punctuations of 'Oh, *khawaja*'. As they watched the woman who is in a relationship but is pregnant to her ex-husband (the father of her first child who died) who is married to another woman: 'Oh, *khawaja*'. The newly married new father tries to reunite with his ex-girlfriend who then gets together with the newly married new father's best friend: 'Oh, *khawaja*'.

And it dawns on me that the battle I am fighting to try to belong as a *Tiengjäng* is so much bigger than me. As much as I try to prove to other *Diäärjäng* I am a decent, upright, good woman, wife and mother, there are other forces positioning me as a *khawaja* and, as *The young and the restless* proves, being a *khawaja* entails certain behaviours that are far outside the realm of what is acceptable for a good *Tiengjäng*. Acknowledging this was to recognise 'that to be white and female is to occupy a social category that is inescapably racialized as well as gendered. It is not about being a white women, it is about being thought of as a white women' (Ware, 1992a, p. xii). Perhaps it does not matter what I do on that day, how many dishes I wash at *Jëëng* community gatherings, how clean I keep my house, how well I look after my children, how faithful I am to Kuol, how much effort I put into learning *Thuongjäng* and the *Jëëng* culture, I will always be just another 'Oh, *khawaja*' and everything that goes along with it. For everything I try to disprove, I am being fought not only by *The young and the restless*, but every other show like it that teaches the women the ways of the 'Oh, *khawaja*'.[1]

INTRODUCTION

> Political and academic representations of race, ethnicity and gender frequently suggest these as alternative or exclusive identities, as Aborigines and members of ethnic communities *and* women, as if women aren't more than half of the first two categories, and as if women don't come from very different racialised or ethnic backgrounds. These categories are also often represented as natural and fixed, disguising the politics of their construction and their shifting and relational qualities. (Pettman, 1992, p. vii)

Since Pettman wrote these words over twenty years ago, there has been a proliferation of research that considers both the intersections of gender, 'race' and ethnicity (for example, Anthias, 2015; Afshar & Maynard, 2000; Das Gupta, 1997; Estima, 2006; Kurien, 1999; Herrera, 2013; Fox & Jones, 2013), as well as the shifting and relational qualities of these categories (for example, Fortier, 2000; Galaty, 1993; Yuval-Davis, 2009). Through considering the negotiations of belonging for six *Diäärjäng* (including myself), this chapter builds on this body of research by examining first the gendered ethnicities implicit in the word *Diäärjäng* and then considering the 'politics of construction' of what it means to be, become and belong as *Diäärjäng* as well as how these have shifted, changed and remained the same as a result of migration.

Toni Morrison (2008b) has suggested that 'it is with some trepidation that anyone should undertake to generalize about still another group' (p. 20). Therefore, it is with some apprehension that I label *Diäärjäng* as yet another group, for fear that this will become a classificatory mode for objectively describing this group of women based on particular behaviours. However, all of the women, including myself, emphasised the significance of being and becoming *Diäärjäng* as a key site in which they negotiated their belongings. The complexities of being, becoming and negotiating belongings as *Diäärjäng* are sufficiently emphasised in this chapter to illustrate that it is impossible to classify this group objectively based on particular behaviours, territoriality, 'race' or any other number of defining characteristics that have historically defined specific groups of people (Gupta & Ferguson, 1997b, 1997c; Bhabha, 1994). Rather, as Brah (1996) has argued, they are a group 'differentiated along a variety of axes such as gender, religion, language, caste or class' (p. 164).[2]

The opening epigraph begins to explore some of these complexities, with the three women describing how being *Diäärjäng* is lived out and shaped by experiences of marriage, mothering, education and labour. The emphasis for the women is on being *Diäärjäng*. They are always already *Diäärjäng* by nature of their locations and kinships of birth, cultural lenses and outlooks, and ways of being in the world. However, their ways of being *Diäärjäng* are challenged and shifted by their own physical migrations as well as the migrations of ideas and other people (Hopkins, 2010). Through the shifts associated with migration being and belonging as *Diäärjäng* for the women has become a process of becoming. The women's narratives illustrated both the continuities and discontinuities in what it meant to be, become and belong as *Diäärjäng*, and their migration stories clearly identified the operation of 'the changing same' in being and becoming *Diäärjäng*.

Frequently, in discourses on women, globalisation, migration, ethnicity and culture, '[r]ather than being seen as the symbols of change, women are constructed in the role of the "carriers of tradition"' (Yuval-Davis, 2009, p. 13). Gedalof (2009) has supported this with her argument that women's roles in the 'reproductive sphere', both in relation to childbirth and childcare, as well as in

> reproducing cultures and structures of belonging, such as the passing on of culturally specific histories and traditions regarding food, dress, family and other inter-personal relationships … tend to be conceptualized in the history of Western thought as being linked to sameness, being, 'mere' repetition. (p. 82)

This chapter considers how the stories of six women with various migratory experiences challenge these ideas of repetition and sameness. The women's stories illustrate that, while change occurs, sameness continues to haunt the change, making their journeys to belong as *Diäärjäng* continual negotiations between being and becoming.

What I write in this chapter will potentially be contentious for many *Jëëng*, particularly males. As Kibria (1999) has acknowledged, '[e]thnicity is a gender-contested realm. It is an arena of conflict between men and women and one over which they struggle to gain control' (p. 318). It is important to repeat and emphasise at the outset of this chapter that this book reflects my own experiences along with the stories of five other women. Therefore, this chapter is *not* intended as an anthropological explanation of the life and culture of *all Diäärjäng*. If anything, this chapter should serve to illustrate that there is, in fact, no one way of being *Diäärjäng*. It is also particularly important at the outset of this chapter to acknowledge again that the lens through which I write and also understand what it means to be a *Tiengjäng* is that of a 'white' Australian woman who is on a journey to learn to become a certain type of *Tiengjäng*.

As Fortier (2000) suggested in her research with Italian women in Britain, '[u]nder the veil of "Italian woman", are multiple lives and negotiations that complicate the meaning of "Italian womanhood"' (p. 119). While my journey towards belonging as a *Tiengjäng* is not the same as the journeys of the women (and arguably none of their journeys are the same either), there are moments in which our journeys intersect. In my journey towards belonging as a *Tiengjäng*, I have little claim on being; rather my process of becoming is emphasised. This becoming was enunciated during a telephone conversation between me, Kuol and my mother-in-law Abuk Atak in 2009:

> Kuol: *Amel a këc nhom määr thoŋmuɔnyjäŋ.* [Mel has not forgotten the Dinka language.]
>
> Abuk Atak (Kuol's Mum): *Bë nhom bɛn määr kadä, ce raan cë ye cök jɔt wën bë mɛt wun jëëŋ?* [How can she forget and she is a person who started a journey to join/become a Dinka person?]

Examining my story alongside those of the other women illustrates these multiplicities. My story shares similarities and differences with those of the other women, and examining the stories together provides multiple ways of looking, seeing and understanding what it is to negotiate belongings through being and becoming *Diäärjäng*.

This chapter explores three main questions:

- Who are *Diäärjäng*?
- What does it mean to be *Diäärjäng*?
- How do 'who is' and 'what it means to be' *Diäärjäng* shift and change as a result of migration?

To answer these questions, this chapter considers the processes of being and becoming *Diäärjäng* through a number of different lenses. The first section explores the two concepts that constitute the compound word *Diäärjäng*: ethnicity and gender. The second section explores how migration has both forced and exacerbated the shifting and changing of what it means to be *Diäärjäng*, and has ultimately made becoming *Diäärjäng* a continual negotiation. The third section considers three particular aspects of being and becoming *Diäärjäng* that the women identified as significant: marriage, labour and mothering. Through an emphasis on 'the changing same', it describes how these three aspects have been shifted and negotiated throughout the women's journeys.

WHO ARE *DIÄÄRJÄNG*? ETHNICITY AND GENDER

The question of 'who are *Diäärjäng*' is more complicated than it seems. I asked some of the women in this research that exact question and on each occasion I was met with a blank gaze. While the question is seemingly obvious, in the current era it has become painfully complex. The easy, essentialising, uncritical answer would be Dinka women. A Dinka is someone who lives in the Dinka lands, speaks Dinka and looks like a Dinka, and a woman in the Dinka context is a female who has had sexual intercourse and is therefore considered 'married', prior to which she is a girl. However, to begin with *Diäärjäng* also means Dinka wife, so theoretically this means that anyone who is the wife of a *Muonyjäng* (Dinka man) is also *Diäärjäng*. Does this mean that everyone who is identified as or identifies as a *Tiengjäng* feels a sense of belonging as a *Tiengjäng*? In my experience, no.

The compound nature of the word *Diäärjäng* immediately emphasises what many writers have recently observed: ethnicity is gendered and gender is ethnicised (Fortier, 2000; Brah, 1996; Anthias & Yuval-Davis, 1992; Anthias, 2002a).[3] In the case of the six women involved in this research it is impossible to examine being and becoming *Jëëng* without examining the gendered construction of being *Jëëng*. Equally it is impossible to examine what it is to be *diäär* (women/wives) without examining how this is experienced through being *Jëëng*. To begin to consider the question of 'who is *Diäärjäng*?' it is necessary to break this compound word into its two components, *diäär* and *Jäng*.

First, I consider the *Jëëng* component. Recent research which considers the intersections of gender and ethnicity particularly in relation to migration (Das Gupta, 1997; Fortier, 1999, 2000, 2006; Kurien, 1999; Oso & Ribas-Mateos, 2013) tends to use a very broad conception of the term ethnicity. For example, Fortier's (1999, 2000, 2006) work focuses on the production and representation of the gendered ethnicities of a specific community of Italian women in London. Das Gupta (1997) asked the question of four second-generation Indian women in the United States 'What is Indian about you?' and theorised their responses in relation to a transnational, gendered approach to ethnicity. Kurien's (1999) approach was slightly more specific, examining the role of gender in the formation of ethnic communities and identities among Hindu Indian immigrants in the United States. Hopkins (2010) questioned how women's sense of Somaliness changed as a result of migration from Somalia to London and Toronto. These four approaches utilise a very national conception of ethnicity—the ethnicity of the participants correlates with a larger national community (i.e. Italian, Indian and Somali). This national conception of ethnicity, as defined by Fortier, Das Gupta, Kurien and Hopkins, does not represent the lived experiences of the women involved in this research, who spent much of their lives being persecuted as an ethnic minority group in Sudan (as illustrated in the previous chapter). Therefore it is critical, particularly for the women involved in this research, to differentiate between nationality and ethnicity.

Spurlock (2010) is one of the few academics who has examined non-national ethnicities in relation to gender and migration in his doctoral thesis which considered the gender adaptation of Chaldean migrants from Iraq to the United States. The Chaldeans, he suggests, 'see themselves as descendants of the native peoples of Iraq predating Arab influence' (p. 2) and this shared historicity serves as the basis on which the affirmation of everyday traditions and customs takes place. He further identifies that, while Chaldeans had originally lived in territorially defined villages in Iraq, since the 1920s many have migrated to towns but they maintain connections with their villages of origin. They therefore originate from a historically, culturally and territorially distinct group within the larger nation of Iraq. Spurlock's consideration of Chaldean ethnicity is similar to my consideration of the ethnicity of the women involved in this research. Rather than considering the lives of the women through the lens of a national Sudanese ethnicity I have drawn on the women's descriptions as well as my own experience in the *Jëëng* community to emphasise the centrality of being and becoming *Jëëng*.

With these diverse views on what ethnicity encompasses, one of the key challenges in considering belonging to an ethnic group lies in formulating an understanding of the term ethnicity. As Anthias (2002b) has observed:

> Ethnicity is a highly contested term: sometimes denoting a sense of belonging to an ethnic group; sometimes meaning shared cultural ingredients; sometimes being depicted as a social place structured by the existence of ethnic hierarchies, and so on. (p. 497)

Early conceptualisations of ethnicity, particularly drawing on the work of anthropologists, focused on the boundedness of groups: culturally, phenotypically, territorially and linguistically (Brettell, 2007a; Malkki, 1997; Gupta & Ferguson, 1997b). The interest of these anthropologists lay in observing, defining and describing the 'beliefs and institutions' encompassed within these particular boundaries (Donnan & Wilson, 1999, p. 20). This conception was challenged by the foundational work of Fredrick Barth (1969a) in his edited book *Ethnic groups and boundaries: The social organization of culture difference*. Barth's work continues to inform many contemporary conceptions and understandings of ethnicity.[4] Barth described ethnic groups as categories of both self-identification and ascription by others. These categories are defined by social processes through which borders and boundaries are marked and maintained between self and other (Barth, 1969b; see also Brah, 1996; Brettell, 2007a). He asserted that these boundaries do not circumscribe a group, marking ethnicity as 'the automatic by-product of pre-existing cultural difference' (Brettell, 2007b, p. 11), but are rather constructed and maintained through social interactions which differentiate 'us' from 'them' (Donnan & Wilson, 1999). Ethnicity was, therefore, created through a process which presupposed 'an other in defining not only who one is, but also who one is not' (Spear & Waller, 1993b, p. 137). However, as much contemporary theoretical research (see, for example, Brah, 1996; Brettell, 2007a; Lamont & Molnár, 2002) as well as the remainder of this chapter illustrate, the border between 'who is' and 'who is not'—the line between 'us' and 'them'—is 'a narrow strip along a steep edge. A border line is a vague and undetermined place created by the residue of an unnatural boundary. It is a constant state of transition' (Anzaldúa, 1999, p. 3).

Recent theories have begun to consider less bounded and more complex notions of ethnicity, which has been increasingly important in the current era of globalisation. With increased migrations and movements of people, media, culture and resources around the world, borders and boundaries that distinguish one ethnic group from another have become progressively more blurred (Gupta & Ferguson, 1997b, 1997c; Clifford, 1997; Appadurai, 1991; Gupta & Ferguson, 1997a). While this has challenged the notion of ethnicity, Ang (2001) has emphasised that 'ethnicity is a very powerful mode of collective identification in the globalizing world of today' (p. 199). This chapter, in part, examines just how migration, as a consequence of globalisation, has shifted and blurred the boundaries that have defined who can belong as *Diäärjäng*.

Spear and Waller (1993a) drew together a particularly useful edited text, *Being Maasai: Ethnicity and identity in East Africa*, in which a number of authors explore and challenge conceptions of Maasai ethnicity. These authors consider how what it means to 'be Maasai' has shifted and changed but also continued as a result of increased interactions with groups of 'others' and changes to livelihoods. While Waller (1993) concludes that there have been changes, for example, to the ways in which 'being Maasai' is centred around particular ways of living such as agriculturalism and pasturalism, he continues to argue that '[o]ne should not, however, see these changes as representing a complete break with the past, or exaggerate their effect. There may be a thread of continuity here' (p. 292). Many of the chapters in Spear and Waller's book have been critical in informing my understanding of the shift and change that occurs through 'how each community constructs its own ethnicity and what that means to its members' (Waller, 1993, p. 294). However, Waller's book only considers how Maasai ethnicity has shifted for those who continue to live in their traditional homelands in East Africa, and it also does not provide a particularly useful gendered consideration of what it means to 'be Maasai' outside of that context.

Jëëng literally means people. As Southall (1976) observed, the word people 'is the most common type of genuine ethnic name all round the world, but since we are all people it only distinguishes one speech community from another. Where the language changes, so will the ethnic label' (p. 464). Effectively when someone says 'I am *Jääng*', they are not saying 'I am from the *Jëëng* ethnic group', they are just saying 'I am a person' in their linguistically distinctive way (p. 487). As *Jëëng* interacted with other groups of 'people' (i.e. the neighbouring group *Naath* which means 'the people' in the Nuer language), and subsequently the British colonisers in the 1800s, the name *Jëëng* (or its anglicisation as Dinka) began to signify a group of people who shared linguistic, territorial and cultural similarities and thereby they became a group of 'people' with shared ethnicity (Galaty, 1993; Bolaffi et al., 2003; Guibernau & Rex, 2010; Guibernau, 2010).

While some researchers have proposed that the people of southern Sudan do not use classifications such as *Jëëng* to describe themselves (Fanjoy, 2008; Southall, 1976), for the women involved in this research, as with many other southern Sudanese whom I have met over the previous twelve years, this is not the case. While being *Jëëng* may not necessarily be the main or only group with which the women identified in all situations, it remained a central site in which belonging was desired, sought and negotiated. One of the women, for example, was first resettled by the Australian government in an area of Australia in which there were very few *Jëëng*. She described how living in this location, in which there were few other *Jëëng* with whom she could talk, interact and formulate a sense of belonging, resulted in her suffering from mental and physical health issues. Subsequently she decided to relocate her family to Adelaide:

> In Bute[5] I didn't have a lot of people who talk to me in *Thong Muonyjäng.*[6] There were not many *Muonyjëëng* in Bute, it was just me. So I told my sponsor who helped me to come there that I wanted to go to Adelaide because there were *Muonyjëëng* in Adelaide. So I had high blood pressure and if I just sat there stressed with no-one to talk to and relieve me, I may die of that. That's why I came to Adelaide. (Kuol translated)

This illustrated the significance of desiring belonging among other *Jëëng*, but also the importance of shared language in this connection. Nyanut also emphasised the importance both of being a *Jääng* and of language when she opened her first interview with the following sentence:

> *A yeen apath. Ɣen a be jam Thuong Muonyjäng. Thuong da. Ɣen Dinka.* [OK. I'm going to speak in the Dinka language. Our language. I'm a Dinka.]

This excerpt illustrated that, for Nyanut, being a *Jääng* (Dinka) was important. This was emphasised in part through language—'I'm going to speak in *Thong Muonyjäng*. Our language'. Wa Thiong'O (1994) identified that '[t]he choice of language and the use to which it is put is central to a people's definition of themselves in relation to their natural and social environment, indeed in relation to the entire universe' (p. 4). Three of the women (including Nyanut) spoke primarily in *Thuongjäng* during most of their interviews. The other two women used English, reverting to *Thuongjäng* only to express things they could not competently explain in English. Chambers (1996) has described that 'it is the uncanny property of language not merely to expose the "structure" of the mind but to both reveal and occlude the world in which we are constituted' (p. 50). Linguistically, as the first language of five of the women, plus the language I have devoted much time to learning in my journey of becoming a *Tiengjäng*, the use of *Thuongjäng* clearly emphasised the world in which the women are constituted—that of *Jääng*.

As I noted above, being and becoming *Jëëng* is also gendered. This chapter limits itself primarily to a consideration of who are *Diäärjäng*—the female perspective on being and becoming *Jëëng*. Feminist writers (particularly those who are not 'white' women) have been arguing for many years (see for example Collins, 1986, 1990; hooks, 1989; Oyewúmí, 2003b, 2003c)[7] that 'women do not belong to a universal category … the significance of being female varies with technology, setting, class, context, task, rank, age, profession, kinship, wealth and economies' (Steady, 1993, p. 98). By specifically considering what it means to be female and *Jëëng* through the journeys of multiple women's lives, in this chapter I aim to broaden conceptions of what it means to be a woman and most specifically a *Jëëng* woman. Waller (1993) has emphasised that in literature on various African ethnicities there is an 'uncritical acceptance of an adult male view' (p. 299) and he goes on to suggest that this needs to be challenged as women's understanding and experience of particular ethnicities is different to that of men. This chapter contributes to broadening these conceptions of ethnicity.

MIGRATION IN BEING AND BECOMING *DIÄÄRJÄNG*

The women's narratives all highlighted the shifting nature of being and becoming *Diäärjäng* across translocations through time and space. Their narratives confirmed the writing of many current cultural theorists who argue that migration results in both the continuity and discontinuity of identities (see, for example, Bauman, 2011; Trinh, 1994).[8] This point will be further elaborated in the following section by considering how certain aspects of being *Diäärjäng* have changed and yet remained the 'same' as a result of migration. The women's stories, however, illustrated two main things which most of the current academic writing on migration and identity shifts does not recognise.

First the women's narratives illustrated that migration, even on a small scale (i.e. between urban and rural South Sudan), had been shaping their identity as *nyïr* (girls) and *diäär* (women) *Jääng* since they were born. In contrast to much contemporary research which emphasises very large-scale transnational migration, these smaller scale migrations haunted how the women negotiated their belongings in relation to being and becoming *Diäärjäng*. Secondly, the women's narratives illustrated how migration and transnational movements of *other* people shifted the roles of *Diäärjäng* who had not actually made migratory movements themselves. This section considers two main dialogues which illustrated the effects of both smaller migrations and the movement of others in shifting what it meant to be and become *Diäärjäng*.

Migration effected and shaped the ways of being and becoming *Diäärjäng* before the women even left Sudan. For example, the women described the significance of urban–rural migrations in their early lives in Sudan. Four of the women had spent time living in urban towns before they were married. Nyalong and Achol's families lived predominantly in Aweil town, Atong spent time living with her Aunt in Khartoum, and Abuk spent time living in towns in the south with her brothers while they were at school. Regardless of whether the women spent most or little of their lives in the towns, all of the women had retained connections with and had experience living in *Pan Muonyjäng* (the village). The significance of the connection between urban and rural has not gone unnoticed by researchers in other regions of Africa, with Geschiere and Gugler (1998) observing that '[a] special characteristic of urbanisation in Africa is the continuing commitment of many urbanites to "the village"' (p. 309).[9] As Nyalong commented:

> But you have your people, cousins, your father or grandfather in *Pan Muonyjäng*. Because all of us have a grand … someone in *Pan Muonyjäng*. Not all the people in the city, no. Your brother or your cousin in *Pan Muonyjäng* still. Like grandma, like my grandma, they doesn't like city. Live in *Pan Muonyjäng*.

As a result of Nyalong's continued ties to family living in *Pan Muonyjäng*, she spent time living in both the town and in *Pan Muonyjäng*. This was also the experience of Achol and Atong. Nyalong discussed, in great detail, some of the differences that she experienced as a girl who mostly lived in the town but stayed in *Pan Muonyjäng* during school holidays:

> Nyalong: So the life, because I have two life. One when I grow up, then when my father close the school today, then we buy sugar, oil, everything, salt, and take us to *Pan Muonyjäng* until the school opens [laughs]. He doesn't want us to stay in the city.
>
> Melanie: So you knew the life in *Pan Muonyjäng* as well?
>
> Nyalong: Yes yes yes.
>
> Melanie: So you did the pounding[10] and …?
>
> Nyalong: I'm very good in that [laughs] because you don't have something to eat. So and the hard one is to make the house, you know, with grass, that one I didn't know. But the rest of things, I'm better. But the bad thing I don't like in *Pan Muonyjäng* is lion. Oh very scary. Yeah, so I think the life in *Pan Muonyjäng* is not good. Oh oh oh it's very bad life there. It's danger. Life from *Pan Muonyjäng* oh oh oh. Not like the city you know … So and when you go *Pan Muonyjäng* you can see the difference of city and *Pan Muonyjäng* for women. I feel bad for women. They're suffering. It's true. Like women if you have *dora* [period], no what no anything. Girl or women from *Pan Muonyjäng*, they are suffering … When you go *Pan Muonyjäng* and you have like boyfriend in *Pan Muonyjäng* there, then they said oh, talk very difficult one. Very difficult one, not like *Thuong Muonyjäng* the easy one. No. Hard *Thuong Muonyjäng*.
>
> Melanie: Why they don't want you to understand or?

Nyalong: Yeah cause in *Pan Muonyjäng* it's different than in city one. In city one we make simple, but in *Pan Muonyjäng* no [laughs]. It's hard.

Melanie: You know last time when I was talking to you, you said in the school holidays you go to *Pan Muonyjäng* and you said the people in *Pan Muonyjäng*, sometimes they don't wear clothes.

Nyalong: Yeah naked.

Melanie: So when you go back to *Pan Muonyjäng*, do you go with clothes or?

Nyalong: No, like especially our *Pan Muonyjäng*, we don't have clothes.

Nyalong discussed differences in labour, access to resources (i.e. sugar, salt, oil and materials), language and clothing. These differences between urban and rural areas were crucial to the women's lives and continued to haunt them for the rest of their lives. These hauntings meant different things for different women at different times—sometimes they were negative and entailed loss and lack of access to particular forms of capital, other times they were positive and enabling. Their urban or rural backgrounds and experiences shaped their marriage partners, their labour expectations, the ways they could support their families in exile and their experiences in resettling and gaining employment in Australia. The difference in the lives of *nyïrjäng* (Dinka girls) from the towns and *nyïrjäng* from *Pan Muonyjäng* was central to how the women became *Diäärjäng* and what type of *Diäärjäng* they became. Some of the ways in which these urban–rural differences haunted the everyday lives of the women are further explored in the following section.

While the physical movement of the women themselves unequivocally shifted their being and becoming as *Diäärjäng*, interestingly some of the women's narratives also described how the movement of other people resulted in a shifting of what were considered acceptable roles and behaviours for *Diäärjäng*. The following conversation between myself, Nyalong and two other women, Amath and Aluel, primarily described how the movement of other people (in this case senior male SPLA members to Eritrea) forced a shift in what the women described as 'rights of the women' as *Diäärjäng*:

Aluel: We have a right now.

Melanie: But before …

Aluel: Women is not right. They don't have rights.

Melanie: But why do you think it's changing?

Aluel: Because it's a lot of education. We moving around to the world, we see the world.

Amath: You see different.

Aluel: You see different in the world. Yeah that's why it is a problem, it's opening the mind. The mind is now is open, it's not like before. Before we stay in Sudan and we can't go around in the world to see the world how the world is going on. But now the war is coming, it's good. It's given chance for the people. War is bad, killing a lot of people, but it's good. Everybody it's the world is know anything. About the city, about the what to build the city or to build the country. How to bring the country is go up. The people is not. But before everyone is just stay in Aweil and Wau and Juba. Khartoum. Only Sudan only. Can't go anywhere.

Nyalong: One day we had the this one. And then they just the women go to Eritrea. When the Eritrea make peace with the Ethiopia. Then our women go there. Is it Eritrea or South Africa, something like that? No Eritrea. When they go there for politics, SPLA women, they just and then they put two men there. So when the first one to receive them is a woman. With this everything solider one. And then when they go to office and explain why they're coming, it's a woman who is very high, high position. Because they fight, the women fight.

Melanie: The women fight?

Nyalong: Oh the women fight. In Eritrea and Ethiopia. The women yeah. So our men, when they came to Nairobi, then they call us to meeting. This is a funny one. And then was very surprised. First time to see a woman with bodyguard and what and she's a woman. From that time he said, these our women now I support them to go where. To know everything. Because the women there, they have rights, so in that situation now, they said yes, so the different culture, different country, different what. So they make everything to change. They make everything change. Like the kids or women here now, they cannot believe some times in Sudan. You know the difference. Before no … here. The man they say what and what. But here no.

While at the outset this conversation was about the political involvement of *Diäärjäng*, it illustrated how the expectations and involvement of *Diäärjäng* in politics and the rebel movement shifted. Aluel suggested that this change took place as a result of 'moving around to the world', further suggesting that seeing the world resulted in 'opening the mind'. This could also be seen to allude to the movement of the women themselves. The women proposed that, as the SPLA men saw what was acceptable to women in Eritrea, their minds were 'opened' and as a result the men decided that it was okay for 'our women' to undertake these roles also. For these three women, the migration and movement of other *Jëëng* (not only themselves) out of their home regions in southern Sudan and into contact with other groups of people with different ways of living forced both *Muonyjäng* and *Diäärjäng* to shift their expectations of what was acceptable behaviour for *Diäärjäng* and just how *Diäärjäng* should be involved in the political realm.

The above dialogue explores the effect of the movement of only a small group of people on a short journey to a country neighbouring Sudan, and yet the shift the women describe is significant. As the five women involved in this research journeyed themselves to locations much further afield, many other shifts, changes and negotiations in being and becoming *Diäärjäng* took place. These shifts ultimately changed just what it means to be *Diäärjäng* and who can belong as *Diäärjäng*.

THE ASPECTS OF BEING AND BECOMING *DIÄÄRJÄNG*

> When I was the age of Dau [her son—about 10 years old], I used to say that when I grow up I'll get married, I'll stay at my place with my husband and children. (Achol, Kuol translated)

> All those duties that a woman does at home, I did all of them. Cooking, pounding grains, fetching water. If you didn't pound, then you can grind on a stone, just to make flour for cooking food for eating. We used to fetch firewood and cut grass for building. The roofing in *Pan Muonyjäng*, the putting on of the grass, is done by women. (Abuk, Kuol translated)

These excerpts from two of the women's narratives highlight some of the key aspects of being and becoming *Diäärjäng*. The three key aspects that are considered in the following subsections are: becoming *Diäärjäng* through marriage, labouring and the duties of being and becoming *Diäärjäng*, and being and becoming *Diäärjäng* through mothering. While feminist political projects have struggled to denaturalise and debiologise women's roles (Yuval-Davis, 2009), the women's narratives clearly illustrated that these domestic and biological aspects were key realms in which they earned, established, maintained and acquired their belongings as *Diäärjäng*.[11] These spheres have also been identified by other researchers, feminists and ethnographers as important areas in which women negotiate their everyday lives (Gedalof, 2009; Nzegwu, 2004; Oyewúmí, 2003a, 2000).[12] Despite the sometimes obvious burden, the women, including myself, took pride in being successful and accomplished in these roles.[13] Metz and Gaie (2010) suggest that the significance of the roles of marriage and procreation in African societies can be linked to the relational epistemology of *ubuntu*. They argue that:

> While in the West marriage is often seen as an optional matter for an individual, Ubuntu/Botho … entails that one has a basic duty to wed, and many African societies believe in such a duty. After all, seeking out community with others would seem to mean creating the most intimate forms of interaction one can with someone … Furthermore, many African societies believe that one has a basic duty to create children. (p. 279)

Marriage and procreation are embedded in the relational ethic of *cieng*, and therefore constitute a critical component of being *Diäärjäng*. In addition, providing for husbands and children through various forms of labour including food provision and household maintenance were also described as being salient features of what it means to be *Diäärjäng*. This is also in keeping with the epistemology of *cieng*. As van Vlaenderen and Cakwe (2003) have argued, '[c]ongruent with the philosophy of *Ubuntu*, the woman's identity is formed through her service to the well-being of the family' (p. 72). While marriage, procreation and forms of labour were all important in how the women lived in *cieng*, the women's narratives illustrated how migration had resulted in shifts and changes in both expectations of women in carrying out these duties and how women themselves enacted these roles. The following three subsections illustrate the operation of 'the changing same' through both continuities and discontinuities in marriage, labour and mothering throughout the migratory journeys of the women.

Becoming Diäärjäng through Marriage

For all of the women, myself included, marriage was the only way of becoming *Diäärjäng*. Before being married, all of the other women were *nyïrjäng* (Dinka girls) and I was a *nyan khawaja* ('white' girl). The differentiation between girls and women is based, in part, on marriage, but also represents the difference between a female who has had sexual intercourse and one who has not. Both Nyalong and Atong clearly illustrate the linguistic differentiation between a girl as someone who is not married and a woman as someone who is married:

> Nyalong: Like a girl, it's a good life for her but, woman, when you get married, ohh [laughs]

> Atong: Not anybody's married. We come married there. All the girls coming is girl. Nobody marriage.

Ideally, girls are not supposed to have sexual intercourse until they are married. As Nyalong recalled, 'especially our *Pan Muonyjäng*, we don't have clothes. If you are a girl. Because if you wear a clothes, they say you are a woman you go with boys, so, it's open. Just everybody can see.' Nyalong described that if you are a girl (i.e. have not had sexual intercourse) you do not wear clothes so that everyone can see you have nothing to hide. She suggested that if you wear clothes then people would say that you are a woman (i.e. have had sexual intercourse) and therefore have something to hide.

The women's marriages, and who they were able to marry, were haunted by a number of factors including their locations (whether in Sudan or exile, rural or urban), their family backgrounds (relatively affluent families or subsistence farmers) and their education levels (whether or not they had been to school). While the women were living in *Pan Muonyjäng* it was virtually guaranteed that they would marry a *Muonyjäng* (Dinka man). There were very few men living in the Dinka lands who were not *Muonyjäng* and it was therefore unlikely that they would marry someone from another ethnic group. However, the women's location and status as either town or village girls shaped the type of *Muonyjäng* they were likely to marry. Nyalong and Aluel, for example, who grew up predominantly in the town, suggested that their status as 'town girls' who had been to school limited them to only being able to marry 'town boys'.

> Aluel: But in *Pan Muonyjäng* they want to marry the girl with the cow when you go to school, they don't marry again.
>
> Nyalong: A *sharmotha* [prostitute].
>
> Melanie: Just because you go to school?
>
> Nyalong: Yeah.
>
> Aluel: When you go to *Pan Muonyjäng*, the *Pan Muonyjäng* people said girl with the. They don't believe anything for.
>
> Melanie: So what about then when the girl who's been to school is ready to get married, do they always marry the man from the city?
>
> Aluel and Nyalong: Yeah yeah yeah.
>
> Aluel: When you stay to the city, you must to marry the man from the city. The city one.
>
> Melanie: OK.
>
> Aluel: But the man in the city marry the *Pan Muonyjäng* girl.
>
> Melanie: So the man he doesn't mind.
>
> Aluel: But the man in *Pan Muonyjäng* they not allowed to marry the city girl.
>
> Nyalong: Yeah because you don't know how to do like build a house and what what.
>
> Aluel: Bring the water in the river and everything.

Aluel and Nyalong suggested that boys from *Pan Muonyjäng* do not like to marry girls from the town who have been to school as they are considered 'prostitutes' who do not know how to build houses, fetch water or carry out other duties expected of a woman in *Pan Muonyjäng*. This resonates with *Jëëng* anthropologist Deng's (1998) observation that '[e]ducation for women in particular was frowned upon as it was feared that it would morally corrupt the girls and render them worthless for traditional marriage, which embodied the real value of a woman' (p. 116). Nyalong and Aluel's conversation, as with those of the other two women who were married in Sudan, illustrated that even in Sudan there were different ways of being and becoming *Diäärjäng*. The type of *Diäärjäng* they could become was shaped by their marriage partner which was in turn shaped, in part, by their location as either town or village girls.

The other two women I interviewed were married in Ethiopia. They each described the differences between getting married to someone while in exile and marrying while in Sudan. They described differences in the marriage processes, the relatives who were involved in organising the marriage, and in their lives as new wives. Atong, for example, recalled her experiences of marriage and as a new *Tiengjäng*:

> Melanie: And was it different in Ethiopia than it would have been if you were still in Sudan? After you got married, do you think it would have been different if you'd been in Sudan than when you were in Ethiopia, or it's the same?
>
> Atong: Yeah. It's different. A lot of difference. In Ethiopia because we in the another place, we didn't do exactly like Sudan. If can Sudan, we have a big party, a big wedding, then if can you go to your husband house your parents can give you two children, girls, to go to help you at home. Now when we in Ethiopia, no anything like that. Because everybody is busy, if can you go to the house you can work with yourself. No anybody can help you.

Labouring duties such as cooking and pounding grain play a significant part of the roles required of a new *Tiengjäng,* so in Sudan girls from the family of birth of the woman are sent to assist her with the duties of a newly married wife. In Ethiopia, where many people had travelled without their immediate family members, this process did not occur. This meant that new wives like Atong were required to undertake these duties without the support of their family members.

When *Jëëng* migrated to Australia, there were further shifts in marriage processes and the marriage roles of *Diäärjäng*. As Abuk (Kuol translated) recalled:

> In our land, your daughter cannot just go and walk by herself. In our place, the girl cannot just go away and say I've gone to my boyfriend's place. There's no such thing. Unless it's someone who is ready to get married, and if the girl goes, she goes to establish her home and she doesn't come back. There's no boyfriend. Now here, even a married woman can just leave her husband and get another boyfriend. You can find girls just loitering in the city, which is unheard of in our land.

For Abuk, many of the moral standards that she deemed necessary to become *Diäärjäng* were challenged by migration to Australia. For girls to be able just to go to their boyfriend's house (and by going to their boyfriend's house Abuk implies that they would have sexual intercourse) without any intention of marrying that boy undermined Abuk's notion of what it means to become *Diäärjäng*. In her description that 'even a married woman can just leave her husband and get another boyfriend' Abuk's very conception of what marriage entails is challenged, threatening her notion of what it means to be *Diäärjäng*.

Similarly, Achol recounted the story of a girl she knew in Australia who got pregnant at the age of 16:

Achol: Now is born child. You don't have a husband. Her husband is tell this one 'I don't want you. I don't want you with your child. I'm not ready to marriage.'

Melanie: And now what can she do, the husband doesn't want her and she has a child? What can she do?

Achol: It's stay alone now. She didn't stay with her family. Stay alone, it's now look like girls now. Walking on the road she look like girls.

Achol's tone while describing this story illustrated her unhappiness at this young woman's situation. By becoming pregnant outside of marriage and then being refused by the young man who was the father of the child (and therefore supposed to become the husband) this girl threatened the ideal image of what it meant to be a *Tiengjäng*. While the young woman was now a *tik* (wife) in the sense of having had sexual intercourse and had subsequently given birth to a child, by not having a husband she was challenging Achol's taken-for-granted assumption of what being a *Tiengjäng* entailed. Further to this Achol described how the continued behaviour of the young woman 'walking on the road' and looking 'like girls', was inappropriate for a young *Tiengjäng* with a child.

Abuk and Achol's unhappiness about these shifts in what it means to be *Diäärjäng*, which they perceive have occurred as a direct result of migrating to Australia, reflect not only discontent with the shifts in behaviours of young women in Australia. Marriage is a form of relation in which *cieng* has traditionally taken precedence. Marriage is seen as a relational binding of not only two people, but their extended families, clans and kinship groups. In Abuk and Achol's observations, marriage is not being taken seriously by young *Jëëng* in Australia. As a result it would appear to Abuk and Achol that the very premise of *cieng*, their very way of life and being, is under threat with the younger generation not heeding the relational ethic which marriage should entail.

However, there were also positive aspects of change to marriage systems which the women acknowledged had taken place as a result of their migration to Australia. For example, Nyalong, Aluel and Amath's conversation (quoted in the opening epigraph) described how the opportunities available to their daughters to complete their education, work and learn about 'life' before getting married would improve the lives of their daughters.

Perhaps most significantly, certainly for me, the migration of *Jëëng* to Australia has resulted in increased interactions between *Jëëng* and people from other ethnic groups including 'white' Australians. It is through these interactions that I, a 'white' Australian girl, have started my own journey of becoming a *Tiengjäng*. These interactions have resulted in increased cross-cultural, cross-ethnic group and cross-'race' marriages and notably challenged conceptions of who can belong as *Diäärjäng*. As Yuval-Davis (2009) observes, women are often 'controlled in their role as reproducers of ethnic, national and religious boundaries' (p. 10) and crossing and challenging these conceived boundaries ultimately challenges the 'specific politics of belonging' within those groups.

Nyalong raised the idea of cross-'racial' marriage, suggesting (quoted in the opening epigraph) that, while she still hoped that her daughters in Australia will get married as they would have in Sudan, she did not know whether they would marry a 'black man', a 'white man', or a 'different one'. Nyalong's narrative seemed to infer that she was happy for her daughters to marry anyone; however, my own experiences recounted in the Preface of the book illustrate that marriage across conceived 'racial', cultural and ethnic boundaries challenges ideal concepts of what it means to be or become *Diäärjäng*.

While cross-ethnic group marriages are becoming increasingly common for *Jëëng* in Australia, they are pushing, challenging and shifting the borders of what it means to be and become a *Jääng*. This shift is ultimately uncomfortable for all of those involved. To me, the experience of living on the edge of becoming but not quite being a *Tiengjäng*, of challenging the very borders which have historically separated who is and who is not a *Tiengjäng*, represents the borderlands described by Anzaldúa (1999). She describes these borderlands as 'where the Third World grates against the first and bleeds. And before a scab forms it haemorrhages again, the lifeblood of two worlds merging to form a third country—a border culture' (p. 3). While Anzaldúa's reference is to the US–Mexican border, her description is no less relevant to those of us who live along and challenge the borders between different ethnic groups. Who is from the Third World and who is the First may be debatable; both feel the grating, the bleeding and the haemorrhaging of the two worlds merging. While I do not think this grating results in the emergence of a third country, or in this case culture or ethnic group, I do believe that these interactions challenge the very conception of what it means to be *Diäärjäng* and who can belong as *Diäärjäng*. And ultimately this grating forces change, even when no change may be desired.

Labouring: The Duties of Being and Becoming Diäärjäng

When I asked each of the women what made someone a good Dinka woman or wife, invariably they would answer with 'a woman who can pound grain, fetch water, cook and look after their husband and children'. For example, Abuk (Kuol translated) recounted:

> That is the things we did in *Pan Muonyjäng*. Building, cooking, grinding, pounding. All those duties that a woman does at home, I did all of them.

However, building traditional houses, cooking on open fires and grinding and pounding grain were not relevant to what it meant to be *Diäärjäng* across all of the locations in which the women resided. Achol, for example, grew up in the town where she did not learn many of these duties. In town there were grinding machines to grind grain, and the main task for girls was often to attend school. She married a man who lived in the town, but when war broke out she went to live in *Pan*

Muonyjäng with her husband and his family who had remained in the village. Achol explained the shift in expectations of her growing up as a girl in the town and then moving to *Pan Muonyjäng* after she was married:

> Achol (Kuol translated): When I was a child in Mading Aweil, I grew up in Aweil city. My father sent me to school. My dad was a business man in Aweil. And I stayed there and I studied in *sanawulia* [Arabic for Year 1]. I studied until I finished. No, no I haven't finished, I went midway. Then I got married to my husband. The year I was married was the year that the war broke out. And when there was no peace anymore we went to *Pan Muonyjäng*. We went to my husband's place. We went to his place in *Pan Muonyjäng*. We stayed there. I pounded grain and cultivated and cooked and milked cows. I did everything that a Dinka woman could do. And made my own house. I learned to do everything that a woman could do in *Pan Muonyjäng*.
>
> Melanie: Did you learn *ahol rap* [pounding sorghum] in Aweil, or was it your first time when you got married?
>
> Achol (Kuol translated): It was my first time to do it in *Pan Muonyjäng*. I never pounded grains in Aweil. Some people, they learn in Aweil. Not me. I went to school. They had a grinding mill in Aweil. So when the war broke out, we left and went to *Pan Muonyjäng*. My husband had a place in Aweil too. When I was in *Pan Muonyjäng*, my husband's father used to tell people 'Don't make her do such things, she's a girl from the town. Let her stay, let her do nothing.'

As a 'girl from the town', Achol's father-in-law did not hold high expectations of her ability to undertake the duties expected of girls from the village. However, Achol prided herself on learning and undertaking these expected roles of *Diäärjäng*: pounding, cultivating, cooking and milking cows. I can relate to Achol's experience from my own experiences during journeys to *Pan Muonyjäng* where I have stayed with Kuol's family. While I initially had no experience in pounding grain, fetching firewood and the other duties expected of *Diäärjäng* in *Pan Muonyjäng*, I knew of these expectations and wanted to be able to perform them to prove my value as a *Tiengjäng*. On all of our trips to *Pan Muonyjäng* I have endeavoured to perform these duties, some with more success than others. The importance and pride that women take in these duties is reflected in the following journal entry I made after a community gathering in Adelaide.

> A bit later the girlfriends of two *Jääng* young men arrived. Both appeared to be from migrant backgrounds but were not African. I had been talking to the *Diäärjäng* who were there in *Thuongjäng*. The women then started talking *at* one of the other girlfriends in *Thuongjäng* asking when she was going to learn to speak *Thuongjäng* and take her children to see their grandmother in Sudan. She did not understand a word of what they were saying, but I did. On one hand it was embarrassing, while on the other, I was proud. I felt included and

> as if the women were proud of me. They started telling stories about me. One of the women came up and started telling a story she'd heard when she had returned to her home in Nyamlel (a town in Aweil region) for a visit recently. She had been cooking on a wood fire one day and started coughing and her eyes watered with the smoke. She said that her husband had laughed at her and said that Kuol Baak's wife had come to Sudan and fetched firewood, cooked on a fire and fetched water for everyone, why couldn't she. While this might have been a bit of over-kill (I cooked on a fire for everyone in Kuol's family on one night only and most of the time I just fetched firewood for myself), nonetheless the obvious pride of the community in my efforts to carry out the activities of a *Tiengjäng* in *Pan Muonyjäng* was there.

The labouring expectations of *Diäärjäng* continued through their migrations into countries of exile. While the core labour activities for the women still centred around providing and cooking food, cleaning and maintaining the household and child rearing, the types of labour changed. For example, in exile there was no need to pound grain, as in refugee camps grain was mostly provided already ground, and in towns such as Nairobi and Cairo grain was purchased in its ground form. I reflected on my own experiences as a *Tiengjäng* in exile during six weeks living with my in-laws in Arua, a medium sized town in northern Uganda with an exilic population of approximately 7,000 Sudanese.

> At the end of 2010 and beginning of 2011, Kuol, Akon and I spent about six weeks living with Kuol's family whom we had taken to live in Arua to improve their opportunities for education. At the time that we stayed in the household there were between nine and twelve people living in the three-bedroom house. As the eldest wife of that household I was responsible for the day-to-day running of the house. From the daily trips to the market to purchase food (there was no fridge to store food in), to the cooking of meals, cleaning the house, to taking care of children, anything related to people and the home was my responsibility. Kuol's two sisters and sister-in-law would help as directed with all of these tasks but I was expected to take control of them. In an environment and a culture in which I was not entirely comfortable, this was quite a challenge. Granted when I was really unwell or obviously was not handling things, Kuol would pitch in and help a bit with food preparation, cleaning and child minding—but not without being chastised for doing so. Generally on a day-to-day basis, Kuol and the other males in the house sat and chatted or played dominoes while the females of the house were expected to work tirelessly.
>
> For me, this was cause for great discontent during our stay. In Australia, Kuol and I worked mostly equally in paid employment and domestic labour. In Arua, however, where he and a majority of other *Muonyjäng* were not working in any paid employment, nor were they working on farms that traditionally in Sudan

would provide a family with their livelihoods, the duties required of males were non-existent, while those required of females seemed never-ending.

While I was the only one who seemed to complain endlessly about the burdens I found myself having as the eldest female, I was not the only female in the family who suffered the duties of the gender-based labour divisions. While from the moment Kuol's brother woke up in the morning (as late as he desired) to the moment he slept (usually the last person in the family to sleep) he looked after only himself—deciding when and where he wanted to go, what he wanted to do and moving freely without informing anyone of his whereabouts. Kuol's two sisters, on the other hand, were at the beck and call of others (albeit they sometimes responded somewhat begrudgingly) from the moment they awoke in the morning (or were woken to start their daily tasks) until the moment they went to sleep. Whether to light charcoal fires for cooking, heat water for bathing, make tea, sweep the floor or bring someone drinking water, the girls were expected to be on their feet most of the day and respond almost instantly to any requests, or face being shouted at and told what bad girls they were.

The women's labouring experiences in exile were also shaped by their location as either urban (in towns) or rural (in refugee camps) refugees. In addition, their labouring duties were also shaped by the presence or absence of their husbands. Four of the women spent much of their time in exile without their husbands. Abuk's husband was killed as a soldier during the war. Atong's husband married other wives[14] and spent most of his time on the frontline as an SPLA soldier. Achol's husband also married another wife and returned to *Pan Muonyjäng*. Nyalong lived with her husband for some of the period during which she was in exile; however, her husband died while her children were still young, leaving her struggling to support her young family. She recalled this struggle:

Nyalong: So I just begging, begging, just beg.

Melanie: So you just go from person to person.

Nyalong: Yeah, I just go, because some they know my husband, some they are friend of my father, so they know, they know what happened. Yeah. And when I go and they see me, maybe, like Ayok [her daughter] she was very good, she get A in her report. [laughs] So I just take that one, like school fee they just pay for me. And they just talk to me like let your kids to be school. They just advise me better than my people.

Melanie: So even like the rent and anything like that, you just have to ask people.

Nyalong: Yeah. Rent, food, everything. Everything [laughs]. It was very, very. Yeah when I think now, oh. I said God help me. Very hard.

Melanie: Ten years you stay like that.

Nyalong: Yep. Mmm. It's hard.

Melanie: And cause you were looking after six children?

Nyalong: It was eight. Oh it was hard. Some they help my other kids, but some, no. But I was, I thank God, just help … And my husband was when he died, he was saying, 'I know you will take care of my kids.' So you know one time when I asked 'How?' Cause I don't know [laughs] … I said 'Don't say that'. When I think, oh Mel, oh. So I said 'No, no, don't say that because I'm not educated what, no what, how can I take. No please, you're not going to die. You take care of your kids.' [laughs]. So when he was dying he said 'No, I know you will take care of my kids'.

Without farms to provide them with their livelihoods and food supplies as in Sudan, and without husbands who were employed to support their families financially, the women were forced to engage in more diverse forms of 'labour' to sustain their families. For Nyalong, this meant 'begging' and requesting money from other Sudanese and also from Kenyans to support her family financially. Atong, on the other hand, used to travel for 24 hours by bus every month from the regional town she was staying in back to Kakuma Refugee Camp to collect her family's rations from the UNHCR feeding centre. Abuk (Kuol translated), the only woman who had been in formal employment before coming to Australia, described how in Khartoum and then in Egypt she had to take on employment to support her family.

> So in Khartoum I used to brew beer for sale, and the police used to come and catch brewers and beat them up. And people were put in jail and sent to court. So I stopped brewing and went to work in the church. So I used to cook for students in the church. I did that for a while until I came to Egypt. In Egypt I also used to cook for students in a school that was run by the church. Before I came to Australia, the three years I spent in Egypt, the work I did was cook for students.

On arriving in Australia, the labour duties of *Diäärjäng* once again shifted. After the initial adjustment in learning to access and utilise resources, tasks such as food collection, cooking and child rearing became easier (with access to shopping centres, fridges, stoves, childcare centres, etc.). However, the labouring demands shifted to the need to be able to generate income to support and access these resources. As a result of their low English and literacy levels, and limited formal work experience, the women struggled to find employment in Australia. They relied on welfare payments[15] to support their families financially. However, they were required to undertake study to be eligible for these payments. Most of the women had therefore been studying English and other adult education courses since arriving in Australia. Many of the women saw this education as somewhat redundant and tokenistic and would rather have been working in formal employment. As Abuk (Kuol translated) recounted:

> The school is good, but I can't understand anything. The school is good for children, but it's not good for big people. We don't understand a lot of concepts. The reason we go to school sometimes is just so you don't stay at home and do nothing and Centrelink thinks you're doing nothing. You have to be doing something, either work or go to school.

Atong and Nyalong were the only two women who had been able to gain formal employment for periods in Australia, although both had found this challenging for various reasons.

> Nyalong: Yeah, yeah. Like now I'm happy to do something for them [her children]. When they finish, they will work, so I think I thank God I finish my what. Yeah. Because like now I can stay with Centrelink but not good. Not good, yeah. I need to do something. Like now I was thinking to do nurse, you know, to do the course. Oh.
>
> Melanie: The enrolled nursing or something like that.
>
> Nyalong: Mmm. Because the carer is, I like it but it's my height.
>
> Melanie: Hard for the body.
>
> Nyalong: Yeah, it is a problem for my body.

Nyalong described that she was happy to be able to work, as through her employment she was able to provide for her children and this was better than staying on Centrelink benefits. What she found challenging was the type of work that she was able to access with limited skills and education. She worked in aged care and, as a tall woman, she found this work demanding on her body, particularly her back. Atong spoke of similar frustrations in only being able to access employment in places such as factories with very low earning potential. Some of the jobs Atong had been able to obtain were unreliable both in the number of shifts she would get and in income. This meant that she was financially better off remaining on welfare.

The women's stories illustrated a significant shift in the types of labouring duties that were required of them, from *Pan Muonyjäng* to countries of exile and then to Australia. Labouring remained significant, but the ways in which labour was conducted shifted. Interestingly the women described their pride in completing the everyday labouring duties in *Pan Muonyjäng* as somehow being more fulfilling than the menial employment or redundant education that they were forced to undertake in Australia. Contrary to the argument of many feminists that liberation from the oppression of 'traditional' ways of life empowers women (Mohanty, 1991, 1995), it would seem from the women's narratives that their transition to 'modern' ways of living in fact undermined how they felt about themselves as women in providing for their families through labour. Ultimately, when it came to labouring, while the types of duties had changed, the end outcome of the duties had remained the same—to provide for their families through the provision of food, household maintenance and child rearing.

Being and Becoming Diäärjäng through Mothering

As the African feminist Oyérónkẹ́ Oyewùmí (2003a) has noted, '[m]otherhood occupies a special place in African cultures and societies. Regardless of whether a particular African society displays a patrilineal or matrilineal kinship system, mothers are the essential building block of social relationships, identities, and indeed society' (p. 1; see also Rukuni, 2007, p. 33). In the patrilineal *Jëëng* context, a woman marries into her husband's family. However, she does not become a full member of her husband's family until she has safely delivered the first child. Burton (1982) suggests that '[u]ntil she conceives her first child, the woman is treated more as a respected guest than as kin' (p. 484).[16] There is some truth in this, but the descriptions of many *Diäärjäng* I have met, and also my own experience, suggest that as new wives they do not feel like 'respected guests', but rather they are observed and judged on their ability to perform the other duties of *Diäärjäng* such as the labouring described above.

In my own experience, following my marriage to Kuol I was repeatedly asked by other *Diäärjäng* in Sudan, exile and Australia when I was having a baby. Frequently comments were made inferring that *khawaja* women do not seem to make having children a high priority, and to this day judgements are passed about the number of children I may or may not have. *Jëëng* perceive that the *khawaja* system of having children (later in life and smaller families) is not commensurate with the *Jëëng* system in which 'the desire for a large family is the norm … and the woman is expected to become pregnant shortly after marriage—preferably within a few months to a year' (Jok, 1999a, p. 200). Kuol and I had been 'married' (i.e. living together) for over four years before I became pregnant, and in the *Jëëng* context this is a particularly long time. The relief among the *Jëëng* community in Australia when I finally became obviously pregnant with Akon was palpable. I recall walking into a community gathering when I was about five months pregnant, with an obvious baby belly, and being greeted with laughter and smiles all round.

Procreation for *Jëëng*, argues Deng (1984), is 'more than childbearing and childrearing' but becomes a means of 'immortality' (p. 9). He further suggests that procreation is one of the main goals for all *Jëëng*. In addition, Jok (1999a) found in his research with *Diäärjäng* in war-torn Sudan during the mid-1990s that women were frequently either forced to, or were prepared to, put their own health at risk 'to ensure the continuity of the family name, and gain acceptance as worthy community members' (p. 197). This is part of the relational, communal ethic governed by *cieng*. With this emphasis on procreation, it is clear why being and becoming a mother was significant for the women in determining what it meant to belong as *Diäärjäng*. However, even aspects of procreation and mothering have made significant shifts as a result of the women's migratory journeys.

The importance of childbearing for *Diäärjäng* can be seen in the following except from Achol's narrative. Achol had difficulty conceiving her first child and the following passage illustrates the significance of this challenge for her:

Melanie: OK. So you stay a long time before you had Mayar. For 9 …

Achol: No no 11 years. 11 years I didn't have child. It's 12 years, I born child. Already 12 years.

Melanie: Yeah it's a long time.

Achol: It's born child, maybe it's big child.

Melanie: Yeah. So you were very happy to get Mayar?

Achol: Yeah I'm very happy. When I will stay I didn't born child, uhh, I know I'm thinking I'm born child.

Melanie: OK. Yeah it's good.

Achol: Not one day I'm cry, one day I didn't tell this one 'I'm not born child'. No. I didn't think like that one. Other people it didn't born child is cry, it's not happy. But that one not for me.

Melanie: What about for your husband, when you didn't have a child was he surprised or …? Because I know the man he wants to have children to give the name and.

Achol: Yes when I will born child, he's happy. He's happy. When I will born child, I born child in Nairobi … I'm dreaming … I'm dream. In 1993, I'm dream like I born child, other person coming I born child. I born child, this one I dream first … (speaks Dinka)

Achol (Kuol translated): I had a dream that I was on the way to Kajokeji [a town in the south of Sudan] and I had a small child. I dreamt of a toddler, one year old, and my husband told me 'The child is hungry, give him some *madudo* [porridge]'. And then I asked 'So what can I make *madudo* with?' And they said 'Just use that one and make it'. So I made it and the little child drank the *madudo*. After 3 months, I had another dream that a child was brought wrapped in a cloth, and the women that brought the child were women from the hospital, nurses. There were doctors, I was dreaming like I was in the hospital on the hospital bed, so when the nurses brought the child to me they asked me to breastfeed and I breastfed the child. So I dreamt like that, and when I opened my eyes, I found it was a lie. [laughs] When I opened my eyes, I found it was a lie. Just a lie. So I was surprised. Then I spent another year, then I got pregnant. After 2 months the 'Antonov' bomber came and bombed the people. We were hiding in the dugout where people bury themselves for safety. My husband said 'it's better you go to Uganda'. So I went and spent 3 months in

> Uganda, then I went to Nairobi. Then I went and stayed in Nairobi. I gave birth in a hospital, and it was the same hospital I saw exactly in my dream. Even the nurses that I saw were the ones that brought the child to me. [laughs] The same, same hospital that I had a dream is the hospital that I delivered in. Then when I realised that, I thought of the dream of more than 2 years before. Then I compared the dream with the reality. Then I saw the people from the hospital that brought the child to me and I had a prefect comparison of the dream and the reality.

While Achol stated that she was not the sort of woman who cried because she had not been able to have a child, her emphasis on the dreams she had prior to delivering her first child would suggest that not having a child did weigh on her mind. In fact, her dreams were haunted by the imagining and belief that she would one day mother a child. Her desire to become a mother was evident in the disappointment she expressed when she awoke from dreaming she had delivered a baby to find it was 'a lie'. Achol reflected that, although it was eleven years from when she was married to when she conceived, she had always believed that one day she would have a child. During the eleven years in which she was trying to conceive, she followed her husband from Sudan, to Ethiopia, back into Sudan to the frontlines of the war, to Kenya and then back to Sudan. She did not leave her husband's side in the hope that she might conceive a child. This illustrates the importance for *Diäärjäng* of becoming mothers.

Achol, in another part of her narrative, also reflected on the experiences of other women who delivered their babies while fleeing from refugee camps in Ethiopia following the outbreak of civil war there in the early 1990s:

> Achol (Kuol translated): And it was raining and there was no shelter. It would rain, and we would just be standing there in the rain. If there was a big tree with leaves, we could sit under there. Some women delivered on the way.
>
> Melanie: Under the tree? They just have the baby under the tree?
>
> Achol (Kuol translated): Yes women deliver under the tree. There was nothing for the breastfeeding mother to eat. The child would be wrapped in whatever cloth you could find and you keep going.
>
> Melanie: Were the babies OK?
>
> Achol (speaks English): Ee, baby is OK and other baby is not here.
>
> Achol (speaks *Thuongjäng*—Kuol translated): Some babies are here now, some who were born there. And now they don't want to listen to their mothers in Australia. Some were born on the way. It was a true suffering.

She described how women went through processes of 'true suffering' to deliver their children on the horrendous journeys they made to escape war. During these journeys to exile, in spite of the fact that there was little food for pregnant and breastfeeding mothers to eat, the women continued to get pregnant and have children. This is most likely due to cultural expectations that *Diäärjäng* will have large families as a result of what Yuval-Davis (2009) refers to as:

> 'people as power' in which women are mobilized in various ways to bear more children … where there is an urgent need for more members of the collectivity to settle, to work, to fight against another collectivity, to keep ethnic hegemony in the collectivity. (p. 10)

It would appear that historically and on a practical level[17] *Diäärjäng* have had large families for several reasons. The first reason is the high child and infant mortality rate—the more children a woman gave birth to, the more likely she was to have a reasonable number of children who survived. Several authors suggest that this issue is compounded during periods of war (Jok, 1999a; Scrimshaw, 1978; Hutchinson, 1996). Secondly, where livelihoods were traditionally made through agrarian lifestyles and subsistence farming, having more children to help on the farm ensured increased labourers. Thirdly, children provided resources and care for their parents as they got older (Agozino, 2000). Daughters bring in cattle wealth through the dowries received for their marriages, and in old age parents live with their sons and their families who provide food, accommodation and day-to-day care. All of these issues resulted in existing reproductive pressures on *Diäärjäng* prior to the civil war. However, Jok (1999a) suggests that with the outbreak of war and displacement of people during the war these reproductive pressures increased.

Only one of the women delivered children while living in Sudan, three of the women delivered all of their children while living in countries of exile, and one woman delivered a majority of her children while living in exile and one child while living in Australia. As such, it is difficult to suggest either shifts or continuities in childbirth experiences or childbirth demands on the women during their journeys from Sudan to Australia.

Childbirth, however, is only one aspect of mothering. Child rearing was another aspect of mothering the women focused on significantly. As only one of the women had experienced raising children in Sudan, the main shifts in child rearing described by the women emphasised differences between what they had observed and experienced themselves as children in Sudan, then their experiences in exile and finally their experiences in Australia. The most significant shift in childrearing experiences occurred when the women and their families journeyed to Australia. For example, Achol in the narrative quoted above described how some of the children who were born during the difficult journeys of women into exile are now here in Australia where they 'don't want to listen to their mothers'.

For *Jëëng*, much of the day-to-day child rearing is done by females. As *Jëëng* ave migrated this has increasingly become the case. Many *Diäärjäng* have come to Australia as single mothers, either because their husbands died during the war or because their husbands stayed in Sudan.[18] Four of the women were raising their children in Australia as single mothers. All of the women described frustrations and challenges in trying to raise their children in Australia. They felt as if the Australian government (through government agencies such as Centrelink), refugee and resettlement service providers and what they perceived as 'the Australian way of life' had undermined their mothering as *Diäärjäng.*[19] Abuk (Kuol translated), for example, stated:

> If it is a woman, a woman only drinks beer after she has 6 to 7 children. By that time you are a big person. A man can also wait until he is married and has children and then he can start drinking. Women who are 40 and above, they are the ones who are socially allowed to drink beer, because at that stage they have children who can look after them. Here children are the ones who are drinking in clubs and we don't have clubs in *Pan Muonyjäng*. This issue of clubs, you have to tell the *khawaja*, that it is not a good thing, and we don't like it.
>
> And you also don't allow kids to have their own accommodation; no we don't like that one. In our place, your daughter only leaves your house once they are married. They don't just leave their mum and dad's house before they get married. The same thing for the boy, your son only leaves your house once he's married. Anyone who is not married cannot just leave home, but here in Australia it doesn't work like that. These rules, I don't like them.
>
> We want the Australian government to allow us to look after our children like we used to. If the need be to beat your child, then you should beat your child and your child shouldn't be taken away or run away. And if you get angry with your child, you should get angry with your child and still remain at home with your child. Now we don't talk with our children because if you try to tell your child off he just says 'I don't care!' And they just go, but we don't have that in our home. We don't have it in our land, you've gone to our place, you've seen it, we don't have it. This, you have to tell the Australian people, our children are not turning out the way we want them, and the children are not the only ones doing it to themselves, Australia is also doing it to them.
>
> If Australia was not contributing, Australia should be telling a child that leaves home to go back home. Then the children would learn that it's not good to leave home and they wouldn't go away. If a child goes and doesn't find accommodation and food, they will come back home. But now Australian people, they just give the child their own card,[20] then they can get their own money. Because they have their own card, then they can go because they can buy their own food, they can rent their own house, they can buy tobacco, they can buy beer. It's their own card to do whatever they want to do and nobody can ask them. These things they are very difficult for *Muonyjäng*. Our children that are not staying at home anymore, we really don't like to see them that way, it hurts our hearts to see them living that way. Every woman whose child is not staying at home is not happy. But we don't know what to do.

Abuk's narrative clearly illustrated her frustrations about mothering in Australia, where she felt as if her children did not listen to her, and they were supported to refuse her guidance and discipline. As she poignantly noted, 'it hurts our hearts to see them living that way'—in ways which do not conform with ideals that they had for their children as *Jëëng* These ideals are shaped by the relational ethic of *cieng* which requires respect for parents and elders and encourages particular ways of living together. These include children not moving out of their family homes before they are married, people not drinking alcohol until they have established significant standing within the community, and disciplining children. This shift in mothering, and the concomitant shift in *cieng*, Abuk felt had been forced on her, and it was not something that she was happy with. She longed to be able to look after her children like she 'used to', and if that meant getting angry with her child or beating them, as she had previously been able to, she believed she should be able to do that. She called on me, as a 'girl' from Australia and a *khawaja* who has also been to 'our place' and 'seen' the mothering practices and the way of life there, to appeal to the *khawaja*, the Australian people, for their support so that *Jëëng* children will 'turn out the way we want'. Nyalong also described these challenges of mothering in Australia:

> Nyalong: I don't have any problem, only problem is the one our kids, you know. You know our kids. Yeah because I don't know it's from our community or from Australian people because we cannot come and change the law, you know. We cannot come and say 'do this, do this' but the only because our kids come and say they are free, you know. They say 'We have a free life' or a free what. So they are free to do like now they are doing, they're lost, even the life, you know. And even they make us, like the mothers, not telling good, you know. Yeah not telling good. Like when somebody died, you feel like, I don't know how can. My all is come up, but how we are coming from there to here. We are not coming for problems, we are running from problems. And we are running because of them [children]. No women come here without the kids, no. Because they are the ones, the life, the one who bring us here. But when they did that one, that is why only that upset me up to now. Yeah I'm not happy for that one. But I cannot say the Australia, I just ask God why? And I don't know when we are in camp our kids are very good and they listen, but now they are here they eat, they go to school, treatment and they think that they don't appreciate that one. Yeah, that is why now.
>
> Melanie: Like they forgot the life …
>
> Nyalong: They forgot everything now. So that one. Sometimes when I see it, no I'm not happy for that one. But I thank God for that one. Maybe it will change.

Nyalong explained that there were no *Diäärjäng* who came to Australia without children. She elucidates that they came to Australia to improve the lives of their children, and now it upsets her that here, in Australia, her children have forgotten the difficulties of the lives they fled and now take for granted the opportunities to eat, go to school and receive health treatment. Instead she suggested that children are focused on their 'freedom' to make their own choices and that is taking them down pathways that the women are not happy with. Through the children's insistence that they are 'free' and have a 'free life', Nyalong suggests that 'they're lost'. Like Abuk's narrative, Nyalong expresses that through the freedoms children believe they have gained in Australia, many have forgotten the *Jëëng* way of life encompassed by *cieng*, and the women were not happy with this change.

A large number of *Diäärjäng* became widows during the war and this left these women as the sole carers of the children. In addition, increased numbers of women have become sole carers as they have journeyed to Australia, leaving their husbands in Africa. As the main and sometimes only child rearers, if a child does not behave in an acceptable manner the child's behaviour is often blamed on the mother. Equally, if the child is well behaved and successful the mother may be praised. As Atong explained:

> If can woman take care about the children, if can children coming out, she don't have any respect, sometimes the man can say 'This one is because it's the woman take care about these children. These ones are not coming well.' Now if can the child coming good thing, the father he can say 'My children, it's my wife is very good wife.' He can be pride to you.

The fact that many of the *Jëëng* children in Australia are behaving in ways that people 'are not happy with' is to a large extent blamed on the mothering of the *Diäärjäng* in Australia. The shift in acceptable childrearing practices from Sudan and countries of exile to Australia has left the women without the skills that they feel are necessary for successful mothering in Australia. They feel as if the skills and success they had as mothers in Africa are ultimately undermined by what the 'Australian system' expects and allows them to do as mothers in Australia. Coming to Australia has forced a shift in the relation between parents and children that they are not comfortable with. Ultimately this forced shift has left them feeling as if they cannot be the sort of mothers they want to be, rendering them feeling inadequate and incompetent in a role which to a large extent defines their belonging as *Diäärjäng*.

CONCLUSION: SHIFTING GENDERED ETHNICITIES

As Gedalof (2009) has argued, 'scholarly accounts of migration often frame migration as a narrative of dynamism, change, mobility and agency, without questioning the gendered politics of this account' (p. 82). Understanding the gendered politics of migration and how resultant shifts and changes occur through a gendered lens is thus of critical importance. However, current accounts of gender shifts in migration often fail to note the critical intersections of gender with 'race', class and ethnicity (Anthias, 1992, 1998a, 1998b, 2002a, 2006, 2008, 2009b; Yuval-Davis, 2001, 2006b). It is particularly important to take into account these intersections when considering the migrations of women from the so-called 'Third World' to the West. There are three main points that I draw out of this chapter in this concluding section.

First, understanding gender in relation to the migration of women from the 'Third World' to the West is haunted by the ghostly matters of 'racial' and 'ethnic' hierarchies. And on this note, it is crucial that ethnicity be understood, for many people in the world, as distinct from nationality. As such, considerations of gender in migration should not be considered outside of the hauntings of these other categories. For me, these intersections were made obvious by the compound nature of the word *Diäärjäng*. While gender is an overarching theme throughout the research which haunts the ways the women were able to negotiate their belongings within all spheres, in part because of the compound word *Diäärjäng*, it is considered in most detail in this chapter. However, future research must also be cognisant of the ways in which all of the distinct categories that researchers are forced to 'box' their research into continue to intersect and haunt each other (Anthias, 2008, 2009a; Brah & Phoenix, 2004; Yuval-Davis, 2006b).

Secondly, migrations of women from the 'Third World' to the West are often viewed as disempowered, oppressed 'Third World women' migrating from 'traditional' ways of life to the emancipatory opportunities opened to them through migration to the 'modern' West (Arnfred, 2002; Mohanty, 1991). Arnfred (2002) has described that:

> embedded in the uni-linear and pre-packed notion of development is a pre-packed conception of gender relations: Woman as *the other*, as universally subordinated, and Third World women as subordinated par excellence. The general idea is that women's subordination belongs to tradition and to the past, whereas women's emancipation or gender equality, as the current terminology has it belongs to modernity and to the future. (p. 3)

In the preceding sections, the women's narratives of their personal journeys from the 'Third World' to the West did not equate to this unilinear shift from 'tradition' to 'modernity', 'subordinated' to 'emancipated'. Rather, they suggested that through different means in different locations along the journey they were both empowered and disempowered. In some instances the journeying and collision of the 'Third World' with the West resulted in what they referred to as 'opening the mind' and subsequent improvements in 'rights' for women (for example, the journeys of the SPLA men to Eritrea resulting in increased involvement for women within the SPLA). But they also argued very strongly that through their journeys to Australia some of their 'rights' as women had been undermined (for example, their roles and the respect that they had in Africa as mothers had been undermined by Australian service providers and government agencies such as Centrelink). Clearly, for the women, while there were shifts in their gendered roles between *Pan Muonyjäng*, exile and Australia, it was not as simple as a shift from 'subordination' to 'emancipation'.

Thirdly, while the focus in migration and identity studies is currently on the shifting, impermanent, processual status of categories such as gender and ethnicity, the women's narratives also identified a degree of sameness. As such, Gilroy's notion of 'the changing same' is particularly useful in considering both the continuities and discontinuities in what it meant to negotiate belongings as *Diäärjäng* throughout the women's journeys. In some instances the women embraced the 'change' while continuing to be haunted by the 'sameness' (for example, in their visions that their daughters would be able to complete their education, travel and choose their future husbands but ultimately that it was still 'a little bit the same' because they hoped that their daughters *would* get married), while in other instances they clung to the 'sameness' while the hauntings of powers outside their control forced the 'change' to come about (for example, in the ways in which the women felt that their mothering was being forced to change by the 'Australian people' and the Australian government while they desperately desired to be able to look after their children like they 'used to').

The women's narratives of these shifts, particularly in relation to marriage and mothering, in Australia also signify a shifting and changing of *cieng*. The women described a shifting in ways of life for the younger generations which, for them, were not commensurate with the ways of being which *cieng* entailed. The shift in practices and understandings of *cieng*, particularly in younger generations of *Jëëng* in Australia, requires more in-depth research to understand how and why these shifts are occurring and the outcomes for the community.

While shifts and changes in 'who is' and 'what it means to be' *Diäärjäng* had taken place through both the spatial and temporal movements of the women, the changes were haunted by the sameness of what it had meant to be and belong as *Diäärjäng* in their home regions in their youth. All of these shifts and changes meant that ways of being *Diäärjäng* were undergoing continual change, but this change was haunted by sameness.

NOTES

1 This extract clearly illustrates the intersections of 'race', gender and ethnicity. These intersections haunt much of my negotiation to become a *Tiengjäng*, but I will not explore them in depth in this chapter. The intersections of ethnicity, gender and 'race' have been well examined by many other academics (see, for example, Anthias, 1992; Brah, 1994; Brettell, 2007a, 2007b; Collins, 1998; Eriksen, 2010; Frankenberg, 1993; Hall, 2000; Spinner, 1994; Ware, 1992a, 1992b).

2 See also Anthias (1998a).

3 See also Afshar and Maynard (2000), Das Gupta (1997), Kurien (1999), Pettman (1992), Spurlock (2010), Waller (1993) and Yuval-Davis, Anthias and Kofman (2005).

4 See for example Anthias (1998a), Brah (1994, 1996), Brettell (2007a), Guibernau (2010) and Wimmer and Glick Schiller (2002).

5 A pseudonym has been used for this area to protect the identity of the woman.

6 The women's use of the word *Thong Muonyjäng* emphasises the gendered nature of being a *Jääng*. *Jëëng* commonly use the word *Muonyjäng* to refer to themselves in everyday language. *Muonyjäng* literally means the man or husband of the people. Its derivative of *Thuong Muonyjäng* (the language of the man/husband of the people) was used by all of the women to describe their language. While *Jëëng* and *Thuongjäng* are the gender-inclusive terms which have been adopted in more recent academic and scholarly fields they have not yet gained wide acceptance in everyday usage.

7 See also Abu-Lughod (1993), Anzaldúa (1999), Cuomo and Hall (1999), Kaplan (1994), Nzegwu (2003) and Trinh (1990).

8 See also Butler (1993), Chambers (1994b), Fortier (2000, 2006), Hall (1996b), Hopkins (2010), Sarup (1994), Trieu (2009) and Waller (1993).

9 See also Geschiere and Nyamnjoh (1998), Gugler (2002), Thomas (2002).

10 Pounding of sorghum into a fine flour which is used to make *kun*, the staple food of *Jëëng*.

11 The works of Edward (2007), Hutchison (2000) and several other African feminist writers (see, for example, Kolawole, 1997; Mbilinyi, 1984; Mire, 2001; Nzegwu, 2003; Sudarkasa, 1996) have also identified these domestic spheres as important sites through which women define their belongings and identifications.

12 See also de Regt (2009), Griffith (1998), Rosander (2009), Sudarkasa (1996), McLaren and Dyck (2004) and Timmermann, Lodewyckx and Wets (2009).

13 To consider why these particular roles were significant to the women more comprehensively would require a more thorough analysis than there is scope for in this book.

14 In the polygamous *Jëëng* family structure, a man typically has more than one wife (Deng, 1984).

15 In Australia welfare payments are received from the government agency 'Centrelink'.

16 See also Edward (2007) and Hutchinson (2000).

17 There are also 'spiritual' reasons for having large families which will not be considered here.

18 Some of the women's husbands stayed in Sudan to continue fighting in the SPLA, while other husbands had other wives still living in various countries in Africa whom they did not want to leave.

19 Ong (2003) found similar experiences among Cambodian 'refugees' in America.

20 'Card' could signify either an ATM card to access cash from bank accounts or a Centrelink 'card' that entitles children to receive their own welfare payments.

CHAPTER 5

NEGOTIATING BELONGINGS THROUGH 'LOCAL' PLACE IN A GLOBALISED WORLD[1]

> Madiŋ Awïl ee pan da.
> Wun Buɔth Anyaar ee baai.
> Madiŋ na bäär ye riɛl,
> Wuön da na bäär ye bäŋ,
> Ka yï kat yï cök ba wut wuör.
> Pan da na bäär yï ye mac,
> Ka yï lir thuat ba piu waan.
> Tiŋ ɣook, Malual Anyaar.
> Ɣok bäŋ, ɣok aa ce dhuk cieën.
> Madiŋ Awïl, wek ko?
> Wun Buɔth Anyaar, week ko?
> (Abuk, 2009)

> Mading Aweil is our home.
> A community who follows buffaloes is home.[2]
> If you come to Mading with power,
> If you come to our community with aggression,
> You will run with your feet faster than an ostrich.
> If you come to our home as fire,
> You will soon become as cold as water.
> See us, Malual[3] following buffaloes.
> We are brave, we do not retreat.
> People of Mading Aweil, where are you?
> People of the community who follows buffaloes, where are you?
> (Kuol translated)

It is a cold winter's afternoon in Adelaide. Members of a select group of the Sudanese community have gathered at a local school hall to celebrate the recovery of a woman who was hit by a car several years previously. It is a festive and celebratory occasion. The long series of obligatory speeches have finished. People have eaten their fill of traditional food cooked by the women. People are happy and satisfied. I sit watching a relatively small group on the dance floor, bopping away to the rhythms of an imported Dinka cassette. Children are running left, right and centre, men are chatting animatedly on the left of the hall, some women are finishing off the last of their meals and others are beginning to clean up. The song ends and the dancers begin to return to their seats when the next song begins. As the rhythm grows and the song becomes clear, every person in the hall, man, woman and child, leaps to their feet, runs to the dance floor and erupts in song. The hall is alive and abuzz with the movements of a group of people obviously touched and inspired by a song. The song they are singing is the one quoted above.

INTERLUDE V: BETWEEN EXCLUSION AND BELONGING IN THE MADING AWEIL COMMUNITY IN ADELAIDE

In the Preface to this book I described how, as a result of Kuol's and my relationship, both of our belongings within the *Jëëng* community became politicised. We went from feeling like a full member of the community in Kuol's case, and a friend of many people in my case, to outsiders who were excluded from virtually everything. Our belongings became painfully politicised through the hauntings of 'race', ethnicity, stereotypes and 'local' community politics. What I did not initially realise when all of this painful exclusion was taking place, was that really the main community we were being excluded from was the Mading Aweil community in Adelaide. Subsequently, over the past eleven years, I have begun to learn many of the intricate ways in which this glocal community operates to ensure its continuity in particular ways through the inclusion of some, the exclusion of others, and the continual negotiations of all of its members to belong.

Given that the underscoring impetus of my research was the question of why it had been so difficult for me to feel a sense of belonging within the community into which I had married, invariably this question arose in my conversations with each of the women. As the following conversation with Atong illustrates, Atong knew that Kuol's and my belonging within the Mading Aweil community had become politicised:

> Melanie: Kuol said before we were together, people informed him of everything. And then as soon as we were together, no one phoned him.
>
> Atong: Oh, why?
>
> Melanie: The phone stopped. Nobody talked to him.
>
> Atong: (laughs) Some people in Aweil community, some things, something is wrong in Aweil community.
>
> Melanie: I don't understand it.
>
> Atong: When Kuol is leader for the community,[4] community was good. Now before Kuol he don't have any car, Kuol he can ride the bicycle. He's a good person.

Melanie: Yeah, that time, we were very upset because, like before every time Kuol was on the phone, someone calling him, asking something or telling something. The day that people knew that me and Kuol were together, his phone stopped.

Atong: Why?

Melanie: About 1 year. No one called him.

Atong: Maybe he's very scary, maybe he can say Mel he can think [pauses] You, you are very good person, no anybody can scaring for you.

Melanie: Ahh, people used to say bad things about me. In the first year or something. Yeah, people said a lot of bad things.

Atong: It's a jealous. You know the Aweil people, the woman group, the Aweil people is not, you have a lot of problem.

Melanie: The politics of those women is too [pause]

Atong: The woman they have a lot of corruption. If can you see the big woman she can walk like this one, is a corruption. No anybody she like another one. She say something lie. Somebody she can tell you something, she do that and do that, if can you go to find, got nothing. No anything. Somebody doing.

Melanie: And I don't, I don't think it's all Aweil, like when I went to *Pan Muonyjäng*, no problem.

Atong: Yeah in *Pan Muonyjäng* is good. Here in Adelaide is very bad.

Melanie: I don't know Sydney or Melbourne. I don't know, but Adelaide, I have a lot of problems with them.

Atong: A lot of problems.

Gradually over the past eleven years I have grown to understand the community of Mading Aweil better, not only in Adelaide, but also in South Sudan and the communities in various locations in countries of exile (such as Kenya and Uganda). Through this I have learnt that it is not only Kuol and my belongings within the glocal Mading Aweil community which are politicised, but everyone within these various communities is engaged in a continual negotiation for belonging.

INTRODUCTION

I first became aware of the salience of the Mading Aweil community[5] in early 2005. Over the previous year I had become a friend and acquaintance to various members of what, until that time, I thought was a unified 'Sudanese' community.

By that stage I had come to know Kuol quite well, but we were not in a relationship. We were both visiting the house of the family that he had sponsored to come to Australia. He excitedly told the wife of that family that he had found some music on a website and that we should go to his house to listen to it. Kuol, the woman and I jumped in the car and drove around the corner to his unit. He logged on to the internet, opening a website which has subsequently affectionately become known in our household as 'the green page'. The website was www.madingaweil.com (2004). I started trying to find out more about Mading Aweil. I looked at the website, I joined the well-attended discussion forums, I downloaded and listened to the music, and I began asking questions of the members of the 'Sudanese' community whom I knew. Slowly I began to find out who and what the Mading Aweil community was, how it functioned in the everyday lives of community members in Sudan, exile and Australia, and the politics of belonging within this community. While the 'technoscapes' and 'mediascapes' (Appadurai, 1996) of the Mading Aweil website and the song quoted in the opening epigraph of the chapter helped to perpetuate the idea of the Mading Aweil community in exile and Australia, the founding of this community of belonging was initially established within a particular territory.

In Chapter 4, it may have appeared that *Jëëng* are a united group; however this is far from the case. *Jëëng* are the largest ethnic group in South Sudan, with a population estimated at between 1.5 and 3 million[6] people. Their dispersion over a large area in South Sudan has resulted in divisions and differences across various locations. The differences range from dialectical language differences, to differences in dowry amounts and other cultural nuances. The first official territorial division of southern Sudan came about under the colonial administrations. These divisions, which largely ignored the pre-existing territorial divisions which had occurred through the territorialisation of particular ethnic groups and sub-groups, saw the southern region of Sudan divided into three provinces: Bahr el Ghazal, Upper Nile and Equatoria (Figure 2). The subsequent postcolonial division of southern Sudan into ten states (Figure 3) is more cognisant of the distribution of the main ethnic groups and sub-groups. Each state is then further divided into counties, the counties are divided into *Payams* (chiefdomships) and these territorial divisions continue down to the level of the village.[7]

All of the women in this research have connections with what was, as of the period of data collection, referred to as Northern Bahr El Ghazal state.[8] This state covered an area of approximately 30,543 km^2 (about the size of Belgium), and according to the controversial 2008 Sudan census has a population of approximately 720,898.[9] Northern Bahr El Ghazal state is comprised of five counties: Aweil Central, Aweil North, Aweil South, Aweil East and Aweil West. The names of these counties (i.e. Aweil) indicate the name which is in common everyday usage among the women in this research for the region of Northern Bahr el Ghazal, and that is Mading Aweil (or Aweil for short). As such, I refer to this region as Mading Aweil in this book.

Nyalong, Nyanut, Achol and Abuk were all born in, and spent most of their foundational years growing up in, the Mading Aweil region. The importance of

Mading Aweil as their birthplace and a region of identification was emphasised from the very outset of the first interviews with both Nyanut and Achol, who opened their stories of life with the following sentences:

> Nyanut (Kuol translated): I was born in Sudan. In Mading Aweil.
>
> Achol (Kuol translated): I'm born in Aweil, I'm born in the city.

Atong was born in and spent most of her formative years in a neighbouring region in the state called Western Bahr El Ghazal (as of the period of data collection). Most specifically she lived in the Wau region of this state and, as such, she referred to her home region as Wau. However she married a man from the Mading Aweil region. I also married a man from the Mading Aweil region. The Mading Aweil community is therefore the one community with which all of the women and myself share a connection. In this chapter I consider the negotiations for belonging within this 'local' territorially based connection to Mading Aweil and how this connection operates on a global scale.

The chapter begins by considering the current theories surrounding the notion of 'local' place in a globalised world. Through this, I suggest that current academic writing does not adequately explain the women's experiences of 'local' place in relation to transnational migration. I consider the salience of the women's experiences of belonging to communities formed through ties to 'local' places in South Sudan and I argue that through migration these ties are deterritorialised and reterritorialised into specific types of glocal communities (Robertson, 1995). Through listening to and experiencing the 'echoes and murmurs' (Gordon, 2008, p. x) of the 'local' in various 'global' locations, I argue that the 'local' continues to haunt the negotiations and desires for belonging of the women throughout their global migrations. Secondly, I focus on a portion of Atong's narrative, which illustrates how these glocal communities became salient through the women's transnational migrations. While Atong did not describe belonging *within* the Mading Aweil community, she described how these territorially derived communities became significant as a result of migratory movements of people.

For the other women, the glocal Mading Aweil community represented a key site in which they negotiated their belongings. In the final section I consider three stories told by the Mading Aweil women in examining how their belongings were negotiated and politicised in relation to this glocal community. The first story is drawn from Achol's narrative which described how members of the Mading Aweil community in Australia denied her inclusion and acknowledgement as a Mading Aweil woman, alluding to the fact that one of her grandparents was a migrant to the Mading Aweil region. The second story considers an excerpt from Nyalong's narrative. She described how, following the death of her husband, she was ostracised by the people of the Mading Aweil community in Nairobi. She was instead forced to seek support from people outside of the Mading Aweil community. The final story considers Nyalong's experience in the Mading Aweil community in Australia following the murder of a young Mading Aweil man in Adelaide. Nyalong described an almost complete breakdown and division of the Mading Aweil community into even more micro levels of territorial belonging based on village and chiefdomship connections. Through these stories I argue that 'local' belongings continue to haunt the women's lives on a global scale, but even negotiating belongings within these 'local' sites are haunted by family histories, marriages, deaths and other 'hidden' agendas. This renders these 'local' belongings impermanent and continually negotiated processes of becoming.

ON 'LOCAL' PLACE IN A GLOBALISED WORLD

Through the women's transnational movements across the globe, their sense of belonging to communities formed through connections to the region of Mading Aweil have been shaped by intersections of the 'global' and the 'local', and through both deterritorialisation and reterritorialisation. This section explores these intersections, considering how the often overlooked 'local' continues to haunt the belongings of individuals in a globalised world.

Early theorists of globalisation argued that the rapid movements of people, capital, commodities and ideas around the globe would lead to a deterritorialisation of people and places (Beck, 1992, 2000; Giddens, 1991) rendering local identities and places obsolete. Through this imagining of globalisation it was argued that the local would be subsumed under the global (Gikandi, 2010) and through this process the heterogeneity of specific times, places, localities and identities would be incorporated into homogeneous forms (Robertson, 1995). These theorists argued that the nation-state was likely to become redundant in a world where people would conceive of themselves as increasingly transnational with the cosmopolitan, transnational and deterritorialised identities that would result from increased travel (Gilroy, 2005; Roudometof, 2005; Schnapper, 1999; Gikandi, 2010). What the previous two chapters have shown is that, in the lives of the women in this research, this is far from the case. The women's narratives are more commensurate with recent research in anthropology and cultural studies which argues that globalisation has resulted in both the deterritorialisation and reterritorialisation of various identities (see, for example, Geschiere & Nyamnjoh, 2000; Inglis, 2008, 2009; Moorti, 2003; Gupta & Ferguson, 1997a). As Gupta and Ferguson (1997a) suggest:

> [i]n the puberized space of postmodernity, space has not become irrelevant it has been *re*territorialized in a way that does not conform to the experience of space that characterized the era of high modernity. It is this reterritorialization of space that forces us to reconceptualise fundamentally the politics of community, solidarity, identity, and cultural difference. (p. 37)

In an increasingly global world where the deterritorialisation and reterritorialisation of space is central, it becomes obvious that the global cannot be conceived of outside of the local and vice versa (Lefébvre, 1991; Smith, 2001, Savage;

Bagnall, & Longhurst, 2005; Wahlbeck, 2002; Robertson, 1995; Gikandi, 2010; Ang, 2011). As Urry (2003) has argued, 'the global and the local are inextricably and irreversibly bound together through a dynamic relationship' (p. 84).

Robertson (1992, 1995) was one of the first theorists to begin to examine thoroughly the idea of the symbiotic relations between the local and the global in the social sciences. He drew on the marketing and business-based Japanese term *dochakuka* which means 'global localization' (1995, p. 28). This word was used to signify 'the tailoring and advertising of goods and services on a global or near-global basis to increasingly differentiated local and particular markets' (p. 28). Robertson's sociological usage of glocalisation highlights not only the intersection of the local and the global, but also the 'interconnected processes of homogenization and heterogenization' (Giulianotti & Robertson, 2007a, p. 134). Over the past two decades, Robertson's notion of the glocal has been built on and adapted across the social sciences from studies of Scottish football fans in America (Giulianotti & Robertson, 2004, 2006, 2007a, 2007b) and a wide range of other sporting fields (Andrews & Ritzer, 2007; Lee, Jackson, & Lee, 2007; Weedon, 2011), to the glocalisation of organised crime (Hobbs, 1998), the glocal hip hop subculture in Australia (Mitchell, 1998), and the glocalisation of fast-food chain McDonald's (Vignali, 2001). Most of these writers consider how global phenomena occur or are acted out in local places.

Several migration theorists have also considered 'local' belongings in relation to transnational movements of people, and while these theorists have not specifically labelled these as glocal belongings, they can well be interpreted in this way. As with many early writers on the glocal, most of these conceptions consider the 'local' as the smaller region or community which particular groups have migrated *to*. For example, Fortier (2000) considers the 'local' belongings of a group of Italian migrants in relation to a church community and language school in London. Savage, Bagnall and Longhurst (2005) describe the 'local' belongings of residents, including migrants, which were formed in relation to 'local' suburbs and neighbourhoods in Manchester.

Giulianotti and Robertson (2004, 2006, 2007a, 2007b) are some of the few theorists who, in recent research, consider how 'local' connections from the location of origin can be 'transplanted', 'transformed' and 'reproduced' in locations of migration. Through their research with North American-based supporters of Scottish football teams they argue that 'these migrants prefer to transplant their old cultural allegiance and identities into this new territory' (2006, p. 170). They liken their argument for the deterritorialisation of 'the local' to anthropological arguments about the deterritorialisation of 'culture', suggesting that 'the local' 'is not a geographically fixed entity, but an aspect of mobile cultural particularity' (2007a, p. 134). Raffles (2002) has also emphasised this point and related it to place by arguing that:

> while the unmooring of culture from place in anthropology has resulted in the thoroughgoing transformation of the idea of culture, notions of place have

> remained largely intact. Indeed, in the context of the current preoccupation with globalisation, the local—a standard surrogate for a conventional notion of place—has tended to be reconfirmed as the site of ethnographic particularity, in sharp distinction to the non-placed abstraction of the global.
>
> However—and this twist in the argument will come as no surprise—the idea of a placebound local is readily subject to a critique that parallels that of the culture concept. (p. 329)

This conception most closely resonates with the experiences of glocal place-based communities described by the women in this research. In this chapter I seek to explore this more complex notion of the unbounded 'local' place in a globalised world. For the women, the 'local' community of desired belonging stemmed from a 'local' territorial connection in the 'home' region which has been made 'global' through the transnational migrations of people from this 'local' region. When this 'local' place goes 'global', it challenges conceptions of the 'local' as a territorially grounded site rooted in time and space. These glocal identifications were then made salient through reterritorialisation in other 'local' locations in other parts of the world. As Giulianotti and Robertson (2007a) have argued, '[m]igration promotes the intensive "deterritorialization" of the local' (p. 134) which is then 'transplanted' (2007b, p. 173), 'relativized' (2007a, p. 134) and reterritorialised in new locations in new ways. For the women these glocal connections were enacted through their negotiations to belong to the Mading Aweil community in other 'local' locations such as refugee camps in Ethiopia, cities like Nairobi in Kenya and Adelaide in Australia. Their connections to the 'local' place of Mading Aweil became increasingly salient as they found their belongings to other more macro sites destabilised as a result of their global migrations.

While the women lived in their home regions in Sudan, the region of Mading Aweil, and other such 'local' regions in South Sudan, were territories that formed the basis of 'imagined communities' (Anderson, 1991). As a 'macro' territorial region, this level of community was not particularly important to how the women negotiated their everyday belongings in South Sudan. While living in their physical home regions, such as Mading Aweil, the women's main sites of desired belonging were within the everyday communities of their families, clan groups and villages. With their dispersion through different regions and other countries, they were no longer able to retain the same emphasis and dependency on their families, villages and clan groups for belonging as smaller numbers from these groups were dispersed. As Probyn (1996) has indicated, 'belonging cannot be an isolated and individual affair' (p. 13). With much smaller numbers and in some cases only individuals from particular families, village and clan groups present in various locations throughout the globe, people sought belongings within a community that still retained 'local' connections but allowed for the sociality that belonging to a group entails.

Producing these groups of 'local' belonging resulted from processes which saw these groups constructed through differentiations from 'other' groups. As Robertson

(1995) has observed, 'much of the conception of contemporary locality and indigeneity is itself historically contingent upon *encounters* between one civilizational region and another' (p. 38; see also Appiah, 1992; Hall, 1996b; Bauman, 2001). Through their global dispersal, people from particular localities, such as Mading Aweil, came into contact with groups of 'Others' from different regions, who spoke different languages or dialects and who held different world views.[10]

The production of place as a result of encounters with others emphasises the relationality of locality and place. As Raffles (2002) elaborates:

> places are relational. They are caught up in complex networks and articulations that tie them to capacious geographies, linking humans and non-humans across time and space. Moreover, places carry multiple meanings and are the sites of numerous overlapping, contradictory, synergistic activities, brought into being through and productive of difference and inequality. These are the sites people travel as they live their complex, mobile lives. And the people that produce and are produced by places, 'local people', are, like the places themselves, anything but local—at least, so long as we continue to think of the local in that conventional sense of narrowly parochial, self-contained, static, and restrictive. (p. 329)

Raffles stresses the sociality of place, describing how people both produce places as well as being produced by place (see also Inglis, 2009; Appadurai, 1996; Savage, Bagnall, & Longhurst, 2005). This relationality of place means that both place itself and belongings in relation to place cannot be and are not stable. The narratives of the women in this chapter explore how through this sociality and relationality the women were excluded, included and negotiated their belongings within the glocal communities of Mading Aweil, and this thereby produced not only their own belongings to place, but also the very production of the place.

'US' AND THE 'OTHER' IN THE PRODUCTION OF GLOCAL COMMUNITIES

Through the processes of deterritorialisation and reterritorialisation associated with global movement and dispersal, and the resultant transplantation, transformation and reproduction (Giulianotti & Robertson, 2006, 2007a) of glocal communities, sites such as the Mading Aweil community became salient sites of desired belonging in the women's everyday lives. This section explores the everyday processes through which glocal communities were produced. It draws on Atong's narrative to illustrate the production of these glocal communities. Atong was from the region of Wau but married a man from Mading Aweil. While her narrative did not emphasise desiring belonging within the Mading Aweil community, it illustrated how, through relationality, deterritorialisation and reterritorialisation, these glocal communities became significant sites of desired belonging.

The strong emphasis that came to be placed on belonging within communities such as Mading Aweil was not solely a result of historical and territorial differences.

Rather, the production and emphasis of these different groups resulted from two simultaneously occurring processes: the emphasis on solidarity and sameness of those from a common region, and the 'articulation of difference' (Grossberg, 1996, p. 94) from those from 'Other' regions, which was based on the 'strong sense of otherness which recognizes that the other exists' (p. 94). These articulations of differences grew from specific historical contexts, in specific times and places which necessitate contextualising (Ang, 2001; Moore, 1988). Atong's narrative illustrated these salient features in the production of glocal communities.

The regional identifications, and belongings within these territorially based communities, began to play a significant role for the women virtually as soon as they left their homes. For Atong, whose home region was in Wau, her connections to Wau first became significant when she embarked on the three-month journey walking from Wau to Ethiopia. People walked to Ethiopia in large groups; the groups were primarily started by soldiers sent to recruit for the SPLA. These recruitment processes invariably extended to include family members of the soldiers and other people who decided that they would have better opportunities for survival in Ethiopia. The groups started in particular locations, and then gathered additional members from other regions as they journeyed across southern Sudan. Atong told me that a number of other young women from Wau had left their homes and families at the same time as her to journey to Ethiopia. The following conversation ensued:

> Melanie: When you were walking, did you walk with like the girls from Wau, do you stay together?
>
> Atong: Yeah, we stay together. We stay together with a girl and our boys from Wau. He's take care for us.
>
> Melanie: So any person from Wau?
>
> Atong: Yeah any person from Wau she was a leader for us. She see us like their sister.
>
> Melanie: So it doesn't matter who your father is or your *Pacher* [clan] or anything? Just anybody from Wau can help?
>
> Atong: Yeah. No we go with a group, like Wau people, we go. If can we meet another people, we can stay together. Then we walk together, we stay to another place, in the same place.

Atong described how, over the course of the journey, people from Wau joined together to support and take care of each other regardless of their village, clan or family of origin. She emphasised the solidarity among people from Wau through her use of terms such as 'our boys' and 'see us like their sister'. Through this process their belongings as people from Wau became significant and were emphasised through their solidarity as people with the same 'local' region of 'origin'.

However, these 'local' regionally based formations of belonging resulted from the contact that groups of people who shared the similarity of being from Wau had with groups of 'Others' from regions such as Mading Aweil. Groups were produced and emphasised through processes of othering those people who were from groups that were perceived as different. A subsequent section of Atong's narrative shows how these 'local' communities were emphasised through perceived difference. While in Ethiopia, Atong met a man and they mutually decided they wanted to marry. The man was from Mading Aweil. In the following excerpts from Atong's narrative, she reflected on the perceptions of her relatives from Wau about her marriage to a man from Mading Aweil:

> Atong: Before when we want to make marriage, my brother,[11] I was staying with my brother at home [in Ethiopia]. My brother he don't like this husband because in my country, in Mading Aweil and Wau. My brother is very scared. He say these people sometimes it can, it's not good. How do you know this person is good?
>
> Melanie: So what did they think is not good about people from Aweil?
>
> Atong: Because he's Mading Aweil, I'm Wau. Now my brother he need me to marriage to Wau.
>
> Melanie: Is there something about people from Aweil, or just because it's someone is not Wau.
>
> Atong: Because if can you far away, like when we in Sudan, we don't know Aweil because Aweil is very far from us. Now if can your child is going to Aweil, maybe you can give problem like you don't have any relative there. A lot of people in my country is very scary to go to Aweil. Because we don't know Aweil how to doing the thing ... You know in our country,[12] I can take you like my country Wau, and Aweil. You have difference. Aweil he can say I want to, maybe he can say I can marry some girl for 100 cow, now it's not exactly 100 cow. Maybe it's 100 cow is 50 cows. Now in my country, if can you say you marry the girl 100 cow, its 100 cow. Now Aweil, he have something. You can ask Kuol, he know.
>
> Melanie: So do you think your parents, would they have been sad that you married someone from Aweil? Would they have been more happy if you married someone from Wau?
>
> Atong's daughter: Yes.
>
> Atong: Yeah it's not bad. Last time, before the war is not starting, Wau he don't like Aweil people. If can you go to Aweil, you can say this girl, she don't have any heart. [Three of Atong's children are in the room, they are all listening and laugh.]

Atong's stepson: *A cïn puöu.* [literally 'have no heart', meaning is not a good person]

Atong: No before he don't like. The Wau people and Aweil people he was very far, he don't know. Now Aweil, we don't know. We don't know Aweil, he don't go to the Wau, he don't know us.

Melanie: So it's a little bit like strangers.

Atong's narrative illustrates the fear of the Other, the unknown stranger, that permeates discourses of otherness and difference (see, for example, Hage, 2009; Bauman, 1991; Balibar, 2005; Derrida, 1976; Yuval-Davis, 1993). Sarup (1994) argues that the foreigner and the stranger are identified as:

> [t]he one who does not belong to the group, who is not 'one of them', the other. The foreigner can be defined only in negative fashion. The foreigner is the Other … An otherwise innocuous trait of the stranger becomes a sign of affliction, a cause of shame. The person bearing this trait is easily recognizable as less desirable, inferior, bad and dangerous. There is cultural exclusion of the stranger. S/he is constructed as a permanent Other. (pp. 99–102)

Atong's husband, and all those from Mading Aweil, were constructed in Atong's reflection of her 'brother's' thoughts as unknown Others. Atong emphasised people from Wau 'not knowing' people from Aweil, and the intersections of this 'not knowing' with fear, in her sentence: 'A lot of people in my country is very scary to go to Aweil. Because we don't know Aweil how to doing the thing.' Atong stressed that Wau and Mading Aweil were very far apart, and as a result of this distance people from the two regions were unlikely to know each other, interact or intermarry.

Atong acknowledged the reservations of her 'brother', and her daughter suggested that Atong's parents would not have been happy about her marrying a man from Mading Aweil. Atong described that before the war any girl from Wau who had decided to marry a man from Mading Aweil would have been defined as 'having no heart' (i.e. being a bad person). But in signifying the time frame of 'before the war', Atong seemed to be arguing that during and after the war this was not the case. Perhaps marriage between and across regions became more acceptable. But Atong had to be able to see beyond the fear of the other, the stranger, the unknown, in order to rationalise and justify her own decision to marry a man from Mading Aweil. She argued that there was similarity between herself and her husband:

Melanie: And what about, when you decided that you loved your husband and you wanted to marry him, did you have some thought like 'Oh, he's a man from Aweil, I don't know maybe he's different?' or?

Atong: [laughs] Last when we go to SPLA, we don't have, we don't care about somebody is different person or different person. Because we see other, he's a family. If can you see from Aweil, Aweil and Wau and Gogrial, it's one place like Bahr El Ghazal. It's called Bahr El Ghazal. You feel you're marriage to your place. We very scary if can you say you want to go to Bor, you see Bor is very far of us. We don't like, like Bor, like Equatoria. Yeah you don't want to go there. Now if can you married from Gogrial from Aweil and Wau, this one is the same area.

Melanie: So although your family thought it was a bit different, like Wau to Aweil, to you because it's Bahr El Ghazal, it's a bit the same.

Atong: Yeah, I thought in my head like that one. My family she said 'Aweil is very far'.

Atong argued that when she joined the SPLA they were encouraged not to see divisions based on regional and ethnic differences between populations in South Sudan. This, however, was not entirely possible as is seen in the remainder of her narrative. Atong went on to suggest that she saw herself and her husband as being from 'one place', the larger region of Bahr El Ghazal which encompassed both Wau and Mading Aweil. She felt that within this larger region of Bahr El Ghazal people knew each other sufficiently to feel like a family, so she felt as if she had married 'to her place'. For Atong, the unknown stranger was found in further places such as Bor (in south-eastern Sudan) or Equatoria (in far southern Sudan). She argued that it would have been different if she had wanted to marry someone from a 'very far' place like Bor. In falling in love and marrying across a perceived border between her own community and that of the Other, Atong had begun to recognise 'the inescapable impurity of all cultures and the porousness of all cultural boundaries [at least within Bahr El Ghazal] in an irrevocably globalized, interconnected and interdependent world' and through this, she was 'able to conceive of our living together in terms of complicated entanglement, not in terms of the apartheid of insurmountable differences' (Ang, 2001, p. 194).

However, as quickly as she denounced the differences between Mading Aweil and Wau, choosing to focus on the similarities of being from Bahr El Ghazal, Atong reverted to emphasising the difference between the two in order to explain subsequent challenges in her marriage. As Schipper (1999) has acknowledged, 'the boundaries between own and foreign are mobile and constantly redefined and manipulated; new situations followed by new interpretations make people modify earlier assumptions' (p. 2). Soon after her marriage to her husband, Atong encountered difficulties in her marriage. Her husband quickly married a second wife and he subsequently continued to marry many more wives over the years. Atong blamed her husband's multiple marriages, and the resultant neglect that she felt had occurred of her and her children, on her husband being from Mading Aweil:

Atong: It's very scary, like me now, how many wife she's going behind me? Like now, the husband is very busy, even he don't think about me. Now if can I married in my country, you don't forget your older wife. You don't forget your older children. We have a difference between Aweil and Wau, because we, if can in Wau you can marry ten wife, you don't forget your older wife. Now the second wife you can know your state. Don't go to another state ...

Melanie: How many wives does he have now?

Atong: Uhuh. It's a lot. A lot. When I go to Sudan, I saw a lot. I went to Malakal, I got something like 3 wife, after I left Malakal, I go to Khartoum, I got something like 4.

Melanie: Ohh. OK.

Atong: When I left Khartoum I came to Aweil, hey, a lot, a lot. I got something in Nyamlel, in Nyamlel, have 2 wife, in Malualkon he have 2 wife, in Aweil, in Aweil city, have 3 wife.

Melanie: OK.

Atong: The same Uganda, he have 3 wife in Uganda. A lot.

Melanie: OK.

Atong: A lot.

Melanie: And do you, because you were the first wife, do you have like a special treatment or something?

Atong: In our country now I'm, you know, we have a different culture. Between Wau and Aweil. In my country, if can you, your husband have a little wife, she come behind, you can get respect. Because the wife coming, you get the big wife in her house, you can get respect. Respect more.

Melanie: Aweil is not the same?

Atong: No. In Aweil, it's not the same. It's not. Before, maybe. Before my mother-in-law, maybe it's good. Now, I don't think. Everything, maybe it's another place is good. When I see in my husband house, it's not good. Not anybody care about anybody ... In my family, he don't do that. In my culture.

Melanie: In Wau?

Atong: In Wau, no anybody needs second wife.

Melanie: OK. Your father was just having only your mother?

Atong: Yeah. My father is just my mother. Then the second wife she come for his brother, he died, he was bigger. A big man. Then he married for his brother.[13]

Arguably, polygamy is prevalent in every group and region of *Jëëng.* Some men choose or are economically only able to have one or a few wives while others chose to display their wealth and 'dignity' through marrying as many wives as possible (Deng, 1984; Biong Deng, 2010). However, for Atong, rather than seeing her husband's choice to have multiple wives as a negative reflection on her husband, she explained his and her own predicament as being a result of the difference in 'cultures' between her home region of Wau and her husband's region of Mading Aweil. She also suggested that in Wau the first wife is respected for her status as the senior wife. However, in Atong's experience she did not feel that she was respected as the first wife. Again she blamed this difference on her husband being from Mading Aweil. Ultimately, it was clear in Atong's narrative how the 'logic of difference, in which the other is defined by its negativity, can only give rise to a politics of resentment' (Grossberg, 1996, p. 97).[14] Atong directed this resentment not only at her husband, but at all those from Mading Aweil.

Atong's narrative illustrated one example of how the journeys of diverse groups of people have intersected on a global scale, and the subsequent interactions have resulted in an emphasis on sameness and difference in the construction of glocal communities. She narrated how, through her marriage to a man from the Mading Aweil community, a marriage that would have been very unlikely to occur had both parties not left their home regions in South Sudan and journeyed to Ethiopia, the conceived otherness and difference between the Wau and Mading Aweil communities were enforced, challenged and ultimately reaffirmed.

CONTESTING AND NEGOTIATING BELONGING IN THE GLOCAL MADING AWEIL COMMUNITY

> The idea of belonging to a 'community' … is never simply the recognition of cultural similarity or social contiguity. It is instead a categorical identity that is characterized by various forms of exclusion and constructions of otherness. (Ilcan, 2002, p. 2)

While Atong's narrative illustrated how sites such as the Mading Aweil and Wau communities were produced as important sites of belonging for the women, the women's belongings within these sites were no less contested or complex than within any of the other sites such as the nation-state and being *Diäärjäng*. Their belongings within these glocal communities continued to be negotiated throughout their various locations in exile and Australia. In each new 'local' site that people migrated to, the glocal Mading Aweil was reterritorialised in particular ways. As Probyn (1990) has argued, '[t]he local is only a fragmented set of possibilities that can be articulated into a momentary politics of time and place' (p. 187). The narratives in the previous sections of this chapter explored some of the momentary particularities of these reterritorialisations in new 'local' sites. The following three narratives explore the politics of belonging specifically within the reterritorialised glocal Mading Aweil communities. The women's narratives illustrate that, once again, their journeys towards desired belongings, even within the more micro community of the glocal Mading Aweil community, were shaped and shifted in such a way that they were continually negotiating their belonging through a process of becoming.

Achol on Glocal Mading Aweil Belonging in Adelaide

One of Achol's grandparents was a migrant to the Mading Aweil area. While this grandparent was not a *Jääng* and was not 'native' to Mading Aweil, they married someone from Mading Aweil, learnt *Thuongjäng* and spent the remainder of their lives living in the region. In addition, this grandparent played a role in establishing one of the main towns in the Mading Aweil region. Subsequently, both of Achol's parents were born in and spent their whole lives living in Mading Aweil, and identified themselves as *Jääng* from Mading Aweil. Achol, in turn, was born in Mading Aweil, identified herself as a *Jääng* girl from Mading Aweil and subsequently married a man from Mading Aweil. Achol believed that she belonged in the glocal Mading Aweil community. However, this was thrown into question one day at a meeting of the Mading Aweil community in Adelaide. There was a 'white' Australian priest, John, present at this meeting who was searching for a volunteer from the Mading Aweil community in Adelaide to accompany him on a trip he was planning to South Sudan. John had suggested that Achol could accompany him. Achol reflected, in an interview, on the discussion that took place during the community meeting following that suggestion:

> It's now other people here, other people in Aweil he tell me, he don't know me in Aweil … It's John tell me 'Go to the Aweil with me'. You buy anything in hospital, go to show people in hospital. I tell him it's ok. I want to go volunteer, I don't have, he didn't give me money, I want to go. It's other people he tell me he didn't know me, Achol where he is going to Aweil. I'm hear that, you coming meeting, I tell him, I tell him now, other people you show me, are you from, you take me from, I want you, you take me my country now. Show me my country now. Not Aweil my country, show me now, now, now show me. It's people is quiet … He tell me, you tell me, show me my country. Is my country, I know my country Aweil. Is my father is born in Aweil. Is my grandmother is marriage in Aweil. Is born in Aweil. Is my mother is born in Aweil. Is my grandparent is coming … I tell him, before my grandparent coming, you come my grandparent. He didn't know (laughs). You don't know *awan milo* [salt], you don't know *chai* [tea]. It's my grandparent is coming, people is give you chai, you drink chai? Is other people quiet. 'Achol, don't talking like that one'. I tell him, this I talk. (laughs) I tell other people, she show me my country, no … It's people from Adelaide, not good people … This one is my country. Not now, I don't have anything. The people in Adelaide, the bad people. Is woman and man, big problem. John is tell me 'Achol coming crazy today'.

> It's this one people talking, Achol she didn't know Aweil. She didn't born in Aweil (laughs).

Achol described how, in spite of her own knowledge that she belonged as a woman of Mading Aweil, other members of the Mading Aweil community in Adelaide managed to question and politicise her sense of belonging. This is in strong contrast to Savage et al.'s (2005) frequently cited text on 'local belonging' which suggests the 'need to fundamentally break from any lingering conceptions of local social relations as defined by the activities, values and cultures of those "born and bred" in an area' (p. 29). They go on to emphasise the idea of 'elective belonging' through which 'individuals attach their own biography to their "chosen" residential location' (p. 29). While Savage et al. emphasise the agency of the individual in choosing where to belong, Achol's narrative showed the opposite, her agency in defining who she was, where home was and where she belonged was undermined by other individuals within the wider Mading Aweil community (Grossberg, 1996). Achol's narrative clearly illustrated the haunting which Gordon (2008) argues is 'a process that links an institution and an individual, a social structure and a subject, and history and a biography' (p. 19).

Through suggesting that they 'didn't know her in Aweil' (i.e. they did not recognise her as a person from Mading Aweil), these other people were trying to undermine Achol's chances of being selected to travel to South Sudan with John (an opportunity that many of the community members were vying for as it entailed a fully paid trip to South Sudan where they would have been able to see family members whom they had not seen for many years). However, in doing this they also undermined Achol's very sense of belonging within the Mading Aweil community. Achol's animated response to those who suggested that she was not an Aweil person illustrated the emotive nature of this connection and desire to belong within this community. Achol had no other territorially based community of belonging and as such she responded with the comment 'you take me my country now. Show me my country now. Not Aweil my country, show me now, now, now show me'. She knew that she had no other 'local' community to which she belonged, so by challenging the other Mading Aweil community members to show her 'her country' if it was not Aweil, she silenced them.

Achol went on to emphasise her connections to Mading Aweil through listing all of her relatives who were born there. She also stressed the time period over which her family had lived in Aweil, suggesting that before her grandparent came there was no salt or tea in Mading Aweil. Achol felt the need to justify her relational connection to Mading Aweil, which was called into question through the haunting of the migration of one grandparent to the region. Other community members, shocked by Achol's outburst, told her not to talk like that, and John later accused her of 'coming crazy'. The emotivity of having her sense of belonging within the Mading Aweil community challenged provoked an extreme and unusual outburst from the usually quiet, friendly and composed Achol.

Nyalong on Glocal Mading Aweil Belonging in Nairobi

Nyalong lived in Nairobi, Kenya at the time of her husband's death. At this time there was a reasonably large glocal Mading Aweil community living in Nairobi. There were also people from the even smaller village region of her husband living in Nairobi at that time. The expectation through the relational ethic of *cieng* was that those closest to both Nyalong and her husband would offer support during difficult times such as that following her husband's death. Nyalong's experience, however, illustrated that support from these communities and people could not be assumed, and as a result of this Nyalong questioned her belongings within the glocal Mading Aweil community in Nairobi:

> Nyalong: Yeah, so Deng Nyanut is my uncle and he's from Wau, you know. But one tribe with my mum.[15] *Paduil.* So I call like yeah my uncle. He's my uncle and he love me. So he just told me, this is my sister daughter, so he just push me like, so I love him, I love him. He's a good man. Then when I came to Nairobi they just helped me better than my people. They helped me better than Aweil people. When my husband died, yeah, these people helped me.
>
> Melanie: The other Sudanese.
>
> Nyalong: The other Sudanese, yeah, they helped me. They helped me too much. So when my husband died, Aweil people run away from me, so these people helped me.
>
> Melanie: Were there many Aweil people in Nairobi by then?
>
> Nyalong: Yeah. There's Akoldit, Ajith Garang, from Maperaguër you know. There's people there.
>
> Melanie: From your husband's area.
>
> Nyalong: Yeah. And when my husband died, forgot everything. That's why I'm not happy with my people, Mel. Even, I was thinking yesterday night, yeah. I was telling my kids, nobody, if you don't want to do your pen and what your life, nobody, because the time I struggled. Salva Kiir,[16] he helped me when I see him. This one like Ajiing Mabok, do you know people from Rumbek from where, help me a lot than my people.
>
> Melanie: Why?
>
> Nyalong: Because they don't want me to be in Nairobi, they want me to go to *Pan Muonyjäng* with kids … And I said no. That is the problem, they don't want me to be there.
>
> Melanie: Why? What did they think is the problem in Nairobi?
>
> Nyalong: Because nobody is going to take care of me and they don't want to take care of me. They don't want to even take care of my kids.

Nyalong felt that 'her people', the people of the glocal Mading Aweil community in Nairobi, forgot the connections and relational responsibility required of them through *cieng* following her husband's death. Instead, she suggested that 'her people' ran away from her. She postulated that this was because people from Mading Aweil knew that they were obliged (through *cieng*) to support her and her children, and because they either did not want to or were not in a position to support them, they 'ran away'. In a subsequent section of her narrative, she recalled that the people from Mading Aweil wanted her and her children to return to her father (who was elderly, unemployed and had many wives of his own to support) in *Pan Muonyjäng*. She refused to do this as her children were at school in Nairobi, and if they returned to *Pan Muonyjäng* they would have returned to a war-torn region in which education was not available and they would have been reliant on Nyalong's aging father for survival. When she refused to return to *Pan Muonyjäng*, the people from Mading Aweil acknowledged that, through *cieng*, the burden of supporting the family would then fall on them, so they instead 'ran away' from Nyalong and her family. Nyalong then described how she was forced to seek assistance from people from other glocal regions (i.e. Salva Kiir who was from Gogrial and Ajiing Mabok who was from Rumbek).

Through the fear of the economic and financial burdens that supporting Nyalong and her children would entail, the people of the glocal Mading Aweil community in Nairobi also denied Nyalong the social and emotional support that she needed and expected in her time of grief. They left Nyalong feeling shunned by 'her own' people, desperate for the sense of comfort and solidarity that belonging within these glocal groups was assumed to entail. Nyalong was instead forced to seek support from 'other Sudanese', calling into question her sense of belonging as a member of the glocal Mading Aweil community.

Nyalong on Glocal Mading Aweil Belonging in Adelaide

Nyalong's frustrations with the glocal Mading Aweil community did not end in Nairobi. During the course of the research, Ngong Akol, a young man originally from Mading Aweil, was murdered in Adelaide. While Ngong's murder brought to the surface a multitude of issues relating to how members of the Mading Aweil community in Adelaide negotiated their belongings (Baak, 2011b, 2011c), for Nyalong, it once again served to illustrate the challenges of belonging in this glocal community. Following Ngong's murder, the members of the community most closely related to Ngong sought financial contributions to pay for the *karama*[17] and Ngong's burial. Initially the community had planned to fly Ngong's body back to Sudan to be buried, but when this became impossible money was collected instead to bring Ngong's mother from Sudan to Australia for his burial. Traditionally for *Jëëng* when someone is in need financially, those who are most closely related to the person either through kinship, regional ties or friendship are obliged to contribute anything they can (Deng, 1984). This obligation is underset by *cieng*. For a person to be able to assist someone when they are in financial need, such as at the time of Ngong's death, engenders a sense of dignity, pride and fulfilment of *cieng*; it demonstrates the significance of the relationship that the giver feels that they have with the receiver (Riak Akuei, 2005; Biong Deng, 2010). For someone's contribution to be refused calls into question the very notion of *cieng* and the relationship between the giver and the receiver.

Nyalong and Ngong were both from the glocal Mading Aweil community, Nyalong, however was not from the smaller *Panyang*[18] section (a chiefdomship) within the Mading Aweil community of which Ngong was a member. Nyalong reflected to me in an interview soon after Ngong's death how the collection of money became a site for division and contested belonging, as some people were considered not sufficiently closely related to Ngong to contribute.

> Nyalong: And even now they talking ... I said when I left Aweil, I just left Aweil one. This new politics, no. And it's true, I don't like. It's true, I don't like. You know because it separate people. Yeah like now, when we do something, *Panyang* say *Panyang*, you know. So you don't have voice to say something cause it's *Panyang*. You know, but when they say Aweil, all of us. Yeah all of us, we have.
>
> Even before, someone said, Ngong is from *Panyang*, so they need *Panyang* to just collect one hundred, one hundred, and I was angry! So I told them, this your politics, I don't like, because Ngong. So I said yes Ngong is from *Panyang*, but he didn't die in *Panyang*. He died here, so here all of us, even if you are north Sudan, we are all Sudanese, and he's a young man, you know, he's a young boy. So I don't want that your politics. You know, I was very angry, I said no, I know Ngong when he was young, so when I have my money I just, only that. And I know he's like my son. Finish. Because of this one, I don't know, I don't know this our people learn from where? OK, when you say, OK, leave *Panyang* to do that one, they cannot. It's not good.

In the first paragraph of this narrative excerpt, Nyalong argued that when she left Aweil it was 'just one'; it was not divided into sub-groups. Nyalong's experience when living in Mading Aweil was haunted by the fact that she grew up in Aweil town where people defined their belongings less by their identification with chiefdomships and more as people from 'the town'. Although they retained connections with the 'home' villages of their families (as illustrated in the previous chapter), Nyalong emphasised that the Aweil town in which she grew up was a 'multicultural' site, where there were increased interactions between people from various groups (clans, villages, regions and families). As a result of these interactions, people tended to define their similarities and solidarity as being 'town' people. This was in contrast to those who grew up in rural areas who tended to emphasise their belongings to chiefdomships, clans, villages and family networks more strongly. Nyalong therefore expressed her frustrations at the divisions of the glocal Mading Aweil community in

Adelaide into smaller groups, such as those based on chiefdomships like *Panyang*. She questioned why, when she did not experience these divisions in Aweil, had they started to become salient in Adelaide, asking 'I don't know this our people learn from where?'

Panyang is one of the few sub-communities of Mading Aweil that has sufficient numbers in Adelaide to form a smaller group. Other chiefdomships, such as Kuol's region of *Athokthou*, have much smaller numbers (there are only about six people from *Athokthou* living in Adelaide). Nyalong is also from one of the chiefdomships with smaller numbers. As such, when those from *Panyang* grouped together and emphasised their belongings as '*Panyang*' people, Nyalong was frustrated by this 'new politics' which undeniably unsettled her sense of belonging within the larger Mading Aweil community.

In the second paragraph of the narrative excerpt above, Nyalong emphasised how this 'new politics' was highlighted following Ngong's murder. She was initially excluded by members of the *Panyang* sub-community from contributing money for the *karama* and Ngong's burial. This attempt by members of the *Panyang* community to exclude others stemmed from the extreme vulnerability they were feeling at the violent death of 'their man'.[19] In trying to strengthen their own bonds and sense of belonging (Sarup, 1994), they tightened their networks so tightly that they excluded others from the broader Mading Aweil community from contributing financially to the collection for Ngong's *karama* and burial. This exclusion, however, called into question *cieng* and the essence of Nyalong's relationship with Ngong, suggesting that her relationship with him was not close enough to warrant her financial contribution. Questioning the closeness of Nyalong's relationship with Ngong destabilised her sense of belonging, forcing her to negotiate her belongings on another level. Nyalong argued that she had known Ngong since he was a young boy and that he was like her son, and she used this to define her relational tie with Ngong and to justify her financial contribution. However, questioning the contributions of those from Mading Aweil who were not from *Panyang* served to destabilise Nyalong's sense of belonging within the Mading Aweil community at that time. She felt that, rather than extending their networks to include all of those who had been affected by Ngong's tragic death, those from *Panyang* exercised a politics of exclusion which ultimately destabilised everyone's belongings.

CONCLUSION: HAUNTED GLOCAL BELONGINGS

Conceptualisations of the glocal have tended to focus on the local place in which people currently live and how global phenomena (think McDonalds) are transplanted, relativised and reterritorialised (Giulianotti & Robertson, 2007a, 2007b) in these specific local places in particular ways. The women's narratives have provided a different way of understanding the glocal, as a phenomenon which is deterritorialised, transported and then reterritorialised from one local place through a global movement to another local place. The original local place, in the women's narratives, in fact became increasingly salient as a result of the global movements of a large group of people to new local places. Considering the glocal in this way forces a consideration of how connections with previous places of residence continue to haunt the subsequent locales in which people resettle, no matter how far or different they may appear to be. Through their global migrations, the women and other southern Sudanese have taken their place-based local belongings with them, uprooted and deterritorialised them from one location, transformed and relativised them and reterritorialised them in new places in new ways.

Atong's narrative illustrates the practical and emotional ways through which these glocal communities became increasingly important sites in which belongings were negotiated. Through increased interactions with groups of Others as a result of migratory journeys, the sameness of being from one local region was emphasised as a grounds for similarity and shared belonging. The regions that the women were born in continued to haunt their negotiations for belonging in regions of exile and in Australia. Ghostly matters of place continue to haunt in spite of and perhaps even because of the movement of people. As Wylie (2007) has suggested:

> What is a place? Perhaps haunting is a pre-requisite to place. That is, a place takes place through a spectral event of displacing. There is place if there is *dislocation*, or sudden uncertainty regarding location in space and time, uncertainty regarding even the reliability of these measurants; in other words if there is a disturbing irruption of doubt or memory, a confounding of past, present and presence all witnessed by a troubled, stricken figure, a figure haunted by this very process. (pp. 180–181)

Certainly haunting is a prerequisite to the ways in which local place-based connections form the basis for glocal communities of desired belonging. Without the dislocation of 'troubled, stricken figures' who are forced into uncertainties of their location in space and time through displacement from their homes and the challenge of surviving without the social support usually found among kin and family, I doubt that these glocal communities would provide such crucial sites for desired belonging.

The women's narratives, however, illustrate that belongings within these glocal communities were not without their politics. Glocal belongings were politicised through the hauntings of family histories and jealousy, *cieng* and a fear of obligation, and the intense desire for stable belongings. While it has been suggested that *cieng* and *ubuntu* can provide a sense of belonging (Segrest, 2002; Tutu, 1999), it has been clearly illustrated in this chapter that, while this may be the ideal and the expectation, it does not always take place in the realities and practice of everyday living. Rather when there is the expectation that certain things should take place through the relational ethic of *cieng*, such as the assistance of a relation who becomes a widow, or the contribution of money for a *karama*, and these are denied or rejected, it requires an even deeper questioning of belonging and the relationality that had been assumed.

This chapter has highlighted the intense desire—that longed-for sense of being together—that underscores the longing in be-longing. As Ilcan (2002) has argued:

> For those at the crossroads of displacement, for those who leave or who are forced to leave one home for another, and for those for whom belonging has been superseded by longing, there are risks involved. There are always risks associated with the journey of longing to belong, of a road that leads toward places less appealing than others and ends with the memories and losses incurred by the places left behind and all the paths forgone. (p. 1)

The women's narratives of their desires for belonging within the Mading Aweil community, or other place-based communities such as Wau, encapsulated the multiple and complex ways in which these longings and desires to belong are enacted and negotiated. They described desires to belong to places that are seemingly left behind, but also globally transported and reterritorialised in particular glocal formations.

The politicisation of belonging in the glocal Mading Aweil community ultimately illustrated the impermanence of belonging, even within this more intimate level of community. The women's narratives highlighted that, even when belongings were assumed and taken for granted, they could be undone in a split second through the actions and words of others. This politics and resultant impermanence meant that the women's belongings at the level of the glocal communities were once again mobile, continually negotiated processes of becoming. Their journeys of becoming—moving towards their desired belongings within the ever-shifting site of the glocal community—were haunted by 'ghostly matters' and spectres of the past that varied from woman to woman and across time and space.

Through this impermanence of place, localities and belongings in relation to glocal places, the women's narratives illustrated how, through global migrations, the local was far from homogenised into a universal global form (Robertson, 1995). Their narratives emphasised that, regardless of their migrations, the local had remained particular, in some cases increasingly so. The ways in which these belongings were negotiated had shifted and changed, with belongings to localities being made more and less possible by certain circumstances in different places. This meant that the women, once again, were forced continually to negotiate the ways in which they were becoming in relation to their desired belongings at this local level.

NOTES

1 This chapter draws on some ideas I have explored in two journal articles (Baak, 2011b, 2011c).

2 It is said in the oral stories of people from the Mading Aweil region that they came to live in that region as a result of their ancestors following herds of buffalo. They believed that by following the buffalo they would find the best grazing ground for their cattle.

3 A sub-group of *Jëëng*.

4 Kuol was the Chairman of the Mading Aweil community in Adelaide before we were in a relationship.

5 I use the term community in this chapter acknowledging the slipperiness and contestation of the term, but also acknowledging that its usage persists because of its ability to evoke a 'thick assortment of

meanings, presumptions and images' that 'ensure that the invocation of "community" is likely to have far more emotional resonance than a more utilitarian term like "group"' (Amit, 2002, p. 13).

6 The reason for the significant disparity between the 1.5 million and 3 million population estimates is that arguably there has never been a successful census or population count in South Sudan. While the Sudan census of 2008 was the first to be all inclusive of southern Sudan since Sudan's independence in 1956, it was controversial and contested (Santschi, 2008) and government leaders in the south suggested that it was inaccurate, flawed and 'unacceptable' (Birungi, 2009; Fick, 2009).

7 An examination of all of these divisions and how they have come about would require much more detail than is possible in this book.

8 In December 2010, President Salva Kiir dissolved the previous 10 states and established 28 new states in South Sudan (Mayom, 2015).

9 This figure was rejected by Northern Bahr El Ghazal state officials who argued that the results of the census were inaccurate and possibly rigged. These officials cited the example that it was impossible that populations in the other states of Sudan had increased since the previous population estimate in 1993 (some by over 90 per cent), while the population of Northern Bahr el Ghazal state had apparently decreased by 3.4 per cent (Mayom, 2009).

10 The processes of 'othering' have been explored extensively in many different fields (see, for example, Ahmed, 2000; Alinia, 2004; Balibar, 2005; Bhabha, 1990; Brah, 1994; Derrida, 1984; Fabian, 1983; Hage, 2009; Trinh, 1994).

11 Atong refers to her cousin as her brother. She had no immediate family members with her in Ethiopia.

12 Most of the women referred to their 'local' regions as 'countries', perhaps because many of the territories that they identified with were not historically recognised as particular regions. Only recently have they come to be referred to as states, counties and *payams*. As such, country is the best English approximation to identify the type of region they were describing.

13 The marriage process Atong described is referred to as 'ghost marriage'. It is a process 'whereby relatives of a dead man marry a wife for his spirit and select one amongst themselves to cohabit with her and beget children to the name of the dead relative' (Deng, 1984, p. 186).

14 McCarthy and Dimitriadis (2000) draw on the work of Nietzsche (1967) to argue that resentment is 'the specific practice of identity displacement, in which the social actor consolidates his identity by a complete disavowal of the merits and existence of his social other. Here, one becomes "good" by constructing the "other" as evil … Indeed, while all processes of identity construction are relational, processes of resentment are explicitly nihilistic and reactive' (pp. 173–174).

15 I.e. he was from a different territorial region, but the same clan group.

16 The current President of South Sudan. He was a high-ranking official in the SPLA at the time he supported Nyalong.

17 *Karama* is an Arabic word which literally means 'dignity'. It is used to describe the gathering which takes place following a person's death to reflect on and remember their life.

18 A pseudonym has been used for this smaller region.

19 In the *Jëëng* context, the connections of men to places and kin are defined by referring to them as the son/man of that place. For example, Ngong was referred to as *raan Paduil Panyang* (man of the *Paduil* people of *Panyang* region).

CHAPTER 6

KOOC[1] *PAN DA*

Negotiating Belonging with 'The People of Our Place'

> The last born, my sister the last born, and my brother. I didn't see anyone now. How they look, how they talk, how they what … My sister the last born, now she have five kids. And even one, I talk with them, her daughter … Oh. I cry, cry, cry. Aunty please send me a money to go to school. You know I feel bad … And I left the stepsister, stepbrother. Oh. And even my mum, my stepmum, the big one. She's sick and she called me, oh God. She need me to give money to go and buy, she's sick with sugar and high blood pressure. Oh. It's the first one, first wife … And I didn't even help her, so [claps hands together indicating she has nothing]. You know I feel … Because when she die or something like that you feel like … not good. Because she's good, I love her. She's good to us. So I love to go and see them. (Nyalong)

INTERLUDE VI: BELONGING AND THE FAMILY OF BIRTH

While on a gradual recovery from anorexia, I felt more bereft than ever in the world. Like hooks (2009), I 'yearned to find my place in this world, to have a sense of homecoming, a sense of being wedded to a place' (p. 2). I repeatedly questioned where I feel a sense of belonging. I do within my immediate family, and the house which I have called home for thirty years. But can home exist only within the insular location of the family unit? Can we ignore the nation and seek home at a level of kinship? Is this my reaction to the consequences of growing up in the 'late modern age', an era in which 'the protective framework of the small community and of tradition' are replaced by 'many larger, impersonal organizations' (Giddens, 1991, p. 33). The individual is left to feel 'bereft and alone in a world in which she or he lacks the psychological support and the sense of security provided by more traditional settings' (Giddens, 1991, p. 33). Has this feeling of bereavement and aloneness turned me against the larger, impersonal organisations in a return to the small community and tradition of the immediate family? Perhaps the macro organisation of the nation-state has left me so lost, lonely and confused that I cannot feel a sense of belonging to it.

In an inadvertent attempt to see if there was somewhere or something to which I could belong, to seek or 'recreate a lost sense of security' (Kinnvall, 2004, p. 744), to find an identity, I travelled. Trinh (1990) suggests that '[t]he search for an identity is … usually a search for that lost, pure, true, real, genuine, original, authentic self, often situated within a process of elimination of all that is considered other, superfluous, fake, corrupted or Westernized' (p. 371). On a perhaps misguided adventure I went to search for my lost past, hoping to find my authentic self.

I went to live and work in England for a year, the homeland of my maternal kin. While I did not feel completely out of place, I could speak the language and looked like the 'natives', I certainly did not feel at home. Likewise, when I travelled to Poland (the homeland of some of my paternal kin), I felt no sense of belonging or connection to place. I felt like a stranger, a tourist, in a place where I did not know the language, the culture or the people. I did not meet any of my relatives there, as we were not able to trace or contact anyone, and it is hard to feel a sense of belonging without a group to belong to, whether family or community (Mouffe, 1994, p. 110). While I was searching for my identity and roots in a particular space and location, I could not find it in one particular place, or group. Perhaps I was searching for an essentialised identity and a sense of belonging to a group that did not exist. Maybe the problem lay once again in being a child of the 'late modern age' (Giddens, 1991).

Kinnvall (2004) suggests that '[g]oing back to an imagined past by using reconstructed symbols and cultural reference points is, in other words, a response to the destabilizing effects of changing patterns of global mobility and migration' (p. 744). I guess my travelling back to the imagined past of my grandparents was my attempt to find an ontological self, my own sense of self, of belonging in the world. I do not know that I achieved this through travelling, through journeying to a place with an imagined past. In fact, I wonder if I have missed what was perhaps my best opportunity to learn about my 'roots', namely stories.

During the period that I undertook this research, both my maternal grandfather and my paternal grandmother died. These deaths, particularly that of my paternal grandmother, have made me question not only the research, but my own history, heritage and belonging. Following is an excerpt from my research journal, written on the day my grandmother died, 17 October 2009:

> My father called me aside and told me. 'I got a phone call from the nursing home at 1.30 this morning and Babushka died in her sleep last night'.
>
> I felt devastated. My Poppa died in March this year, but we had a lot of warning. He had bowel cancer, and so I felt like I said goodbye properly. Babushka, on the other hand, had a stroke about nine years ago, and had sat in a kind of limbo in a nursing home ever since. I visited her infrequently as she had lost her short-term memory and much of her long-term memory. She was a different person than she was before the stroke, and was difficult to converse with. The last time I saw her was in June at Akon's baptism. Akon had seen her three

times since she was born I think. Aside from my lack of visits to her, I also felt a huge guilt or despair or maybe lack of knowing my own heritage. I somehow felt that I did not know my Babushka as much as I would have liked.

I recall an assignment I did in Year 5 putting together my family tree. As part of this, I interviewed Babushka about her life history on little analogue tapes. I recall some of what she told me, but not much. I remember being surprised, but also proud of the amazing life she had lived and the strong, resilient woman she was. She too came to Australia as a refugee after World War II. And her described escapes from German soldiers were just as harrowing as any I've heard from the *Jëëng* women. I felt guilty that I never went back after my Year 5 assignment and got to know her better and found out more about her life. Those memories and stories were lost when she had her stroke nine years ago, but somehow, to me, they were only lost finally with her death. I have lost a very large part of my family history and with it the possibility of finding out a bit more about who I am and where I came from. I have always been told that I am very similar to her in many ways, not only in looks, but in character. I think I have her strength of spirit to get through tough situations, and her perseverance. But in many ways, I have come to realise that I really did not know her that well at all. That is the hardest part of it. Here I am spending all this time interviewing women I'm not even immediately related to, to hear their experiences of being refugee women, but I do not even know my own grandmother's experience.

◈

INTRODUCTION

> Families constitute primary sites of belonging. (Collins, 1998, p. 63)

> A person 'belongs' to their kin group in a way which is not true of other social groups of which they might be a member. Especially in relation to the family of origin, a kin group is the group into which a person is born, in which the membership is in no sense chosen, and where relationships still exist throughout life even if they are left dormant. (Finch & Mason, 1993, p. 169)

In *Thuongjäng*, the word *ruääi* means kinship, marriage and relationship (Biong Deng, 2010). It encompasses relations on diverse levels, from the marriage between a husband and wife, to the relations formed between their two families, from the relationship between mother and child to extended genealogical lineages and clan groups based on these lineages. *Ruääi* can describe relations from the intimacy of the relationship between two people, to the larger 'imagined' (Anderson, 1991) clans and lineages which connect people who shared an ancestor sometimes more than twelve generations previously.

This chapter focuses on one particular set of *ruääi*, those within '*kooc pan da*' (literally 'the people of our place' but it signifies the family or lineage of birth, i.e. the consanguineal kin). In this phrase *koc* (people) signifies all of the people within the family and lineage of birth, from the immediate mother, father and siblings, to stepmothers and stepsiblings, extending all the way out to those connected through extended lineages. Nyalong's narrative in the opening epigraph illustrates that family and kin belongings were not just negotiated within the immediate 'nuclear family' but also through extended family ties and kinship networks. The women's narratives described an intimacy and emotionality in these relations which is not often found in the field of kinship studies, but the networks they described in which they negotiating their belongings lay outside of the traditional academic conception of 'family'. For this reason, this chapter brings together two fields of academia that overlap, but infrequently engage in dialogue: kinship and family studies.

The first section of this chapter focuses on the ways in which kinship and family networks are determined by biological, social and gendered aspects, as well as the ways in which these aspects haunt negotiations for belonging within and among family and kin. This section is broken into two subsections. The first subsection explores the extant literature stemming from the fields of kinship and family studies. It considers the congruencies and differences between the two fields as well as highlighting some of the key aspects of how they are used to illuminate and better understand the women's narratives. The second subsection examines an extended section from Nyanut's narrative which clearly illustrates the hauntings of the biological, the social and gender in shaping her negotiations and desires for belonging within and among her family and kin in Sudan.

The second section of the chapter explores the ways in which migratory journeys shape negotiations for belonging within and among kin and family. Nyalong's narrative in the opening epigraph begins to illustrate some of the complex ways in which migration haunts the women's negotiations for belonging at this level. From the emotions of guilt, helplessness and longing, to the significance of phone calls, the obligations through *cieng* to send remittances and fulfil familial obligations, to the desire for return visits. This section is also broken into two subsections. The first subsection explores existing literature in relation to belonging, migration, families and kin which is mostly drawn from research on transnational families. The second subsection explores several ways in which the women described negotiating their belongings within and among family and kin while being spatially dispersed across the globe. It considers, for example, the obligation to send remittances, the emotionality of phone calls and photos, and the desire to be reunited with family and kin.

As Carsten (2004) has argued, it is

> the close-up, experiential dimension of kinship that too often is excluded from anthropological accounts. This lived experience often seems too mundane or too obvious to be worthy of close scrutiny. But the stories I have sketched

> make clear that kinship is far from being simply a realm of the 'given' as opposed to the 'made.' It is, among other things, an area of life in which people invest their emotions, their creative energy, and their new imaginings. (p. 9)

Like Carsten, it is the stories of the close-up, the lived and the experiential dimensions of kinship to which I turn in this chapter. This chapter is not an analysis of the types and forms of *Jëëng* lineages and kinship networks;[2] rather it is an exploration of how belonging within and among family and kin is a continually negotiated process haunted by the biological, the social and gender which is made ever more complex through the migratory journeys of the women.

THE BIOLOGICAL, THE SOCIAL AND GENDER IN NEGOTIATING BELONGING WITH KIN AND FAMILY

The fields of kinship studies and family studies were historically situated in very distinct areas of academia. A brief consideration of the histories of the two fields illustrates why there has traditionally been very little dialogue between the two. Kinship studies grew out of anthropology, a discourse grounded in the study of the 'Other'. From the early studies of kinship in the 1870s (e.g. Morgan, 1997) through to approximately the 1970s, anthropological studies of kinship were firmly rooted in the study of 'other' groups of people (Langham, 1981).[3] Family studies, on the other hand, were based primarily in the fields of sociology and psychology, and tended to focus on Western, Anglo-Saxon families and conceptions of family (Dunham, Cannon, & Dietz, 2004; Mann et al., 1997). It was seen that 'Others' have kin, while 'We' have family (Carsten, 2004). This history, in part, explains why many non-Western or non-Anglo-Saxon writers reflect on the ways in which neither of these fields account for their conceptions of family and kin. They suggest that anthropology and kinship studies have historically been responsible for exoticising and othering non-Anglo groups (Said, 2003; Appiah, 1992; Sudarkasa, 1996), while discourses of 'family' most commonly privilege Western notions of the nuclear or extended family with its inherent patriarchal kinship ties (Oyewúmí, 2000; König & de Regt, 2009a; Nzegwu, 1996).

For almost one hundred years, anthropologists produced studies of various kinship systems which sought to explore particular consanguineal and affinal relations and classes, the meanings associated with these relations and the ways in which allotment to these classes 'derive specific sets of complementary rights and obligations' (Lévi-Strauss, 1965, p. 13). Kinship studies were undone and changed forever by David Schnëider's (1984) seminal work *A critique of the study of kinship*. As Tapper (2001) suggests, this work brought about the 'undoing of the notion underlying traditional anthropologies of kinship' by returning 'again and again to that haunting fact that anthropologists have come home to find that their discoveries—other peoples' kinship—have turned out, in the end to be nothing more than their shadows' (2001, p. 330). Schnëider (1984) challenged the ways in which kinship studies were conceived by questioning the very ways in which notions of kinship were imagined, understood and reported by Western anthropologists.

This challenge resulted in an unmooring of kinship studies from its historical roots in anthropology from where it has morphed and spread throughout the social sciences into diverse fields such as cultural studies and queer studies. Just some of the more recent studies of kinship include examinations of kinship in transnational adoption (Howell, 2001; Melhuus & Howell, 2009), queer conceptualisations of kinship (Butler, 2002; Cadoret, 2009), and considerations of kinship through assisted reproductive technologies (Edwards, 2000; Strathern, 1992; Bestard, 2009; Cêpaitienė, 2009). Schnëider's (1984) challenge has also resulted in a shift in kinship studies from being studies of 'other' kinship systems, to more reflexive studies of Western and Anglo kinship networks (Edwards, 2000; Schneider, 1968). However, this undoing of the traditional anthropological notions of kinship has also led to a complication of the term kinship, which I explore further in the following sections.

In comparison to kinship studies, family studies have been very slow to diversify and extend the conceptualisation of family. Despite challenges from a multitude of scholars, studies of family still commonly do not extend beyond that of the Western nuclear or extended family. Many theorists argue that conceptions of family privilege the 'nuclear family' (Oyewúmí, 2000, 2002; Sudarkasa, 1996), which African feminists in particular have suggested is a 'specifically European form' (Oyewúmí, 2002, p. 1). Arguably, these conceptions of family do not address the diverse family structure of groups such as *Jëëng* (König & de Regt, 2009a).

Therefore, to understand the women's family networks a broader conception of family is adopted. For the women, *kooc pan da* included not only the immediate family of their biological mother, biological father, and siblings born of the same mother and father, but also the other members of the polygamous family unit including what Nyalong referred to as 'my other mums'[4] or Achol referred to as her father's 'small wife' (i.e. the multiple wives of their fathers), as well as the children of these 'other mums'. Some of the women, such as Nyalong, grew up with their 'other mums' and siblings and therefore invariably had close connections with these members of their family. Others, such as Nyanut, Achol and Atong, did not grow up with the other wives of their fathers and therefore this 'extended family' did not play a particularly important role in their negotiations for belonging. In addition, 'family' was used by the women to include all of the broader members of their lineages (both maternal and paternal). For example, Atong repeatedly referred to a distant cousin as her brother, and Nyalong referred to a very distantly related man from her maternal kin as her uncle. However, it must be noted that it is only from my Western perspective that I am labelling these connections as 'distant'. For the women it did not matter how 'distantly' related they were to someone; that person was family with all the obligations and benefits that this entailed.

The Social and the Biological of Kin and Family

Kinship has long been thought of in both biological and social terms (Lévi-Strauss, 1949; Parsons, 1943; Beattie, 1964). The biological aspect of kinship primarily engages a notion of 'shared biogenetic substance' (Schneider, 1968, p. 23) or genealogical connection, while the social aspect of kinship refers to 'a set of beliefs, values and categories which structure social action' (Harris, 1990, p. 4). Early anthropological work in kinship studies usually located itself as either biological *or* social; however more recent work has tended to problematise the dichotomy between the two. In addition, more recent conceptualisations of the social aspects of kinship have also come to signify the cultural (Carsten, 2004) and performative elements of kinship (Wade, 2005). Edwards (2000), for example, argues that

> being biologically related to a person does not axiomatically make them kin. A claim of belonging (to persons and places) can be made through upbringing as much as birth. The juxtaposition of being born and bred allows for kinship to be conceptualized through both or either. (p. 28)

Further to this, Carsten (2000b) has suggested the use of the term 'relatedness' to consider 'ways of being related without relying on an arbitrary distinction between biology and culture, and without presupposing what constitutes kinship' (p. 5).

Arguably, both the biological and the social play a role in determining who is or is not considered as family or kin. The question becomes what degree of significance to place on which. Over-emphasising the biological has historically resulted in the essentialising way in which kinship has been used to categorise specific groups of people (Wade, 2005). On the other hand, reifying the social aspect of kinship results in kinship becoming indistinguishable from other categories such as community or friendship (Butler, 2002). As Holý (1996) has questioned, to what extent can kinship connections be extended without kinship 'becoming analytically vacuous' (p. 168)? Below I use an excerpt from Nyanut's narrative to illustrate how the social and the biological function alongside each other to determine who is considered kin.

While kinship studies has begun the complex journey of accounting for both the biological and the social in constructions of kin, family studies lags behind in making the acknowledgement of these two aspects in constructs of family. There is therefore a dire need to consider constructions of family in relation to both the biological and the social. By considering the broader concept of family used by the women, it becomes clear that families were constructed through both biological and social processes. For example, I asked Atong how an agreement was reached between her husband's family and her family for their marriage to take place in Ethiopia, given that both her husband's immediate family as well as her own had remained in Sudan. She suggested that in Ethiopia, where very few people had close family members present who would usually be involved in negotiating the marriage process, the situation demanded that more 'distant' relatives undertake these negotiations:

> When we in Ethiopia, I have my family in Ethiopia. I had a cousin, we have brother from Wau. We have our brother he have a wife, we have woman from Wau. Then he [her husband-to-be] can talk with his family, his family can come with to my family.

This is similar to Miller's (2007) findings in Jamaica, where he suggested 'that a father is not the person who impregnated your mother, but the person who acts toward you as a father' (p. 537). For Atong, the word brother, for example, was not specifically interpreted to mean a male born of the same parents as her. Rather, she used the word brother to signify a male relative who acted towards her as a brother. In this way, family was constructed through more of a social need than an immediate biological connection.

Through my consideration of the women's kinship and family networks in the following sections, I argue that there is a necessity for an acknowledgement of both the biological and social components of kinship and family. I argue that the intersections between the biological and social are complex, and these complexities must not be ignored.

The Gender of Kin and Family

While there have been some moves to acknowledge the significance of gender in both kinship (Stone, 2010; Yanagisako & Collier, 2004) and family studies (Mann et al., 1997; Oyewúmí, 2002; Strasser et al., 2009), there is still much scope for further work in these fields. For the women in this research, gender haunted every aspect of their negotiations for belonging within and among *kooc pan da*. The kinship and family-based belongings of *Diäärjäng* are complex. To begin with there is the differentiation between *kooc pan da* and *kooc paan dië* (literally 'the people of my place' meaning a woman's affinal kin).[5] These terms signify the difference between consanguineal relations and affinal relations. As this chapter specifically focuses on negotiating belongings within and among *kooc pan da*, I focus on the gendered nature of that particular site.

Jëëng are a patrilineal society, so when a child is born, they become a member of their father's clan and lineage, but also retain links to their mother's clan and lineage as well as to the female relatives on the father's side (i.e. their paternal grandmother and great-grandmothers) (Deng, 1984). For *Jëëng* these ties are signified not only through the obligations and benefits of being kin, but also through marriage taboos. For example, a child is not allowed to marry someone from their maternal or paternal clan or lineage and its extensions back to their great-grandparents. This was explained to me in a conversation with three women at Nyalong's house. As the women so often do, they started quizzing me on my knowledge of Kuol's lineage. Through this, I was reminded of the continuing importance of the maternal connections (and for a significant number of generations):

Nyalong: Like when she's [Akon] growing like *Patek* [Akon and Kuol's clan]. Her son or her daughter, they're not going to marry *Patek*. Because she's the grandma. No.

Aluel: Like me now, my mother from *Paceny*, my daughter she's not allowed to marriage.

Melanie: So like her [Akon's] grandma is *Pachermeth*, so she wouldn't marry *Pachermeth*?

Nyalong: No. Because they are the uncle. So the different, different one. And to your background and to the mother and father.

Melanie: So does that mean like even *Patek* from Bor or ...?

Nyalong, Aluel and Amath: Any *Patek*.

Amath: Even *khawaja Patek*.

All: [laughs]

Aluel: [In Dinka] What about Kuol's father's mother?

Melanie: I think she's no ...

Aluel: Kuol's father's mum, she's from what?

Melanie: I forgot.

Aluel: You must remember, because one day Akon she is still grown, you tell that. When you got the man from *Pachermeth* or whatever do this one.

Melanie: It's *Pageu* or ...

All: [laughs]

Melanie: I think maybe. But I will ask Kuol when I get home. I confuse them all.

Aluel: You must to know for this. When Akon is still grown, tell Akon, this one your cousin, your cousin.

I later asked Kuol if I was right but, embarrassingly, I was not. Kuol's grandmother was actually from *Paduil*. This conversation illustrated the importance of both male and female kinship ties. Although in primary identifications a person will always identify themselves as a member of their father's clan and lineage, kinship ties with the female members of a lineage remain crucial for social support networks and marriage prohibitions.

In their emphasis on the patriarchal, patrilineal component of kinship connections in much of Africa, most Western anthropologists have missed these crucial continuing connections to maternal lineages. These Western anthropologists typically argue, for example, that:

> From a very early age girls are instilled with the knowledge that they are 'in transit' at home, in order to prepare them for the trauma of separation … The girl is doomed to depart and her children will in many cases belong to her husband's clan, while she belongs nowhere … Her identity is rendered uncertain and vulnerable by two completely contradictory loyalties. Such a permanent feeling of alienation in girls only becomes manageable by unconditionally adopting and internalizing the principles of the dominant ideology. (Schipper, 1999, p. 128)

This argument is not in keeping with the women's narratives of their connection to *kooc pan da*, nor of my own experience and observation of the crucial continuing connections that women retain with the families, kin and lineages of birth. Oyewúmí (2000) also argues strongly against this patriarchal, patrilineal focus, suggesting that regardless of where a woman resides or whom she is married to, women 'belong to their birth families, even though they do not necessarily reside with their kin groups' (p. 1097).

Oyewúmí (2002) further argues that it is the privileging of the Western nuclear family in these discourses that leads to the inherent conception of family as gendered and the dismissal and denial of connections to maternal kin. She comments:

> What is the nuclear family? The nuclear family is a gendered family par excellence. As a single-family household, it is centered on a subordinated wife, a patriarchal husband, and children. The structure of the family conceived as having a conjugal unit at the center lends itself to the promotion of gender as a natural and inevitable category because within this family there are no crosscutting categories devoid of it. (p. 2)

It is, therefore, essential to explore the continued links of a woman to *kooc pan da* as well as to extend conceptions of family outside of the 'nuclear' single-family household. However it is also important to acknowledge that, within the extended family networks described by the women, the ties between the women, their biological mothers and their siblings born of the same mother were usually the strongest. As Burton (1983) argues in his anthropological studies with Nilotic groups including *Jëëng* '[n]o stronger moral tie exists than that between children born by the same mother' (p. 114).[6]

Negotiating Kin and Family

The early anthropological studies on kinship systems and networks, particularly in Africa, focused on analysing and describing kinship in ways that emphasised the permanence of boundaries between categories of kin and ways of being related (Evans-Pritchard, 1990; Lienhardt, 2004). However, as Carsten (2004) has argued:

> In retrospect, it is clear that the unproblematic boundedness of the units described was much more a product of a particular kind of analytic endeavour than a reflection of the much messier realities of the political and social context of colonial and postcolonial Africa. (p. 12)

In more recent work in kinship studies, through the emphasis on the social construction of kinship, it has been argued that, just like any other social relation, kinship is not fixed but remains fluid and under continuous construction (Drotbohm, 2009; Finch and Mason, 1993, 2000; Miller, 2007; Strathern, 1992; Carsten, 1997, 2000a, 2004). Janet Carsten has been at the forefront of this push to acknowledge the processual nature of kinship with her texts *The heat of the hearth: The process of kinship in a Malay fishing community* (1997) and *After kinship* (2004) as well as her edited collection *Cultures of relatedness: New approaches to the study of kinship* (2000a). Carsten has shown how kinship networks and relations form, disperse and develop through flexible, negotiated processes and everyday experiences.

For the women, acknowledging the processual and flexible aspects of kinship is critical in understanding the continually 'negotiated relationships' (Finch & Mason, 2000, p. 164) which underscore their belongings within and among *kooc pan da*. However, as Miller (2007) emphasises, it is important in this focus on kinship as flexible and processual not to neglect the still often present formality and fixity of kinship as well. The women's narratives move between emphasising both the formality/fixity and the flexibility/processuality in negotiations for belonging with family and kin. The following subsection explores both the fixity and processuality of kin and family through an in-depth exploration of a portion of Nyanut's narrative.

NEGOTIATING BELONGINGS THROUGH GENDER, THE BIOLOGICAL AND THE SOCIAL IN *PAN MUONYJÄNG*

Before discussing Nyanut's story, I need to explain, in brief, some of the *Jëëng* cultural norms surrounding naming, marriage and separation. First, for *Jëëng*, name is a key marker of kinship (Burton, 1982). Francis Mading Deng (1984), a *Jëëng* anthropologist, suggests that 'personal names are of great importance to the Dinka' (p. 38). A name represents a person's ties to their clan and lineage. When a child is born their name is chosen by relatives (parents or extended family) from the names of the paternal ancestors and clan. For example, my daughter Akon was named after Kuol's father's mother. The names that we were allowed to choose from were those of the mothers of the males in Kuol's lineage. This first name is then followed by the names of the father, grandfather, great-grandfather and so on all the way back to the founder of the clan. For example, Akon's full name is Akon Kuol Baak Kuol Baak Kɔ̈ɔc Wiɛɛu Baak Kuol Mel Lual Teek. Each of these names represents a generation in the lineage originating with Teek (this is why their clan is referred to as Patek—the home of Teek). As Deng (1984) suggests, when introducing oneself to another, a person will recite their names to 'the degree necessary for identification' (p. 39). As can be seen from Akon's full name, the recurrence of certain names in a lineage mean that, in many instances, people's clans and lineages can be identified from their names. This is pertinent to understanding Nyanut's story that follows.

Secondly, there are some cultural components of marriage and separation that it is necessary to understand in order to consider Nyanut's narrative more fully. Traditionally when a marriage takes place cattle are exchanged between the two families. Biong Deng (2010) describes marriage for *Jëëng* in this way:

> Marriage in Dinka society is an endless process that involves a series of claims, counter-claims, obligations and transfers of cattle between the groom's and bride's families and their extended families—a wave of obligation that usually engulfs the entire lineage and communities. (p. 244)

There is an initial payment of 'betrothal cattle' from the groom's family, after which the couple are considered 'married' (Deng, 1984, p. 96). Following this, discussions take place between the two families to decide the number of cattle to be given to the bride's family. This is known as 'counting the marriage' (Deng, 1984, p. 97). When the cattle are paid by the groom, a reverse payment is made by the bride's kin which is equal to approximately a third of the cattle given by the groom's kin (Deng, 1984; Biong Deng, 2010). It varies between marriages as to which stage in the marriage process the couple begin living together and are allowed to engage in sexual relations. Deng (1984) suggests that a bride does not go to her husband's family until the cattle payments have been completed. My research and experiences however would suggest that this is not always the case, as often families are not able to collect the desired number of cattle in a short period of time, so the bride and groom begin their lives as a family long before the final cattle exchanges take place.

Separation and divorce for *Jëëng* are complicated and strongly abhorred. Deng (1984) suggests that divorce is rare due to the complexities of identifying which party is at fault and deciding ensuing cattle payments or repayments, as well as the complex interrelationships that result between the parents and any children of the union. However, separation is relatively more common. Both separation and divorce are rarely talked about, and discussions of these occurrences in another person's family are seen as bad-mouthing that family. The use of Nyanut's story that follows is, therefore, by no means designed to highlight the separation that occurred in her family, but is rather used to emphasise the resultant search for belonging that took place for Nyanut two generations later and the complications this had for her kinship identifications.

I opened the following part of my conversation with Nyanut with what I thought was a straightforward question with a straightforward answer. The answer that I got demonstrated that even belonging within *kooc pan da*, a site of belonging which I had initially thought was relatively permanent and uncomplicated, was never as simple as it seemed. The first sentence of Nyanut's response is the standard, straightforward response that would be given in an introductory conversation, but what Nyanut went on to explain highlights the haunted complexities of belonging even within the most intimate sphere of *kooc pan da* in *Pan Muonyjäng*. As Peterson (2007) suggests, '[n]o kinship relations … can claim immunity from the spectral' (p. 10).

> Melanie: *Ye nyan pa cër ŋö* [Which clan are you the daughter of]?
>
> Nyanut: My father is the one of *Paduur* [pause]. Do you know in my country, the lady, like you, your father and your mother, they need something to take in your husband place like cows. My father, my grandmum, my father's mum, she's married from the one is *Paduur*. She go there, she get my aunty called Nyanut, then she get my father without something her husband give to her family. Nothing. They are disappointed. To ask all them 'Why you are take my sister without cows? What happened? We need a cows.' The man is give them 10 cows. They said 'the ten cows, they're not enough, so we need more, you can give us more'. They said 'OK, don't worry for that, I can find other cows, if I got some cows, I can give them to you.' They said 'OK'. Now if you ask them to find some cows, now we need to take my grandma and the ten cows. They took my grandma and cows, take them in her place, back to her place. When they are stay there, the one is not coming again. While he has two children, he's not coming again. When my grandma she stayed there, she have two children, she stayed for a long, long year with her family. When they are stay there, my grandma brother said 'We don't need to wait your husband anymore. Now we want to find another man to give us some cows. Because we need the cows. If your husband coming, that time if he bring the cows, we take back the cows.' He said like that. The one is *Paceny* marriage my grandma. Marriage my grandma, she born two children. Then my grandma stopped, she doesn't born another children. She just had four children. Two boys and two girls. One is my father. The one is *Paceny* born two children and the one is *Paduur* born two children. That time when they are coming, the one he doesn't come anymore, the cows stay with my grandma family, all cows, the *Paceny* person cows there and *Paduur* cows there. That they are tell the children, don't tell we are *Paduur*, no.
>
> Melanie: So your father and his sister, they didn't know they were *Paduur*?
>
> Nyanut: Yes. They didn't know. Now you tell we are *Paceny*. When they are stay like that, they are stay, but they knew they are have a different father.

Nyanut began her story by contextualising how her father was born to a *Paduur* man, but when this man did not meet the expectations of her grandmother's family in terms of marriage cattle payments, her grandmother's family took their daughter and her two children back to live with them until the man from *Paduur* could bring them enough cows. Nyanut's grandmother's family waited for many years, but the man from *Paduur* never came with the cattle for his wife and children. Nyanut's grandmother's brother decided after some time that it was necessary for her to marry again as the family needed the cows. She married a man from *Paceny* and had another two children. Nyanut's father and Nyanut's aunty, the two children born of the man from *Paduur*, were told not to tell people that they were from *Paduur*. From the time of their mother's remarriage they had to tell people that they were from *Paceny*. For *Jëëng*, it is important that the children who are 'adopted' into a clan via socialisation publically identify with their adopted clan to avoid ostracism and ridicule. Public identification with their clan of birth, *Paduur*, would equate to advertising their mother's marriage breakdown which is particularly undesirable.

As Wade (2005) suggests, there are 'very important aspects of cultural performance which are involved in creating kin ties that are not just affinal. Kin are not just born, they are made' (p. 610). Nyanut's story told of a family built on kinship ties which were socially constructed to meet societal norms. An undesirable family breakdown resulted in two children whose biological ties were complicated by a father who did not assume the required responsibility for his children. These children were 'adopted' into another clan by a father who took on the social responsibility of raising them as his children, although they were not biologically his. Edwards' (2000) claim of the importance of being 'born and bred', of the 'claim of belonging (to persons and places) … made through upbringing as much as birth' (p. 28) is crucial to understanding the complex intertwinings of the biological and social aspects of kinship. With this background, Nyanut moved on to describe her own journey to learning about her complicated family history:

> Nyanut: When we grow up … I grow up, I asked someone, he's a man, my uncle, he's called Diing, but now he's not alive. I asked my uncle, 'Why are you called Diing'. When I'm still young, but that time I had a question, I asked someone a question. But the one is listen me; he told me the real thing. I said 'Why you called Diing? And my father is called Akol. But now I stayed here I didn't see one is called Akol in my country. Why my father come like that?' Different name. Yes I asked like that. He laughed. He laughed. He said 'Come here *manh wämääth* [the child of my brother].' I sit down. He said 'Can you repeat again?' I said 'yes'. So I repeated. He said 'What do you say before?' I said 'Why you called Diing and I hear other Diing in here, all other people Diing, but my father is called Akol, without another man is called Akol here. I can't see my uncle called Akol, or a grandfather, I can't see.' He said 'You are a good girl' and patted my head like that 'You are a good girl.' I'm still listening. He said 'Don't worry for that.' He didn't tell me. That time I'm not happy. I want to tell me.

One day a man he's talking with me, his wife, his wife born a boy called Ngong. I go, I said 'Baby is called Akol?' He said 'No'. I said 'Why? I need the Akol.' They said 'the Akol is not really my name'. I said 'Why?' They said 'No, no, no.' I said 'OK'. Sometimes, the boy is called Ngong, and sometimes I come I call him Akol. Because I need the reason why my father is Akol only all in my country, in my family. Without no another Akol. I want to know. Why, but when I go to get some people it's called Akol, it's a different clan.

> Even sometimes I go, I'm include in different clan. I don't want to use my clan. Yeah I thought it's *Paceny*, but I don't know, because I'm very, very small girl, I don't know the clan. But the even Garang [Nyanut's four-year-old son] is know now, but he doesn't know the reason why. That is why, I want the someone called like that, but I don't know the clan. Just I need the Akol. Just I need like that. And my father is not there, he's went in Khartoum. He stayed in Khartoum, but I stayed, I'm very, very, very young. My mum is carrying my brother follow me, it's called Deng, in Aweil now. That is I asked someone, I need someone to tell me, no-one. No-one.

Judith Butler (1997) suggests that '[b]eing called a name is … one of the conditions by which a subject is constituted' (p. 3). In a culture where naming is central to kinship identification, what happens when a subject is constituted as belonging to a kinship group with which their name does not fit? Nyanut discovered at an early age that her father's name, Akol, could not be found among those she identified as kin. When she first began to question her sense of belonging, she did not know about clans. She could recite that she was a member of the *Paceny* clan, but did not know why. Rather her insecurities about belonging were rooted in a name. Nyanut described how, as a child, she was troubled by the absence of her father's name among her kin in *Paceny*. She described her uncle's reluctance to answer her question of why she could not find anyone else called Akol among her relatives. She asked her uncle 'Why are you called Diing and I hear other Diing in here, all other people, Diing, but my father is called Akol, without another man is called Akol here? I can't see my uncle called Akol, or a grandfather. I can't see.' Through the *Jëëng* naming system which results in the prevalence of certain names in some kinship groups, Nyanut initially identified that her father's name meant that he did not really 'belong' in the kinship group that he identified with. Nyanut embarked on a search for her father's name that signified her own search for belonging.

Yuval-Davis, Kannabiran and Vieten (2006) describe belonging as 'about emotional attachment' which 'comprises specific political projects aimed at constructing belonging to a particular collectivity or collectivities' (pp. 2–3). For Nyanut, the lack of her father's name in the *Paceny* clan positioned her outside belonging (Probyn, 1996), and her search for her father's name became a project of constructing an attachment to a particular kinship collectivity which she did not find with *Paceny*. As she explained, 'because I need the reason why my father is Akol only … in my family. Without no another Akol. I want to know.' Her desire to belong was so great that, recognising the importance of name, Nyanut nicknamed her cousin, whose real name was Ngong, by her father's name, Akol. As she described, '[w]hile I know I'm the one of *Paceny*. I know already, but I can't see the Akol there.' For Nyanut, although socially belonging to the *Paceny* clan had been instilled in her, not finding her father's name among those she had always known as kin fomented a feeling of being bereft.

When she went to live with her aunty in a neighbouring region which was home to a large number of people from the *Paduur* clan, Nyanut identified a prevalence of the name Akol. She recounted a day when her aunty was listening as she engaged in the self-introductions typical for a *Jääng*:

> Nyanut: Until I'm grow up, I turn ten years, no I turn nine years, that time, my father coming from Khartoum. My father said, now I want to take you in your Auntie's place, she's called Nyanut as well. When he's carrying me, he put my legs in his neck here, and then he sing me in Nyanut house. Then I stay in Nyanut house because Nyanut she has her children is coming grown, old. The one is marriage, just remain two boys. Two boys who doesn't marriage. I stay with her. My aunty lived in *Paduur* place when she got married. The one in *Majangbai*. She go with me, she said 'Nyanut, come. *Bäär manh wämääth* [Come the child of my brother]. Let's go. *Ɣɛn a bë cath kek yïïn* [I'll walk with you].' We walk, we go to *Paduur* place, that time I see Akol, Akol, Akol. I said yes, I got my clan. While I know I'm the one of *Paceny*. I know already, but I can't see the Akol there. I get the Akol here. Then the one person asked me 'What is your name?' I said 'I'm Nyanut Akol.' She said 'What is your clan?' I said '*Paduur*'. Yeah like that. My Aunty listen, when we came back, she sitting in *ɣönhial thok* [entrance to the house on stilts] at night like 7 o'clock. I come sit her, next to her. She said 'Why you said you clan is *Paduur*?' I said 'My aunty, I get a lot of people, a lot of Akol in there in *Paduur* place, now I'm *Paduur*.' She said 'No. You are not *Paduur*.' I'm very, I can't stop *Paduur*, up to now. Even the one is ask me 'What is your clan?' Sometimes I said '*Paduur*' and sometimes I said '*Paceny*'. Because I'm not forgot. That time, my aunty told me, 'When your father born, the one of *Paduur* are born your father and me.' She said me like that. She said 'Me and your father, we are *Paduur*'. That time, I asked 'I said why you are *Paduur* and your sister and your brother they are *Paceny*?' She said 'we have different father'. I said 'Who is the really father?' She said 'the *Paceny*'. I said 'Why the *Paceny*?' She said 'The *Paceny* is stay with us. The *Paceny* is *muk* [literally to carry, but in this case it means to take care of as a guardian]. He look after us. So that is we did like that. We didn't take anything in *Paduur*.' She said like that. I said OK.

Nyanut, thinking that she had identified her clan by finding a prevalence of the name Akol, introduced herself as Nyanut Akol from the *Paduur* clan. When Nyanut and her aunty returned home that night, Nyanut's aunty sat her down and finally explained to Nyanut why she could not find her father's name in the *Paceny* clan. However, having recounted the story of the family separation, Nyanut's aunty emphasised that 'No. You are not *Paduur*.' Nyanut's aunty explained to her that while 'the one of *Paduur* born your father and me', the man from *Paceny* was their real father as the '*Paceny* is stay with us. The *Paceny* is *muk*. He look after us.'

Kinship for Nyanut's aunty meant being taken care of, the sociality of kinship. For Nyanut's aunty, by separating fatherhood from the reproductive act and considering the social responsibilities of fatherhood as 'providing a spatiotemporal nexus of identification, an extended network of relatives and relations within which the lineage-diffused character of a self-othered identity is formed' (Nzegwu, 1996, p. 187), they remained children of *Paceny*. Additionally, identifying as *Paduur* would have served to highlight the marriage breakdown that had taken place within their family and bring shame and embarrassment to the family.

By discovering that biologically she belonged to *Paduur*, but socially she belonged to *Paceny*, Nyanut's experience of kinship was eternally complicated. Nyanut explained how, to this day, she continues to move between identifying as *Paceny* and identifying as *Paduur*; she has connections with both. As she explained, 'Even the one is ask me "What is your clan?" Sometimes I said "*Paduur*" and sometimes I said "*Paceny*".' One identification is biological and the other is social. For Nyanut, kinship identification remained a flexible, negotiated process haunted by both the social and the biological.

NEGOTIATING KINSHIP AND FAMILY BELONGINGS IN MIGRATION[7]

> Theorising the ways in which migration, emotions and belonging are experienced and understood in the context of transnational family life is no small task because it involves several major, and closely interconnected, social scientific concepts—the institution of the family, the processes of transnationalism and migration, emotions and the complex question of belonging. (Skrbis, 2008, pp. 233–234)

This quote from Skrbis encapsulates the key themes and ideas which are covered in the second section of this chapter. Having begun the chapter by expanding conceptualisations of family and illustrating how these should be dialoguing with conceptions of kin, this second part draws these conceptions together with the growing sub-field in family studies of 'transnational families' (Baak, 2015; Baldassar, 2008; Boccagni & Baldassar, 2015; Bryceson & Vuorela, 2002b; König & de Regt, 2009a; Lim, 2009; Skrbis, 2008; Vermot, 2015; Vuorela, 2002).[8] As Skrbis suggests (above), these studies have focused on how transnational family life both shapes and is shaped by migration, emotions and belonging. Having already considered theoretical conceptions of 'the institution of the family' and its intersections with kinship in the opening section of this chapter, as well as 'the complex question of belonging' in the introduction and throughout the book, this section focuses on exploring the concept of transnationalism and specifically transnational families. It then looks at some of the ways that emotion underpins negotiations for belonging within transnational families, drawing into this discourse the *Jëëng* notion of *cieng*.

First, to consider the notion of 'transnational families' it is important to sketch a brief definition of transnationalism. Glick Schiller, Basch and Blanc-Szanton (1992) were the first to introduce the idea of 'transnationalism' to describe 'the processes by which immigrants build social fields that link together their country of origin and their country of settlement' (p. 1). They argued that 'transmigrants … take actions, make decisions, and feel concerns, and develop identities within social networks that connect them to two or more societies simultaneously' (pp. 1–2). Most theorists of transnational families draw heavily on Glick Schiller et al.'s definition, with Skrbis (2008), for example, suggesting that 'the term transnationalism entered the debates in a contemporary sense of multiple and constant transnational interconnectedness, accompanied with a process of deterritorialisation' (p. 234).

Skrbis (2008) further argues that it was not until these conceptualisations of transnationalism emerged that there were sufficient theoretical tools to consider the 'phenomenon of transnational family in all its complexity and diversity' (p. 235). With these tools then, transnational families were defined as 'families that live some or most of the time separated from each other, yet hold together and create something that can be seen as a feeling of collective welfare and unity, namely "familyhood", even across national borders' (Bryceson & Vuorela, 2002a, p. 3). Arguably the conception of the 'transnational family' can easily be translated into a similar but broader conception of transnational kin. Conceptualisations of transnational families invariably brought up questions such as 'How do people create a unity of kinship and family feeling when living apart? … How do individuals leading transnational lives negotiate their sense of belonging?' (Vuorela, 2002, p. 63).[9] Ultimately researchers have argued that migration and transnationalism lead to a reconfiguration of who does or does not belong to the family (Beyers, Venken, & Goddeeris, 2009; König & de Regt, 2009a). These belongings are negotiated through a variety of different processes. Consequently it is argued that 'belonging in transnational families, more than in other contexts, is a question of choice and negotiation' (Drotbohm, 2009, p. 134).

These negotiations for belonging are underscored by emotions. The women's narratives, as with much of the recent literature on transnational families, emphasised the ever-present emotions of negotiating belongings within and among transnational families and kin (Baldassar, 2008; Skrbis, 2008; Svasek, 2010, 2008). Svasek (2008) described that the emotional life of transmigrants is 'characterised by contradiction, as migrants are morally pulled in different directions in social networks that stretch over large distances' (p. 216). This contradiction can be seen in the two groupings of emotion that are described in both the women's narratives and in much of the literature on transnational families. The first grouping, which will be explored in the following subsection, is focused on emotions such as obligation and shame (Fleischer, 2007; Riak Akuei, 2005; Ryan, 2009; Lindley, 2009). These emotions, for the women, were haunted by the *Jëëng* ontology of *cieng* and were acted out through the everyday lived experiences of sending remittances to family and kin who had remained in Africa. The second set of emotions, which are explored in the second subsection, focus on the intense 'missing', desire and longing for kin and family (Baldassar, 2008). These are considered through an exploration of the women's desires for what Baldassar (2008) has referred to as 'co-presence', the longing to be 'with' kin and family through either physical (i.e. reunification) or virtual (i.e. phone calls and photos) means and how this has shaped their negotiations for belonging. The women's narratives, in considerations of both remittance sending and the desire for co-presence, emphasise the desire for belonging within and among *kooc pan da.*

Obligation, Cieng and Remittances

Collins (1998) has argued that 'notions of belonging to a family remain important to issues of responsibility and accountability, individuals feel that they "owe" something to, and are responsible for, members of their families' (p. 71). This is even more salient for those, like the women, who have migrated from difficult and challenging circumstances in disadvantaged countries or refugee situations, where they have left family members, journeying to relatively affluent situations in countries such as Australia. There is a perceived obligation and responsibility to support those who have remained behind (Baak, 2015; Fleischer, 2007; Riak Akuei, 2005). Not doing so results in shame (Lindley, 2009; Ryan, 2009).

Clark (1990) has suggested that:

> If our language and sociology have largely overlooked the emotional content of obligation, people have not. Relying on this to enhance their standing, everyday micro-politicians often remind others of their place by invoking a feeling of obligation. The message is: 'Your place has rules. The rules are bigger than both of us. God/society/everyone knows that people in your place should …' (p. 324)

For *Jëëng* these 'rules', obligations and responsibilities are governed by *cieng. Cieng* entails an ethical responsibility to others and to the greatest extent applies to those who are most closely related through family and kin networks. There have been two very interesting publications which consider the transnational kin and family-based obligations for Sudanese (in particular *Jëëng*) and, while they may or may not be aware of it, both authors emphasise (without naming) the significance of *cieng* (Lim, 2009; Riak Akuei, 2005). The first, by Anglo-American *Tiengjäng* Stephanie Riak Akuei (2005), considers the obligations and expectations of remittances in a multi-sited ethnography of *Jëëng* in Egypt and the US. She suggests that:

> In Cairo, when Dinka refugees depart for resettlement, they are sent off with heavy 'cultural' reminders and directives. Next to prayers to usher them on their new journey, songs, speeches and tributes are conducted that relay messages intended to remind people leaving how in the forthcoming sea of opportunities and options that await them, they should not forget who they are ('Yïn e Muonyjieng!') and what it means to be a Dinka. Among other morsels of advice ('Marry a Dinka!—Have children, teach them the language—don't let them go astray!'), expectations are conveyed to those taking leave that they

> should not forget their responsibilities and obligations—To help your people back home and elsewhere who are suffering. (p. 5)

This observation resounds with my personal experiences of listening to cassette and video recordings brought by those who have journeyed to Australia. These recordings are made by those who have remained in Africa and are sent to remind those who have come to Australia of the continuing obligations they have to support and remain connected to those who have remained. Riak Akuei (2005) further argues that the sheer number of people who request support from the individuals who have migrated means that it is not always possible to support everyone:

> it is the few who do resettle who find they are looked to for assistance by a disproportionately large number of people. This results in predicaments that are not easily resolved in light of constraints and other factors related to the local setting and the importance of meeting one's obligations and thereby being a good moral person (raan Muonjiang apath). (p. 3)

The women's narratives as well as my experience living with Kuol resound with this experience of the overwhelming demands of supporting very large numbers of people in Africa. Achol alluded to these unattainable demands as she reflected:

> Achol: Yes. A lot of people is ringing … I tell him I don't have money.
>
> Melanie: That's the hardest thing. The people every night on the telephone …
>
> Achol: Yeah every night. Me I'm talking with them every night, ringing. 'I ring you back.'

Achol reflected that her way of coping with these demands and the shame and embarrassment of not being able to meet her obligations is to tell people that she will ring them back. In order to avoid the shame of actually telling the person that she has no money, she then does not ring the person back, which indirectly sends the message that she is unwilling or unable to support them. As a member of a transnational *Jääng* family myself, I have experienced what Lindley (2009) refers to as 'the early-morning phonecall', the calls of those who are not cognisant of time differences and therefore ring at any time of the day or night. These endless requests for support and assistance in paying for school fees, rent, food and health treatment come from siblings, parents, aunts, uncles, cousins, distant kin and even friends. Each request is heard knowing that *cieng* obliges them to help in whatever way they can. Not to help brings questions not only about their *cieng* and thereby their *dhëëng* (dignity) or their status as '*raan Muonyjäng apath*' (a good moral person), but about their belongings with kin, family and friends. As Nyalong reflected (quoted in the opening epigraph):

> I talk with them, her daughter … Oh … I cry, cry, cry. Aunty please send me a money to go to school. You know I feel bad … And even my mum, my stepmum, the big one. She's sick and she called me, oh God. She need me to

> give money to go and buy ... she's sick with sugar and high blood pressure ... And I didn't even help her, so [claps hands together indicating she has nothing]. You know I feel ... Because when she die or something like that you feel like ... not good. Because she's good, I love her. She's good to us.

These obligations and responsibilities were also reflected by a participant in Lim's (2009) study of Sudanese resettled in the US (the second of the two studies referred to above). This participant reflected that:

> If I'm eating here, they need to eat too. If I'm having a life here, they need to have the life that I have too. They are a part of me. So if I'm feeling happy here, and they are suffering and they need something and then there are no assistance ... then what am I doing? What do I think of myself? So it is for me to share with them. Even if they don't expect it from me, I expect it for myself. (p. 1036)

This participant further reflected that 'loss of connections is death', maintaining a relationship with his family and kin through meeting these obligations 'keeps me alive otherwise I would be dead' (p. 1038). He reflected on how *cieng*, the ethical responsibility to share anything he had with his family and kin in Africa, maintained his connections with them. *Cieng*, therefore, critically haunts the ways in which resettled *Jëëng* negotiate their belongings with kin and family who have remained in Africa.

For Nyalong, not having been able to support her family, particularly her mother and father, when living in exile—a role she would have played in her traditional role as the daughter of *kooc pan da* had she stayed in Sudan—also added to the guilt and obligation she felt to support them once she was in Australia:

> Like when I was in Kenya, or Sudan, nobody is going to pay for my kids like uni. Nobody to go and pay for me like house until now. So nobody. So it's a different life, you know, I'm in different life. I could not even help my mum, but now I don't say that I help, but I try to do something for them. Yeah so it's a different life and we thank God for that one because we didn't know. I didn't know I would have this life.

While she was in exile, she acknowledged that she struggled to support even her own children, so there was no way that she could possibly help her mother. However, now that she has had the opportunity for a 'different life' in Australia, in which her children are able to attend university and she is in a reasonably comfortable and stable position financially, while she does not promise her mother that she will be able to help (i.e. send her money), she does try her best to send something.

All of the expressions and sentiments in this section resound strongly with my experience in living with Kuol. Uncountable times we have had heated discussions over the amount of money we send to Africa. My experience as a white-Anglo child of typical 'baby boomers' who have done their best to support me financially in any way they can has not prepared me to have this system of obligation and responsibility (i.e. parents responsible for children) flipped on its head. Kuol's experience with his family challenges the very ways I conceive family responsibility and obligation. These differences between Western-Anglo notions of familial obligations and those of the *Jëëng* for example, were highlighted during questions and comments given on a presentation I made at Makerere University in Uganda. A Ugandan man, who had spent time studying in the US, made the following comment:

> I find it striking, because as a white woman from Australia, I know the Western thinking is your sense of autonomy, your space, all of that, you know. Then on the other hand you talked about your husband paying school fees for his brothers. You're one of the very few white women living who find that acceptable. I lived in the US for a while and they would not tolerate that kind of thing. I wonder how you deal with that? Because for me it presents a kind of tension.

My response was that it had and continues to be a slow, difficult and continuous learning experience, just part of what I consider my journey towards becoming a *Tiengjäng*. For Kuol, his family and his kin, however, he is perceived as the one with access to money and resources in the 'affluent West'. He is therefore obliged in both his own eyes and those of other *Jëëng* to support them. Not to do so would bring him shame and this would unsettle his sense of belonging within and among his family and kin.

The Desire for Co-Presence: Phone Calls, Photos and Desiring Reunification

> It takes the form of a longing that lingers with and within belonging—a longing that is both the motive and consequence of belonging and that which resists it. Longing is the inside thought from the outside. It is an outside thought that is in perpetual communication with the interiorities of settlement. (Ilcan, 2002, p. 2)

The emotions of longing and desire have been thoroughly considered both in relation to belonging (Fortier, 2000; hooks, 2009; Ilcan, 2002; Probyn, 1996) as well as transnational families (Baldassar, 2008; König & De Regt, 2009b; Mercer, Page, & Evans, 2009; Skrbis, 2008; Zontini, 2004). In endeavouring to conceptualise the everyday ways in which longing for and missing kin and family is enacted, Baldassar (2008) conceives of the significance of co-presence. She describes this longing, drawing on her research with transnational families living between Italy and Australia:

> The feeling, often referred to as a type of heartache, of longing and missing is commonly expressed as a desire to be with kin or to be back home … the way to manage the heartache of longing for and missing is through sensual contact and co-presence, in other words, through feeling the presence of people and places involving all of the five senses. The expressions of longing and missing

> or absence and loss thus appear to be manifestations of the emotional need for reunion and return or co-presence. (p. 352)

This subsection considers some of the ways in which the women's narratives described the everyday desires for co-presence and how through these they have continued to negotiate their belongings within and among globally dispersed family and kin. Baldassar (2008) suggests four main types of co-presence: physical (physically being together in the same time and place), virtual ('constructed through forms of communication technology' (p. 352) such as phone, email, SMS and online social networking), proxy ('achieved indirectly through objects and people whose physical presence embodies the spirit of the longed for absent person or place' (p. 352) such as photos or significant objects) and imagined (includes acts such as praying for distant relatives but can arguably be considered as a component of the other three types). The women's narratives described, in particular, the salience of phone calls as a virtual medium for obtaining co-presence, photos and videos as proxy mediums and the significance of or desire for reunification with kin and family as the desire for physical co-presence. I will consider these three types of co-presence in relation to the women's narratives below.

Phone calls. Telephones, particularly mobile phones, were the most prevalent way in which the women stayed in contact with and enacted a sense of co-presence with their globally dispersed kin and family. Even during interviews and time spent 'hanging out' with the women most of them received at least one phone call from a family member somewhere in Africa, whether South Sudan or countries of exile. While most commonly these calls were requests for financial support as discussed above, they also provided a way to 'keep in touch' (Baldassar, 2008; Lim, 2009; Shandy, 2003).

As the quotation from Nyalong in the opening epigraph illustrates, these phone calls are frequently emotionally charged. While they allow for the 'virtual' co-presence between the two parties, the virtuality in many ways emphasises the physical distance between them. The initial joy at the immediacy of hearing the other person's voice is often quickly dulled by the stories of the struggles of family and kin who have remained in Africa. The person in Africa usually reminds the person in Australia how difficult life is for them 'over there'. The following conversation with Nyanut illustrates this:

> Melanie: Cause your sister is still in Nairobi now?
>
> Nyanut: In Kakuma.
>
> Melanie: In Kakuma? Oh I think it's really bad in Kakuma.
>
> Nyanut: It's really bad, really bad. Yesterday, no not yesterday, in last week she ring me she told me 'My daughter, my small daughter, the scorpion came'. When she ring me, she still crying there. It's very hard.

The immediacy of hearing her niece's cries in the background after being stung by a scorpion reminded Nyanut not only of the difficulties of living in Kakuma Refugee Camp, but also of the sheer distance between her and her sister and of how helpless she was to assist them. Svasek (2008) has argued that the virtual co-presence that is possible through forms such as the telephone has 'sped up communication amongst distant kin, making them more aware of each other's daily rhythms and concerns' (p. 220). However being 'aware of each other's daily rhythms and concerns' in the case of the women was not always easy, as invariably this meant continual reminders of the challenges their family members continued to face. Juxtaposing this against the relative safety and security they themselves had in Australia entailed a constant questioning and negotiation of how they existed as a family. As a South Sudanese participant in Lim's (2009) study reported of her kin who remained in Africa, 'I want to know how they're doing—but when somebody is suffering there, I am too. Often I can't help. It's really hard … they are family' (p. 1033).

Photos. The walls of every sitting room in every *Jëëng* house that I have been to in both exile and Australia are lined with photos of relatives: fathers, mothers, brothers and sisters, their families and their children. There are copies of birth certificates, university degrees, and anything that reminds them of the family and kin they have left behind. Surrounding themselves with these images helps to formulate some sense of co-presence by proxy. As Baldassar (2008) has argued:

> these 'transnational objects' embody the internalised presence of the absent and longed for people and places … Such objects and other memory triggers represent, by proxy, the longed for kin and the emotion of missing them; they are evidence of love and affection as well as of loss and yearning. Such inanimate objects actually animate the practices, imagining and emotionality of transnational family life. (pp. 257–258)

The significance of photos and other 'proxy' items in negotiating belongings with family and kin was emphasised in my first interview with Achol. She insisted on opening the interview by looking at her family photo album. As we flicked through the album, she would pause to tell me stories about significant photos. Virtually every photo was of a person; there were very few, if any, of places. Each photo captured a memory of that person for Achol, and looking at it gave her some sense of co-presence with that person. For example, she paused when we reached a photo of an elderly man, saying:

> Achol: This one my father. My father photo.
>
> Melanie: Very good.
>
> Achol: He's old man.
>
> Melanie: He's still alive now or …?

Achol: He's still alive … He's 70 … 70 … maybe 73 years.

Melanie: Oh. He's in Aweil?

Achol: In Aweil now. He's 73 years now.

As well as opening the interview process by looking through photos, Achol insisted that I borrow and watch a video of footage that had been shot during her return trip to Sudan the previous year. For her it was important that I see 'her people', particularly her father, to be able to understand better who she was, where she came from and the *kooc pan da* with whom she negotiated her belonging.

Atong also narrated the desire to have photos as a way of remembering people. Her father died while Atong was living in exile and she did not manage to make contact with him from the time that she left her home and family until the time that he died. Just prior to the research period she had made a return visit to Sudan. She described her desire to obtain a photo of her father:

Atong: My father is a good person. If I need, when I went back last time, I need the photo for my father. My mother she said 'The photo in Khartoum'. My stepbrother, she said he has my father photo. If I talk to them, I said if can my father photo, you can give for my photo to take.

Melanie: Or make a copy.

Atong: If can you see my father, he's like Tong [her son]. He's very good person.

Unfortunately during her trip she was unable to obtain a photo of her father. For Atong, a photo would have been a physical, tangible object with which could obtain a sense of co-presence and remember her father in spite of his death. Without a material object which could '"stand for" the absence of being' (Baldassar, 2008, p. 257) physically present, Atong was instead forced to remember her father by likening him to her son.

Desiring reunification and return visits. As with both Baldassar (2008) and Skrbis (2008), the women's narratives illustrated that the most desired form of co-presence was physical. They desired physically being together, particularly with *kooc pan da*, either through their own return visits to Africa or through sponsoring family members to be resettled in Australia through Australia's Special Humanitarian Entrant Program.[10] Nyanut's desire to be reunited with her brother and sister, for example, was so strong that she emphasised in three interviews her desire to bring them out to Australia. She described her fear and reluctance to return to Africa, suggesting that for her, the only hope of reunification was through bringing her family to Australia:

Nyanut: Even now I don't like. I couldn't think to go back in Africa, no.

Melanie: Never?

> Nyanut: Never.
>
> Melanie: You never want to go back?
>
> Nyanut: Because very scared. You think the place you go, your place, you think the people died there, here, here and here … Even I want to bring my brother here. I want to bring my family.

However, her efforts to bring her brother and sister to Australia had been unsuccessful. As she further elaborated:

> Nyanut (Kuol translated): When we came as a family we came all of us, no one remained behind. If it was possible, I would have put my sister and my brother in the form. We would have all come. [speaks English] We can coming here together. Even my history I write my sister and my brother. I said it's there in Kakuma. If I need, I bring them. Bring to stay with me. Because I like them.
>
> Melanie: Did you put a form for your sister?
>
> Nyanut: Yeah.
>
> Melanie: And what's happened?
>
> Nyanut: I don't know it's still in ARA [Australian Refugee Association].
>
> Melanie: Still waiting. Did they put it to the government?
>
> Nyanut: Yeah they put to the government.

Nyanut described that ideally she would like to have been resettled in Australia with her brother and sister, suggesting that she would have liked to include them on 'the form' which she completed to apply for resettlement in Australia. She further described that when completing 'the form' she included information about her brother and sister in the 'history' that she had to write for her application. She had hoped that this would make it easier for them subsequently to seek resettlement.

Her desire for reunification and physical co-presence was hindered by difficult application processes and repeated refusals from the Department of Immigration and Citizenship (DIAC). As Drotbohm (2009) has argued:

> social relations—negotiable as well as prescribed—are structurally determined and in the case of transnational family lives we cannot deny that the powers of the nation state and its definition of relatedness can be decisive for social relations that extend across the borders of different countries. (p. 147)

For Nyanut and her *kooc pan da*, the nation-state of Australia and the state institution of DIAC held 'great definitory powers over social belonging as well as interfamilial dependencies and hierarchies' (p. 134; see also Vuorela, 2002; Svasek, 2008). She further explained that she had submitted a recent form through the Australian Refugee Association, which assists those applying to sponsor family members to come to Australia and, at the time of the interview, the form had been submitted to DIAC for review. Subsequent to the interview, Nyanut found out that this application had been unsuccessful.

Nyanut was frustrated by a system which seemed to be working against her desire for reunification and physical co-presence with her brother and sister. Her frustration, desperation and resignation are poignantly described in the following:

> Nyanut: Even now, I have a chance, I move my sister and move my brother to come here to stay. Because I didn't have anything in my bed, just my sister and my brother. Even I have, I look like a bird now, I collect them to come to stay here.
>
> Melanie: To stay here with you, yeah.
>
> Nyanut: Even I'm very sad, sometimes I'm very sad, I'm very, I'm very hurt. Because my head now, I have now a heartburn about thinking.
>
> Melanie: When you think about them.
>
> Nyanut: Yes. If they in the one of human being they have thinking a lot, you get two. You get the heartburn, or mental problem. Just two things. But now I have a heartburn.

Nyanut's focus was on facilitating physical co-presence through trying to have her brother and sister resettled in Australia. However, most of the other women were focused on obtaining physical co-presence with kin and family through return visits to Sudan. As Nyalong described when reflecting on how good her 'other mum' had been to her and how much she missed her kin and family in Sudan (quoted in the opening epigraph), 'So I love to go and see them'. Baldassar (2001) argues that these 'home visits' are important ways in which migrants negotiate a sense of belonging within and among family and kin. At the time of the interviews only Achol and Atong had made return visits to Sudan, but by the end of the research period all of the women except Nyanut had travelled to Sudan at least once.

Achol (Kuol translated) reflected on her experience of seeing her father again after almost twenty years apart:

> My father was very old. When I saw him last year he was very old. If he lived here with me I would be happy. So I can look after him, but now he has his own wife. And he has other kids. And if I say let me bring you here dad, he wouldn't accept. I would have brought him if he would accept. So I can stay with him in Australia. But he doesn't accept because no-one can remain with his other children.

Rather than being a celebration of the brief period of reunification, Achol's visit instead showed her how much her father had aged during her period of absence. This resulted in an increased desire to bring her elderly father to Australia. While she acknowledged that this would not be what her father would want, she said that having him in Australia with her where she could care for him would make her happy.

Atong's return visit was also a mixed experience. While being happy to be reunited with those she managed to visit, it also reminded her of those she could not see.

> Atong: And last time it's not bad because I get my mum, I see my brother and my whole family. You see I am very happy.
>
> Melanie: Yeah, it's good to see. So your family was all still there, but everything else is change.
>
> Atong: When I go there, I'm not see my father because my father is die in 1999.
>
> Melanie: When you were in Kenya?
>
> Atong: When I'm in Kenya yep. Now I'm not see my another family like my cousin and young brother. I see my young brother when I went Khartoum. He see me, then I don't have any time to see his family because we have, we go.

The absence of her father was a reminder of what she had missed while being in exile and Australia. It also reminded her that there are some people with whom, despite her travels in an effort to meet the desire for physical co-presence, she could no longer be together. She also reflected that due to the brevity of her stay she was unable to meet with all of the kin and family that she desired to see.

While physical co-presence was the most desired form through which the women felt they could physically grasp and negotiate their belongings with family and kin, it was also the most difficult to obtain. Invariably these desires, efforts and even accomplishments of physical co-presence did not lessen the challenges of negotiating belonging within and among transnationally dispersed *kooc pan da*.

CONCLUSION: NEGOTIATING FAMILY AND KIN

> Most of us imagine the family as a place of safety, closeness, intimacy; a place where we can comfortably belong and be accepted just as we are. If we think of family ties as given, not chosen, they have this much at least in common with our other attachments: nation, race, class, gender. And yet we know quite well that in real life matters are rarely quite so simple. (Kuhn, 2002, p. 1)

This chapter has illustrated the ways in which belonging within and among kin and family are rarely quite as simple as is often assumed. From family and kin networks in *Pan Muonyjäng* to those that span across transnational locations, belonging within these sites was a complex and continually negotiated process. Conceiving of family and kin in such a way that allowed for a consideration of the hauntings of social, biological and gendered aspects illustrated that belonging within this site was never fixed or permanent.

If family and kin are conceived of as purely biological processes, this relegates belonging within and among family and kin to simply being. However, it is obvious from the women's narratives, as with the current discourse of family and kin, that there is also a very strong social component to the ways in which family and kinship networks are formulated. To conceive of kinship and family as purely social, however, means that it loses its distinction from other categories such as friendship. The women's narratives, particularly Nyanut's, have illustrated how seeking, desiring and negotiating belongings within and among families are haunted by both the biological and the social.

In addition, drawing on the narratives of the women and critique from African feminists, it is clear that Western conceptions of family and kin have haunted the ways in which kinship and family are understood as gendered sites. While family studies research would seem to illustrate that desires for belonging are most strongly felt within the nuclear family of marriage (i.e. husband and biological children) or the nuclear family of birth (i.e. mother, father and siblings), the women's narratives illustrated the need for broader conceptions of 'family'. While for some of the women, such as Nyanut, belonging was most strongly desired with those kin from within the immediate nuclear family, for others, such as Nyalong, the family of desired belonging was wider, incorporating 'other mums' and nieces and nephews. The women's stories illustrated that no singular model of family or kin was adequate to understand all of their connections of desired belonging. While this chapter specifically focused on the desires for belonging within and among *kooc pan da* for the women, who was included and emphasised within *kooc pan da* differed from woman to woman.

While negotiating belonging within and among *kooc pan da* in Sudan was inherently complex, global dispersion of family and kin complicated this further. The ways in which belongings were negotiated on this transnational scale were haunted by emotions including obligation, desire and longing. The women described the obligation, underscored by *cieng*, which they felt to financially support kin and family who had remained in various locations in Africa. Meeting this obligation to a large extent enhanced the women's sense of belonging with those whom they had sent remittances to. Not fulfilling the obligations of *cieng*, however, resulted in significant shame and guilt which served to destabilise the women's sense of belonging with family and kin.

The desire the women felt for belonging within and among *kooc pan da* transnationally was enacted through the ways in which they negotiated a sense of co-presence. Through the virtual, proxy and physical means of phone, photos and reunification, the women endeavoured to negotiate a sense of belonging with those who remained in Africa. However, even these were made problematic by the emotional reminders of the difficult circumstances in which their *kooc pan da* were living, as well as the power of state institutions in determining under what circumstances people can be reunited. The ways and forms in which the women obtained a sense of co-presence were continual reminders of the ways in which their situations, circumstances and negotiations for belonging were haunted by ghostly matters which remained largely beyond their control.

NOTES

1 Pronounced *koch.*

2 For a problematic analysis of *Jëëng* kinship see Lienhardt (2004).

3 Just some of the anthropological studies of kinship specifically examining groups in Africa include: Lienhardt's (2004) exploration of Dinka kinship systems in 'The Western Dinka', Evans-Pritchard's (1990) frequently cited examination of Nuer kinship in *Kinship and marriage among the Nuer*, Radcliffe-Brown's (1950) *African systems of kinship and marriage*, Brain's (1972) exploration of Bangwa kinships systems in the Cameroon in *Bangwa kinship and marriage* and Goody's (1969) Ghanaian-focused *Comparative studies in kinship.*

4 Nyalong emphasised that she addressed these 'other mothers' as Ma (mother). However, a clear distinction is made between one's biological mother and the 'other mothers'.

5 For a woman in identifying which kin group she is speaking about '*da*' (our) signifies the collective of the birth family whereas '*diё*' (my) signifies the singularity of a woman marrying out of her birth family and into the new lineage of her affinal kin.

6 See also Oyewúmí (2000).

7 Some of the ideas explored in this section have been published in a journal article (see Baak, 2015).

8 See also three special issues of journals released in 2015, 2010 and 2009. 'Moving feelings: Emotions and the process of migration' (Baldassar & Boccagni, 2015), a special issue of *Emotion, Space and Society*; 'Families, foreignness, migration: Now and then' (Venken, Beyers, & Goddeeris, 2009), a special issue of *The History of the Family* journal; 'Family dynamics in transnational African migration to Europe' (König & De Regt, 2009b), a special issue of *African and Black Diaspora: An International Journal*; and 'On the move: Emotions and human mobility', a special issue of the *Journal of Ethnic and Migration Studies* (Svasek, 2010).

9 See also Drotbohm (2009, p. 134).

10 See note 4 on page xi for a brief description of this resettlement process.

CHAPTER 7

NEGOTIATING BELONGINGS THROUGH *CIENG*

> Ultimately haunting is about how to transform a shadow of a life into an undiminished life whose shadows touch softly in the spirit of a peaceful reconciliation. In this necessarily collective undertaking, the end, which is not an ending at all, belongs to everyone. (Gordon, 2008, p. 208)

INTERLUDE VII: A HAUNTED ENDING THAT IS ONLY THE BEGINNING …

In February 2012, Kuol, Akon and I, as well as another Australian man, travelled to the new nation of South Sudan. One evening at dusk, we found ourselves caught in a tricky situation (which I will not elaborate on here) with a group of young *Jëëng* men in the streets of Juba, the capital of South Sudan. After some prolonged physical and verbal altercations, Kuol caught the attention of a young man who stated that he was a sergeant in the army and seemed to have taken leadership of the group. Kuol started speaking with this young man in *Thuongjäng*, and it was as if all other interactions among the group ceased. Kuol said something along the lines of:

> I heard that you are a sergeant in the army. We are age-mates, so we must have been in the Red Army together. In those years when we were struggling to fight for our country's freedom there were times when we had nothing to eat. There was a year that we had very little to eat; when we were all walking bones, when we were all dying of starvation. And yet we did not live together like this. We did not cause people fear, particularly women and children. Why is it that now, after we have finished fighting and won freedom for our country, you start living like this? This is not good *cieng*. This is not how we live together in *cieng*.

The young man hung his head, returned to humility, and immediately returned us safely to our hotel.

***

Three weeks later, in Johannesburg on our way back to Australia, we decided it was time for a day of relaxation and we took Akon to the Gold Reef Theme Park. Late in the day we walked into a large open room in which the walls were lined with photos of Johannesburg's gold mining era. As I walked through the door I was caught by the phrase in large lettering on the wall: '*Motho ke motho ka batho babang*', a Sotho-Tswana phrase which was translated to mean 'A person is a person through other people'. I felt that ghostly feeling that has haunted me throughout my research journey as I have encountered a personal experience that resonated with my research. Having just returned from living in a village in South Sudan alongside having spent an intensive four years of the research period living and learning *cieng*, I thought to myself, 'Yes, that is it. That is *cieng* and I'm starting to understand it.' I felt as if I was beginning to belong to and through this collective way of being. Two minutes later, Kuol walked into the room and was caught by the same phrase. Having read it, he turned to me and said 'That is what you don't get.' Just like that, my belonging was undone.

Initially I was shattered, but then I realised that perhaps we were both right. Understanding *cieng* is one thing; actually 'getting' it may be another. I interpret Kuol's 'get' as being much deeper than simply understanding. There is understanding on an academic level, but then there is understanding in practice, accepting other people's practice of *cieng*, accepting the practice of *cieng* when it impacts directly on me, and actually practising *cieng* myself. I believe Kuol was referring to all these other elements in his use of the word 'get'. My journey to learn about, understand and practise *cieng* will never arrive at a destination, because if there is anything the women's narratives have taught me throughout this research process it is that nothing is fixed, nothing is permanent; even *cieng* continues to shift, change and 'become' as does my understanding and practice of *cieng*.

INTRODUCTION

At the heart of *Negotiating belongings*' meditation on belonging is an engagement with the *Jëëng* ontology of *cieng*. Through exploring the belongings of a group of *Jëëng* women it has been possible to hear and understand how they situate themselves first and foremost through their relations with others. This chapter engages further with the concept of *cieng*, drawing together arguments about what this concept of relationality can offer to both methodological approaches to research as well as the ways in which belonging is understood.

Motha (2010) has argued that a move towards an 'epistemology and ontology of postcolonial becoming' is timely and necessary (p. 287). In this chapter I draw together the lessons that have been learned in the previous chapters of the book to propose how these epistemologies and ontologies of postcolonial becoming may be learned, what they will contribute to the formation of knowledge, and how they may shift the very ways in which being, becoming and belonging are understood.

The chapter is divided into three main sections. The first section explores the methodological contributions made by this book by articulating how *Negotiating belongings* has enabled 'new' ways of 'hearing' the narratives of a particular group of

Jëëng women. Through this it has been possible to hear these narratives as embedded in particular non-Western epistemologies and ontologies. Through 'new'[1] ways of 'hearing' it becomes possible to hear narratives without coopting or reducing them to Western frameworks, but rather allowing different epistemologies and ontologies to be articulated from within colonised spaces. These emerging epistemologies and ontologies are able to challenge what has previously been the Western-dominated notions of what it means to be and know. In addition, the first section explains how a relational ethic was necessary to be able to 'hear' in 'new' ways, but also how understanding the relational ontology of *cieng* has further highlighted the importance of embedding the research within a relational ethic.

The small second section attends to what many of the women alluded to throughout the research process, which is the 'becoming' of *cieng*. It reveals the ways in which *cieng* has shifted and changed as a result of the migration of the women, their families and their communities to a place in which their very way of being is challenged. It suggests that additional exploration of epistemological and ontological shifts as a result of migration and globalisation requires a great deal of further and urgent research.

The final section revisits the main argument of the book, returning to a consideration of the intersections between the haunted journeys of being, becoming and belonging. It also articulates how an understanding of the relational ontology of *cieng* can contribute to understandings of being, becoming and belonging.

'NEW' WAYS OF 'HEARING' AND THE NEED FOR RELATIONAL ETHICS: METHODOLOGICAL AND EVERYDAY INSIGHTS

Negotiating belongings makes two important contributions to rethinking the ways in which research should be done, particularly with those who are from different cultural, linguistic and epistemological backgrounds to the researcher. While primarily the book poses these as methodological insights, they can, and should, be related to everyday interactions as well as to research interactions.

My initial methodological approaches (i.e. centring in an ethic and method of friendship) clearly illustrate that at the outset of the research I understood, at least to some extent, the importance and significance of 'relationships' for *Jëëng*. By utilising an ethic of friendship and grounding the research within a method of friendship, I had already ensured that a relational ethic was central to how the research was conducted. While at the outset I chose to use these approaches based on my prior and continuing relationships and friendships with the women, what these approaches enabled, alongside my own position as an inside-out researcher and becoming a *Tiengjäng*, was a means to 'hear' the narratives of a particular group of women in ways that the prevailing traditions of listening had never before allowed. 'Hearing' in 'new' ways subsequently enabled me to gain an even clearer insight into why the use of 'relational ethics', such as an ethic of friendship, was so salient for research with this group of *Jëëng* women. In addition, hearing in these ways illustrates why and how this type of 'relational ethic' can challenge and shift the ways in which other 'non-Western' groups are 'known'.

The following subsection reflects on why 'new' ways of 'hearing' are so important and how they might be done, arguing that translation—not just linguistic, but also epistemological—is essential for groups of Others to be really 'heard'. In addition, I argue that through these different ways of 'hearing', that enable, and even require, the understanding of different epistemologies and ontologies, the necessity of a 'relational ethic' and how this may be enacted becomes clearer. While arguably, in this research it was through 'new' ways of 'hearing' that the importance and reasons for the need for a 'relational ethic' became clear, without a 'relational ethic' to begin with it would not have been possible to 'hear' the women's narratives in 'new' ways. Therefore the two approaches and their resultant outcomes are intrinsically intertwined. While this section focuses on how 'new' ways of 'hearing' and relational ethics have been enacted and the outcomes of these in the research environment, these insights also offer a way towards formulating a different ethics of everyday interaction with Others, that would allow Others to simply be others (Wise, 2008).

'New' Ways of 'Hearing' and the Necessity of Translation

> Translation is essential for us to live in respect of each other. We have to translate each other to ourselves, to transform our behaviour into living a life acknowledging that to be human is to be vulnerable. And to be vulnerable is to be fully human. (Krog, 2008, p. 236)

Western thought and knowledge production has always been underpinned by the valuing of particular knowledges and devaluing, or even complete dismissal, of others. Research has always privileged Western knowledge and devalued Indigenous knowledges (Wilson, 2005; Smith, 2003; Said, 2003). In this way, knowledge and its production has always been politicised. The politics of knowledge is constituted by *who* wields the power to determine and construct certain discourses and *how* this power is wielded (Sanger, 2007). This is underset by three main questions: Who speaks? To whom? And for what purposes? Added to this, and as noted in Chapter 2, a number of authors have recently acknowledged that the issue is not so much who can speak, but rather who will listen and hear 'since only if there are listeners will people's voices be registered' (Couldry, 2009, p. 579; see also Mama, 2009; Krog, 2011).

Since the seminal work of Edward Said (2003), it has frequently been observed that 'on the whole, the modern social sciences have historically evolved in crucial ways to produce knowledge about the dominated Other in order to legitimize subordination' (Chimni, 2009, p. 23). Following Said's critique, many writers (particularly postcolonial and feminist) have started to challenge the types of knowledge that are produced (Collins, 1990; Haraway, 1991; Raffles, 2002; Spivak, 1988; Krog, 2011), the ways in which this knowledge is produced (for example, the burgeoning field of 'critical and indigenous methodologies'[2]), and for what purposes (Bishop, 2011; Stonebanks, 2008; hooks, 1984, 1989). The challenge for researchers, particularly those of us who are not indigenous and have been raised in the Western traditions of knowledge production, is how to address and respond to these challenges. Recent work by Krog and colleagues (Krog, 2008, 2011; Krog, Mpolweni-Zantsi, & Ratele, 2008) has made it increasingly clear that confronting these challenges of knowledge production requires not only different ways of 'doing' research (i.e. methodologies), but ways of 'hearing' the voices of Others that are not limited by Western colonial ontologies and epistemologies.

At the outset of the research I had only acknowledged the need for different ways of 'doing' research. I thought that by engaging the methodologies of 'living oral (hi)stories of life', ethnography and autoethnography within an ethic of friendship I would be able to challenge sufficiently the ways in which the voices of a particular group of subaltern women have traditionally been 'heard'. Doing this, I thought, would be sufficient to disrupt how these women have traditionally been 'known' in Western discourses.

As I have argued throughout the book, the five *Diäärjäng* who have experiences of war, forced migration and resettlement in Australia, who are women, wives and mothers originally from Africa, have traditionally been 'known' and 'understood' in Western discourses in particular ways. These ways of 'knowing' frequently see the women, and others like them, as victims, traumatised, in need of liberation and modernisation, illiterate, oppressed, or a myriad of other deficit understandings. Through this objectification they are frequently denied the voice required to be active participants in knowledge construction and as such they are denied the opportunity to speak *to* or *with* and remain objects to be spoken *about* and *for* (hooks, 1990; Alcoff, 1991). Through this speechlessness the women 'become [and remain] a site where certain forms of knowledge are reproduced and justified' (Rajaram, 2002, p. 251), and in this way they are denied their 'right to complex personhood' (Gordon, 2008, p. 4).

As the research progressed, it became clear that particular methodological approaches (ways of 'doing') alone were not enough to really 'hear' and therefore overcome this politics of knowledge and denial of complex personhood. As Gordon (2008) has acknowledged:

> The persistent and troubling ghosts in the house highlighted the limitations of many of our prevalent modes of inquiry and assumptions they make about the social world, the people who inhabit these worlds, and what is required to study them. The available critical vocabularies were failing (me) to communicate the depth, density, and intricacies of the dialectic of subjection and subjectivity (or what in my business we call structure and agency), of domination and freedom, of critique and utopian longing. Of course, it is not

> simply the vocabularies themselves that are at fault, but the constellation of effects, historical and institutional, that make a vocabulary a social practice of producing knowledge. (p. 8)

The available critical vocabularies certainly did fail me, as they have failed so many other researchers. Throughout the research it has struck me time and again how researchers, seemingly with the best intentions, go to great lengths to try and really 'hear' the narratives of their participants through different methodological, theoretical and disciplinary approaches, and yet they ultimately produce the same forms of 'knowledge'.[3] Somehow the voices of their participants are still not 'heard'. My journey through the research alongside a reading of Krog, Mpolweni-Zantsi and Ratele's (2008) reflections on 'hearing' Mrs Konile's testimony at the South African Truth and Reconciliation Commission has helped to clarify just why it is so hard to really 'hear'.

Really 'hearing' cannot be done simply by using 'critical and indigenous methodologies' (Denzin, Lincoln, & Smith, 2008)—through different ways of 'doing'. Nor can it be done simply through using a constellation of theoretical approaches for a 'different' way of 'knowing' and understanding. Nor is an interdisciplinary approach that brings together multiple modes of inquiry adequate to address these 'hearing' issues. While all of these are useful, they do not overcome perhaps the biggest challenge to 'hearing'. Most researchers come to the research with a set of epistemological 'lenses' which are produced within particular, usually Western, frames that do not allow the researcher to 'see' or 'hear' the narratives of their participants outside of the ways in which they are already 'known'. The location, the role and the position of the researcher is therefore 'epistemically salient' (Alcoff, 1991, p. 7). As Mauthner and Doucet (2003) have articulated, there is an 'inseparability of epistemology, ontology and research practice' (p. 424).

Western ways of 'doing' research, of 'knowing' and 'hearing' people, are haunted by particular Western epistemologies and ontologies. This 'ontological image' places at its core the notion 'of a separate, self-sufficient, independent, rational "self" or "individual"' (Mauthner & Doucet, 2006, p. 125). Western ontology and epistemology

> places high priority on individuality and reason and is inclined to presuppose that European values could be applied universally. The tension between the particular and the universal is assumed to be dissolved since the particular is supposed to be universal. (Krog, Mpolweni-Zantsi, & Ratele, 2008, p. 532)

When the researcher exists within these ontologies and understands through these epistemologies, how, if at all, is it possible to 'hear' the narratives of those who do not exist in the world within the confines of these particular epistemologies and ontologies? Through my own research experience as well as a number of articles written by Krog and colleagues (Krog, 2008, p. 2011; Krog, Mpolweni-Zantsi, & Ratele, 2008), I argue that it *is* possible to 'hear' narratives that are situated in different ontological and epistemological standpoints than the dominant Western discourse.

The articles by Krog (2008, 2011) and Krog, Mpolweni-Zantsi and Ratele (2008) emphasise the necessity of not only linguistic but also epistemological and ontological translation and interpretation. Krog (2011) reflects on the testimony of Mrs Konile which, when she first heard it at the South African Truth and Reconciliation Commission, she states was 'the most incoherent testimony' she 'had to report on' (p. 382) (in her role as a national radio reporter).[4] Krog (2008) 'suspected that' Mrs Konile's 'testimony was important … and that, perhaps, one needed other tools to make sense of it' (p. 535). So she subsequently collaborated with two Xhosa-speaking colleagues (Mpolweni-Zantsi and Ratele) who were familiar with both the linguistic and ontological expressions of Mrs Konile. The three researchers used their 'different disciplines, backgrounds, cultures, and languages to gradually devise a way to "hear" Mrs. Konile' (Krog, Mpolweni-Zantsi, & Ratele, 2008, p. 534). Through retranslating and reinterpreting both the linguistic aspects of Mrs Konile's narrative as well as the epistemology through which it was 'heard', they were able to 'interpret the narrative via its embeddedness in an indigenous worldview' and, through this, the narrative became 'breathtakingly ethical and fair' (Krog, 2008, p. 231). Through Krog and her colleagues' careful retranslation and analysis it became clear that 'the dominant discourse has no way of "hearing" Mrs. Konile because her narrative defies all the elements that render narratives "audible" within the dominant tone' (Krog, Mpolweni-Zantsi, & Ratele, 2008, p. 545).

I had several similar experiences during the research process and compilation of *Negotiating belongings*. Perhaps the most salient was during the remote translation of Abuk's first interview which I was completing with Kuol. In the introduction to Chapter 3 I reflected that 'arriving home having completed my first interview with Abuk I felt a little deflated, as if everything she spoke of was superficial and anecdotal and was not a reflection on her personal life story'.[5] In Chapter 3 I postulate that this is because Abuk's narrative centred on describing a desire to belong at the less intimate level of the nation-state. I had also previously felt that because of this manner of speaking I had not got to 'know' and become as close 'friends' with Abuk as I had with the other women. On reflection, and having now progressed through the whole journey of the research, I do not think this is the full story. While interpreting Abuk's narrative I reflected to Kuol my disappointment and the sense of distance I felt in Abuk's manner of speaking. Kuol paused at one moment during the interpretation and made the following aside:

> You say she doesn't talk about her life, but actually she tells it in third person. Like they help you and [pause] And when she says that you think it's not about her, but she tells the story in the third person, she doesn't tell it in the first person that they helped me and they took me to the hospital and [pause] She just says that the Christians in Egypt are good they can help you, they can support you, they go to church. It sounds like she's talking about the lives of

> Christians in Egypt not about her life. But in actual fact what she's telling you is what was done to her. Yes, they helped her with her operation, they were there when she needed them, they go to church together. It's a funny way of talking. Some people talk like that. They don't like saying I did this and I went like that. They just put it out there in the third person.[6]

Having never encountered anyone who talks about themselves in this way I just took this as an unusual manner of speaking specific to Abuk. However, reading Krog's reflection on a similar but more-or-less opposite hearing of Mrs Konile's narrative, I was forced to reconsider my initial analysis. Krog reflects on noticing Mrs Konile's repeated emphasis on the word 'I' in her TRC testimony:

> As a white person steeped in individuality, I initially did not even notice the frequency of the word 'I', but when I did it merely confirmed to me that the notion of African collective-*ness* was overrated, despite the emphasis it receives from people like Nelson Mandela and Archbishop Desmond Tutu. The conclusion Ratele reached, however, was the opposite, and it was a conclusion I could not have reached, and, up until now, also one that no other White TRC analyst had reached. (Krog, 2011, p. 384)

Ratele's (in Krog, Mpolweni-Zantsi, and Ratele 2008) conclusion on Mrs Konile's use of the word 'I' was that:

> The word *I* is actually not talking about her real psychological individuality. Mrs. Konile is using *I* as a form of complaint. She is saying, I don't want to be I. I want to be us, but the killing of my son, made me into an I. This deed has removed me and I can't get back to where I belong. (p. 544)

Ratele further reflects:

> it is precisely because of a lack of understanding about the *self-in-community* and the *unity-of-the-world* that makes Mrs. Konile sound incoherent. Indeed, what racism, apartheid, and colonialism did and do is to destroy those specific values, because it is incomprehensible that *one lives for others*. It is very difficult for the Western mind or psyche to accept that *others make one*. In Western psychology, the individual comes first and is foremost, the family is constituted by individuals, and the world is made up by individual minds. (p. 543)

While Mrs Konile emphasised the 'I', a speech pattern which Krog and Ratele had acknowledged was unusual for an older Xhosa-speaking woman from rural South Africa, they were able to use this to understand how Mrs Konile's son's murder had made her feel as if she no longer belonged through the Xhosa relational ontology of *ubuntu* through which 'one lives for others' (p. 543).

Going back to and 'hearing' Abuk's narrative again with an understanding of this particular speech pattern as well as an acknowledgement of her embeddedness within the relational ontology of *cieng*, her 'third person' manner of speaking suddenly makes sense. She does not exist in the world outside of her relations with others, so she never speaks of herself as an 'I'; it is always 'us' or 'we'. While none of the other five *Diäärjäng* utilised this manner of speaking, it is important to remember that Abuk was the oldest of the participants and spent the smallest portion of her life exposed to Western epistemologies and ontologies. As such it may be possible that the other women could comfortably present their narratives in a manner which they knew was conducive to Western understandings. Alternatively it is possible that patterns of speech may differ across generations, or between those who grew up different regions of *Pan Muonyjäng*. In addition, Abuk's interviews were conducted entirely in *Thuongjäng* while most of the other women either spoke almost entirely in English or switched between English and *Thuongjäng*. As such, perhaps in making the linguistic shifts between *Thuongjäng* and English the other women were forced to shift the epistemological way in which they presented their narratives. The possible reasons for why Abuk spoke in the 'third person' while the other women's narratives were told in the 'first person' are multiple and require further exploration than is possible in this book. However, the most important observation that I make on this somewhat belated revelation is that 'hearing' Abuk's narrative through this understanding now offers a very different way of 'knowing' Abuk. It offers a way of 'knowing' Abuk that centres on her understanding of self in relation to others. It offers a different understanding of how Abuk negotiated her belongings, as for Abuk her life was lived first and foremost in relation to others. She always already belonged through relations to different others at different times.

This is just one of the many ways in which the importance of epistemological awareness in really 'hearing' the women's narratives was emphasised throughout the research period. As both Krog and I too have realised, interpreting and translating a narrative that is embedded in a particular non-Western epistemology and ontology requires the assistance of those who are familiar with both the Western and the 'indigenous' ontology. As Krog (2008) has argued,

> translation is a crucial strategy for survival—not only for all the untranslated narratives, but to free us from those who assume that they can translate the untranslated through their own perspectives, or worse, those who believe untranslated means not worthy of the trouble of translation. Translation creates space for one's heart in a language. Who you are, what you yearn for, does not simply die in a cul-de-sac of a powerless language. Translation lets the osmosis of human knowledge take place between cultures. Translation ensures that all kinds of concepts are being brought into one's language for which one has to discover equivalents. (p. 236)

In my case this ontological translation and interpretation was provided primarily by Kuol, alongside my numerous everyday experiences and interactions with *Jëëng* (many of which have also subsequently been 'interpreted' by Kuol in our everyday conversations and analyses of 'life'). Ontological and epistemological interpretation and translation provides insights into ways of being in the world that offer much for challenging not only the politics of knowledge, but also in formulating understandings of how it may be possible to be in the world in different ways. There has been significant acknowledgement of the role of gender in translation, particularly in relation to the translation of written texts (see, for example, Simon, 1996; von Flowtow, 1997, 1991; Arrojo, 1994), and there has also been minimal consideration of the role of epistemology in translation (Gikandi, 1991); however even Gikandi's paper only considers the role of epistemology in literary translation. Acknowledgement of the importance of epistemological and ontological interpretation and translation in everyday interactions is virtually non-existent, with the exception of the work of Krog and colleagues (Krog, 2008, 2011; Krog, Mpolweni-Zantsi, & Ratele, 2008). *Negotiating belongings* has demonstrated, through 'hearing' and 'being with' a particular group of *Jëëng*, the inescapability and necessity of ontological and epistemological interpretation and translation, illustrating that each encounter with the Other needs to seek a space of 'hearing' and understand this as always-already compromised or infused with cultural specificity.

Research must be conducted with a recognition that we are all engaged in processes of translating and interpreting Others. By understanding the ontological and epistemological situatedness of ourselves and Others, and remembering that we are always forced to translate and interpret these through how we understand the world, it becomes possible 'to transform our behaviour into living a life acknowledging that to be human is to be vulnerable. And to be vulnerable is to be fully human' (Krog, 2008, p. 236). An acknowledgment of these vulnerabilities enables us to see the complex personhood of those who have previously been reduced to being understood through only Western epistemologies and ontologies.

Relational Ethic

Acknowledging the relational ontology and epistemology of *Jëëng* has also required a reconsideration of the ethic in which the research was conducted—a relational ontology and epistemology also requires a relational ethic. In Chapter 2 I outlined my use of both friendship as ethic and a method of friendship, drawing on the work of Tillman-Healy (2001, 2003). I concluded that these approaches were necessary because I had been a friend or acquaintance of all five women before commencing the research relationships and that these friendships were continually built and developed over the course of the research and continued after the conclusion of the research. However, as I got further into the research it became increasingly clear that these approaches were even more necessary given the relational ontology of *cieng* through which the women exist in the world. Existing in the world in a way in which relationships are central and the self does not exist outside these relationships requires a particular form of everyday ethics which is first and foremost relational. Maintaining relations is at the heart of what it means to exist. These relational ethics must therefore also be central to conducting research with *Jëëng*. Not to conduct the research within a relational ethic would be to ignore the relational ontology in which *Jëëng* exist. Further, a deeper understanding of *cieng* has also enabled me to see what a relational ethic which is embedded within the relational ontology of *cieng* may offer to better understanding the ways in which research can be conducted as, itself, a relational ethic. As Swanson (2009) has argued of using what she refers to as 'a disposition of Ubuntu', research approaches which acknowledge and utilise relational ethics result in 'less objectifying ways of being in research' (p. 18).

Frosh (2011) has argued that 'relational ethics, which is concerned with the quality of the connections that people ("human subjects", as they seem to be known) form with one another, centres on acknowledgement, witnessing and responsibility' (p. 225).[7] In contrast to ordinary ethics, a relational ethic holds that relations and connections with other people are central to an ethical way of coexisting in the world. Centring a research relationship on this relational ethic means acknowledging the research participants as fellow 'human subjects'. For Frosh (2011), '[t]he ethical relationship is built on the capacity to recognize the other as a subject' (p. 227). There is also a responsibility to portray this subjectivity in the ways in which the research is written. Further, a relational ontology demands and acknowledges that this subjectivity is formulated within the relationality in which people exist.

Through recognising this subjectivity it becomes possible to start acknowledging and challenging the ghostly matters which haunt the ways in which the Other is known. A recognition of this relationality, and therefore subjectivity, can serve as a tool which makes possible the 'reconciliation' necessary to 'transform a shadow of a life into an undiminished life' (Gordon, 2008, p. 208). Research within a relational ethic, whether an ethic of friendship, or any other ethic, with relationality with research participants at its heart, can thereby challenge the types of objectifying research which have typically resulted in the 'knowing' of subaltern groups in particular ways.

However, as the women's narratives and my own experiences have clearly illustrated, the relational ethic demanded by *cieng*, as with any ethic, is an ideal which is practised by humans. The degree and extent to which *cieng* is practised varies between people and situations. *Cieng* can be both good (*cieng path*) and bad (*cieng rac*); it can be used to include (as in the sending of remittances as a way of maintaining transnational family connections) and exclude (as in Nyalong's exclusion from financially contributing to Ngong's *karama* based on her not being from the same region as him). I have personally been a recipient of *cieng rac* (in my initial exclusion from the community following my relationship with Kuol) and *cieng path* (in the ways in which the women welcomed me into their homes and entered into open and honest dialogue for the research, as well as the innumerable times people have given up their beds to accommodate me in their homes across Africa and Australia). As a human ethic, it can only ever be an ideal which is reliant on the practice of humans. As an ideal, however, it has much to offer.

What Do 'New' Ways of 'Hearing' and a Relational Ethic Contribute?

Research conducted in a relational ethic which allows 'new' ways of 'hearing' with attention to translation and interpretation provides a way 'to uncover and speak the buried histories of those that have been "othered"—denied their essential humanity through oppression' (Caracciolo, 2009, p. xii). As Oelofsen (2009) has argued, '[t]rying to apprehend the other's reality will mean that if we engage with the other, we will see her humanity, and that she demonstrates *different ways* of being human' (p. 184). Seeing and 'hearing' Others through their embeddedness in their own ways of being in the world acknowledges a complexity that recognises their full humanness. Understanding through these relational ontologies, it becomes clear that we all have an ethical responsibility, whether as researchers, friends, family or simply fellow human beings to hear the voices of those least often 'heard' by Western discourses, to recognise the complexities of the stories they tell and the lives they live, and through this to 'realize that there are no Others, only others, finding their way through their ordinary everyday lives' (Wise, 2008, p. 154).

Through different ways of 'doing' and 'hearing' as well as through the critically important process of translation and interpretation it became possible to 'hear' the women's narratives through an epistemology that places relationality at its centre. While arguably I have not been able to 'hear' in 'new' ways consistently throughout the book, the importance of these 'new' ways of 'hearing' as well as a relational ethic have come out as the most important observation and learning in the research process. 'Hearing' in 'new' ways and conducting research through a relational ethic offers 'new' and different contributions to Western discourses for understanding other 'ways of knowing and being' (Swanson, 2009, p. 11). As Swanson (2007) has further argued, 'hearing' and understanding these other ways of 'knowing and being' 'contributes to disrupting and decolonizing hegemonic meanings, and provides an opportunity for renewal and transformation in our desire for egalitarianism and human dignity. It affords a way of knowing that helps us learn to become human' (p. 65).

Motha (2010) has suggested that Antjie Krog (2009), in her book *Begging to be black*, is attempting 'an epistemic move towards another ontology of being. She is seeking to de-centre herself and a colonizer's way of seeing, knowing and being' (p. 286). I would argue that all of Krog's (2008, 2011; Krog, Mpolweni-Zantsi, & Ratele, 2008) recent academic work has also been written in this vein. Drawing and building on this work, *Negotiating belongings* has also been an articulation of a struggle to de-centre myself and challenge the colonially embedded way of seeing and knowing the Other, as well my very way of being in the world. This de-centring of the researcher, the resultant shift in knowledge and ways of knowing, enables the hearing of another way of being. It enables an opening up of different ontological understandings that make possible new ways of relating and being in the world together.

THE 'BECOMING' OF *CIENG*

Before turning to the main conclusion of the book, which explores what an understanding of the relational ontology of *cieng* offers to considerations of being, becoming and belonging, this section briefly explores the 'becoming' of *cieng*. In this section I consider how the women's narratives alluded to the change that the relational way of being, underscored by *cieng*, is undergoing as a result of the migration of people and ideas. This shift in ontology and epistemology, as a result of the increased movements associated with the current era of globalisation, requires increased and urgent further exploration before these non-Western ontologies and epistemologies are subsumed or denied their relevance by the more boisterous and imposing Western ontology of individualism.

The ontology and epistemology of *cieng*, this way of knowing and being in the world, has historically been rooted in particular ways of life and living together in particular places (i.e. family, kin and lineage-based communities and villages). This way of life has seen unprecedented upheaval in the past 60 years with the mass displacement of *Jëëng*, as a result of civil wars in Sudan, and their global dispersal to countries across the world—countries which frequently encourage, and even require, significantly different ways of living that do not embrace relational ontologies such as *cieng*.

Deng (2009) has suggested that the *Jëëng* value system of *cieng* was 'conservative and oriented away from change and development', further arguing that 'the effectiveness of the value system diminished as people moved away from the family and the lineage-oriented sense of the community' (p. 52). On this point I disagree with Deng. Throughout the book, the women's narratives have illustrated that, in spite of massive geographical movements, the *Jëëng* value system has remained central for the group of women in this research. The women's narratives have also emphasised that *cieng* has been forced to adapt, and in many instances successfully adapted, to accommodate change. For the women in this research, *cieng* remained central, indeed critical, to how they are in the world and how they relate to others. *Cieng* haunts negotiations of belonging at every level, from the family to glocal communities, through ethnic group and gendered belonging to citizenship and national identity.

While *cieng* remained essential to how the women existed in the world despite their migration to Australia, the women described some significant changes to the ways and degree to which *cieng* is enacted in everyday life. The women were most outspoken and frustrated with one particular shift, and they articulated this when they described their relations with their children and the younger generations (Chapter 4). Most of the women described feeling as if their children did not respect them, a respect that would have been previously demanded by *cieng* and is definitely a requirement of *cieng path* in *Pan Muonyjäng*. This lack of respect was demonstrated through the children refusing their mothers' guidance and discipline. Most of the women also noted that when they arrived in Australia their children emphasised their 'freedom' and their 'rights', something which the women put down to the focus in the West on individualism and independence. These values of independence and individualism are in stark contrast to the values of *cieng* which emphasise relationality and interdependence. This shift, for the women, was a direct challenge to *cieng* and their way of being and, as Abuk articulated, 'it hurts our hearts to see them living that way'. It hurts their hearts to see their children living in ways which are not commensurate with the ontological ways of being with which they are familiar.

The shift in *cieng* can also be seen in the changes and increased demands and obligations that are placed on *Jëëng* for remittances once they migrate to Australia and other Western countries, as well as in how *Jëëng* are forced to respond to these obligations (i.e. by saying they will phone people in Africa back and then not calling them back as Achol described in Chapter 6). In *Pan Muonyjäng*, when people lived in close proximity to their relations, everyone's financial position was blatantly clear to all those who lived around them. A person would not be asked to assist someone else unless it was obvious that they were in the position to do so. When *Jëëng* migrate to countries like Australia, a distant location where someone's financial status is not immediately obvious to those who have remained in Africa, and where it is assumed that, as with all Western countries, the quality of life is much better and there is access to unlimited financial resources, the requests for financial support are endless. In order to live in *cieng path*, many *Jëëng* feel an obligation to meet these requests, but most are forced to recognise that it is not financially or physically possible to meet each and every request. As such, many *Jëëng* live with the feeling that they are not meeting the relational obligation which *cieng* demands. In fact not meeting these obligations can be seen by others as *cieng rac* and, in spite of their best efforts, people often feel their status and self-perception as *raan dhëëng* (a dignified person) lessening as a result of not being able to meet these unattainable demands. These demands would not have been placed on people had they not migrated to relatively 'affluent' countries such as Australia.

Nyalong also alluded to a shift in *cieng* when she described the breakdown in community signified by the refusal of her financial contribution for Ngong's *karama* (Chapter 5). With a short but poignant sentence she questioned 'I don't know, I don't know this our people learn from where?' She states that when she left Mading Aweil, she left 'Aweil one' (i.e. united), where people related to others as people through *cieng*, regardless of their home regions of origin. By stating that 'I don't know this our people learn from where' Nyalong is postulating that somewhere along their migratory journey from South Sudan, members of the Mading Aweil community in South Australia have stopped holding the relationality required by *cieng* as central to the ways in which they coexist with others, and have let divisions and politics undermine the sense of belonging that *cieng* could provide.

While these moments in the women's narratives illustrate a diminution in kind and strength of *cieng*, the concept remains core in spite of where or how the women have journeyed. The women's narratives explored some of the shifts that are taking place in the 'becoming' of *cieng*. Nevertheless, pressing questions remain. These questions include:

- How will the first generation of *Jëëng* in Australia (and other countries in the West) retain a relational ontology in the face of the pull, and the almost necessity, in the West for individualism?
- Is it possible for the two ontologies (relational and individualistic) to coexist or are they mutually exclusive?
- Will *cieng* remain the primary ontology for subsequent generations of *Jëëng* in Australia?
- How will *cieng* shift as it comes in contact with other ontologies and epistemologies?

With its primary focus on belonging, this research has led to a point where these questions can now take shape and be asked and approached in richer, relational ways. The questions are apposite; indeed they are critical to a fuller understanding of how *Jëëng* exist in the world and negotiate their migratory journeys.

BEING, BECOMING AND BELONGING: HAUNTED JOURNEYS AND CONTRIBUTIONS OF *CIENG*

To conclude the book, I turn once again to consider what has been the central theme, the haunted journeys of negotiated belongings. *Negotiating belongings* has presented multiple ways to rethink some of the taken-for-granted ideas around belonging through providing an entrée into a certain series of experiences – experiential moments of telling. My understandings of these moments of telling, heard through the women's narratives and reflections on my own experiences, have been constrained by a lack of existing disciplinary resources which allow an understanding, challenging and critique of, among other things, African diaspora, mixed-'race' relationships, experiences of displacement and forced migration. The book has therefore cobbled together a conglomerate of tools from across disciplines and discourses to formulate an understanding that allows, and even encourages, the complexities of everyday life to be heard. Through using an interdisciplinary approach with an overall focus on belonging, it has been possible to hear, understand and explore aspects of women's lives which add significantly to current understandings of belonging.

Negotiating belongings has brought together the narratives of two particular groups of women that do not frequently engage in dialogue: a white-Australian *Tiengjäng* – a woman in a mixed-'race', 'cross-cultural' relationship (a group whose experiences remain under-theorised and elided from almost all academic discourse) and five other *Diäärjäng* who, through a variety of migratory pathways, have found themselves displaced from their homes in *Pan Muonyjäng* and resettled in Australia (a group whose experiences are almost always explored and understood through a deficit understanding situated within particular ontological and epistemological frameworks). Hearing and analysing these complex and overlapping, but not synonymous, narratives alongside each other has offered insights into being, becoming and belonging which support existing research. But through different ways of hearing these narratives, *Negotiating belongings* has also enabled an understanding which makes two further critical contributions to studies of belonging.

This final section explores the ways in which *Negotiating belongings* supports and concurs with existing theories of belonging, building on understandings of the multiplicity, the relationality, the fragility and the temperamentality of belonging. It also makes further contributions to discourses of being, becoming and belonging through considering the imperative of acknowledging the complex and diverse ways in which ghostly matters haunt negotiations for belonging. Finally I argue that the relational ontology of *cieng* presents 'new' ways for considering being, becoming and belonging and that, in its ideal form, *cieng* offers a way of being through which it may be possible for everyone to belong through a relationality as human beings.

Desires, Multiplicity, Relationality, Fragility and Continued Negotiations for Belonging

The women's narratives have helped me to concur with many of the key theorists on belonging who argue that belongings are negotiated within and among people, in relation to place. They are multiple and desired, but also fragile and can therefore never be a fixed and permanent state (Probyn, 1996; Fortier, 2000; Yuval-Davis, 2006; Yuval-Davis, Kannabiran, & Vieten, 2006; Anthias, 2006; hooks, 2009). *Negotiating belongings* contributes to and furthers the explorations of these preceding theorists through considering different momentary tellings from a different group of people heard through a different epistemology.

The women's narratives across all of the chapters clearly illustrate a common desire to belong. While the collectives to which the women described desiring belonging were frequently different, the desire to belong was unanimous. This was clear in the way each woman's narrative as a whole was generally built around emphasising a desire for belonging among a particular collective (for Nyanut this was within *kooc pan da*, Nyalong and Atong both described desiring belonging within 'glocal' communities such as Mading Aweil, Achol and I emphasised belonging as *Diäärjäng*, and Abuk stressed a desired belonging to the nation-state). The desire to belong was also clear through particular snippets and sentences within each of the women's narratives. Portions of the women's narratives that emphasise this intense desire to belong abound, but what follows are a few examples. Abuk's phrase '[b]ut we've been here for years and we are not refugees anymore. Now I've been here for about five years and I'm not a citizen, I'm still a refugee' emphasises the intense desire to belong to the nation-state of Australia through citizenship (Chapter 3). Nyalong's angry response of 'yes Ngong is from *Panyang*, but he didn't die in *Panyang*. He died here, so here all of us, even if you are north Sudan, we are all Sudanese' highlights her desire to belong to a collective that mourns the death of a young man despite her recognition that she cannot belong through the shared identification as *Panyang* (Chapter 5). Nyanut's identification and questioning at a young age that 'I need the reason why my father is Akol only all in my country, in my family. Without no another Akol' stresses the desire to belong through a shared ancestral name to a lineage group (Chapter 6). And my own acknowledgement in the Preface that 'I wanted to be recognised as a *Tiengjäng*, a Dinka wife, to feel some sense of belonging within the *Jëëng* community' illustrates the desire to belong that has governed my whole journey through the book.

By exploring the belongings of the women through a multitude of different collectives including friendship, nationality, citizenship, gender, ethnicity, 'glocal' place-based communities and the family, *Negotiating belongings* has also concurred that belongings are multiple (Probyn, 1996; Yuval-Davis, 2006). All of the women's narratives described simultaneous negotiations for belonging to different collectives, whether desiring belonging as *Diäärjäng* while still belonging in and to Australia, or desiring a sense of belonging within and among *kooc pan da* while still remaining *raan Mading Aweil* (people of Mading Aweil). Belongings were multiple, but having a sense of belonging within one group did not absolve the desire to belong to another group simultaneously.

Like hooks (2009), the women's narratives all emphasised how belonging was negotiated in relation to both people and places. For example, negotiating belonging with the people of Mading Aweil was done on the basis that all the people within that collective had a connection with a particular place, Mading Aweil. These belongings were also negotiated within particular spatial and temporal locations, whether at a party in a school hall in Adelaide on in the homes of southern Sudanese in Nairobi. These temporal, spatial and relational changes meant that belonging always could be, and frequently was, destabilised and politicised (Probyn, 1996; Yuval-Davis, 2006, 2009; Yuval-Davis, Kannabiran, & Vieten, 2006).

Finally, the conceptualisation of belonging with which *Negotiating belongings* has most clearly resounded is that belonging is an ongoing, continually negotiated process 'which is always already becoming' (Fortier, 2000, p. 2; Probyn, 1996). Throughout the book the narratives of the *Diäärjäng* have illustrated that we are all always on a continually negotiated journey of becoming towards desired belongings. This journey sees us shift between the 'momentary positionality' (Fortier, 2000, p. 2) of being, and the 'always already becoming' (p. 2). All of the women's stories have illustrated that belonging is never permanent. It is a continually negotiated process, a process of becoming which is negotiated in relation to Others. It is a journey towards belonging in which, at any given moment, we are all always only being, but ultimately this being is intertwined in a spatial and temporal nexus in which we are always becoming. As Krog (2009) has argued, '[t]hings continue to become the other, while continuing to be what they are' (p. 99).

As human beings, at any given moment we can only ever 'be'. But in the ever-changing world in which we live and, given the temporal and spatial discontinuities of this world, the being is forced to shift and change; being is only ever for a given moment (Chambers, 1996). Being instead shifts across time and space to becoming. We move then between being and becoming. As Wright (2004) has observed, becoming 'asks us to understand any and all negotiations of the subject … as negotiations always already in the making, and not the final word' (p. 26). As becoming beings then we are all always and only negotiating our individual journeys of becoming towards desired belongings.

Ghostly Matters

Exploring the intersections of being, becoming and belonging through six diverse and complex narratives has allowed a development of previous theorisations by emphasising how these journeys toward belonging are negotiated in relation to Others and haunted by the ghostly matters of the social. The continual negotiation for belonging alongside the fact that it is negotiated in relation to people and places (neither of which are permanent) is what makes belongings particularly fragile (Probyn, 1996). It is also what leads to the politics of belonging (Castles & Davidson, 2000; Crowley, 1998; Yuval-Davis, 2006). While acknowledgment of this fragility and politics of belonging is possible, in part, through a reflection on the negotiations of individuals, to do so without an acknowledgement of the larger social systems of power which control and determine the ways in which belongings can be negotiated is to understand belonging in a vacuum.

Acknowledgment of being and belonging as projects of becoming allows an understanding that being, becoming and belonging are always and only continued 'negotiations of the subject' (Wright, 2004, p. 26). However this ignores the fact that these negotiations take place in a world where 'not all subjects are equally subjected by the regimes of power that regulate the conditions of their existence' (Freiwald, 2001, p. 36). The ways in which subjects can negotiate their belongings are determined by the ghostly matters which haunt the journey. These are the processes that link 'an institution and an individual, a social structure and a subject, and history and biography' (Gordon, 2008, p. 19). All of us are haunted, and, as Gordon (2008) argues:

> To be haunted is to be tied to historical and social effects … these ghostly aspects of social life are not aberrations, but are central to modernity itself … The ghostly phantom objects and subjects of modernity have a determining agency on the ones they are haunting, which is everyone, making our lives just what they are at any given moment—a tangle of structured feelings and palpable structures. (pp. 190–201)

Not all beings have the same agency in negotiating their becomings and belongings. Some are haunted by historical and social effects to such an extent that the question arises: 'How do you begin to be/long when everything around you conspires to keep you alien?' (Philip, 1992, p. 22). Through the women's narratives and my own reflections I have explored just some of the ways in which journeys toward desired belongings are shaped, limited, directed and controlled by the ghostly matters of social life.

When followed through the routes of narratives of whole lives of a particular group of women, the fragilities of belonging, the politics of belonging and the questions of where borders and boundaries are drawn between 'us' and 'them' force an acknowledgement of the ghostly matters that haunt the ways that belongings can be negotiated. Hearing these whole-of-life narratives forces an acknowledgement that belonging is, for some groups of people, to some collectivities, unattainable. For others it remains an elusive desire controlled and determined by wider social repressions such as colonialism, racism, capitalism and patriarchy. Acknowledging and exploring these ghostly matters, and how they shape the ways in which belongings can be negotiated, allows a move beyond the politics of belonging. It allows a distancing from the politics that exist within particular groups and encourages a broader analysis of the 'way in which abusive systems of power make themselves known and their impacts felt in everyday life' (Gordon, 2008, p. xvi).

Ghostly matters have recurred throughout *Negotiating belongings*. They can be seen from the complex ways in which colonial legacies contribute to civil war and displacement, to the bureaucratic need for labels such as 'refugee' or 'asylum seeker' to overcome the quandary of the stateless unknown, to the ways in which racialised histories created through colonial hierarchies determine national identities. They are found in the shifts in gendered ethnicities which are haunted by gendered and classed expectations, dependent on locations of birth (town or village), educational opportunities, marriage partners and parents—where the roles of *Diäärjäng* have changed both directly and indirectly as a result of migration forcing the women to acknowledge, enact and engage the desired as well as the undesired changes, changes that have come about through cultural collisions. There are ghosts in the haunting of a song which calls the descendants of 'a community who follows buffalos', drawing together a community whose origins in a distant 'imagined' community becomes salient in the diasporic way in which local communities are globalised, deterritorialised and then reterritorialised in new local situations in new ways. There is a haunting in the always present ghostly calls of those kin and family who have, oftentimes reluctantly, been left in Africa. Their haunting presence through phone calls, photos, remittances and a desire for reunification is an emotive spectre in the daily lives of every *Jëëng*.

Examining belongings across a variety of sites, in a variety of locations, for a number of women has made obvious the multiple and varied ways in which the ghostly matters 'have a determining agency on the ones they are haunting' (Gordon, 2008, p. 190). Exploring my narrative alongside of the women's has served to illustrate the continuities and discontinuities between my narrative and theirs, and exploring the narratives of five different women with very different life histories has also illustrated the continuities and discontinuities that exist across the women's narratives. By exploring the discontinuities between the narratives it becomes evident that there are multiple ways in which ghostly matters including colonial legacies, 'racialised' histories, gender and class conspire to define who can belong.

There are staggering discontinuities between my own almost unquestionable belonging to the nation-state of Australia and the women's struggles to obtain a sense of belonging within any nation-state in which they have lived. My own belonging within the nation-state of Australia is haunted as a grandchild of immigrants in a colonised nation; however my very subjectivity and agency in the nation of Australia as a 'white' Australian-born woman determines my ability to question my sense of belonging in this hegemonically white nation where 'race' continues to dominate the ways in which belongings are negotiated. This is juxtaposed against the women's narratives of unbelonging across every nation-state in which they have resided. Their belongings have been limited and determined by old and new 'racisms' which define how they can belong as citizens and nationals in Australia, as cultural, linguistic and 'racialised' minorities, in their countries of initial asylum where their status as refugees denied them the agency to negotiate belonging, and in Sudan where a colonial inheritance meant that power structures denied them citizenship in their countries of birth and persecuted them as 'African' in a nation-state which desired an 'Arab' identity. When juxtaposing these narratives against each other the determining agency of abusive structures of modern power becomes brutally clear.

In turn, the women's almost guaranteed belonging as *Diäärjäng*, regardless of what it means to be, become and belong as *Diäärjäng* across spatial and temporal shifts, when juxtaposed against my own continued journey to become and belong as a *Tiengjäng*, illustrates the multiple and complex hauntings of 'racism'. Why do I continue to be a good *nyan khawaja* (white girl) who, unlike most *nyïr khawaja*, is 'better' than many *nyïr Jëëng* (*Jëëng* girls)? Why can I not simply be Mel who is a good person? 'Racial' and 'cultural' discourses continue to haunt in multiple directions in complex ways.

Hearing the hauntings of the women's narratives enables a recognition of the ways in which they are tied to the historical and social effects which result from modern systems of abusive power. Recognition is the first step required for reconciliation, and reconciliation will enable the women, and others like them, to step out from the shadows which have for so long hidden the complexities of their lives to live an 'undiminished life', a life in which their agency to negotiate their belongings is not threatened by these ghostly matters (Gordon, 2008).

The journey between being and becoming is haunted by 'ghostly matters' of the social that shape everyday lives. Being is, therefore, a haunted journey of becoming which moves towards momentary and ever-shifting desired belongings. The stories of these pages, of *Diäärjäng*, exemplify hauntedness. Their haunting continues well beyond the pages of this research to remind us of the complexities and routines of being, becoming and belonging.

Being, Becoming and Belonging through Cieng

While a sense of belonging has been identified as an essential desire for most people (hooks, 2009; Probyn, 1996), and even more so for those who have been displaced (Pollock, 1994; Ilcan, 2002), for those to whom relationality is central to their way of being in the world, belonging is even more important. The women's narratives have illustrated that, for those whose way of being is grounded within the relational ontology of *cieng*, desiring belonging remains important, and belonging is underscored by this relational way of being. Whenever belonging becomes politicised or destabilised so does the sense of relationality with those to whom belonging was desired or negotiated. When this relationality is destabilised, so too is *cieng*. While understanding that the women's desires and negotiations for belonging could not be comprehended outside of the concept of *cieng*, there is also much that *cieng* can offer to conceptualisations of being, becoming and belonging.

Belonging has always been acknowledged as a relational concept (Nsamenang, 2008; hooks, 2009; Rose, 2000; Probyn, 1996; Garbutt, 2009). However, authors such as Simondon (1992) and Nancy (2000) have aptly noted that being and becoming can also only be understood as in relation. Nancy (2000) has argued that '[b]eing cannot be anything but being-with-one-another, circulating in the with and as the with of this singularly plural coexistence' (p. 3). Venn (2010), in turn, reads Simondon's theory (which he translated from the original French) as 'supporting an ontology of being as becoming in relation to others' (pp. 151–152).[8] As a relational ontology through which one can only 'be' in relation to others, *cieng* provides a useful tool for understanding being and becoming as relational.[9]

Negotiating belongings has begun to develop an interdisciplinary understanding of how *cieng* is enacted in everyday life. Developing an understanding of *cieng* has been central to understanding the ways in which the women are in the world. Through *cieng*, the women and other *Jëëng* described how they only exist through their connections and relations with other people. As the *Thuongjäng* saying states, '*raan ee ya raan e raan da*' (a person is a person through other people) or, to quote a *Jëëng* participant in Lim's (2009) study, 'loss of connections is death' (p. 1038). Lim's participant, like many *Jëëng* I have spoken with in the past twelve years, summed up the essence of the relational epistemology and ontology of *cieng*; without connections to and relations with other people being is not possible. *Cieng* therefore provides a doorway to seek how *Jëëng* make sense of the self (i.e. as in relation to others). However, to avoid overly idealising *cieng*, the women's narratives also illustrate that the relationality that the ideal form of *cieng* requires is not always adhered to, and when this occurs exclusion and unbelonging are felt.

It follows that if we can only 'be' in relation to others then we can also only 'become' through these relations. Through this view of being and becoming as relational, it follows that the formation of subjectivity is also relational. Subjectivity is formed through a 'relational connectedness' (Ware, 1992, p. 119) with others. If we acknowledge the relationality of 'being' it becomes possible to overcome many of the ghostly matters that require the dismissal of the subjectivity of some groups of people.

Cieng can provide a 'new' and different way of thinking about how lives can and should be lived in relation to other people. It acknowledges the salience of relationality and through this provides a different practice of understanding humanity. If we are all only people in relation to other people, then to dehumanise other people is also to dehumanise ourselves. *Cieng* demands a degree of reciprocity and responsibility as underscored by a relational ethic which provides a means of reconciliation that may serve to overcome the hauntings of racism, colonialism, sexism and classism by emphasising the collectivity of shared humanity. The reciprocity and responsibility and relational ethic that is demanded through only being able to 'be' through others would enable us to overcome the ghostly matters and enable us to see the Other as human. This reciprocity and responsibility entailed by *cieng* is beautifully articulated in Deng's (2009) quotation from a Dinka chief:

> If you see a man walking on his two legs, do not despise him; he is a human being. Bring him close to you and treat him like a human being. That is how you will secure your own life. But if you push him onto the ground and do not give him what he needs, things will spoil and even your big share, which you guard with care, will be destroyed. (pp. 45–46)

Cieng thereby provides an opportunity to see shared humanity as relational and beyond difference.

While writers such as Gandhi (2006) and Derrida (2005) have explored the possibilities for overcoming difference through a shared relationality through explorations of the 'politics of friendship', friendship is only one possibility in the multitude of relations between human beings. Understanding all relations as embedded within relational ontologies such as *cieng* enables a move beyond friendship, which postulates a certain type of relation, towards an acknowledgement that all relations entail reciprocity, responsibility and ethics. As Martin (2003) has argued, '[t]hrough a relational ontology, connections are restored, relatedness reciprocated and maintained' (p. 211). Focusing on relational ways of being allows an acknowledgement of 'what it means to be human and to be in relationship with an-Other' (Swanson, 2007, p. 55). Through relationality there is scope to see beyond difference towards a shared humanity. As Venn (2010) has argued:

> This approach to the relationality of the living—of players as 'neither wholes nor parts' (Haraway, 2003, p. 8)—and to the human as one entity intertwined among the cohort of organisms and objects of the world, as always more-than-one, implies the co-implication of vulnerabilities and thus a rejection of all forms of colonialism and anthropocentrism, that is, of difference-as-antagonism or as excuse for ontological violence through exploitation of one kind or another. (p. 157)

But it remains to be seen whether it will ever be possible to get beyond the binaries of difference that have been created through a legacy of hierarchies. The question remains, will it ever be possible to get beyond difference sufficiently to all belong to an all-encompassing collectivity?

Cieng offers a different way of understanding ways to coexist ethically in the world. This relational way of living together offers a way of being, becoming and belonging that would enable *Jëëng* and other migrants to be in Australia and the world with ease, unhampered by the confines of citizenship, nationality, 'race', religion, gender, sexuality, ethnicity or any of the other constructs that haunt the ways in which they are able to make their lives. *Cieng*, in its ideal form, provides a way through which a white Australian woman can belong as a *Tiengjäng* regardless of the ways in which her 'race' and ethnicity haunt how she is understood. Being in the world relationally, where reciprocity, responsibility and relational ethics remain central, allows those whose lives have been diminished by ghostly matters to negotiate their belongings in ways which rely on nothing more than their subjectivity, their agency and their shared humanity.

NOTES

1 Again, I am not suggesting that these ways of 'hearing', 'doing' and 'knowing' are entirely new. Rather, they have been suggested before, but not widely undertaken. I use 'new', therefore, with an acknowledgement that their 'newness' can be contested. However, these approaches are 'new' in the application to and utilisation in the type of research which has been undertaken in *Negotiating belongings*.

2 See for example, Denzin, Lincoln and Smith (2008), Mkabela (2005) and Smith (2003).

3 See for example Bailey (2012), Macdougall (2008), Marlowe (2009a, 2009b, 2010a, 2010b) and Westoby (2005, 2008).

4 Mrs Konile gave her testimony in Xhosa which was interpreted into English and then transcribed in English.

5 Following is a passage quoted from the interpreted (by Kuol) transcript of Abuk's narrative which illustrates how she spoke in the second and third person:

> The females go and do cleaning of clothes and things in Arabs' houses. And you don't get paid a lot of money. You get 100 pounds in a month. If you don't want to go and work in Arab's house, and you want to brew and make your own business, then the police will come and catch you. They will go and beat you and put you in prison for a month or two, and fine you. When you pay the fine, then you can be released from jail.

> During a later conversation (which was not recorded), Abuk revealed that she had personally been arrested for brewing alcohol in Khartoum.

6 Abuk did not only speak in the third person, but also in the second person and sometimes in the first person plural.

7 See also Routledge (2004) who argues that 'relational ethics thus requires that we are sensitive to the contingency of things, and that our responsibility to others and to difference is connected to the responsibility to act' (p. 86).

8 Venn (2009) further argues in a separate article that relationality runs counter to all that neoliberalism represents. He suggests that

> [u]nderlying the radical ontology I am defending one finds a view of life, human and otherwise, that asserts the co-implication, co-constitution and co-dependence of living beings in a world we all inhabit … One implication is the idea of relationality as a defining feature of the living and the recognition that cooperation and collaboration are what essentially characterizes life in common. (p. 227)

9 There are a number of authors who have begun to note the salience of relationality (see, for example, Venn, 2009; Glissant, 1987; Irigary, 2002).

REFERENCES

Abu-Lughod, L. (1993). *Writing women's worlds, Bedouin stories*. Berkeley, CA: University of California Press.

Abuk, C. (Producer). (2009). *Mading Aweil ee Pan Da*. Retrieved November 15, 2011, from http://soundcloud.com/terminator-a-k-a-t-m

Achebe, C. (2010 [1960]). No longer at ease. In C. Achebe (Ed.), *The African trilogy* (pp. 149–286). New York, NY: Everyman's Library, Alfred A. Knopf.

Afshar, H., & Maynard, M. (2000). Gender and ethnicity at the millennium: From margin to centre. *Ethnic and Racial Studies, 23*(5), 805–819.

Agozino, B. (2000). What women's studies offer men: Entremesa discussion. *West Africa Review, 2*(1). Retrieved from http://www.westafricareview.com/vol2.1/agozino.html

Ahluwalia, P. (2001). When does a settler become a native? Citizenship and identity in a settler society. *Pretexts: Literary and Cultural Studies, 10*(1), 63–73.

Ahmed, A. G. M., & Rahman, M. A. (1979). Small urban centres: Vanguards of exploitation. Two cases from Sudan. *Africa: Journal of the International African Institute, 49*(3), 258–271.

Ahmed, S. (2000). *Strange encounters: Embodied others in post-coloniality*. New York, NY: Routledge.

Akyeampong, E. K. (2006). Race, identity and citizenship in Black Africa: The case of the Lebanese in Ghana. *Africa, 76*(3), 297–323.

Alcoff, L. M. (1991). The problem of speaking for others. *Cultural Critique, 20*(Winter), 5–32.

Ali, S. (2006). Racializing research: Managing power and politics? *Ethnic and Racial Studies, 29*(3), 471–486.

Alinia, M. (2004). *Spaces of diasporas: Kurdish identities, experiences of otherness and politics of belonging* (PhD thesis). Göteborg University, Göteborg.

Allender, S. C. (1998). *Australia's migrants and refugees: Opening the door to lifelong learning*. Paper presented at the How Adults Learn Conference, Georgetown University Conference Center, Washington, DC. Retrieved from http://www.ed.gov/pubs/HowAdultsLearn/Allender.pdf

Amit, V. (2002). Anthropology and community: Some opening notes. In V. Amit & N. Rapport (Eds.), *The trouble with community: Anthropological reflections on movement, identity and collectivity* (pp. 13–25). London: Pluto Press.

Anderson, B. (1991 [1983]). *Imagined communities: Reflections on the origin and spread of nationalism*. London: Verso.

Andrews, D. L., & Ritzer, G. (2007). The grobal in the sporting glocal. *Global Networks, 7*(2), 135–153.

Ang, I. (2001). *On not speaking Chinese: Living between Asia and the West*. London: Routledge.

Ang, I. (2011). Navigating complexity: From cultural critique to cultural intelligence. *Continuum: Journal of Media and Cultural Studies, 25*(6), 779–794.

Ang, I., & Stratton, J. (2001). Multiculturalism in crisis: The new politics of race and national identity in Australia. In I. Ang (Ed.), *On not speaking Chinese: Living between Asia and the West* (pp. 95–111). London: Routledge.

Anthias, F. (1992). Connecting 'race' and ethnic phenomena. *Sociology, 26*(3), 421–438.

Anthias, F. (1998a). Evaluating 'diaspora': Beyond ethnicity? *Sociology, 32*(3), 557–580.

Anthias, F. (1998b). Rethinking social divisions: Some notes towards a theoretical framework. *The Sociological Review, 46*(3), 505–535.

Anthias, F. (2002a). Beyond feminism and multiculturalism: Locating difference and the politics of location. *Women's Studies International Forum, 25*(3), 275–286.

Anthias, F. (2002b). Where do I belong?: Narrating collective identity and translocational positionality. *Ethnicities, 2*(4), 491–514.

Anthias, F. (2006). Belongings in a globalising and unequal world: Rethinking translocations. In N. Yuval-Davis, K. Kannabiran, & U. M. Vieten (Eds.), *The situated politics of belonging* (pp. 17–31). London: Sage.

REFERENCES

Anthias, F. (2008). Thinking through the lens of translocational positionality: An intersectionality frame for understanding identity and belonging. *Translocations: Migration and Social Change, 4*(1), 5–20.

Anthias, F. (2009a). Intersectionality, belonging and translocational positionality: Thinking about transnational identities. In G. Rosenthal & A. Bogner (Eds.), *Ethnicity, belonging and biography: Ethnographical and biographical perspectives* (pp. 229–250). Berlin: Lit Verlag.

Anthias, F. (2009b). Translocational belonging, identity and generation: Questions and problems in migration and ethnic studies. *Finnish Journal of Ethnicity and Migration, 4*(1), 6–15.

Anthias, F. (2015). Interconnecting boundaries of identity and belonging and hierarchy-making within transnational mobility studies: Framing inequalities. *Current Sociology, 64*(2), 172–190.

Anthias, F., & Yuval-Davis, N. (1992). *Racialized boundaries: Race, nation, gender, colour and class and the anti-racist struggle*. London: Routledge.

Anzaldúa, G. (1999 [1987]). *Borderlands la frontera: The new mestiza* (2nd ed.). San Francisco, CA: Aunt Lute Books.

Appadurai, A. (1991). Global ethnoscapes: Notes and queries for a transnational anthropology. In R. G. Fox (Ed.), *Interventions: Anthropologies of the present* (pp. 191–210). Santa Fe: School of American Research.

Appadurai, A. (1996). *Modernity at large: Cultural dimensions of globalization*. Minneapolis, MN: University of Minnesota Press.

Appiah, K. A. (1992). *In my father's house: Africa in the philosophy of culture*. New York, NY: Oxford University Press.

Appiah, K. A. (2005). *The Ethics of identity*. Princeton, NJ: Princeton University Press.

Arnfred, S. (2002). Simone De Beauvoir in Africa: 'Woman = the second sex?' Issues of African feminist thought. *JENdA: A Journal of Culture and African Women Studies, 2*(1). Retrieved from http://www.africaknowledgeproject.org/index.php/jenda/article/view/69

Arrojo, R. (1994). Fidelity and the gendered translation. *TTR: Traduction, Terminologie, Rédaction, 7*(2), 147–163.

Asante, M. K. (2011). Maat and human communication: Supporting identity, culture, and history without global domination. *Intercultural Communication Studies, XX*(1), 49–56.

Australian Associated Press. (2008a, November 13). Boy, 14, charged with Adelaide murder. *Perth Now*. Retrieved from http://www.perthnow.com.au/news/top-stories/boy-14-charged-with-murder/story-e6frg12l-1111118042195

Australian Associated Press. (2008b, November 14). Police confident of charges within days over Daniel Awak death. *The Australian*. Retrieved from http://www.theaustralian.com.au/news/charges-expected-over-14yos-stabbing/story-e6frg6p6-1111118036964

Australian Human Rights Commission. (2008). *Face the facts: Questions and answers about asylum seekers and refugees*. Retrieved August 25, 2010, from http://www.hreoc.gov.au/racial_discrimination/face_facts/chap3.html

Baak, M. (2010, July 15–16). *Murder, community talk and belonging: An exploration of Sudanese community responses to murder.* Paper presented at the Migrant Security 2010: Citizenship and Social Inclusion in a Transnational Era National Symposium, University of Southern Queensland, Faculty of Arts, Public Memory Research Centre, Toowoomba, Australia.

Baak, M. (2011a). *Belonging: From exile to diaspora*. Paper presented at the 2011 Migration Update: South Australia and Beyond Conference, Adelaide, South Australia.

Baak, M. (2011b). Diasporic mourning and negotiating belongings in response to murder. *Social Alternatives, 30*(2), 9–12.

Baak, M. (2011c). Murder, community talk and belonging: An exploration of Sudanese community responses to murder in Australia. *African Identities, 9*(4), 417–434.

Baak, M. (2011d). *Negotiating belonging: Citizenship, documentation and 'new racisms' for Sudanese women in exile*. Paper presented at the African Centre for Migration & Society Seminar Series, Johannesburg.

Baak, M. (2011e). *Negotiating belongings from 'home' through asylum to settlement*. Paper presented at the 2011 Refugee Conference: Looking to the Future, Learning from the Past, University of New South Wales.

Baak, M. (2011f). *Searching for belonging from Sudan through exile to Australia: Becoming nationals, being and becoming citizens*. Paper presented at the Transitions: From Refugee to Citizen Symposium, University of South Australia, Adelaide.

Baak, M. (2015). Transnational families, remittances, cieng and obligation for Dinka women in Australia. *Emotion, Space and Society, 16*, 123–129. doi:http://dx.doi.org/10.1016/j.emospa.2014.08.001

Babacan, H. (2010). Immigration, nation state and belonging. In A. Babacan & S. Singh (Eds.), *Migration, belonging and the nation state* (pp. 7–30). Newcastle upon Tyne: Cambridge Scholars Publishing.

Bailey, O. G. (2012). Migrant African women: Tales of agency and belonging. *Ethnic and Racial Studies, 35*(5), 850–867.

Baird, M. B. (2011). Lessons learned from translators and interpreters from the Dinka tribe of southern Sudan. *Journal of Transcultural Nursing, 22*(2), 116–121.

Baldassar, L. (2001). *Visits home: Immigration experiences between Italy and Australia*. Melbourne: Melbourne University Press.

Baldassar, L. (2008). Missing kin and longing to be together: Emotions and the construction of co-presence in transnational relationships. *Journal of Intercultural Studies, 29*(3), 247–266.

Balibar, E. (2001). Outlines of a topography of cruelty: Citizenship and civility in the era of global violence. *Constellations, 8*(1), 15–29.

Balibar, E. (2005). Difference, otherness, exclusion. *Parallax, 11*(1), 19–34.

Balibar, E. (2007). Is there a 'neo-racism'? In T. Das Gupta, C. E. James, R. C. A. Maaka, G.-E. Galabuzi, & C. Andersen (Eds.), *Race and racialization: Essential readings* (pp. 83–88). Toronto: Canadian Scholars' Press.

Barth, F. (1969a). Introduction. In F. Barth (Ed.), *Ethnic groups and boundaries: The social organization of culture difference* (pp. 9–38). Boston, MA: Little, Brown and Company.

Barth, F. (Ed.). (1969b). *Ethnic groups and boundaries: The social organization of culture difference*. Boston, MA: Little, Brown and Company.

Barthes, R. (1972). Jeunes Chercheurs. *Communications, 19*, 1–5.

Barthes, R. (1981). *Camera lucida: Reflections on photography* (R. Howard, Trans.). New York, NY: Hill and Wang.

Bassil, N. (2009). *The crisis of the Sudanese post-colonial state and conflict in Darfur* (PhD thesis). Macquarie University, Sydney.

Bateson, M. C. (1989). *Composing a life*. New York, NY: Grove Press.

Batrouney, T., & Goldlust, J. (2005). *Unravelling identity: Immigrants, identity and citizenship in Australia*. Melbourne: Common Ground.

Bauder, H. (2013). Nation,'migration'and critical practice. *Area, 45*(1), 56–62.

Bauman, Z. (1991). *Modernity and ambivalence*. Cambridge: Polity Press.

Bauman, Z. (2001). *Community: Seeking safety in an insecure world*. Cambridge: Polity Press.

Bauman, Z. (2011). Migration and identities in the globalized world. *Philosophy and Social Criticism, 37*(4), 425–435.

Baumeister, A. (2003). Ways of belonging: Ethnonational minorities and models of 'differentiated citizenship'. *Ethnicities, 3*(3), 393–416. doi:10.1177/14687968030033006

Beattie, J. H. M. (1964). Kinship and social anthropology. *Man, 64*(July–August), 101–103.

Beck, U. (1992). *Risk society: Towards a new modernity*. London: Sage.

Beck, U. (2000). *What is globalization?* Cambridge: Polity Press.

Behar, R. (1996). *The vulnerable observer: Anthropology that breaks your heart*. Boston, MA: Beacon Press.

Bell, M. M. (1997). The ghosts of place. *Theory and Society, 26*(6), 813–836.

Bennett, S.-J., & Tait, M. (2008). The Australian citizenship test. *Queensland Law Student Review, 1*(2), 75–87.

Beoku-Betts, J. (1994). When black is not enough: Doing field research among Gullah women. *NWSA, 6*(Fall), 413–433.

Berg, N. E. (2010). *The politics and poetics of belonging: An auto-ethnographic exploration of personal identity and family* (Honours thesis). Wesleyan University, Middletown, CT.

REFERENCES

Berger, L. (2001). Inside out: Narrative autoethnography as a path toward rapport. *Qualitative Inquiry, 7*(4), 504–518.

Bernstein, B. (2003a [1975]). *Class, codes and control: Volume III Towards a theory of educational transmission.* Oxon: Routledge.

Bernstein, B. (2003b [1990]). *Class, codes and control: Volume IV The structuring of pedagogic discourse.* Oxon: Routledge.

Bestard, J. (2009). Knowing and relating: Kinship, assisted reproductive technologies and the new genetics. In J. Edwards & C. Salazar (Eds.), *European kinship in the age of biotechnology* (pp. 19–28). Oxford: Berghahn Books.

Betts, K., & Birrell, B. (2007). Making Australian citizenship mean more. *People and Place, 15*(1), 45–61.

Beverley, J. (2008). *Testimonio*, Subalternity, and narrative authority. In N. K. Denzin & Y. Lincoln (Eds.), *Strategies of qualitative inquiry* (3rd ed., pp. 257–269). London: Sage.

Beyers, L., Venken, M., & Goddeeris, I. (2009). Families, foreignness, migration. *The History of the Family, 14*(2), 125–131.

Bhabha, H. (1990). The other question: Difference, discrimination and the discourse of colonialism. In R. Ferguson, M. Gever, M.-h. T. Trinh, & C. West (Eds.), *Out there: Marginalization and contemporary cultures* (pp. 71–88). New York, NY: The New Museum of Contemporary Art.

Bhabha, H. K. (1994). *The location of culture*. London: Routledge.

Biong Deng, L. (2005). The challenge of cultural, ethnic and religious diversity in peacebuilding and constitution-making in post-conflict Sudan. *Civil Wars, 7*(3), 258–269.

Biong Deng, L. (2008). Are non-poor households always less vulnerable? The case of households exposed to protracted civil war in southern Sudan. *Disasters, 32*(3), 377–398.

Biong Deng, L. (2010). Social capital and civil war: The Dinka communities in the Sudan's civil war. *African Affairs, 109*(435), 231–250.

Birungi, M. (2009). South Sudan President: Census results 'unacceptable'. *The New Sudan Vision.* Retrieved from http://www.newsudanvision.com/index.php?option=com_content&view=article&id=1655:south-sudan-president-census-results-unacceptable-&catid=1:sudan-news-stories&Itemid=6

Bishop, R. (2011). *Freeing ourselves*. Rotterdam, The Netherlands: Sense Publishers.

Blankenberg, N. (1999). In search of a real freedom: Ubuntu and the media. *Critical Arts: A South-North Journal of Cultural & Media Studies, 13*(2), 42–64.

Boatcă, M., & Roth, J. (2015). Unequal and gendered: Notes on the coloniality of citizenship. *Current Sociology, 64*(2), 191–212. doi:10.1177/0011392115614781

Boccagni, P., & Baldassar, L. (2015). Emotions on the move: Mapping the emergent field of emotion and migration. *Emotion, Space and Society, 16*, 73–80. doi:http://dx.doi.org/10.1016/j.emospa.2015.06.009

Bolaffi, G., Bracalenti, R., Braham, P., & Gindro, S. (Eds.). (2003). *Dictionary of race, ethnicity & culture*. London: Sage.

Bond, R. (2006). Belonging and becoming: National identity and exclusion. *Sociology, 40*(4), 609–626.

Brah, A. (1994). Time, place, and others: Discourses of race, nation, and ethnicity. *Sociology, 28*(3), 805–813. doi:10.1177/0038038594028003010

Brah, A. (1996). *Cartographies of diaspora: Contesting identities*. London: Routledge.

Brah, A., & Phoenix, A. (2004). Ain't I a woman? Revisiting intersectionality. *Journal of International Women's Studies, 5*(3), 75–86.

Brain, R. (1972). *Bangwa kinship and marriage*. London: Cambridge University Press.

Breidlid, A. (2005a). Education in the Sudan: The privileging of an Islamic discourse. *Compare: A Journal of Comparative Education, 35*(3), 247–263.

Breidlid, A. (2005b). Sudanese migrants in the Khartoum area: Fighting for educational space. *International Journal of Educational Development, 25*(3), 253–268.

Brettell, C. B. (2006). Political belonging and cultural belonging: Immigration status, citizenship, and identity among four immigrant populations in a southwestern city. *American Behavioral Scientist, 50*(1), 70–99.

Brettell, C. B. (2007a). Introduction: Race, ethnicity, and the construction of immigrant identities. In C. B. Brettell (Ed.), *Constructing borders, crossing boundaries: Race, ethnicity, and immigration* (pp. 1–23). Lanham, MD: Lexington Books.

Brettell, C. B. (Ed.). (2007b). *Constructing borders, crossing boundaries: Race, ethnicity, and immigration*. Lanham, MD: Lexington Books.

Breuilly, J. (1993). *Nationalism and the state*. Manchester: Manchester University Press.

Bruner, E. M. (1986). Ethnography as narrative. In V. W. Turner & E. M. Bruner (Eds.), *The anthropology of experience* (pp. 139–156). Urbana, IL: University of Illinois Press.

Bryceson, D. F., & Vuorela, U. (2002a). Transnational families in the twenty-first century. In D. F. Bryceson & U. Vuorela (Eds.), *The transnational family* (pp. 3–30). Oxford: Berg.

Bryceson, D. F., & Vuorela, U. (Eds.). (2002b). *The transnational family*. Oxford: Berg.

Burton, J. W. (1982). Nilotic women: A diachronic perspective. *The Journal of Modern African Studies, 20*(3), 467–491.

Burton, J. W. (1983). Same time, same space: Observations on the morality of kinship in pastoral Nilotic societies. *Ethnology, 22*(2), 109–119.

Butler, J. (1993). *Bodies that matter*. London: Routledge.

Butler, J. (1997). *Excitable speech: A politics of the performative*. New York, NY: Routledge.

Butler, J. (2002). Is kinship always already heterosexual? *Differences: A Journal of Feminist Cultural Studies, 13*(1), 14–44.

Butler, J. (2010 [2009]). *Frames of war: When is life grievable?* (2nd ed.). London: Verso.

Butler, J., & Spivak, G. C. (2007). *Who sings the nation-state?: Language, politics, belonging*. Oxford: Seagull Books.

Cadoret, A. (2009). The contribution of homoparental families to the current debate on kinship. In J. Edwards & C. Salazar (Eds.), *European kinship in the age of biotechnology* (pp. 79–96). Oxford: Berghahn Books.

Caracciolo, D. M. (2009). Introduction: Becoming human. In D. M. Caracciolo & A. M. Mungai (Eds.), *In the spirit of Ubuntu: Stories of teaching and research* (pp. xi–xv). Rotterdam, The Netherlands: Sense Publishers.

Carsten, J. (1997). *The heat of the hearth: The Process of kinship in a Malay fishing community*. Gloucestershire: Clarendon Press.

Carsten, J. (2000a). Introduction: Cultures of relatedness. In J. Carsten (Ed.), *Cultures of relatedness: New approaches to the study of kinship* (pp. 1–36). Cambridge: Cambridge University Press.

Carsten, J. (2004). *After kinship*. Cambridge: Cambridge University Press.

Carsten, J. (Ed.). (2000b). *Cultures of relatedness: New approaches to the study of kinship*. Cambridge: Cambridge University Press.

Castles, S. (1992). *The challenges of multiculturalism: Global changes and Australian experiences*. Canberra: University of Wollongong.

Castles, S., & Davidson, A. (2000). *Citizenship and migration: Globalization and the politics of belonging*. London: Macmillan Press.

Cêpaitienė, A. (2009). Imagining assisted reproductive technologies: Family, kinship and 'local thinking' in Lithuania. In J. Edwards & C. Salazar (Eds.), *European kinship in the age of biotechnology* (pp. 29–44). Oxford: Berghahn Books.

Ceuppens, B., & Geschiere, P. (2005). Autochthony: Local or global? New modes in the struggle over citizenship and belonging in Africa and Europe. *Annual Review of Anthropology, 34*, 385–407.

Chambers, I. (1994a). Leaky habitats and broken grammar. In G. Robertson, M. Mash, L. Tickner, J. Bird, B. Curtis, & T. Putnam (Eds.), *Travellers' tales: Narratives of home and displacement* (pp. 245–249). London: Routledge.

Chambers, I. (1994b). *Migrancy, culture, identity*. London: Routledge.

Chambers, I. (1996). Signs of silence, lines of listening. In I. Chambers & L. Curti (Eds.), *The post-colonial question: Common skies divided horizons* (pp. 47–62). London: Routledge.

Chase, S. E. (2008). Narrative inquiry: Multiple lenses, approaches, voices. In N. K. Denzin & Y. Lincoln (Eds.), *Collecting and interpreting qualitative materials* (3rd ed., pp. 57–93). London: Sage.

Chimni, B. S. (2009). The birth of a 'discipline': From refugee to forced migration studies. *Journal of Refugee Studies, 22*(1), 11–29.

Chow, R. (1993). *Writing diaspora: Tactics of intervention in contemporary cultural studies*. Bloomington, IN: Indiana University Press.

REFERENCES

Chow, R. (1998). *Ethics after idealism: Theory-culture-ethnicity-reading.* Bloomington, IN: Indiana University Press.

Clandinin, D. J. (Ed.). (2007). *Handbook of narrative inquiry: Mapping a methodology.* Thousand Oaks, CA: Sage.

Clandinin, D. J., & Connelly, M. (2000). *Narrative inquiry: Experience and story in qualitative research.* San Francisco, CA: Jossey-Bass.

Clandinin, D. J., & Murphy, M. S. (2009). Comments on Coulter and Smith: Relational ontological commitments in narrative research. *Educational Researcher, 38*(8), 598–602.

Clandinin, D. J., & Rosiek, J. (2007). Mapping a landscape of narrative inquiry: Borderland spaces and tensions. In D. J. Clandinin (Ed.), *Handbook of narrative inquiry: Mapping a methodology* (pp. 35–75). Thousand Oaks, CA: Sage.

Clark, C. (1990). Emotions and micropolitics in everyday life: Some patterns and paradoxes of 'place'. In T. D. Kemper (Ed.), *Research agendas in the sociology of emotions* (pp. 305–336). Albany, NY: State University of New York Press.

Clarke, P. A. (2007). Indigenous spirit and ghost folklore of 'settled' Australia. *Folklore, 118*(2), 141–161.

Clifford, J. (1989). Notes on travel and theory. *Inscriptions, 5.* Retrieved from http://www2.ucsc.edu/culturalstudies/PUBS/Inscriptions/vol_5/clifford.html

Clifford, J. (1997). *Routes: Travel and translation in the late twentieth century.* Cambridge, MA: Harvard University Press.

Clifford, J., & Marcus, C. E. (Eds.). (1986). *Writing culture: The poetics and politics of ethnography.* Los Angeles, CA: University of California Press.

Collins, C. (1976). Colonialism and class struggle in Sudan. *MERIP Reports, 46,* 3–17+20.

Collins, P. H. (1986). Learning from the outsider within: The sociological significance of black feminist thought. *Social Problems, 33*(6), S14–S32.

Collins, P. H. (1990). *Black feminist thought: Knowledge, Consciousness, and the politics of empowerment.* London: Unwin Hyman.

Collins, P. H. (1998). It's all in the family: Intersections of gender, race, and nation. *Hypatia, 13*(3), 62–82.

Collins, R. O. (2007 [1971]). *The southern Sudan in historical perspective.* London: Transaction Publishers.

Corfield, S. (2008). *Negotiating existence: Asylum seekers in East Anglia, UK* (PhD thesis). University of Adelaide, Adelaide.

Couldry, N. (2009). Rethinking the politics of voice. *Continuum: Journal of Media and Cultural Studies, 23*(4), 579–582.

Crowley, J. (1998). The politics of belonging: Some theoretical considerations. In A. Geddes & A. Favell (Eds.), *The politics of belonging: Migrants and minorities in contemporary Europe* (pp. 15–39). Avebury: Ashgate.

Cuomo, C. J., & Hall, K. Q. (1999). Introduction: Reflections on whiteness. In C. J. Cuomo & K. Q. Hall (Eds.), *Whiteness: Feminist philosophical reflections* (pp. 1–12). Maryland, MD: Rowman and Littlefield Publishers.

Das Gupta, M. (1997). 'What is Indian about you?' A gendered, transnational approach to ethnicity. *Gender and Society, 11*(5), 572–596.

Davidson, B. (1992). *The Black man's burden: Africa and the Curse of the nation-state.* New York, NY: Times Books.

Davidson, B., & Munslow, B. (2004). The crisis of the nation-state. In G. Mohan & T. Zack-Williams (Eds.), *The politics of transition in Africa* (pp. 188–194). Sheffield: ROAPE Publications.

Davis, C. (2005). Hauntology, spectres and phantoms. *French Studies, 59*(3), 373–379.

De Andrade, L. L. (2000). Negotiating from the insider: Constructing racial and ethnic identity in qualitative research. *Journal of Contemporary Ethnography, 29*(June), 268–290.

de Ngor, M. (2006). Globalization and the African kinship network system: Will it sustain? *Sudan Tribune.* Retrieved from http://www.sudantribune.com/spip.php?iframe&page=imprimable&id_article=16826

de Regt, M. (2009). Refugee, woman and domestic worker: Somali women dealing with dependencies in Yemen. *African and Black Diaspora: An International Journal, 3*(1), 109–121. doi:10.1080/17528630903319904

Deal, J. L. (2010). Torture by *cieng*: Ethical theory meets social practice among the Dinka Agaar of South Sudan. *American Anthropologist, 112*(4), 563–575.

Deng, F. M. (1984). *The Dinka of the Sudan*. Prospect Heights, IL: Waveland Press.

Deng, F. M. (1995). *War of visions: Conflict of identities in the Sudan*. Washington, DC: The Brookings Institution.

Deng, F. M. (1998). The cow and the thing called 'what': Dinka cultural perspectives on wealth and poverty. *Journal of International Affairs, 52*(1), 101–129.

Deng, F. M. (2007, March 12–13). *Southern Sudan and the cultural change of governance*. Paper presented at the Conference on the Current Peace and Security Challenges in the Horn of Africa, Addis Ababa.

Deng, F. M. (2009). Francis Mading Deng. In W. L. Twining (Ed.), *Human rights: Southern voices: Francis Deng, Abdullahi An-Na'im, Yash Ghai, Upendra Baxi* (pp. 4–52). Cambridge: Cambridge University Press.

Denzin, N. K. (1995). On hearing the voices of educational research. *Curriculum Inquiry, 25*(3), 313–329.

Denzin, N. K., & Lincoln, Y. (2008). Introduction: The discipline and practice of qualitative research. In N. K. Denzin & Y. Lincoln (Eds.), *Collecting and interpreting qualitative materials* (3rd ed., pp. 1–43). London: Sage.

Denzin, N. K., Lincoln, Y. S., & Smith, L. T. (Eds.). (2008). *Handbook of critical and indigenous methodologies*. Thousand Oaks, CA: Sage.

Department of Immigration and Citizenship. (2006). *Citizenship: Becoming an Australian citizen*. Retrieved June 21, 2011, from http://www.citizenship.gov.au/

Department of Immigration and Citizenship. (2009). *The Special Humanitarian Program (SHP)*. Retrieved from http://www.immi.gov.au/media/publications/pdf/shp-client-info-sheet.pdf

Department of Immigration and Citizenship. (2011a). *Report settlers by country of birth (settlement) by calendar year of arrival from 01-Jan-1995 to 01-Jan-2011*. Retrieved March 7, 2011, from http://www.immi.gov.au/settlement/

Department of Immigration and Citizenship. (2011b). *Report settlers by country of birth (settlement) by calendar year of arrival from 01-Jan-1995 to 01-Jan-2011 limited by ethnicity (direct): Dinka (Sudanese)*. Retrieved March 7, 2011, from http://www.immi.gov.au/settlement/

Department of Immigration and Citizenship. (2011c). *Report settlers by country of birth (settlement) by calendar year of arrival from 01-Jan-1995 to 01-Jan-2011 limited by state (South Australia) all local government areas*. Retrieved March 7, 2011, from http://www.immi.gov.au/settlement/

Derrida, J. (1976). *Of grammatology* (G. C. Spivak, Trans., 1st ed.). Baltimore, MA: John Hopkins University Press.

Derrida, J. (1984). Deconstruction and the other: An interview with Jacques Derrida. In R. Kearney & P. Ricoeur (Eds.), *Dialogues with contemporary continental thinkers in the phenomenological heritage: Paul Ricouer, Emmanuel Levinas, Herbert Marcuse, Stanislas Breton, Jacques Derrida* (pp. 107–126). Manchester: Manchester University Press.

Derrida, J. (1988). The politics of friendship. *The Journal of Philosophy, 85*(11), 632–644.

Derrida, J. (1994). *Specters of Marx: The state of the debt, the work of mourning and the new international* (P. Kamuf, Trans.). London: Routledge.

Derrida, J. (2001). *On cosmpolitanism and forgiveness*. London: Routledge.

Derrida, J. (2005). *The politics of friendship* (G. Collins, Trans.). New York, NY: Verso.

Deutsch, C. P. (1981). The behavioral scientists: Insider and outsider. *Journal of Social Issues, 37*, 172–191.

Dewey, J. (1981). *The later works, 1925–1953*. Carbondale, IL: Southern Illinois University Press.

Donnan, H., & Wilson, T. M. (1999). *Borders: Frontiers of identity, nation and state*. Oxford: Berg Publishers.

Drotbohm, H. (2009). Horizons of long-distance intimacies: Reciprocity, contribution and disjuncture in Cape Verde. *The History of the Family, 14*(2), 132–149.

Dube, S. (1999). Travelling light: Missionary musings, colonial cultures and anthropological anxieties. In R. Kaur & J. Hutnyk (Eds.), *Travel worlds: Journeys in contemporary cultural politics* (pp. 29–50). London: Zed Books.

Due, C. (2008). 'Who are strangers?': 'Absorbing' Sudanese refugees into a white Australia. *ACRAWSA E-Journal, 4*(1), 1–13. Retrieved from http://www.acrawsa.org.au/ejournalFiles/Volume%204,%20Number%201,%202008/ClemenceDue.pdf

Duneier, M., & Back, L. (2006). Voices from the sidewalk: Ethnography and writing race. *Ethnic and Racial Studies, 29*(3), 543–565.

Dunham, C. C., Cannon, J. H., & Dietz, B. (2004). Representing the other in sociology of the family texts. *Teaching Sociology, 32*(4), 374–384. doi:10.1177/0092055x0403200403

Dyck, I., & McLaren, A. T. (2004). Telling it like it is?: Constructing accounts of settlement with immigrant and refugee women in Canada. *Gender, Place and Culture, 11*(4), 513–534.

Edward, J. K. (2007). *Sudanese women refugees: Transformations and future imaginings*. New York, NY: Palgrave Macmillan.

Edwards, J. (2000). *Born and bred: Idioms of kinship and new reproductive technologies in England.* Oxford: Oxford University Press.

Ellis, C. (2007). Telling secrets, revealing lives: Relational ethics in research with intimate others. *Qualitative Inquiry, 13*(3), 3–29.

Eriksen, T. H. (2010). Ethnicity, race and nation. In M. Guibernau & J. Rex (Eds.), *The ethnicity reader: Nationalism, multiculturalism and migration* (pp. 46–53). Cambridge: Polity Press.

Estima, C. (2006). *Performing what we applaud, applauding what we perform: Exploring the narratives of gendered ethnicities on the Toronto stage, post 9/11* (Masters thesis). York University, Toronto.

Etking, A. (2009). Post-Soviet hauntology: Cultural memory of the Soviet terror. *Constellations, 16*(1), 182–200.

Evans-Pritchard, E. E. (1940). The Nuer of the southern Sudan. In M. Fortes & E. E. Evans-Pritchard (Eds.), *African political systems* (pp. 271–296). London: Oxford Univeristy Press.

Evans-Pritchard, E. E. (1990 [1951]). *Kinship and marriage among the Nuer*. Gloucestershire: Clarendon Press.

Evans-Pritchard, E. E. (2010 [1940]). The Nuer: Time and space. In R. R. Grinker, S. C. Lubkemann, & C. B. Steiner (Eds.), *Perspectives on Africa: A reader in culture, history, and representation* (2nd ed., pp. 71–82). West Sussex: Wiley-Blackwell.

Fabian, J. (1983). *Time and the emerging other*. New York, NY: Columbia University Press.

Faist, T. (2000). Transnationalization in international migration: Implications for the study of citizenship and culture. *Ethnic and Racial Studies, 23*(2), 189–222.

Fanjoy, M. (2008). *Conceptions of belonging among Sudanese refugees in Canada: Evidence and methods*. Retrieved from http://www.utoronto.ca/ethnicstudies/Fanjoy_2008.pdf

Faubion, J. D. (2001). Toward an anthropology of ethics: Foucault and the pedagogies of autopoiesis. *Representations, 74*(1), 83–104.

Fick, M. (2009). S. Sudan census bureau releases offical results amidst ongoing census controversy. *Enough!* Retrieved from http://www.enoughproject.org/blogs/s-sudan-census-bureau-releases-official-results-amidst-ongoing-census-controversy

Finch, J., & Mason, J. (1993). *Negotiating family responsibilities*. London: Routledge.

Finch, J., & Mason, J. (2000). *Passing on: Kinship and inheritance in England.* London: Routledge.

Finke, J. (2000–2003). *Kenya's ethno-linguistic groups: The Nilotes*. Retrieved November 10, 2010, from http://www.bluegecko.org/kenya/contexts/nilotes.htm

Fleischer, A. (2007). Family, obligations, and migration: The role of kinship in Cameroon. *Demographic Research, 16*(13), 413–440.

Fortier, A.-M. (1999). Re-membering places and the performance of belonging(s). *Theory, Culture and Society, 16*(2), 41–64.

Fortier, A.-M. (2000). *Migrant belongings: Memory, space, identity*. Oxford: Berg.

Fortier, A.-M. (2006). Community, belonging and intimate ethnicity. *Modern Italy, 11*(1), 63–77.

Foucault, M. (1982). Afterword: The subject and power. In H. L. Dreyfus & P. Rabinow (Eds.), *Michel Foucault: Beyond structuralism and hermeneutics* (pp. 208–226). London: Harvester Wheatsheaf.

Foucault, M. (1991). Truth and power. In P. Rabinow (Ed.), *The Foucault reader* (pp. 51–75). London: Penguin.

Fox, G. (2011). Remembering ubuntu: Memory, sovereignty and reconciliation in post-Apartheid South Africa. *Platforum: Journal of Graduate Students in Anthropology, 12*, 100–117.

Fox, J. E., & Jones, D. (2013). Migration, everyday life and the ethnicity bias. *Ethnicities, 13*(4), 385–400.

Fozdar, F., & Spittles, B. (2009). The Australian citizenship test: Process and rhetoric. *Australian Journal of Politics & History, 55*(4), 496–512. doi:10.1111/j.1467-8497.2009.01529.x

Frankenberg, R. (1993). *White women, race matters: The social construction of whiteness*. Minneapolis, MN: University of Minnesota Press.

Franzosi, R. (1998). Narrative analysis—or why (and how) sociologists should be interested in narrative. *Annual Review of Sociology, 24*(1), 517–554.

Freiwald, B. T. (2001). Becoming and be/longing: Kate Bornstein's *Gender outlaw* and *My gender workbook*. *Biography, 24*(1), 35–56.

Frosh, S. (2011). The relational ethics of conflict and identity. *Psychoanalysis, Culture & Society, 16*(3), 225–243.

Gade, C. B. N. (2010). *Ubuntu and the South African truth and reconciliation process* (Masters thesis). Aarhus University, Denmark. Retrieved from http://www.konfliktloesning.dk/files/UBUNTU_2010_Chr._Gade_speciale.pdf

Galaty, J. G. (1993). 'The eye that wants a person, where can it not see?': Inclusion, exclusion, and boundary shifters in Maasai identity. In T. Spear & R. Waller (Eds.), *Being Maasai: Ethnicity and identity in East Africa* (pp. 174–194). London: James Currey Ltd.

Gamson, J. (1998). *Freaks talk back: Tabloid talk shows and sexual nonconformity*. Chicago, IL: University of Chicago Press.

Gandhi, L. (2006). *Affective communities: Anticolonial thought, fin-de-siècle radicalism, and the politics of friendship*. Durham, NC: Duke University Press.

Garang, J. (Ed.). (1992). *The call for democracy in Sudan*. London: Kegan Paul International.

Garbutt, R. (2009). Social inclusion and local practices of belonging. *Cosmopolitan Civil Societies: An Interdisciplinary Journal, 1*(3), 84–108.

Gedalof, I. (2009). Birth, belonging and migrant mothers: Narratives of reproduction in feminist migration studies. *Feminist Review, 93*, 81–100.

Geschiere, P. (2009). *The perils of belonging: Autochthony, citizenship, and exclusion in Afirca & Europe*. Chicago, IL: University of Chicago Press.

Geschiere, P., & Gugler, J. (1998a). Introduction: The urban-rural connection: Changing issues of belonging and identification. *Africa: Journal of the International African Institute, 68*(3), 309–319.

Geschiere, P., & Nyamnjoh, F. (1998). Witchcraft as an issue in the 'politics of belonging': Democratization and urban migrants' involvement with the home village. *African Studies Review, 41*(3), 69–91.

Geschiere, P., & Nyamnjoh, F. (2000). Capitalism and autochthony: The seesaw of mobility and belogning. *Public Culture, 12*(2), 423–452.

Giddens, A. (1991). *Modernity and self-identity: Self and society in the late modern age*. Cambridge: Polity.

Gikandi, S. (1991). The epistemology of translation: Ngũgĩ, Matigari, and the politics of language. *Research in African Literatures, 22*(4), 161–167.

Gikandi, S. (2010). Between roots and routes: Cosmopolitanism and the claims of locality. In J. Wilson, C. Sandru, & S. L. Welsh (Eds.), *Rerouting the postcolonial: New directions for the new millennium* (pp. 22–35). Oxon: Routledge.

Gilroy, P. (1990). Nationalism, history, and ethnic absolutism. *History Workshop Journal, 30*, 114–120.

Gilroy, P. (1993). *The Black Atlantic: Modernity and double consciousness*. Cambridge: Harvard University Press.

Gilroy, P. (2000). *Against race: Imagining political culture beyond the color line*. Cambridge, MA: The Belknap Press of Harvard University Press.

Gilroy, P. (2003). Race is ordinary: Britain's post-colonial melancholia. *Philosophia Africana, 6*(1), 31–45.

Gilroy, P. (2005). A new cosmopolitanism. *Interventions: The International Journal of Postcolonial Studies, 7*(3), 287–292.

Ginsberg, E. K. (1996). Introduction: The politics of passing. In E. K. Ginsberg (Ed.), *Passing and the fictions of identity* (pp. 1–18). Durham, NC: Duke University Press.

Giroux, H. A. (1993). Living dangerously: Identity politics and the new cultural racism: Towards a critical pedagogy of representation. *Cultural Studies, 7*(1), 1–27.

Giroux, H. A. (2006). Reading Hurricane Katrina: Race, class, and the biopolitics of disposability. *College Literature, 33*(3), 171–196.

Giulianotti, R., & Robertson, R. (2004). The globalization of football: A study in the glocalization of the 'serious life'. *The British Journal of Sociology, 55*(4), 545–568.

Giulianotti, R., & Robertson, R. (2006). Glocalization, globalization and migration: The case of Scottish football supporters in North America. *International Sociology, 21*(2), 171–198.

Giulianotti, R., & Robertson, R. (2007a). Forms of glocalization: Globalization and the migration strategies of Scottish football fans in North America. *Sociology, 41*(1), 133–152.

Giulianotti, R., & Robertson, R. (2007b). Recovering the social: Globalization, football and transnationalism. *Global Networks, 7*(2), 144–186.

Glick Schiller, N., Basch, L., & Blanc-Szanton, C. (1992). Transnationalism: A new analytic framework for understanding migration. *Annals of the New York Academy of Sciences, 645*(1), 1–24.

Glissant, E. (1987). *Poetics of relation.* Ann Arbor, MI: University of Michigan.

Goody, J. (1969). *Comparative studies in kinship.* London: Routledge and Kegan Paul.

Gordon, A. F. (2008 [1997]). *Ghostly matters: Hauntings and the sociological imagination.* Minneapolis, MN: University of Minnesota Press.

Griffith, A. I. (1998). Insider/outsider: Epistemological privilege and mothering work. *Human Studies, 21*, 361–376.

Grossberg, L. (1996). Identity and cultural studies—Is that all there is? In S. Hall & P. Du Gay (Eds.), *Questions of cultural identity* (pp. 87–107). London: Sage.

Guerin, B., Guerin, P., Abdi, A., & Diiriye, R. O. (2003). Identity and community: Somali children's adjustments to life in the Western world. In J. Gao, R. Le Heron, & J. Logie (Eds.), *Windows on a changing world* (pp. 184–188). Aukland: New Zealand Geographical Society.

Guerin, P., & Guerin, B. (2007). Research with refugee communities: Going around in circles with methodology. *The Australian Community Psychologist, 19*(1), 150–162.

Gugler, J. (2002). The son of the hawk does not remain abroad: The urban-rural connection in Africa. *African Studies Review, 45*(1), 21–41.

Guibernau, M. (2010). The concept of ethnicity. In M. Guibernau & J. Rex (Eds.), *The ethnicity reader: Nationalism, multiculturalism and migration* (pp. 13–15). Cambridge: Polity Press.

Guibernau, M., & Rex, J. (2010). Introduction. In M. Guibernau & J. Rex (Eds.), *The ethnicity reader: Nationalism, multiculturalism and migration* (pp. 1–9). Cambridge: Polity Press.

Gupta, A., & Ferguson, J. (1997a). Beyond 'culture': Space, identity, and the politics of difference. In A. Gupta & J. Ferguson (Eds.), *Culture, power, place: Explorations in critical anthropology* (pp. 33–51). Durham, NC: Duke University Press.

Gupta, A., & Ferguson, J. (1997b). Culture, power, place: Ethnography and the end of an era. In A. Gupta & J. Ferguson (Eds.), *Culture, power, place: Explorations in critical anthropology* (pp. 1–29). Durham, NC: Duke University Press.

Gupta, A., & Ferguson, J. (Eds.). (1997c). *Anthropological location: Boundaries and grounds of a field of science.* Berkeley, CA: University of California Press.

Gurtong. (2011). *Dinka* (Jieng, Muony-Jang). Retrieved August 10, 2011, from http://www.gurtong.net/Peoples/PeoplesProfiles/DinkaJieng/tabid/189/Default.aspx

Haddad, E. (2003). Refugee protection: A clash of values. *The International Journal of Human Rights, 7*(3), 1–26.

Hage, G. (2000). *White nation: Fantasies of white supremacy in a multicultural society.* Annandale, NSW: Routledge.

Hage, G. (2002). Citizenship and honourability: Belonging to Australia today. In G. Hage (Ed.), *Arab-Australians today: Citizenship and belonging* (pp. 1–15). Carlton South: Melbourne University.

Hage, G. (2003). *Against paranoid nationalism: Searching for hope in a shrinking society.* Annandale, NSW: Pluto Press Australia.

Hage, G. (2009, October 13). *Negotiating the other: One more effort to exorcise the colonial evil spirit.* Workshop, University of South Australia, Adelaide.

Haggis, J., & Schech, S. (2010). Refugees, settlement processes and citizenship making: An Australian case study. *National Identities, 12*(4), 365–379.

Halfmann, J. (1998). Citizenship universalism, migration and the risks of exclusion. *The British Journal of Sociology, 49*(4), 513–533.

Hall, S. (1993). Culture, community, nation. *Cultural Studies, 7*(3), 349–363.

Hall, S. (1996). Introduction: Who needs 'identity'? In S. Hall & P. Du Gay (Eds.), *Questions of cultural identity* (pp. 1–17). London: Sage.

Hall, S. (2000). Old and new identities, old and new ethnicities. In L. Back & J. Solomos (Eds.), *Theories of race and racism: A reader* (pp. 144–153). London: Routledge.

Hall, S. (2002). Political belonging in a world of multiple identities. In S. Vertovec & R. Cohen (Eds.), *Conceiving cosmopolitanism: Theory, context and practice* (pp. 25–31). Oxford: Oxford University Press.

Halpern, J., & Weinstein, H. M. (2004). Rehumanizing the other: Empathy and reconciliation. *Human Rights Quarterly, 26*(3), 561–583.

Hand, F. (2007). Story-telling as an antidote to disempowerment. *Afroeuropa: Journal of Afroeuropean Studies, 1*(1).

Haniff, N. Z. (1985). Toward a native anthropology: Methodological notes on a study of successful Caribbean women by an insider. *Anthropology and Humanism Quarterly, 10*, 107–113.

Hansen, T. B., & Stepputat, F. (Eds.). (2005). *Sovereign bodies: Citizens, migrants, and states in the postcolonial world.* Princeton, NJ: Princeton University Press.

Hanson-Easey, S., & Augoustinos, M. (2010). Out of Africa: Accounting for refugee policy and the language of causal attribution. *Discourse Society, 21*(3), 296–323.

Haraway, D. (1991). *Simians, cyborgs and women: The reinvention of nature*. New York, NY: Routledge.

Haraway, D. (2003). *The companion species manifesto: Dogs, people, and significant otherness.* Chicago, IL: Prickly Paradigm Press.

Harris, A., & Nyuon, N. (2010). Working it both ways: Intercultural collaboration and the performativity of identity. *Australiasian Review of African Studies, 31*(1), 62–81.

Harris, C. C. (1990). *Kinship.* Milton Keynes: Open University Press.

Hart, L. K. (2006). *Against hauntology and historicide: Urban indigeneity in the white imagining.* Retrieved from http://julieshiels.com.au/street/Hauntology-and-Historicide.pdf

Hart, M. (2005). The nomad at home. In M. Hart & M. Ben-Yoseph (Eds.), *Psychological, political, and cultural meanings of home* (pp. 127–141). Binghamton, NY: The Haworth Press.

Hartnell, H. E. (2006). Belonging: Citizenship and migration in the European Union and in Germany. *Berkeley Journal of International Law, 24*(1), 330–400.

Hegel, G. W. F. (1975 [1830]). *Lectures on the philosophy of world history: Introduction* (H. B. Nisbet, Trans.). Cambridge: Cambridge Univeristy Press.

Heidegger, M. (1962). *Being and time*. Oxford: Blackwell Publishing.

Henderson, M. G. (1995a). Introduction: Borders, boundaires, and frame(work)s. In M. G. Henderson (Ed.), *Borders, boundaries, and frames: Essays in cultural criticism and cultural studies* (pp. 1–32). New York, NY: Routledge.

Henderson, M. G. (Ed.). (1995b). *Borders, boundaries, and frames: Essays in cultural criticism and cultural studies*. New York, NY: Routledge.

Herod, A. (1999). Reflections on interviewing foreign elites: Praxis, positionality, validity, and the cult of the insider. *Geoforum, 30*, 313–327.

Herrera, G. (2013). Gender and international migration: Contributions and cross-fertilizations. *Annual Review of Sociology, 39*, 471–489.

Hickman, M. J., & Walter, B. (1995). Deconstructing whiteness: Irish women in Britain. *Feminist Review, 50*(Summer), 5–19.

Hobbs, D. (1998). Going down the glocal: The local context of organised crime. *The Howard Journal, 37*(4), 407–422.

Hofmeyr, M. (2007). From hauntology to a new animism? Nature and culture in Heinz Kimmerle's intercultural philosophy. *The Journal for Transdisciplinary Research in Southern Africa, 3*(1), 1–38.

Holland, N. J. (2001). The death of the other/father: A feminist reading of Derrida's hauntology. *Hypatia, 16*(1), 64–71.

Holt, P., & Daly, M. (1988). *A history of the Sudan: From the coming of Islam to the present day* (4th ed.). Essex: Longman Group.

Holý, L. (1996). *Anthropological perspectives on kinship*. London: Pluto Press.

hooks, b. (1984). *From margin to center*. Boston, MA: South End Press.

hooks, b. (1989). *Talking back: Thinking feminist, thinking black*. Boston, MA: South End Press.

hooks, b. (1990). *Yearning: Race, gender, and cultural politics*. Boston, MA: South End Press.

hooks, b. (2009). *Belonging: A culture of place*. New York, NY: Routledge.

Hopkins, G. (2010). A changing sense of Somaliness: Somali women in London and Toronto. *Gender, Place and Culture, 17*(4), 519–538.

Howe, S. (2003). Edward Said: The traveller and the exile. *OpenDemocracy: Free Thinking for the World*. Retrieved from http://www.opendemocracy.net/node/1516

Howell, S. (2001). Self-conscious kinship: Some contested values in Norwegian transnational adoption. In S. Franklin & S. McKinnon (Eds.), *Relative values: Reconfiguring kinship studies* (pp. 203–223). Durham, NC: Duke University Press.

Human Rights Watch. (2002). *Hidden in plain view: Refugees living without protection in Nairobi and Kampala*. Retrieved July 29, 2010, from http://www.unhcr.org/refworld/docid/3e314172e.html

Humphrey, C. (2007). Insider-outsider: Activating the hyphen. *Action Research, 5*(1), 11–26.

Hutchinson, S. (1996). *Nuer dilemmas: Coping with money, war, and the state*. Berkeley, CA: University of California Press.

Hutchinson, S. (2000). Identity and substance: The broadening bases of relatedness among the Nuer of southern Sudan. In J. Carsten (Ed.), *Cultures of relatedness: New approaches to the study of kinship* (pp. 55–72). Cambridge: Cambridge University Press.

Hutchinson, S. (2001). A curse from god? Religious and political dimensions of the post-1991 rise of ethnic violence in South Sudan. *The Journal of Modern African Studies, 39*(2), 307–331.

Hutchinson, S. (2007). 'Food itself is fighting with us': A comparative analysis of the impact of Sudan's civil war on South Sudanese civilian populations located in the north and the south. In V. Broch-Due (Ed.), *Violence and belonging: The quest for identity in post-colonial Africa* (pp. 131—152). New York, NY: Routledge.

Hyde, R. (2009, October). Surviving anorexia nervosa. *Adelaide's Child: The Best Guide for Parents, 8*, 14.

Ifekwunigwe, J. O. (1999). *Scattered belongings: Cultural paradoxes of 'race,' nation and gender*. London: Routledge.

Ignatieff, M. (1993). *Blood and belonging: Journeys into the new nationalism*. New York, NY: Farrar, Straus & Giroux.

Ilcan, S. (2002). *Longing in belonging: The cultural politics of settlement*. London: Praeger.

Inglis, T. (2008). *Global Ireland: Same difference*. New York, NY: Routledge.

Inglis, T. (2009). *Local belonging, identities and sense of place in contemporary Ireland* (IBIS Discussion Paper: Politics and Identity Series; 4). University College Dublin, Institute for British-Irish Studies, Ireland. Retrieved from http://irserver.ucd.ie/dspace/bitstream/10197/2414/1/P%26D_Disscussion_Paper_4.pdf

Irigary, L. (2002). *The way of love*. London: Continuum.

Jackson, H. C. (1923). The Nuer of the Upper Nile Province. *Sudan Notes Rec, 32*, 59–107.

Jackson Jr., J. L. (2005). A little black magic. *The South Atlantic Quarterly, 104*(3), 393–402.

Jackson, M. (1995). *At home in the world*. Sydney: HarperPerennial.

Jacobsen, K. (1996). Factors influencing the policy responses of host governments to mass refugee influxes. *International Migration Review, 30*(3), 655–678.

Jeppsson, O., & Hjern, A. (2005). Traumatic stress in context: A study of unaccompanied minors from southern Sudan. In D. Ingleby (Ed.), *Forced migration and mental health: Rethinking the care of refugees and displaced persons* (pp. 67–80). New York, NY: Springer.

Johnson, D. H. (2003). *The root causes of Sudan's civil wars*. Oxford: James Currey.

Jok, J. M. (1999a). Militarism, gender and reproductive suffering: The case of abortion in western Dinka. *Africa, 69*(2), 194–212.

Jok, J. M. (1999b). Militarization and gender violence in South Sudan. *Journal of Asian and African Studies, 34*(4), 427–442.

Jok, J. M. (2007). *Sudan: Race, religion, and violence*. Oxford: Oneworld Publications.

Jones, L. (1967). *Black music*. New York, NY: William Morrow & Company.

Kamwangamalu, N. M. (1999). Ubuntu in South Africa: A sociolinguistic perspective to a pan-African concept. *Critical Arts: A South-North Journal of Cultural and Media Studies, 13*(2), 24–41. Retrieved from http://web.ebscohost.com.ezlibproxy.unisa.edu.au/ehost/detail?vid=4&hid=14&sid=e9a61c15-9118-4fd3-aeda-752a5ab3d360%40sessionmgr15&bdata=JnNpdGU9ZWhvc3QtbGl2ZQ%3d%3d#db=aph&AN=2742897

Kannabiran, K., Vieten, U. M., & Yuval-Davis, N. (2006). Introduction. *Patterns of Prejudice, 40*(3), 189–195.

Kaplan, C. (1994). The politics of location as transnational feminist practice. In I. Grewal & C. Kaplan (Eds.), *Scattered hegemonies: Postmodernity and transnational feminist practices* (pp. 137–152). Minneapolis, MN: University of Minnesota Press.

Kaplan, C. (1996). *Questions of travel: Postmodern discourses of displacement*. Durham, NC: Duke University Press.

Keely, C. B. (1996). How nation-states create and respond to refugee flows. *International Migration Review, 30*(4), 1046–1066.

Keevy, I. (2008). *African philosophical values and constitutionalism: A feminist perspective on ubuntu as a constitutional value* (PhD thesis), University of the Free State, Bloemfontein.

Kelly, R. C. (1985). *The Nuer conquest: The structure and development of an expansionist system*. Ann Arbor, MI: University of Michigan Press.

Kenway, J., Bullen, E., Fahey, J., & Robb, S. (2006). *Haunting the knowledge economy*. Oxon: Routledge.

Kibria, N. (1999). Migration and Vietnamese American women: Remaking ethnicity. In S. Coontz, M. Parson, & G. Raley (Eds.), *American families: A multicultural reader* (pp. 318–330). New York, NY: Routledge.

Kiesinger, C. E. (1998). From interview to story: Writing Abbie's life. *Qualitative Inquiry, 4*(1), 71–95.

Kinnvall, C. (2004). Globalization and religious nationalism: Self, identity, and the search for ontological security. *Political Psychology, 25*(5), 741–767.

Knapp, G.-A. (2005). Race, class, gender: Reclaiming baggage in fast travelling theories. *European Journal of Women's Studies, 12*(3), 249–265.

Kochalumchuvattil, T. (2010). The crisis of identity in Africa: A call for subjectivity. *Kritike: An Online Journal of Philosophy, 1*, 108–122. Retrieved from http://www.kritike.org/journal/issue_7/kochalumchuvattil_june2010.pdf

Kolawole, M. E. M. (1997). *Womanism and African consciousness*. Trenton, NJ: Africa World Press.

König, R. S., & de Regt, M. (2009a). Family dynamics in transnational African migration to Europe: An introduction. *African and Black Diaspora: An International Journal, 3*(1), 1–15. doi:10.1080/17528630903368232

König, R. S., & De Regt, M. (2009b). Special issue. Family dynamics in transnational African migration to europe. *African and Black Diaspora: An International Journal, 3*(1), 1–136.

Krog, A. (2004). *African forgiveness—Too sophisticated for the West*. Opening Speech for the 4th International Literature Festival, Berlin. Retrieved from http://www.literaturfestival.com/intern/reden/krog-engl

Krog, A. (2008). My heart is on my tongue: The untranslated self in a translated world. *Journal of Analytical Psychology, 53*(2), 225–239.

Krog, A. (2009). *Begging to be Black*. Cape Town: Random House.

Krog, A. (2011). In the name of human rights: I say (how) you (should) speak (before I listen). In N. K. Denzin & Y. S. Lincoln (Eds.), *The Sage handbook of qualitative research* (4th ed., pp. 381–386). London: Sage.

Krog, A., Mpolweni-Zantsi, N., & Ratele, K. (2008). The South African Truth and Reconciliation Commission (TRC): Ways of knowing Mrs. Konile. In N. K. Denzin, Y. S. Lincoln, & L. T. Smith (Eds.), *Handbook of critical and indigenous methodologies* (pp. 531–546). Thousand Oaks, CA: Sage.

Kuhn, A. (2002 [1995]). *Family secrets: Acts of memory and imagination*. London: Verso.

Kurien, P. (1999). Gendered ethnicity: Creating a Hindu Indian identity in the United States. *American Behavioral Scientist, 42*(4), 648–670.

Labanyi, J. (2001). Coming to terms with the ghosts of the past: History and spectrality in contemporary Spanish culture. *Arachne @ Rutgers, 1*(1). Retrieved from http://arachne.rutgers.edu/vol1_1labanyi.htm

Labaree, R. V. (2002). The risk of 'going observationalist': Negotiating the hidden dilemmas of being an insider participant observer. *Qualitative Research, 2*(1), 97–122.

Lai, C.-J. (2011, July 11–14). *Infinite haunting: Ethical face and political faces*. Paper presented at the 4th Annual International Conference on Literature, Languages and Linguistics, Athens, Greece.

Lammers, E. (2005). Studying refugees and asylum seekers: Notes on the politics of knowledge. *Global Migration Perspectives, 39*. Retrieved from http://www.gcim.org/attachements/GMP%20No%2039.pdf

Lamont, M., & Molnár, V. (2002). The study of boundaries in the social sciences. *Annual Review of Sociology, 28*, 167–195.

Landau, L. B. (2006). Transplants and transients: Idioms of belonging and dislocation in inner-city Johannesburg. *African Studies Review, 49*(2), 125–145.

Landau, L. B., & Freemantle, I. (2010). Tactical cosmopolitanism and idioms of belonging: Insertion and self-exclusion in Johannesburg. *Journal of Ethnic and Migration Studies, 36*(3), 375–390.

Landau, L. B., & Jacobsen, K. (2004). Refugees in the new Johannesburg. *Forced Migration Review, 19*, 44–46.

Langham, I. (1981). *The building of British social anthropology*. Dordrecht: D. Reidel Publishing Company.

Large, D. (2009). China's Sudan engagement: Changing northern and southern political trajectories in peace and war. *The China Quarterly, 199*, 610–626.

Lee, N., Jackson, S. J., & Lee, K. (2007). South Korea's 'glocal' hero: The Hiddink syndrome and the rearticulation of national citizenship and identity. *Sociology of Sport Journal, 24*, 283–301.

Lefébvre, H. (1991). *The production of space* (D. Nicholson-Smith, Trans.). Oxford: Blackwell Publishing.

Lévi-Strauss, C. (1949 [1969]). *The elementary structures of kinship* (J. H. Bell, J. R. von Sturmer, & R. Needham, Trans.). Boston, MA: Beacon Press.

Lévi-Strauss, C. (1965). The future of kinship studies: The Huxley Memorial Lecture. *Proceedings of the Royal Anthropological Institute of Great Britain and Ireland, 1965*, 13–22.

Lévinas, E. (1991). *Otherwise than being or beyond essence* (A. Lingis, Trans.). Dordrecht: Kluwer Academic Publishers.

Lienhardt, G. (2004 [1958]). The western Dinka. In J. Middleton & D. Tait (Eds.), *Tribes without rulers: Studies in African segmentary systems* (pp. 97–135). London: Routledge.

Lim, S.-L. (2009). 'Loss of connections is death': Transnational family ties among Sudanese refugee families resettling in the United States. *Journal of Cross-Cultural Psychology, 40*(6), 1028–1040.

Limbu, B. (2009). Illegible humanity: The refugee, human rights and the question of representation. *Journal of Refugee Studies, 22*(3), 257–282.

Limerick, B., Burgess-Limerick, T., & Grace, M. (1996). The politics of interviewing: Power relations and accepting the gift. *Qualitative Studies in Education, 9*(4), 449–460.

Lindley, A. (2009). The early-morning phonecall: Remittances from a refugee diaspora perspective. *Journal of Ethnic and Migration Studies, 35*(8), 1315–1334.

Lovejoy, A. O. (2009 [1936]). *The great chain of being: A study of the history of an idea*. New Brunswick, NJ: Transaction Publishers.

Lower, G., & Akerman, P. (2008, November 14). Payback concerns after Sudanese death. *The Australian*. Retrieved from http://www.theaustralian.com.au/news/payback-concerns-after-sudanese-death/story-e6frg6p6-1111118032570

Luttrell, W. (2000). 'Good enough' methods for ethnographic research. *Harvard Educational Review, 70*(4), 499–523.

Macdougall, N. (2008). *Getting to know you: The journey from African refugee to African-Australian* (PhD thesis). Murdoch University, Perth.

Macintyre, S., & Simpson, N. (2009). Consensus and division in Australian citizenship education. *Citizenship Studies, 13*(2), 121–134.

Mading Aweil Website. (2004). Retrieved August 17, 2011, from http://www.madingaweil.com/

Madut-Arop, A. (2006). *Sudan's painful road to peace: A full story of the founding and development of SPLM/SPLA*. Charleston, SC: BookSurge.

Malkki, L. H. (1995a). *Purity and exile: Violence, memory, and national cosmology among Hutu refugees in Tanzania*. Chicago, IL: University of Chicago Press.

Malkki, L. H. (1995b). Refugees and exile: From 'refugee studies' to the national order of things. *Annual Review of Anthropology, 24*, 495–523.

Malkki, L. H. (1996). Speechless emissaries: Refugees, humanitarianism, and dehistoricization. *Cultural Anthropology, 11*(3), 377–404.

Malkki, L. H. (1997). National geographic: The rooting of peoples and the territorialization of national identity among scholars and refugees. In A. Gupta & J. Ferguson (Eds.), *Culture, power place: Explorations in critical anthropology* (pp. 52–74). Durham, NC: Duke University Press.

Mama, A. (2009). *Building excellent, diverse and just communities: A conversation among artists, academics and activists*. Plenary Session at 2011 Annual Meeting of the American Sociological Association, Las Vegas, NV. Retrieved from http://videoarchive.asanet.org/presentations/2009_d1.html

Mann, M. (1997). Has globalization ended the rise and rise of the nation-state? *Review of International Political Economy, 4*(3), 472–496.

Mann, S. A., Grimes, M. D., Kemp, A. A., & Jenkins, P. J. (1997). Paradigm shifts in family sociology? Evidence from three decades of family textbooks. *Journal of Family Issues, 18*(3), 315–349. doi:10.1177/019251397018003005

Mansfield, N. (2008). 'There is a spectre haunting …': Ghosts, their bodies, some philosophers, a novel and the cultural politics of climate change. *Borderlands EJournal, 7*(1). Retrieved from http://www.borderlands.net.au/vol7no1_2008/mansfield_climate.htm

Mares, P. (2002). *Borderline* (2nd ed.). Sydney: University of New South Wales Press.

Marlowe, J. M. (2009a). Accessing 'Authentic' knowledge: *Being* and *doing* with the Sudanese community. *The Australian Community Psychologist, 21*(1), 39–49.

Marlowe, J. M. (2009b). Conceptualising refugee resettlement in contested landscapes. *The Australasian Review of African Studies, 30*(2), 128–151.

Marlowe, J. M. (2010a). Beyond the discourse of trauma: Shifting the focus on Sudanese refugees. *Journal of Refugee Studies, 23*(2), 183–198.

Marlowe, J. M. (2010b). *'Walking the line': Southern Sudanese narratives and responding to trauma* (PhD thesis). Flinders University, Bedford Park, South Australia.

Marshall, T. H. (1998 [1963]). Citizenship and social class. In G. Shafir (Ed.), *The citizenship debates: A reader* (pp. 93–111). Minneapolis, MN: University of Minnesota.

Martin, K. L. (2003). Ways of knowing, ways of being and ways of doing: A theoretical framework and methods for indigenous re-search and indigenist research. *Journal of Australian Studies, 76*, 203–214.

Mason, V. (2007). Children of the 'idea of Palestine': Negotiating identity, belonging and home in the Palestinian diaspora. *Journal of Intercultural Studies, 28*(3), 271–285.

Matereke, K. (2009). 'Embracing the Aussie Identity': Theoretical reflections on challenges and prospects for African-Australian youths. *The Australasian Review of African Studies, 30*(1), 129–143.

Matsuoka, A., & Sorenson, J. (2001). *Ghosts and shadows: Construction of identity and community in an African diaspora*. Toronto: University of Toronto Press.

Mauthner, N., & Doucet, A. (2006 [1998]). Reflections on a voice-centred relational method: Analysing maternal and domestic voices. In J. Ribbens & R. Edwards (Eds.), *Feminist dilemmas in qualitative research: Public knowledge and private lives* (pp. 119–146). London: Sage.

Mauthner, N. S., & Doucet, A. (2003). Reflexive accounts and accounts of reflexivity in qualitative data analysis. *Sociology, 37*(3), 413–431. doi:10.1177/00380385030373002
Maylor, U. (2009). What is the meaning of 'black'? Researching 'black' respondents. *Ethnic and Racial Studies, 32*(2), 369–387.
Mayom, J. P. (2015, October 4). President Kiir creates 28 states of South Sudan. *Gurtong*. Retrieved February 2, 2016, from http://www.gurtong.net/ECM/Editorial/tabid/124/ctl/ArticleView/mid/519/articleId/17532/President-Kiir-Creates-28-States-In-South-Sudan.aspx
Mayom, M. (2009). Northern Bahr El Ghazal State officially rejects population census results. *Gurtong*. Retrieved from http://www.gurtong.net/ECM/Editorial/tabid/124/ctl/ArticleView/mid/519/articleId/141/Northern-Bahr-el-Ghazal-State-Officially-Rejects-Population-Census-Results.aspx
Mbembe, A. (2000). At the edge of the world: Boundaries, territoriality, and sovereignty in Africa. *Public Culture, 12*(1), 259–284.
Mbilinyi, M. (1984). Research priorities in women's studies in eastern Africa. *Women's Studies International Forum, 7*(4), 289–300.
McCarthy, C., & Dimitriadis, G. (2000). Governmentality and the sociology of education: Media, educational policy and the politics of resentment. *British Journal of Sociology of Education, 21*(2), 169–185.
McCrone, D., & Kiely, R. (2000). Nationalism and citizenship. *Sociology, 34*(1), 19–34.
McDowell, D. E. (1995). *'The changing same': Black women's literature, critisicm, and theory*. Bloomington, IN: Indiana University Press.
McLaren, A. T., & Dyck, I. (2004). Mothering, human capital, and the 'ideal immigrant'. *Women's Studies International Forum, 27*, 41–53.
McMaster, D. (2001). *Asylum seekers: Australia's response to refugees*. Carlton South: Melbourne University Press.
Melhuus, M., & Howell, S. (2009). Adoption and assisted conception: One universe of unnatural procreation. An examination of Norwegian legislation. In J. Edwards & C. Salazar (Eds.), *European kinship in the age of biotechnology* (pp. 144–161). Oxford: Berghahn Books.
Mercer, C., Page, B., & Evans, M. (2009). Unsettling connections: Transnational networks, development and African home associations. *Global Networks, 9*(2), 141–161.
Meredith, M. (2005). *The state of Africa: A history of fifty years of independence*. London: Free Press.
Merleau-Ponty, M. (2002 [1962]). *Phenomenology of perception*. London: Routledge.
Merton, R. (1972). Insiders and outsiders: A chapter in the sociology of knowledge. *American Journal of Sociology, 78*(July), 9–47.
Metz, T., & Gaie, J. B. R. (2010). The African ethic of *ubuntu/botho*: Implications for research on morality. *Journal of Moral Education, 39*(3), 273–290.
Michaels, A. (1996). *Fugitive pieces*. Toronto, ON: McClelland & Stewart.
Miller, D. (2007). What is a relationship? Is kinship negotiated experience? *Ethnos, 72*(4), 535–554.
Mire, A. (2001). In/through the bodies of women: Rethinking gender in African politics. *Polis: Cameroonian Political Science Review, 8*(Special issue), 1–19.
Mitchell, T. (1998). *Australian hip hop as a 'glocal' subculture*. Paper presented at the Ultimo Series Seminar, University of Technology, Sydney.
Mkabela, Q. (2005). Using the Afrocentric method in researching indigenous African culture. *The Qualitative Report, 10*(1), 178–189.
Modood, T. (2005). *Multicultural politics: Racism, ethnicity, and Muslims in Britain*. Minneapolis, MN: University of Minnesota Press.
Mohanty, C. T. (1991). Under western eyes: Feminist scholarship and colonial discourses. In C. T. Mohanty, A. Russo, & L. Torres (Eds.), *Third World women and the politics of feminism* (pp. 51–80). Bloomington, IN: Indiana University Press.
Mohanty, C. T. (1995). Feminst encounters: Locating the politics of experience. In L. J. Nicholson & S. Seidman (Eds.), *Social postmodernism: Beyond identity politics* (pp. 68–86). Cambridge: Cambridge University Press.
Moore, H. (1988). *Feminism and anthropology*. Cambridge: Polity Press.

Moorti, S. (2003). Desperately seeking an identity: Diasporic cinema and the articulation of transnational kinship. *International Journal of Cultural Studies, 6*(3), 355–376.

Moran, A. (2002). As Australia decolonizes: Indigenizing settler nationalism and the challenges of settler/indigenous relations. *Ethnic and Racial Studies, 25*(6), 1013–1042.

Moran, A. (2005a). *Australia: Nation, belonging, and globalization*. New York, NY: Routledge.

Moran, A. (2005b). White Australia, settler nationalism and Aboriginal assimilation. *Australian Journal of Politics and History, 51*(2), 168–193.

Moreton-Robinson, A. (2003). I still call Australia home: Indigenous belonging and place in a white postcolonizing society. In S. Ahmed, C. Castañeda, A.-M. Fortier, & M. Sheller (Eds.), *Uprootings/ regroundings: Questions of home and migration* (pp. 23–40). Oxford: Berg.

Morgan, H. L. (1997 [1871]). *Systems of consanguinity and affinity of the human family*. Nebraska, NE: University of Nebraska Press.

Morrison, T. (2006 [1987]). *Beloved*. London: Everyman's Library.

Morrison, T. (2008). What the Black woman thinks about women's lib. In C. C. Denard (Ed.), *What moves at the margin: Selected nonfiction* (pp. 18–29). Jackson, MS: University Press of Mississippi.

Motha, S. (2010). 'Begging to be black': Liminality and critique in post-Apartheid South Africa. *Theory, Culture and Society, 27*(7–8), 285–305.

Mouffe, C. (1994). For a politics of nomadic identity. In G. Robertson, M. Mash, L. Tickner, J. Bird, B. Curtis, & T. Putnam (Eds.), *Travellers' tales: Narratives of home and displacement* (pp. 103–113). London: Routledge.

Munos, D. (2011). Gender, migration and agency: Developing a 'hauntology' of new becomings in Shauna Sigh Baldwin's 'Devika' and in Ginu Kamani's 'Just between Indians'. *Acta Scientiarum. Language and Culture, 33*(1), 23–29.

Nancy, J.-L. (2000). *Being singular plural* (R. D. Richardon & A. E. O'Byrne, Trans.). Stanford: Stanford University Press.

Naples, N. A. (1997). A feminist revisiting of the insider/outsider debate: The 'outsider phenomenon' in rural Iowa. In R. Hertz (Ed.), *Reflexivity and voice* (pp. 70–94). Thousand Oaks, CA: Sage.

Ndhlovu, F. (2009). The limitations of language and nationality as prime markers of African diaspora identities in the state of Victoria. *African Identities, 7*(1), 17–32.

Nietzsche, F. (1967). *On the genealogy of morals*. New York, NY: Vintage.

Nsamenang, A. B. (2008). In a globalised world, local culture must be the anchor of identity. *Early Childhood Matters, 111*, 13–17.

Nussbaum, B. (2003). African culture and *ubuntu*: Reflections of a South African in America. *Perspectives, 17*(1), 1–12.

Nyaba, P. (2000). *The politics of liberation in South Sudan: An insider's view*. Kampala: Fountain Publishers.

Nyamnjoh, F., & Rowlands, M. (1998). Elite associations and the politics of belonging in Cameroon. *Africa: Journal of the International African Institute, 68*(3), 320–337.

Nzegwu, N. (1996). Questions of identity and inheritance: A critical review of Kwame Anthony Appiah's *In my father's house*. *Hypatia, 11*(1), 175–201.

Nzegwu, N. (2003). Sisterhood. In O. Oyemúmí (Ed.), *African women & feminism* (pp. vii–viii). Trenton, NJ: Africa World Press.

Nzegwu, N. (2004). Cultural epistemologies of motherhood. *JENdA: A Journal of Culture and African Women Studies, 5*. Retrieved from http://www.africaknowledgeproject.org/index.php/jenda/article/ view/92

O'Neill, M., & Spybey, T. (2003). Global refugees, exile, displacement and belonging. *Sociology, 37*(1), 7–12. doi:10.1177/0038038503037001385

O'Riely, M. F. (2007). Postcolonial haunting: Anxiety, affect and the situated encounter. *Postcolonial Text, 3*(4), 1–15.

Oelofsen, R. (2009). De- and rehumanization in the wake of atrocities. *South African Journal of Philosophy, 28*(2), 178–188.

Ong, A. (2003). *Buddha is hiding: Refugees, citizenship, the new America*. Berkeley, CA: University of California Press.

Oommen, T. K. (1997). *Citizenship, nationality, and ethnicity: Reconciling competing identities*. Cambridge: Polity Press.

Oso, L., & Ribas-Mateos, N. (Eds.). (2013). *The international handbook on gender, migration and transnationalism: Global and development perspectives*. Cheltenham, UK: Edward Elgar.

Overgaard, S. (2004). *Husserl and Heidegger on being in the world*. Dordrecht: Kluwer Academic Publishers.

Oyewúmí, O. (2000). Family bonds/conceptual binds: African notes on feminist epistemologies. *Signs: Journal of Women in Culture and Society, 25*(4), 1093–1098.

Oyewúmí, O. (2002). Conceptualizing gender: The Eurocentric foundations of feminist concepts and the challenge of African epistemologies. *JENdA: A Journal of Culture and African Women Studies, 2*(1). Retrieved from http://www.codesria.org/IMG/pdf/OYEWUMI.pdf

Oyewúmí, O. (2003a). Abiyamo: Theorizing African motherhood. *JENdA: A Journal of Culture and African Women Studies, 4*. Retrieved from http://www.africaknowledgeproject.org/index.php/jenda/article/view/79

Oyewúmí, O. (2003b). Introduction: Feminism, sisterhood, and *other* foreign relations. In O. Oyewúmí (Ed.), *African women & feminism* (pp. 1–24). Trenton, NJ: Africa World Press.

Oyewúmí, O. (2003c). The white woman's burden: African women in western feminist discourse. In O. Oyewúmí (Ed.), *African women & feminism* (pp. 25–44). Trenton, NJ: Africa World Press.

Palmary, I. (2011). 'In your experience': Research as gendered cultural translation. *Gender, Place and Culture, 18*(1), 99–113.

Parsons, T. (1943). The kinship system of the contemporary United States. *American Anthropologist, 45*(1), 22–38.

Peach, C. (2000). Discovering white ethnicity and parachuted plurality. *Progress in Human Geography, 24*(4), 620–626.

Pearson, D. (2005). Citizenship, identity and belonging: Addressing the mythologies of the unitary nation state in Aotearoa/New Zealand. In J. H.-f. Liu, T. McCreanor, T. McIntosh, & T. Teaiwa (Eds.), *New Zealand identities: Departures and destinations* (pp. 21–37). Wellington: Victoria University Press.

Peterson, C. (2007). *Kindred specters: Death, mourning, and American affinity*. Minneapolis, MN: University of Minnesota Press.

Pettman, J. (1992). *Living in the margins: Racism, sexism and feminism in Australia*. St Leonards: Allen and Unwin.

Philip, M. N. (1992). *Frontiers: Essays and writings on racism and culture*. Stratford, Ontario: Mercury.

Phillips, M. (2010). *Dropped from the moon: (Mis)representations of 'African' refugees in Australia*. Paper presented at the 33rd AFSAAP Conference: Engaging Africa/Engaging Africans: Knowledge, Representation, Politics, Victoria University, Melbourne.

Pickard, J. (2006). *Southern Sudanese concepts of cieng/ciang in America: The transcultural experience of well-being and adaptive functioning* (PhD thesis). University of South Dakota, Vermillion, SD.

Pollock, G. (1994). Territories of desire: Reconsiderations of an African childhood. In G. Robertson, M. Mash, L. Tickner, J. Bird, B. Curtis, & T. Putnam (Eds.), *Travellers' tales: Narratives of home and displacement* (pp. 63–89). London: Routledge.

Portelli, A. (1991). *The death of Luigi Trastulli, and other stories: Form and meaning in oral history*. Albany, NY: State University of New York Press.

Portelli, A. (1997). *The battle of Valle Giulia: Oral history and the art of dialogue*. Wisconsin, WI: University of Wisconsin Press.

Porter, E. (2007). Women's truth narratives: The power of compassionate listening. *Critical Half: Bi-Annual Journal of Women for Women International, 5*(2), 21–25.

Pries, L. (2015). Boundaries of belonging, migration and types of social spaces. In U. Lehmkuhl, H.-J. Lüsebrink, & L. McFalls (Eds.), *Of 'contact zones' and 'liminal spaces': Mapping the everyday life of cultural translation* (pp. 29–48). Munster, Germany: Waxmann Verlag.

Pries, L., & Pauls, R. (2013). Introduction: New dynamics of migration and belonging. In L. Pries (Ed.), *Shifting boundaries of belonging and new migration dynamics in Europe and China* (pp. 1–25). London: Palgrave Macmillan UK.

Probyn, E. (1990). Travels in the postmodern: Making sense of the local. In L. J. Nicholson (Ed.), *Feminist/post-modernism* (pp. 176–189). New York, NY: Routledge.

Probyn, E. (1995). Queer belongings: The politics of departure. In E. A. Grosz & E. Probyn (Eds.), *Sexy bodies: The strange carnalities of feminism* (pp. 1–18). London: Routledge.

Probyn, E. (1996). *Outside belongings*. New York, NY: Routledge.

Probyn, E. (2005). *Blush: Faces of shame*. Minneapolis, MN: University of Minnesota Press.

Radcliffe-Brown, A. R. (1950). *African systems of kinship and marriage*. London: Oxford University Press.

Radway, J. (2008). Foreword. In A. Gordon (Ed.), *Ghostly matters: Haunting and the sociological imagination* (pp. vii–xiii). Minneapolis, MN: University of Minnesota Press.

Raffles, H. (2002). Intimate knowledge. *International Social Science Journal, 173*, 325–335.

Rajaram, P. K. (2002). Humanitarianism and representations of the refugee. *Journal of Refugee Studies, 15*(3), 247–264.

Ramose, M. B. (2001). An African perspective on justice and race. *Polylog*. Retrieved from http://them.polylog.org/3/frm-en.htm

Riak Akuei, S. (2005). Remittances as unforeseen burdens: The livelihoods and social obligations of Sudanese refugees. *Global Migration Perspectives, 18*. Retrieved from http://www.gcim.org/attachements/GMP%20No%2018.pdf

Riccardi, A. (2002). Translation and interpretation. In A. Riccardi (Ed.), *Translation studies: Perspectives on an emerging discipline* (pp. 75–91). Cambridge: Cambridge University Press.

Richmond, A. H. (2002). Globalization: Implications for immigrants and refugees. *Ethnic & Racial Studies, 25*(2), 707–727.

Riessman, C. K. (1987). When gender is not enough: Women interviewing women. *Gender and Society, 1*(June), 172–207.

Robertson, R. (1992). *Globalization: Social theory and global culture*. London: Sage.

Robertson, R. (1995). Glocalization: Time-space and homogeneity-heterogeneity. In M. Feathersone, S. Lash, & R. Robertson (Eds.), *Global modernities* (pp. 25–44). London: Sage.

Ronell, A. (1993). *Dictations: On haunted writing* (2nd ed.). Lincoln: University of Nebraska Press.

Rosander, E. E. (2009). Gender relations and female autonomy among Senegalese migrants in Spain: Three cases from Tenerife. *African and Black Diaspora: An International Journal, 3*(1), 91–107. doi:10.1080/17528630903319862

Rose, G. (2000). Place and identity: A sense of place. In D. Massey & P. Jess (Eds.), *A place in the world? Places, cultures and globalization* (pp. 87–132). Oxford: Oxford University Press.

Rotberg, R. I. (2002). The new nature of nation-state failure. *The Washington Quarterly, 25*(3), 85–96.

Roudometof, V. (2005). Transnationalism, cosmopolitanism and glocalization. *Current Sociology, 53*(1), 113–135.

Routledge, P. (2004). Relational ethics of struggle. *Autonomous Geographies*. Retrieved from http://www.autonomousgeographies.org/files/routledge_2004.pdf

Ruay, D. D. A. (1994). *The politics of two Sudans: The South and the north 1821–1969*. Uppsala: Nordiska Afrikainstitutet (Scandinavian Institute of African Studies).

Ruitenberg, C. (2009). Education as séance: Spectres, spirits, and the expansion of memory. *Interchange, 40*(3), 295–308.

Rukuni, M. (2007). *Being Afrikan*. Johannesburg: Penguin Books.

Ryan, L. (2009). How women use family networks to facilitate migration: A comparative study of Irish and Polish women in Britain. *The History of the Family, 14*(2), 217–231.

Sackey, B. M. (2012). Colonialism. In M. D. Palmer & S. M. Burgess (Eds.), *The Wiley-Blackwell companion to religion and social justice* (pp. 456–468). West Sussex: Blackwell Publishing.

Said, E. W. (1983). Travelling theory. In E. Said (Ed.), *The world, the text, and the critic* (pp. 157–181). Cambridge, MA: Harvard University Press.

Said, E. W. (2000). *Reflections on exile and other literary and cultural essays*. London: Granta.

Said, E. W. (2003 [1979]). *Orientalism*. London: Penguin Books.

Salbi, Z. (2006). *The other side of war: Women's stories of survival & hope*. Washington, DC: National Geographic.

Salih, R. (2001). Moroccan migrant women: Transnationalism, nation-states and gender. *Journal of Ethnic and Migration Studies, 27*(4), 655–671.

Salih, R. (2003). *Gender in transnationalism: Home, longing and belonging among Moroccan migrant women.* London: Routledge.

Sanger, L. (2007). Who says we know: On the new politics of knowledge. *Edge*. Retrieved from http://www.edge.org/3rd_culture/sanger07/sanger07_index.html

Santschi, M. (2008). Briefing: Counting 'new Sudan'. *African Affairs, 107*(429), 631–640.

Sartre, J.-P. (2005 [1943]). *Being and nothingness: An essay on phenomenological ontology* (H. E. Barnes, Trans.). Oxford: Routledge.

Sarup, M. (1994). Home and identity. In G. Robertson, M. Mash, L. Tickner, J. Bird, B. Curtis, & T. Putnam (Eds.), *Travellers' tales: Narratives of home and displacement* (pp. 93–104). London: Routledge.

Savage, M., Bagnall, G., & Longhurst, B. (2005). *Globalization and belonging.* London: Sage.

Schipper, M. (1999). *Imagining insiders: Africa and the question of belonging.* London: Cassell.

Schnapper, D. (1999). From the nation-state to the transnational world: On the meaning and usefulness of diaspora as a concept. *Diaspora, 8*(3), 225–238.

Schneider, D. M. (1968 [1980]). *American kinship: A cultural account* (2nd ed.). Chicago, IL: University of Chicago Press.

Schneider, D. M. (1984). *A critique of the study of kinship.* Ann Arbor, MI: University of Michigan Press.

Schramm, K. (2008). Leaving area studies behind: The challenge of diasporic connections in the field of African studies. *African and Black Diaspora: An International Journal, 1*(1), 1–12.

Scrimshaw, S. (1978). Infant mortality and behavior in the regulation of family size. *Population Development Review, 4*, 383–403.

Scroggins, D. (2004). *Emma's war: Love, betrayal and death in the Sudan.* London: HarperCollins Publishers.

Segrest, M. (2002). *Born to belonging: Writings on spirit and justice.* New Brunswick, NJ: Rutgers University Press.

Seligman, C. G., & Seligman, B. Z. (1932). *Pagan tribes of the Nilotic Sudan.* London: Routledge & Kegan Paul.

Shacklock, G., & Thorp, L. (2005). Life history and narrative approaches. In B. Somekh & C. Lewin (Eds.), *Research methods in the social sciences* (pp. 156–163). London: Sage.

Shandy, D. J. (2003). Transnational linkages between refugees in Africa and in the diaspora. *Forced Migration Review, 16*, 7–8.

Sharkey, H. J. (2008). Arab identity and ideology in Sudan: The politics of language, ethnicity, and race. *African Affairs, 107*(426), 24–43.

Sharra, S. (2009). Towards an African peace epistemology: Teacher autobiography and uMunthu in Malawian education. In D. M. Caracciolo & A. M. Mungai (Eds.), *In the spirit of ubuntu: Stories of teaching and research* (pp. 23–38). Rotterdam, The Netherlands: Sense Publishers.

Simon, S. (1996). *Gender in translation: Cultural identity and the politics of transmission.* London: Routledge.

Simondon, G. (1992). The genesis of the individual (M. Cohen & S. Kwinter, Trans.). In J. Crary & S. Kwinter (Eds.), *Incorporations* (pp. 297–319). New York, NY: Zone Books.

Siu, L. (2005). Queen of the Chinese colony: Gender, nation, and belonging in diaspora. *Anthropological Quarterly, 78*(3), 511–542.

Skrbis, Z. (2008). Transnational families: Theorising migration, emotions and belonging. *Journal of Intercultural Studies, 29*(3), 231–246.

Smith, L. T. (2003). *Decolonizing methodologies: Research and indigenous peoples.* London: Zed Books.

Smith, M. P. (2001). *Transnational urbanism: Locating globalization.* Oxford: Blackwell Publishing.

Smyth, M. (2005). Insider-outsider issues in researching violent and divided societies. In E. Porter, G. Robinson, M. Smyth, A. Schnabel, & E. Osaghae (Eds.), *Researching conflict in Africa: Insights and experiences* (pp. 9–23). Toyko: United Nations University Press.

Soderqvist, T. (1991). Biography or ethnobiography or both? Embodied reflexivity and the deconstruction of knowledge-power. In F. Steier (Ed.), *Research and reflexivity* (pp. 143–163). London: Sage.

Southall, A. (1976). Nuer and Dinka are people: Ecology, ethnicity and logical possibility. *Man, 11*(4), 463–491.

Soysal, Y. N. (2001). Changing citizenship in Europe: Remarks on postnational membership and the national state. In J. Fink, G. Lewis, & J. Clarke (Eds.), *Rethinking European welfare: Transformations of Europe and social policy* (pp. 65–75). London: Sage.

Spear, T., & Waller, R. (1993a). Being Maasai: Introduction. In T. Spear & R. Waller (Eds.), *Being Maasai: Ethnicity and identity in East Africa* (pp. 137–139). London: James Currey Ltd.

Spear, T., & Waller, R. (Eds.). (1993b). *Being Maasai: Ethnicity and identity in East Africa*. Oxford: James Currey Ltd.

Spencer, P., & Wollman, H. (2002). *Nationalism: A critical introduction*. London: Sage.

Spinner, J. (1994). *The boundaries for citizenship: Race, ethnicity, and nationality in the liberal state*. Maryland, MD: Johns Hopkins University Press.

Spivak, G. C. (1988). Can the subaltern speak? In C. Nelson & L. Grossber (Eds.), *Marxism and the interpretation of culture* (pp. 271–314). London: Macmillan.

Spivak, G. C. (1990). *The post-colonial critic: Interviews, strategies, dialogues* (S. Harasym, Ed.). New York, NY: Routledge.

Spurlock, C. J. (2010). *From the Tigris to the rouge: An exploratory study of Chaldean gendered ethnicity and gender transition* (PhD thesis). Michigan State University, East Lansing, MI.

Stacey, J. (1988). Can there be a feminist ethnography? *Women's Studies International Forum, 11*(1), 21–27.

Steady, F. C. (1993). Women and collective action: Female models in transition. In S. M. James & A. P. A. Busia (Eds.), *Theorizing Black feminisms: The visionary pragmatism of Black women* (pp. 90–101). London: Routledge.

Steiner, N. (2009). *International migration and citizenship today*. Oxon: Routledge.

Stone, L. (2010). *Kinship and gender: An introduction*. Boulder, Co: Westview Press.

Stonebanks, C. D. (2008). An Islamic perspective on knowledge, knowing, and methodology. In N. K. Denzin, Y. S. Lincoln, & L. T. Smith (Eds.), *Handbook of critical and indigenous methodologies* (pp. 293–321). Thousand Oaks, CA: Sage.

Strasser, E., Kraler, A., Bonjour, S., & Bilger, V. (2009). Doing family: Responses to the constructions of 'the migrant family' across Europe. *The History of the Family, 14*(2), 165–176.

Strathern, M. (1992). *Reproducing the future: Essays on anthropology, kinship and the new reproductive technologies*. Manchester: Manchester University Press.

Styles, J. (1979). Outsider/insider: Researching gay baths. *Urban Life: A Journal of Ethnographic Research, 8*(July), 135–152.

Sudarkasa, N. (1996). The 'status of women' in indigenous African societies—Implications for the study of African American women's roles. In N. Sudarkasa (Ed.), *The strength of our mothers: African and African American women and families* (pp. 165–180). Trenton, NJ: Africa World Press.

Surra, C. A., & Ridley, C. A. (1991). Multiple perspectives on interaction: Participants, peers, and observers. In C. M. Montgomery & S. Duck (Eds.), *Studying interpersonal interaction* (pp. 25–55). New York, NY: Guilford Press.

Svasek, M. (2008). Who cares? Families and feelings in movement. *Journal of Intercultural Studies, 29*(3), 213–230.

Svasek, M. (2010). Special issue. On the move: Emotions and human mobility. *Journal of Ethnic and Migration Studies, 36*(6), 865–1011.

Swanson, D. M. (2007). Ubuntu: An African contribution to (re)search for/with a 'humble togetherness'. *Journal of Contemporary Issues in Education, 2*(2), 53–67.

Swanson, D. M. (2009). Where have all the fishes gone? Living ubuntu as an ethics of research and pedagogical engagement. In D. M. Caracciolo & A. M. Mungai (Eds.), *In the spirit of ubuntu: Stories of teaching and research* (pp. 3–22). Rotterdam, The Netherlands: Sense Publishers.

Taiwo, O. (1998). Exorcising Hegel's ghost: Africa's challenge to philosophy. *African Studies Quarterly: The Online Journal for African Studies, 1*(4). Retrieved from http://www.africa.ufl.edu/asq/v1/4/2.htm

Tapper, M. (2001). Blood/kinship, governmentality, and cultures of order in colonial Africa. In S. Franklin & S. McKinnon (Eds.), *Relative values: Reconfiguring kinship studies* (pp. 329–354). Durham, NC: Duke University Press.

Taringa, N. T. (2007). Possibilities and limitations for intercultural dialogue from the perspective of ubuntu philosophy. *Swedish Missiological Themes, 95*(2), 185–196.

Tetreault, M. A., & al-Mughni, H. (1995). Gender, citizenship and nationalism in Kuwait. *British Journal of Middle Eastern Studies, 22*(1/2), 64–80.

Thomas, P. (2002). The river, the road, and the rural-urban divide: A postcolonial moral geography from southeast Madagascar. *American Ethnologist, 29*(2), 366–391.

Tierney, W. G. (1999). Guest editor's introduction: Writing life's history. *Qualitative Inquiry, 5*(3), 307–312.

Tillmann-Healy, L. M. (2001). *Between gay and straight: Understanding friendship across sexual orientation*. Walnut Creek, CA: AltaMira Press.

Tillmann-Healy, L. M. (2003). Friendship as method. *Qualitative Inquiry, 9*(5), 729–749.

Timmerman, C., Lodewyckx, I., & Wets, J. (2009). Marriage at the intersection between tradition and globalization: Turkish marriage migration between Emirdag and Belgium from 1989 to present. *The History of the Family, 14*(2), 232–244.

Trieu, M. M. (2009). *Identity construction among Chinese-Vietnamese Americans: Being, becoming, and belonging*. El Paso, TX: LFB Scholarly Publishing LLC.

Trinh, M.-h. T. (1990). Not you/like you: Post-colonial women and the interlocking questions of identity and difference. In G. Anzaldua (Ed.), *Making face, making soul = haciendo caras: Creative and critical perspectives by feminists of color* (pp. 371–375). San Francisco, CA: Aunt Lute Foundation Books.

Trinh, M.-h. T. (1992). *Framer framed*. New York, NY: Routledge.

Trinh, M.-h. T. (1994). Other than myself/my other self. In G. Robertson, M. Mash, L. Tickner, J. Bird, B. Curtis, & T. Putnam (Eds.), *Travellers' tales: Narratives of home and displacement* (pp. 9–28). London: Routledge.

Turcotte, G. (2007). Ghosts of the great south land. *The Global South, 1*(1), 109–116.

Turner, B. S. (1992). Outline of a theory of citizenship. In C. Mouffe (Ed.), *Dimensions of radical democracy: Pluralism, citizenship, community* (pp. 33–62). London: Verso.

Turner, V. W. (1982). *From ritual to theatre: The human seriousness of place*. New York, NY: Performing Arts Journal Publications.

Tutu, D. (1999). *No future without forgiveness*. London: Rider.

United Nations High Commissioner for Refugees. (1996). *Convention and protocol relating to the status of refugees*. Retrieved from http://www.unhcr.org.au/pdfs/convention.pdf

United Nations High Commissioner for Refugees. (2006). *South Sudan as of September 2006*. Retrieved February 11, 2016, from http://www.unhcr.org/4540c6ee4.html

Urry, J. (2003). *Global complexity*. Cambridge: Polity Press.

U.S. Central Intelligence Agency. (1994). *Sudan (Political) 1994*. Retrieved September 21, 2011, from http://www.lib.utexas.edu/maps/africa/sudan_pol_94.jpg

US Committee for Refugees. (2001). *World refugee survey 2001: An annual assessment of conditions affecting refugees, asylum seekers and internally displaced persons*. Washington, DC: Immigration and Refugees Services of America.

van Vlaenderen, H., & Cakwe, M. (2003). Women's identity in a country in rapid social change: The case of educated Black South African women. *Psychology & Developing Societies, 15*(1), 69–86. doi:10.1177/097133360301500105

Venken, M., Beyers, L., & Goddeeris, I. (2009). Special issue. Families, foreignness, migration. Now and then. *The History of the Family, 14*(2), 125–244.

Venn, C. (2009). Neoliberal political economy, biopolitics and colonialism. *Theory, Culture & Society, 26*(6), 206–233. doi:10.1177/0263276409352194

Venn, C. (2010). Individuation, relationality, affect: Rethinking the human in relation to the living. *Body and Society, 16*(1), 129–161.

Vermot, C. (2015). Guilt: A gendered bond within the transnational family. *Emotion, Space and Society, 16*, 138–146. doi:http://dx.doi.org/10.1016/j.emospa.2015.04.001

Vignali, C. (2001). McDonald's: 'Think globcal, act local'—The marketing mix. *British Food Journal, 103*(2), 97–111.

von Flowtow, L. (1991). Feminist translation: Contexts, practices and theories. *TTR: Traduction, Terminologie, Rédaction, 4*(2), 69–84.

von Flowtow, L. (1997). *Translation and gender: Translation in the 'era of feminism'*. Ottawa, ON: University of Ottawa Press.

Vuorela, U. (2002). Transnational families: Imagined and real communities. In D. F. Bryceson & U. Vuorela (Eds.), *The transnational family: New European frontiers and global networks* (pp. 63–82). Oxford: Berg.

wa Thiong'O, N. (1994). *Decolonising the mind: The politics of language in African literature*. Nairobi: East African Educational Publishers.

Wade, P. (2005). Hybridity theory and kinship thinking. *Cultural Studies, 19*(5), 602–621.

Wahlbeck, Ö. (2002). The concept of diaspora as an analytical tool in the study of refugee communities. *Journal of Ethnic and Migration Studies, 28*(2), 221–238.

Waller, R. (1993). Conclusions. In T. Spear & R. Waller (Eds.), *Being Maasai: Ethinicity and identity in East Africa* (pp. 290–302). London: James Currey Ltd.

Warburton, N. (2001). Jean-Paul Sartre Being and nothingness. In *Philosophy: The classics* (2nd ed., pp. 217–228). London: Routledge.

Ware, V. (1992a). *Beyond the pale: White women, racism and history*. London: Verso.

Ware, V. (1992b). Moments of danger: Race, gender, and memories of empire. *History and Theory, 31*(4), 116–137.

Weedon, G. (2011, March). 'Glocal boys': Exploring experiences of acculturation amongst migrant youth footballers in Premier League academies. *International Review for the Sociology of Sport*, 1–17.

Westoby, P. (2005). *Narratives of distress within the Sudanese community of Brisbane and Logan*. Retrieved from http://espace.library.uq.edu.au/eserv.php?pid=UQ:34513&dsID=Sudanese_Refugee_Narratives_of_Distress_-_Brisbane_and_Logan.doc

Westoby, P. (2008). Developing a community-development approach through engaging resettling southern Sudanese refugees within Australia. *Community Development Journal, 43*(4), 483–495.

Wilson, A. C. (2005). Reclaiming our humanity: Decolonization and the recovery of indigenous knowledge. In P. A. French & J. A. Short (Eds.), *War and border crossings: Ethics when cultures clash* (pp. 255–264). Maryland, MD: Rowman and Littlefield Publishers.

Wimmer, A., & Glick Schiller, N. (2002). Methodological nationalism and beyond: Nation-state building, migration and the social sciences. *Global Networks, 2*(4), 301–334.

Windle, J. (2008). The racialisation of African youth in Australia. *Social Identities, 14*(5), 553–566.

Wise, J. M. (2008). *Cultural globalization: A user's guide*. Carlton, Victoria: Blackwell Publishing.

Wright, M. M. (2004). *Becoming Black: Creating identity in the African diaspora*. Durham, NC: Duke University Press.

Wylie, J. (2007). The spectral geographies of W.G. Sebald. *Cultural Geographies, 14*(2), 171–188.

Yanagisako, S. J., & Collier, J. F. (2004). Toward a unified analysis of gender and kinship. In R. Parkin & L. Stone (Eds.), *Kinship and family: An anthropological reader* (pp. 275–293). Oxford: Blackwell Publishing.

Yuval-Davis, N. (1993). Gender and nation. *Ethnic and Racial Studies, 16*(4), 621–632.

Yuval-Davis, N. (1997). Women, citizenship and difference. *Feminist Review, 57*(Autumn), 4–27.

Yuval-Davis, N. (2001). Contemporary agenda for the study of ethnicity. *Ethnicities, 1*(1), 11–13.

Yuval-Davis, N. (2006a). Belonging and the politics of belonging. *Patterns of Prejudice, 40*(3), 197–214.

Yuval-Davis, N. (2006b). Intersectionality and feminist politics. *European Journal of Women's Studies, 13*(3), 193–209.

Yuval-Davis, N. (2009). Women, globalization and contemporary politics of belonging. *Gender, Technology and Development, 13*(1), 1–19. doi:10.1177/097185240901300101

Yuval-Davis, N. (2011, February 4). *Exile, diaspora and the politics of belonging*. Paper presented at Migration: A Joint Birkbeck College/University of East London Symposium, London. Retrieved May

26, 2011, from http://backdoorbroadcasting.net/2011/02/nira-yuval-davis-exile-diaspora-and-the-politics-of-belonging/

Yuval-Davis, N., Anthias, F., & Kofman, E. (2005). Secure borders and safe haven and the gendered politics of belonging: Beyond social cohesion. *Ethnic and Racial Studies, 28*(3), 513–535.

Yuval-Davis, N., Kannabiran, K., & Vieten, U. M. (2006). Introduction: Situating contemporary politics of belonging. In N. Yuval-Davis, K. Kannabiran, & U. M. Vieten (Eds.), *The situated politics of belonging* (pp. 1–14). London: Sage.

Zavella, P. (1993). Feminist insider dilemmas: Constructing ethnic identity with 'Chicana' informants. *Frontiers, 13*(3), 53–76.

Zetter, R. (2007). More labels, fewer refugees: Remaking the refugee label in an era of globalization. *Journal of Refugee Studies, 20*(2), 172–192.

Zontini, E. (2004). Immigrant women in Barcelona: Coping with the consequences of transnational lives. *Journal of Ethnic and Migration Studies, 30*(6), 1113–1144.

Zuor, R. Y., & Chan, H. G. (2006). *South Sudan: A legitimate struggle*. Baltimore, MD: Publish America.

Zusak, M. (2005). *The book thief.* Sydney: Picador.

APPENDIX A

THE WOMEN'S JOURNEYS

The women undertook a variety of physical journeys of migration before they finally resettled in Australia. This appendix explores these various journeys, an understanding of which is imperative to considering the ways in which they were able to negotiate their belongings within particular sites. While journeying provides a useful conceptual tool, it is also critical to acknowledge the challenging physical journeys of migration undertaken by the women. As Achol (Kuol translated) stated in an interview:

> So, the wife of my brother,[1] I have been to hell and back … Just you see how many years I spent walking and how many places I've gone to. I have been to a lot of places.

While each of the women's journeys from Sudan, through exile, to Australia was different, there were similar reasons for their displacement, exile and resettlement. This appendix introduces a history of Sudan which intersperses the 'official' written history with the narratives of the women. This approach shows both the continuities and discontinuities between the women's [hi]stories and the 'official' history and also formulates a more personal and nuanced [hi]story which helps to understand how and why the women left their country of birth. Following this there is a brief description of the various pathways the women took to seek asylum in neighbouring countries in Africa before being resettled in Australia.

Geographically, Sudan[2] is the largest country in Africa and borders nine other countries. It is situated in the north of the African continent, directly across the Red Sea from Saudi Arabia (Figure 1). As a result of its geographical location, the people of the northern regions of Sudan have been interacting with people from the Middle East for thousands of years (Deng, 1995). 'Arab' traders who travelled to Sudan settled among the indigenous peoples of the north, intermarrying with the indigenous people in the area and producing what Deng (1995) refers to as a 'genetically mixed African-Arab racial and cultural hybrid' (p. 2). Achol recounted this narrative of intermixing as we sat watching a DVD of a young Sudanese boy singing in Arabic in a competition in the capital of Sudan, Khartoum. I commented that the boy looked like a *Muonyjäng*.

> Achol: [He] is *Muonyjäng*. Many, many years ago in Khartoum, it's *Muonyjäng* is live in Khartoum. *Muonyjäng* is live in Khartoum, *Muonyjäng* is live with the cow in Khartoum. It's would like you, you know Athokthou [Kuol's home region], you would the other people is go to Khartoum, *Muonyjäng*, you stay

with the cow. The *wutich* [cattle camp] [She implies that some *Muonyjäng* would stay in the southern regions of Sudan, like Athokthou, while others would take the cattle to the northern regions and set up cattle camps at certain times of the year]. The Arab coming with the *awan milo* [salt], with the coming anything coming with the boat.

Melanie: On the Nile.

Achol: Walking in the river on the Nile. It's coming Khartoum, is looking other *Muonyjäng* is people is telling buy everything [i.e. the *Muonyjäng* living in Sudan did not have anything, so they would buy everything from the Arab traders]. You buy everything in the *Muonyjäng*, *Muonyjäng* they don't have anything in Sudan, in Khartoum. It's *Muonyjäng*, Nuba [another indigenous group in Sudan] mixing in Khartoum. Yeah people in Sudan, Sudanese. Stay here. Every Sudanese stay with the cow not anything. Not anything in Sudan. Cow. Just cow and goat.

Melanie: And then the Arabs come.

Achol: Its Fur [another indigenous group, now the main population in Dafur], Nuba stay here in Khartoum. It's *Muonyjäng*. Mixing. Arab coming *awan milo* [salt], sugar, is coming you buying *Muonyjäng*. It's stay with the *Muonyjäng* maybe one year or two year you looking for girl from *Muonyjäng*. (laughs). Is girl, is girl not good. Looking with the girl, is marriage the girl. Every person [Arab trader] marriage girl, girl, girl. Sudanese girl marriage, you born children. When he will born children is stay maybe… is staying the Sudan. Yeah. Stay to the Sudan. This one, this one the Arab, not Arab.

Melanie: Then that's when it started.

Achol: It starting Arab, Arab, Arab.

Melanie: Maybe they came from Iran or Iraq coming down the Nile.

Achol: Yeah, yeah, it's coming from Iran, Iraq, it's place maybe Yemen, yeah it's coming. It's stay here. Finish. It's stay in Sudan, Arab, Arab, Arab. Not Arab. This the great-great-great Arab [i.e. the great-great-great-grandparent was an Arab].

Melanie: Long time, long time ago.

Achol: (laughs) Long time.

What Achol identifies is the biggest challenge for national identity in Sudan. While the Arabised northern Sudanese may be considered by others as a 'genetically mixed African-Arab racial and cultural hybrid' (Deng, 1995, p. 2), the northern Sudanese 'see themselves primarily as Arabs and resist any attempt by the majority non-Arab population to identify the country with black Africa' (Biong Deng, 2005, p. 262).

Differentiation between 'Arabs' and 'Africans' is signified not only by skin colour and ethnicity, but also by religion (Deng, 1995, p. 16).

The northern 'Arabs' maintained their Islamic faith which further differentiated them from the southern 'Africans' who predominantly held animist beliefs before colonisation. During colonisation missionaries introduced Christianity to the southern regions, and as a result many southerners converted to Christianity. While religious differences seemingly signified further differences between the predominantly Muslim 'Arab' north and the Christian and animist 'African' south, as Achol's narrative illustrates, the divide was never that clear cut.

> Achol: When I was in Sudan, I am Muslim.
>
> Melanie: OK.
>
> Achol: When I will run away. When I will born my son … when I will born my son, when I will pregnant in Kenya, when I will born my son in I am coming to Christian.
>
> Melanie: OK. When you were Muslim in Aweil, how was it? Like because some people were making fighting with the Arab, how was it for you in Aweil?
>
> Achol (Kuol translated): When people were fighting, it was not Christian and Muslim. It was in the end, it was one of the factors that people mentioned was the cause for fighting, but it was basically the south and the north, and the Muslims in the south were southerners, so many of them were fighting against the northerners. So I was part of southerners even though I was a Muslim. We are not Arabs. A lot of people in Aweil are Muslim.

For hundreds of years the 'Arab' population remained in the north of the country, coming to the south only to trade goods. Natural barriers, such as swamps and deserts, limited 'Arab' migration and settlement in the south of Sudan (Deng, 1995). In 1821 Sudan was colonised by the Turko-Egyptian forces (often referred to as the Ottoman Empire). This colonisation process began in the north which was easily accessible from Egypt due to the River Nile, but took over twenty years to spread to the south due to the formidable nature of the terrain and the people. Southern Sudan and its peoples remained largely isolated from the rest of the world until the 1840s, when access to the south was opened up by the Ottoman Empire, and European merchants and missionaries began trading and proselytising in southern Sudan (Holt & Daly, 1988; Jok, 2007; Madut-Arop, 2006; Ruay, 1994; Collins, 2007).

In the 1860s a small number of European and Middle-Eastern ivory traders recruited and armed large numbers of 'Arab' servants from the north of Sudan to assist in the poaching of ivory from the Nilotic regions in the south of Sudan (Collins, 2007). It has been suggested that this was the origins of the distrust and fear which still dominate north–south relations to this day (Collins, 2007). From the initial ventures for ivory the 'Arabs' were encouraged by the Europeans to intrude further into the southern regions of Sudan establishing stations, seizing wives and slaves and collecting ivory (p. 15). While the initial trade between Turko-Egyptians and southern Sudan was in ivory, by 1860 the largest trade out of southern Sudan was in slaves (Ruay, 1994). It is estimated that over the duration of the slave trade more than 400,000 slaves were transported from Sudan to Egypt and then on to the USA and countries in Europe (Ruay, 1994). The slave trade wreaked havoc among the populations in the south of Sudan, and added to the southerners' mistrust of the northern 'Arabs'. The slave trade was finally stopped in 1898.

In 1881 the northern Sudanese, under the direction of Muhammad Ahmed al-Mahdi (also known as 'the Mahdi'), overthrew the Turko-Egyptian forces and for 15 years Sudan was largely free of colonising forces (Collins, 2007). However, under the leadership of 'the Mahdi', Islam was used as a divisive element against the south of Sudan (Deng, 1995, p. 11).

In 1899 Sudan was colonised once again when a 'condominium' agreement was signed between Great Britain and Egypt entitled 'Agreement for the Administration of the Sudan' (Ruay, 1994, p. 34). This colonial intervention, known as the 'reconquest' (Deng, 1995), ended slavery and resulted in the definition of Sudan's current national boundaries and division into the 'Arabicised' north and the 'African and Negroid' south (Ruay, 1994, p. 35). As Mbembe suggests (2000):

> With the demarcation of districts, the levying of taxes, the spread of cash crops, a monetary economy, urbanization, and education, economic and political functionality were ultimately combined, the administrative power and the social power weaving together a fabric that was henceforth to dominate the colonial state. However, the decisive factor was the internal boundaries the colonial enterprise defined within each country … membership in a race and an ethnic group served as the condition of access to land and resources. (pp. 265–266)

From 1900 to 1949 the south of Sudan was governed separately from the north under the 'southern policy' which aimed to keep the south and the north separate before eventually annexing the south to one of the other British colonies in East Africa (Collins, 1976; Deng, 1995; Ruay, 1994). Unfortunately this never occurred due to the rapid exit of the British from Sudan as they struggled in the aftermath of World War II. What they left behind, however, was a legacy of racially based power imbalance.

In the racial and cultural hierarchy prevalent during the period of colonisation, the 'African' population was positioned as inferior to the 'Arab' population, who were in turn positioned as inferior to the 'white' population (Hegel, 1975; Schramm, 2008). This 'racial hierarchy' permeated all levels of European thought and discourse at the time. A British administrator in Sudan described this apparent difference between the 'Arab' north and the 'African' south in the early 1900s. He stated:

> The task in the North was simple compared with that in the South. The northern Sudanese at least knew what administration was, and they were civilized in

> some degree. The primitive southerners ... were quite untamed, and a handful of British officers, each with a few soldiers, went off into the unknown to gain the confidence of such people as they might meet. (cited in Collins, 1976, p. 8)

As Achol explained, the northern 'Arabs' were treated differently by the colonisers, and appeared to cooperate more with the colonial powers.

> Achol: When I will white people coming, white people coming is *Muonyjäng* not good. *Muonyjäng* is tell white people 'Go out here from my country'. Is white people is good, is taking anything, go back. Tell him 'You Arab is come on here' he looking for Arab. Maybe the white people is stay in South Sudan is now is South Sudan is development, is bigger. It's now tell white people go out, this now, where now? This one big problem.
>
> Melanie: It's a big problem. Because maybe they didn't leave anything to the people from the south, all the power.

Achol described that the *Muonyjäng* were very aggressive toward the 'white' people, making it difficult for the colonial authorities to operate in southern Sudan. She expressed regret at this, suggesting that maybe if the *Muonyjäng* had been more accommodating to the 'white' people, then southern Sudan might now be more developed. On the other hand, she briefly described that the 'Arabs' worked more cooperatively with the 'white' people. What Achol is alluding to is that under British colonial rule and the 'southern policy' southern Sudan was left largely undeveloped. The British administration preferred to leave the southern Sudanese to tribal rule, as in this way they were easier to manage. However in the north much effort was made to develop the region through the provision of infrastructure and development of an education system. Again this resounds with Mbembe (2000), who observes that '[o]ne of the main legacies of colonization has been to set in motion a process of development that is unequal, depending on the regions and countries involved' (p. 268).

Further to this, as Aluel noted in a group interview I did with Nyalong:

> Because we adopted the ... Arab decision. Because the Arab is say the country all the country. Arab they know everything, all the Arab is develop first than *Muonyjäng*. Arab they go to school first than *Muonyjäng*. That's the problem. We take the policy, Arab policy all.

She suggests that because the 'Arabs' (the north) were developed before the '*Muonyjäng*' (the south), and because they had greater access to education during the colonial period, the *Muonyjäng* (the south) were forced to accept many of the 'Arab' policies and 'decisions' in the postcolonial era. The modern nation-state of Sudan was founded on what Gilroy (2000) might refer to as these 'attempts to differentiate the status of peoples, their cultures, fates, destinies, and different racial and national spirits' (p. 64).

In 1948 the process of independence was started and by 1953 Sudan had acquired full self-government (Ruay, 1994). However, Madut-Arop (2006) suggests that, 'like most sub-Saharan African nations, it has been hard to convince the Sudanese people of various nationalities that they belong to this post-colonial structure' (p. 39). The colonial strategy of encouraging tribalism resulted in many Sudanese being more loyal to their ethnic and tribal regions than to the state, and as a result the state used harsh, often violent, measures to control the various peoples within its territories (Madut-Arop, 2006).

When elections for the first Sudanese parliament took place in 1953, there were 97 seats in the House of Representatives, and of these only 22 were given to southerners (Ruay, 1994). The positions held by southerners were largely tokenistic and these Members of Parliament had little influence over government policies and decisions. There have been attempts by successive governments since independence to 'dominate, Islamize, and Arabize the South' (Deng, 1995, p. 11). These attempts at assimilation and oppression have been met with great resistance in the south and the result has been what Deng (1995, p. 11) refers to as an 'internecine war of visions' in which 'state-supported racialization of social relations has been a deadly project … and has prompted people to carry out terrible acts of violence, to deny services, and to determine a person's status in the nation' (Jok, 2007, p. 12).

In 1955 the first of many years of conflict between the north and south broke out (Deng, 1995; Ruay, 1994; Zuor & Chan, 2006; Collins, 2007). The ensuing civil war is often referred to as 'Anya-nya I' ('snake poison') by southern Sudanese (Ruay, 1994; Jok, 2007; Collins, 1976; Riessman, 1987; Surra & Ridley, 1991). It is suggested that the first civil war was a 'direct reaction to the process of decolonization that had sought to replace British colonialism with another form of colonialism—Arab nationalism' (Madut-Arop, 2006, p. 53). Most of the women in this research project were born during this war and some of their earliest recollections are of this war. For example, Nyalong cited the following as her first memory.

> Nyalong: So in Anyanya its war one in Sudan. So I remember one thing when I was with my mum because my father was to be like SPLA [Sudan People's Liberation Army] fighting with Arabs. One day I wake up with my grandma and we were coming to visit my auntie. And then when we came to sleep, you know where you sleep in *Pan Muonyjäng*, the house, the one up.
>
> Melanie: *Hon nhial* [house on stilts].
>
> Nyalong: Yeah. And when I sleep my grandma used to say '*ca pac, ca pac?*' (whispered) [Are you awake, are you awake?]. And when she used to say like that I open and wake up. When she just call me 'Nyalong', so the Arab came. And you know what they just come and knock the door and call and then they just burn the house. And I was even not start standard one. So I don't know how old are me that time. But I remember that one.
>
> Melanie: Less than five.

> Nyalong: Yeah, less than five. But I remember that I still remember it. That one I'm not happy for that one you know.
>
> Melanie: So did they burn down your grandmother's house?
>
> Nyalong: No, that one we slept in that house [it was someone else's house that they were staying with on the way to Nyalong's auntie's house] and tomorrow we continued to go to my auntie's house. My grandmum just call me 'Nyalong, Nyalong', and then we run out. And then she tried to wake up the man in the house or the woman and they just (makes snoring noise). So we just ran and my grandma she always carried a blanket, a red one. I remember just sit like this (sits huddled up), and then my grandma cover me like this. So you cannot see, you can see maybe tree or something like that. Yep, and then they just burn the house. So I don't know they burn the people inside or what they do, what.
>
> Melanie: Ohhh ... when they couldn't wake up.
>
> Nyalong: Yeah. From that time, I still remember that one and I was very young. I still remember that one.

Not only does this memory paint Nyalong's earliest memories as being of war, but it also demonstrates that from a young age the dichotomy between themselves, the 'Africans', and the Other, the 'Arabs', was made very clear. Nyalong stated that her father was in the rebel movement 'like SPLA' (this was the Anyanya rebel movement) fighting the 'Arabs'. And it was the 'Arabs' who would come and knock on the doors and burn down the houses, and the 'Arabs' who they would have to run from at night.

In 1972 the Addis Ababa Agreement was signed between the northern government of Jaafar Muhammad Nimeiri and the Southern Sudan Liberation Movement (SSLM), ending the first civil war (Zuor & Chan, 2006; Deng, 1995; Jok, 2007). This agreement granted the south regional autonomy. In the 11 years that followed, Nimeiri gradually reneged on many of the components of the Addis Ababa Agreement, eventually imposing *shari'a* (Islamic law) and declaring Sudan an Islamic state (Deng, 1995). In 1983 civil war broke out again between the north and south, this time between the government troops of the northern army and the Sudan People's Liberation Army (SPLA). All of the women in this research left Sudan during the ensuing 21 years of war. It is estimated that this war resulted in the war-related deaths of over two million people, the internal displacement of over four million people, and over half a million refugees displaced to neighbouring countries (Biong Deng, 2008; Large, 2009).

Four of the women recounted having to leave their homes in southern Sudan as a direct result of the war. For these four women, their journeys were perilous and they witnessed numerous friends and relatives die along the passage to countries of initial asylum. Nyanut, Atong and Achol all spent approximately three months walking, at different times, from their homes in *Pan Muonyjäng* to refugee camps in Ethiopia, a journey of approximately 800 kilometres. The following lengthy quotation from Nyanut's story[3] details just a small part of the difficult journey she made from her home in *Pan Muonyjäng* to Ethiopia. It took great courage for Nyanut, Atong and Achol to share some of their traumatic memories of their walks with me, and I quote this story at length as it is critical to understanding the nature of the journeys that the women have made.

> After three weeks we left a place called Yirol and walked to the Nile. It took us about one month, or a bit more, walking every day. We would wake up in the morning and walk until night time. Sometimes at night, we were told that the place we had arrived at was not safe, the elder, the one in charge would blow a whistle to get our attention. Then the people would gather quickly and he would tell us 'We have a problem here. We can't stay here. We will walk at night.' Sometimes people would come and tell the soldiers that the Arabs were coming, so then we would have to keep walking through the night until we arrived at another place. We would arrive in the morning then rest during the day and walk again the next night. A lot of children would sleep while they were walking on the road. Even me, sometimes I would sleep like that. Some would be crawling along the road. It was really tough. Sometimes when the soldiers could see the children were too hungry and tired and couldn't keep walking, we would all sit down on the road in a group and sleep. Then the soldiers would go out into the bush surrounding us to keep watch. No one could make a fire or smoke because then the Arabs could see it or smell it.
>
> During the wet season, when it was flooding and people were walking in the water deep to the knee, and people were attacked, blood would just flow over the water. If you wanted to find somewhere to fetch water and drink, it's not safe from the blood that is already in the water. The water was not clean anyway, apart from blood, and for that reason a lot of people got tapeworms.
>
> One time when we were walking, we were near a place called Ajakageer, there were no trees, no water, no people, no grass, no animals—we call it *sara* [desert]. It's just red sand. In the day it's very hot and at night it's very cold and windy. The wind would come—*poow, poow, poow*. There's nothing there, even lions don't come there because there's no water. If anything goes there, it must die, quickly. When you walk you see the trees slowly disappear behind you and nothing in front of you. Slowly you leave the trees, then you see nothing in front of you and nothing behind you. You take three days or seven days walking and you don't see a tree.
>
> We carried water, but the water finished. You walk side by side, you don't follow anyone because the place is so wide. A lot of people died in *sara*. I started eating mud. It was really hard there. We walked for a lot of days without eating or sleeping. A lot of people died on the way and you would just walk over them and keep going. Some people died on the way because of thirst and

> hunger. The hardest thing was thirst. We walked and you could jump over a dead person and leave them on the way there. And there's nothing you can do to help them. People used to drink the urine, you just make sure nothing drops, and you get all the urine and drink it. Human urine. Did you hear that? If you haven't died of hunger, or thirst, you will die of a gunshot from the enemy. If you have some water you can put it in their ear, but that's all. We were all very thin, just bones.
>
> There were groups who had gone through *sara* before us. As we walked, we would find the bones of other people who had gone before. I saw the bones, the skulls and the teeth. When I saw the skulls, I would see the lines on the forehead.[4] You know we are all different, four lines on each side of the forehead is people from Aweil, Bor are different, and Apuk are different. So when I found a skull with lines in a certain pattern, I knew it was someone from Aweil, from Malual. When I saw those bones I was very scared. We walked for about three days and nights. You don't stop walking. You can't sleep, you keep walking until you don't even feel like sleeping anymore. You walk until you're tired, then you keep walking until the tiredness goes, then you keep walking until it comes back again. God was there, it was God who helped the people. We didn't cross *sara* all the way. We went up to a place called Kasingnor, then when we got to Ajakgiir, the Red Cross brought some water in a *barmil*—a metal drum—and some biscuits. Then they brought a convoy to take us to Kormashi.
>
> When they bring the water, you put some water on someone's head first before they start drinking. They bring the water in drums and bring it to us. They throw it off the truck. If people don't have the power to open the drum they shoot it, and when the water starts flowing out, you drink it. You put in a hose and you suck on the hose, when the water starts flowing you distribute water so people can drink. Sometimes the Red Cross people, instead of throwing the drums down, they actually stop the truck and alight and open the drums and distribute the water. In that way, they serve people. Then people eat biscuits and the Red Cross brings sugar so that people can drink tea. The people that they find alive survive, and the people that are already dead are dead. No one has energy to bury them. And when people go and the bodies remain behind, the birds feast on them. It's very tough, many people were eaten by birds. The birds eat them. You know that one, the bird, the big one.[5]

Nyanut fled her home walking to Ethiopia with her sister, brother and brother-in-law. They had decided that, following the war-related deaths of four immediate family members, it was no longer safe to stay in Sudan. Nyanut recounted 'so that's how we left our home, it was because of the war. Because of the war at home, our home went bad.'[6] After only a couple of years living in a refugee camp in Ethiopia, outbreak of civil war in Ethiopia displaced her again and she was forced to flee to Kenya where she then lived in Kakuma Refugee Camp for about 15 years before being resettled in Australia.

When Achol left Sudan she walked to Ethiopia to join her husband who had gone to Ethiopia for training with the SPLA. Like Nyanut, she stayed in Ethiopia for several years before also being displaced again as a result of the Ethiopian civil war. Achol moved around to several different locations in Uganda, Kenya and even attempted to return to southern Sudan before finally staying in Nairobi before she was resettled in Australia.

Atong, at the age of approximately 16, decided that she wanted to join the Sudan People's Liberation Movement (SPLM) after having witnessed family members being murdered by the northern army. She walked to Ethiopia where she undertook military training, but was not allowed to fight on the frontline. She was also displaced from Ethiopia following the outbreak of civil war. She also sought asylum in Kakuma Refugee Camp for a number of years before transporting her family to a regional town in Kenya and finally to Nairobi before being resettled in Australia.

Abuk was forced to flee her home in *Pan Muonyjäng* and travel to Khartoum in the north of Sudan after her husband, an SPLA soldier, was killed, leaving her with a young family to support. She stayed in Khartoum for a number of years before deciding that Khartoum was not a safe place to bring up her children. They journeyed to Cairo in Egypt where they lived for several years before being resettled in Australia.

Nyalong was the only woman who did not recount leaving home as a direct result of the war. She initially travelled to Kenya with her husband for employment purposes. However, while they were living in Kenya it became unsafe for her or her husband to return to Sudan. While in Kenya, she sought refugee status and after almost 20 years living in Nairobi she was resettled in Australia.

NOTES

1 Many *Jëëng*, even those not directly related to Kuol through kinship ties, refer to me as *Tieng wämääth* (wife of my brother). This is said both endearingly, and to emphasise obligations that I have as a woman who has married into the *Jëëng* community.

2 Sudan was divided into the new countries of Sudan and South Sudan on 9 July 2011. However, for the substantive period of this research including the data collection period, as well as for most of the duration of the lives of the women involved in the project, Sudan was one country. As such, the map illustrates the pre-2011 country of Sudan.

3 This quotation is taken from the story that I composed from several of Nyanut's interviews. I chose to use the composed story in this instance so that I could provide a more concise example of Nyanut's journey.

4 Initiation marks are made on the foreheads of young men and these marks often penetrate to the skull.

5 Vultures.

6 Nyanut made this statement in *Thuongjäng* and it was subsequently translated by Kuol.

APPENDIX B

THE HAUNTED NATURE OF INTERPRETING, TRANSLATING AND TRANSCRIBING

> Whether you translate one language into another language, whether you narrate in your own words what you have understood from the other person, or whether you use this person … to serve the direction of your [work], you are dealing with cultural translation. (Trinh, 1992, p. 128)

Translating, interpreting and transcribing brought a number of challenges to the research largely due to language and cultural differences between the women and me. Interpreting and translating haunt multilingual, cross-cultural research in various ways (Baird, 2011). Throughout the research there were disjunctures between levels of translation and interpretation such as between how I heard the women's narratives and how Kuol heard the women's narratives. In addition there will be disjunctures between how I have read and interpreted the women's narratives compared with how the reader may interpret the narratives. Some of the reasons for these disjunctures as well as some of the methods I have employed to overcome them are explored in this appendix.

Put simply, translation is the transformation of a written document from one language to another (Riccardi, 2002). Kuol, as a qualified and experienced *Thuongjäng* translator, was able to translate the information sheet and consent form required by the University of South Australia Ethics Committee from English into *Thuongjäng*, although this was largely a redundant activity as none of the women were literate in *Thuongjäng*. Kuol was also able to check my spelling of *Thuongjäng* words in the book and my translations of *Thuongjäng* words into English.

Interpretation, however, was more complicated and took place on a number of levels. A narrative, Sarup (1994) suggests, 'has to be interpreted' (p. 16). Each narrative was interpreted to begin with, by me during the conversation. After this, some of the interviews that were conducted in *Thuongjäng* were interpreted by Kuol. Subsequent to this they were interpreted again by me through transcription and then I interpreted them again through writing them into stories. My final interpretation of them has been by weaving them through this book.

First I address Kuol's role as an interpreter. For one interview with Abuk, Kuol was present as a language interpreter to carry out what Riccardi (2002) refers to as liaison interpreting, where the interpreter mediates between two people in a face-to-face conversation, often making not only language, but also cultural interpretations (p. 75). This was probably one of the most difficult and least successful interviews

I conducted with any of the women. As an interpreter Kuol was able to make decisions about what to interpret of my questions and Abuk's answers, and how to interpret them. For example, Kuol felt uncomfortable as a male asking an older female some of the questions I was trying to ask, so instead he adapted and modified them, and once or twice even chose not to interpret them. I decided after this interview that it was not suitable to conduct interviews about events in the women's lives with a male interpreter present, regardless of how he was related to either the woman or me.

Kuol also interpreted the other interviews in which the women responded in *Thuongjäng*. Although my understanding of the *Thuongjäng* language was sufficient to conduct the interviews, I missed some parts of the dialogue which were too complicated for me to understand and some of the nuanced language that was used at times. I wanted to ensure that I had an accurate understanding of all aspects of the women's stories when transcribing, analysing and writing up the research, so Kuol assisted by interpreting. This interpreting was done through what Riccardi (2002) refers to as remote interpreting, where the interpreter is more separated from the event being interpreted. Kuol performed these interpretations subsequent to the interview by listening to the recordings of the conversations with the women and recording his interpretation on a digital recorder as he listened. In this way he was not present in the conversations with the women, so he did not inhibit or change the nature of the conversations by his presence. The women knew that Kuol would be listening to the conversations to help me with interpreting them, but this did not seem to affect the conversations.

At times, Kuol also acted as a 'culture broker' (Krog, 2008, p. 235), an interpreter of particular cultural nuances and events, ways of being and thinking. During the interpretations of the women's narratives Kuol included his own translations, interpretations and explanations of particular aspects of the narratives. This was imperative, as Krog (2008) has argued, as the 'interviewer brings his or her own questions and assumptions, often underpinned by colonial, racist, gender or religious notions' (p. 235) to an interview. As a result of this, she further suggests that:

> even a well translated narrative can be experienced as discriminatory and ethically problematic when read through a particular, in this case a western, perspective. But the moment there is an attempt to interpret the narrative via its embeddedness in an indigenous worldview, it becomes breathtakingly ethical and fair. (p. 231)

Kuol's interpretations of the interviews as a 'culture broker' enabled me to understand the women's narratives as they were embedded in the indigenous worldview of *cieng*.

Kuol's interpretations were also significantly affected by his own background and experiences. For example, when interpreting the women's portrayals of their experiences of marriage, portrayals that Kuol did not necessarily agree with, Kuol interrupted his interpretation of the women's narratives to add his point of view on marriage in *Jëëng* societies, a perspective that was shaped by his gender.[1] I will quote the transcript of another point in one of Kuol's interpretations as it highlights how his own experiences haunted his interpretation. Nyanut had been talking of her experiences of arriving as a refugee in Kenya, an experience Kuol shared with her. The recording had been playing for some time without Kuol stopping to interpret, when suddenly he stopped:

> Kuol: Ohh. [rewinds tape]
>
> Melanie: What? You thought she was speaking English?
>
> Kuol: I start thinking about these things.
>
> Melanie: What do you mean?
>
> Kuol: I relive it.
>
> Melanie: Oh you remember how … is that why you don't like doing it? Is it hard for you?
>
> Kuol: No it's alright. It's not hard, it's just that it engages me and I relive it.
>
> Melanie: It brings back memories.
>
> Kuol: Yeah.
>
> Melanie: Bad or … ?
>
> Kuol: Mmm … nah. It just makes it a bit daunting, like is it really work? Is it something …? To me it's just so simple.
>
> Melanie: To you it's in your memory so you think why the hell do I need to listen and write these stories.
>
> Kuol: And what is this really … So part of it is just, to me it's boring. Sorry, but it's boring. Is that on record?
>
> Melanie: You think my research is boring? [laughs]
>
> Kuol: To me. To me it's boring.
>
> Melanie: I thought it was interesting.
>
> Kuol: It will be interesting to whoever will be the reader, but it's boring.

I, too, was engaged in a process of interpretation throughout the research. Through conversations, transcribing, analysis and writing, I was involved in an ongoing process of interpretation of the women's narratives that was haunted by my own background and experiences. I interpreted the women's narratives and experiences through lenses shaded by my own language, 'race', class, gender and lived experience (Dyck & McLaren, 2004).

To begin with I interpreted the women's language, both when they talked in *Thuongjäng* and when they spoke in what I like to affectionately refer to as Dinglish, a Dinkacised version of English. For example, Nyanut was explaining how she used to eat a type of fruit:

Nyanut: You can put in your mouth [pulls a face like sucking on something].

Melanie: Just suck it.

Nyanut: Suck it. Oh. Suck it [laughs]. You clear my English.

Again in a conversation with Nyanut, as she was reading back a part of her completed life story she exclaimed:

Nyanut: Mel you listening my English, it's very really.

Melanie: It's good?

Nyanut: Yeah the same.

Melanie: OK, good.

Nyanut: Yes then when I told you, but you correct it.

Melanie: Yeah I just corrected a little bit.

Nyanut: Yes you make a lot of things because talking, I miss a big word about talking, but reading it's good.

Melanie: It's good yes. Your reading is very good.

Nyanut: But talking. Oh.

Melanie: Yeah no but, look, I can understand your talking fine.

Nyanut: But you understand because you are listening all the one is talking with you. But some people no.

Due to my previous experiences living and working with *Jëëng* who spoke English as a second, third or fourth language, I was able to interpret and make sense of their English language and write it in a way which for them still represented what they had said to me. I heard their narratives through my interpretation of their Dinglish and it is through this that I have developed my understanding. My understanding of their narratives was helped not only through my understanding of Dinglish, but also through my developing understanding of their world view of *cieng*. Throughout the book I endeavour to guide the reader through how I have formulated my interpretations and understandings of most of the narratives. However other readings are possible, and in fact necessary. In each instance, where the women are quoted, I have heard, understood and utilised the narratives in a particular way for a particular purpose, but there are multiple ways of understanding many of the narrative excerpts. In some instances, for example, narrative excerpts have been included in multiple sections of the book, emphasising the different meanings and interpretations that are possible through contributions to multiple theoretical understandings.

To try to enable the reader to make their own meaning from the narratives (meanings that may differ from my interpretations) I have kept the women's narratives in their own words as much as possible, with translations done only when the women spoke in *Thuongjäng*. In addition, I have included the full transcripts (often quite lengthy) of many of the quotations including my own questions and interjections to encourage the formulation of multiple understandings and interpretations (Clandinin & Murphy, 2009).

I also interpreted the women's narratives in light of my own experiences. At times this was easy, such as when I was imagining Achol's struggles to learn, as a newly married woman, how to pound grain in *Pan Muonyjäng*, something she had never done as a girl growing up in the town. This was an experience I shared with her, having also gone to *Pan Muonyjäng* as a newly married woman where I tried to pound grain, something I had never done as a girl. At other times interpreting was very difficult; again I quote from an interview with Nyanut as she explained her experiences walking across a desert on her trek to Ethiopia:

> Nyanut: No town, yes *sara*. Yes it's called *sara*. You can't see on your front, then you can't see the back. You see the tree, just tree, tree, you leave tree a little bit, slowly, slowly, until you leave tree and you can't see anything.
>
> Melanie: Oh, it's like, you know *The gods must be crazy.*
>
> Nyanut: Yep.
>
> Melanie: The, when the skunk, that one is bite his, that black and white thing is bite his ankle and he's walking, walking, and then he gives the beer to the animal, you know *Gods must be crazy.*
>
> Nyanut: [grabs my leg] That is … that is *sara*! *Sara*, no tree, no anything. Yep. You must to get the tree a long a long, you take three days or seven days, you walk there, no tree.
>
> Melanie: And no water. Do you carry some water or?
>
> Nyanut: Yes. But the water is finished. The water finish there.

Initially I struggled to comprehend Nyanut's explanation of *sara*, as she did not name it as a desert, and it was not anything I had ever seen or experienced. It was not until I likened what she was describing to an image we had watched on a movie together during a previous visit that I was able to comprehend the vastness of the desert she was explaining. There were some experiences that the women spoke of in their narratives that I was never able to comprehend fully, such as Abuk's experiences living as an internally displaced person in Khartoum and a refugee in Cairo, both places that I have never been to or experienced, and Achol's experience of finding her husband in a car with his leg blown off by a landmine. I did not share these experiences with the women, nor had I ever experienced anything similar, and this made it more difficult for me to relate to these experiences and comprehend them, particularly on an emotional level.

Once I had interpreted the stories through my listening during the conversation, I again interpreted them while transcribing the conversations. I completed the transcriptions as soon as possible after the conversations, while the conversations still remained fresh in my memory. This was a tedious, time-consuming and often frustrating task that nonetheless added many layers to my understandings of the women's stories (Kiesinger, 1998, p. 92). Ultimately I ended up with over 300 pages of transcripts from the interviews. Transcribing the women's stories meant that I listened to each story twice or, in the case of the interviews that Kuol remotely interpreted, three times as I sat with him while he completed the interpretation. Transcribing the interviews which Kuol had interpreted gave me an opportunity to listen again to the women's *Thuongjäng* immediately followed by Kuol's English translation to assess the accuracy of Kuol's interpretations. Through this slow, careful listening I could better understand the nuances of the women's *Thuongjäng*, and at times I chose to amend some of Kuol's interpretations. Through the transcribing process I was able to identify gaps and inconsistencies in my questioning and the women's responses and follow these up in subsequent interviews.

In composing the women's stories, I was once again engaged in a process of interpretation as I took the women's narratives and arranged, rearranged and reworded them into a story. This process was haunted by my own desires for a coherent, chronological story of life.

NOTE

1 The politics of gender and culture in translation have been well considered in Palmary (2011).

INDEX

Printed in Australia
AUOC02n0659190816
278293AU00005B/9/P